# *Good Morning* HANOI

IAIN FINLAY AND TRISH CLARK

# Good Morning HANOI

## A YEAR ON THE AIRWAVES IN THE NEW VIETNAM

SIMON & SCHUSTER
AUSTRALIA

GOOD MORNING HANOI
First published in Australia in 2006 by
Simon & Schuster (Australia) Pty Limited
Suite 2, Lower Ground Floor
14–16 Suakin Street
Pymble NSW 2073

A CBS Company
Sydney  New York  London  Toronto

Visit our website at www.simonsaysaustralia.com

© Iain Finlay and Trish Clark 2006

All rights reserved. No part of this publication may be reproduced, stored in a retrieval system, or transmitted in any form or by any means, electronic, mechanical, photocopying, recording or otherwise, without the prior written permission of the publisher.

Cataloguing-in-Publication data:

Finlay, Iain, 1935- .
    Good morning Hanoi : a year on the airwaves in the new
    Vietnam.

    Bibliography.
    Includes index.
    ISBN 0 7318 1272 7.

    1. Radio stations - Vietnam. 2. Volunteers - Vietnam.
    3. Vietnam - Social life and customs - 21st century.
    I. Clark, Trish, 1942- . II. Title.
959.7

Cover design by Christabella Designs
Internal design by Kirby Jones
Typeset in 11 on 16 Sabon by Kirby Jones
Printed in Australia by Griffin Press

10 9 8 7 6 5 4 3 2 1

*For Macs and Milla ... the road ahead,
ten thousand miles.*

Also by Iain Finlay and Trish Clark
(as Iain Finlay and Trish Sheppard):

*Africa Overland*
*South America Overland*
*Across the South Pacific*

Also by Trish Clark (as Trish Sheppard):
*Andrea*
*Children of Blindness*
*Australian Adventurers*
*Motherhood*

Also by Iain Finlay:
*The Azanian Assignment*
*Savage Jungle*

# CONTENTS

*Acknowledgments* ........ *ix*
*Prologue* ........ *xiii*
*Introduction* ........ *xvii*
*Orientations* ........ *xix*

March: First impressions ........ 1
April: Prisoners, victims and heroes ........ 33
May: A program proposal ........ 64
June: A death ........ 89
July: Heroic Mothers ........ 120
August: Sins of the Dead ........ 142
September: Independence Day and first prize ........ 167
October: Oz aid and trade ........ 185
November: An office blow-up ........ 202
December: A funeral and a wedding ........ 233
January: Tet — confidence in humanity ........ 268
February: A visit to Luan's village ........ 290
March: Women's Day ........ 318
April: A courtyard party ........ 341
May: Dien Bien Phu and au revoirs ........ 361

*Epilogue* ........ *377*
*Bibliography* ........ *382*
*Index* ........ *387*

Quotations at the beginning of each chapter are traditional Vietnamese proverbs collected in *Sketches for a Portrait of Vietnam* by Huu Ngoc.

# ACKNOWLEDGMENTS

First and foremost we must thank Australian Volunteers International (AVI), the Australian aid agency without whom our assignment with the Voice of Vietnam would not have happened. This is an extraordinary organisation that sends upwards of 800 Australians overseas every year to help in myriad ways in Africa, the Middle East, Asia, and the Pacific as well as in needy locales within our own country.

We'd like to give a huge thankyou to Rebecca Hales, who shared all these experiences and more with us and who gave unstintingly of her time to read and comment on the manuscript.

Thanks also for the hospitality of Noel White on the north coast of New South Wales and especially of Jack Bowers, admirable principal of Jane Franklin Hall at the University of Tasmania, Hobart, his wife Sally, their daughter Alice, as well as all the staff for welcoming us to the college and providing us a place with such a magnificent view over the Derwent, where most of the writing of this book was undertaken.

Out of deference to social and political sensitivities and in accordance with the Vietnamese tradition of aliases, a few names have been changed.

'Goooood Moorrrning Viiietnam!' was the trademark greeting of American DJ Adrian Cronauer, broadcasting in Vietnam during the 1960s on the US Armed Forces Radio Network. Robin Williams made it famous with his 1988 hit movie of the same name.

Although this book has no connection to the film or to Adrian Cronauer's story, its title is intended as a small nod of recognition to someone who was broadcasting in English more than thirty years ago in a very different Vietnam.

But, most importantly, to the Voice of Vietnam English Service, VOV5.

...a million thanks for a wonderful year and our best wishes for the future.

*There are those among them who chose the road of glory.*
*They dreamed to bend rivers and mountains to their will.*
*Why now recall their ruthless games of power?*
*The heart is crushed remembering the blows of fate.*

From '*Van Te Thap Loai Chung Sinh*', a 3000-verse epic called
*Kieu: a Funeral Oration Call to Wandering Souls*
BY NGUYEN DU 1765–1820

# PROLOGUE

Trish had taken the phone call around midmorning. It was from Peter Dwan, from Australian Volunteers International (AVI) in Melbourne. 'How does Hanoi sound?' he had said. 'It's with the English Service of the Voice of Vietnam — the radio network. It's for a year, and it's for both of you.'

In a sense, we couldn't have asked for a better set-up, or a more interesting project. The two of us working at the same job, albeit on different, overlapping shifts, and both working in the field we knew best. In addition, the contracts were for just over a year in Hanoi, the capital of one of the most fascinating, dynamic and rapidly changing countries in South-East Asia.

How did this all happen? Well, one of the few benefits of being old farts is that, as with most people, quite a lot has happened over the years and you also get to the stage where you feel that, because such a lot *has* happened and because a fair amount of it has involved a good deal of pressure and stress, you think that having a quiet time for a while might not be such a bad idea.

A false premise, as it turned out, but we had this in mind, and the fact that over the years we have both said that, 'when we get older' we should volunteer to work with some international aid organisation for a while, something like Oxfam or Save the Children. Part of the motivation for this idea was the result of some horrific experiences we had as journalists in the refugee camps of Bangladesh during the 1971 Indo–Pakistan War and also in a

Vietnam at war. The end result was that at the beginning of 2002, having gradually backed away from all our television production commitments, we found ourselves in a position where we could put our names down as potential volunteers to go overseas and, hopefully, do something useful for a country that needed a bit of help in that area.

By 'that area', we meant radio or television. We put our applications in with AVI, who could theoretically have sent us off to all sorts of places in Africa, the Middle East, Asia or the South Pacific. We were pushing the envelope a bit, expecting to get two jobs in the same place. But that's the way it happened. It took almost a year before anything came up, and when it did, it was totally inconvenient, because we'd just moved from Sydney onto a little two-hectare farm up on the far north coast of New South Wales. Two weeks into the move, with scores of boxes still unpacked, the phone call came through.

Iain was covered head to toe in crackerdust — small white gravel stones crushed almost to dust — when Trish ran inside to answer the phone. He looked like a ghostly image of a coalminer as he shovelled another load of it off the back of the ute to make a thick bed for the new 25,000-litre water tank to squat on. Overnight our lives had become full of conversations about crackerdust. And mulch. We'd had no inkling that there were so many varieties of mulch. Then there were the rampant cane toads and varying suggestions about what to do with them (including pick them up in a plastic bag and pop them in the freezer) and the two-metre pythons (coil them round your arm, drive down to the rainforest and let them slide away). And when you'd covered all that, there was always the drought to discuss and of course the imminent flood.

So Hanoi looked like a good option! Outer Mongolia would have too. In fact they had asked us six months previously if we'd go to Mongolia and we'd said yes. But nothing came of it. And how fortunate that they now wanted two people. From the job description, we foolishly assumed we could do it on our ear, without stress, and have plenty of time to enjoy living again in Asia. We would even have taken it on if they'd only wanted one of us. We could have job-shared and had even more time out. But this was far better. And Hanoi; well, we immediately thought that it was somewhere we could probably convince our son and daughter-in-law was an okay place to bring the grandchildren.

Trish put the phone down, went across to the barn and called over to Iain, 'D'you want to go to Hanoi?'

He didn't stop shovelling. 'I need to finish this load,' he said, 'and then I have to take a look at the pump in the dam. Can we go this afternoon?'

# INTRODUCTION

If ever the term 'the power of positive thinking' could be applied to a country, it should surely be Vietnam. Today, it is a country that is powering into the future at full throttle, trying to make up for lost time. Its more than 80 million people are among the hardest-working in Asia, if not the world; determined to turn their country from an agrarian society into an industrialised nation, with a knowledge-based economy, by the year 2020. In the past ten years Vietnam has halved its poverty level, doubled its income per capita, and become the second-largest exporter of rice in the world. Prominent Western resident of Hanoi Lady Borton, in her 2001 pamphlet 'To Be Sure', quotes a former southern revolutionary peasant, greeting a delegation of Westerners: 'My country has developed more in the last ten years than in the previous thousand.'

It's thirty years since Vietnam slipped off the front pages of our newspapers and from our nightly news bulletins. It's back now as a 'good news' story, and this book is about the new Vietnam. Or at least about the capital, Hanoi, and the team of mostly young people with whom we worked and who welcomed us into their lives and shared their joys and hopes, their fears and dreams, their everyday lives, their histories and their plans for the future. It's about how we came to know these people and to see the new Vietnam from the inside out, and hopefully you will be able to see something of their country as well as the outside world through their eyes and ours.

We went to Vietnam as volunteers, aid workers in a sense, classified as editors/radio programmers to work with the English language service of the Voice of Vietnam. We were there to teach, or at least to share our knowledge, but in the long run we found that we learnt as much, if not more, than we taught. At the same time we were able to fit in sufficiently well that we were encouraged to develop and put to air a new daily radio program. We also found ourselves unexpectedly welcomed, after a time, into another community living around a little courtyard where we had rented a house; a group that was like an extended family in a medieval village, right in the centre of the city. And it is the small intricacies of the lives of these two quite separate groups of Hanoians that form much of the fabric of this book.

This is not intended to be a travel book, or a history book. Nor is it a political treatise or a cultural guide and yet it is all of these, plus a personal view of life in the bustling capital of Vietnam, as witnessed through our everyday experiences over a period of fifteen months. As such, we hope it puts a human face and dimension to the massive changes that are happening in Vietnam.

The regular English language radio program we developed and ran for just on a year was something of a breakthrough in that it was the first time Westerners had broadcast on the government-run national radio network on a daily basis. Our volunteer status also gave us acceptance at a level not otherwise open to foreigners, and this rather inconsequential little radio program opened other more generally inaccessible areas to us, allowing us the privilege of being able to move easily between the various worlds within worlds which make up the fascinating and many-layered jigsaw puzzle of Hanoi.

We were unavoidably categorised as expatriates and were able to slot quite readily into that world when the occasion demanded. But what gave us greater pleasure was that we were also able to find our place in a very different milieu, gain acceptance and develop friendships with our Vietnamese colleagues and neighbours to the extent that we all added something to each other's lives.

# ORIENTATIONS

Vietnam is a long, thin country stretching some 1600 kilometres from its northern border with China to its southern delta, just above the equator. Its land area, of around 327,000 square kilometres, is about one and a half times larger than the Australian state of Victoria, yet still slightly smaller than Japan. To say it is long and thin is not quite accurate because the thin part is only in the middle, where the country is squeezed to a width of about 50 kilometres, between the mountains along the border with Laos and the South China Sea, which in Vietnam is known as the 'East Sea'. The curved shape of Vietnam makes it appear like an 'S', with larger land areas at the top and the bottom: the rich northern Red River delta and the even more productive Mekong River delta in the south. It has also been described as being like a bamboo pole with baskets of rice at either end.

These rice bowls were attractive to outsiders and foreign invaders; Chinese from the north, and the Cham people of Indo–Malay origin from the west. In the central and border areas, however, life was usually more difficult and the territory was consequently less attractive to invaders. But the people who did inhabit and carve a living out of these more marginal regions now present a complex ethnic diversity that is unique in Asia.

Of Vietnam's 83 million people, between six and eight million are made up of fifty-four distinct minority ethnicities. The numbers in the groups vary widely from the dwindling 382 Pupeo and the minuscule 194 Odu, to the more than half a million in each of the Hoa, Tay and Thai communities, as well as the H'Mong and Dao people, with whom visitors to the Sapa district, close to the Chinese border, have become most familiar.

With shaved eyebrows and hairlines and sporting large and complex red turbans, or wearing indigo hand-dyed and elaborately embroidered clothes — worn, incidentally, for their everyday work and not just for the tourists — these are the groups that have adapted in quite different ways to changing times. They have learnt marketplace skills and basic phrases in a raft of foreign languages to barter in a good-natured manner with all comers. But they are comparatively small in number, and so, despite proactive government legislation, the minority peoples remain socially, politically and economically marginalised.

The history of the majority Kinh, or Viet, people goes back to at least 1000 BC, when a brilliant Bronze Age, wet-rice Dong Son culture bloomed in the area between the Yangtse and the Red River delta. For the following thousand years the state was dominated by China, a fact that continues to resonate strongly within the Vietnamese psyche.

In the tenth century, Vietnam won its independence from China on the battlefield and, for a further thousand years, under its own national dynasties, the Viet people spread south, devastating the Cham culture that had developed in the central coastal regions of the country, to eventually settle the fertile delta area of the Mekong. Throughout those centuries, although the cultural impact of their northern neighbour, China, was extremely strong, Vietnam managed to resist actual invasion until, in 1862, the French arrived with their warships.

For a little over eighty years France colonised Vietnam, dividing it into the three client states of Tonkin, Annam and Cochin China. These remained parts of their Indochinese colonial empire until their ignominious defeat at Dien Bien Phu, in a battle which proved to be a turning point in history, not just for Vietnam but for the whole concept of colonisation worldwide.

But then, almost as a hideously destructive afterthought, came the Americans. Vietnam, as the Vietnamese are very anxious to point out, is more than the Vietnam War. It's nevertheless true that, in the second half of the twentieth century, it has suffered more from war than almost any other country. More than two million people died during the 'American' War, as the Vietnamese prefer to call the hostilities that raged through the 1960s and early 1970s. And more bombs were dropped on North Vietnam during that period than were dropped on Nazi Germany in all of World War II. Sadly, the suffering continues to this day, in the long-term effects of Agent Orange and unexploded ordnance.

In hindsight, it is relatively easy to see Vietnam's century-long struggle against French colonial regimes, from the mid–1800s to 1954, as simply being a war of independence; a continuation of their 2000 years of conflict with the Chinese for the right to govern themselves.

With the collapse of French rule, America had been alarmed at the prospect of communism sweeping down through Indochina, Thailand and Malaysia — the so-called 'Domino Theory' — so they poured vast quantities of men and materiel into the mix, only to find that the whole thing involved much more than just containing communism. On the one hand it was a civil war between the North and the South, complicated by the major Cold War protagonists taking sides, but beyond that, it was still a war of independence, with the Vietnamese wanting to rule themselves.

The truth of this perspective was vividly demonstrated six years after the United States pulled out of Vietnam and four years after the fall of Saigon when, in 1979, China invaded Vietnam's northern provinces after it took umbrage over the fact that Vietnam had overthrown the Pol Pot regime in Cambodia. At that time Vietnam fought a fierce, bloody but successful campaign against its former communist ally and won.

But victory in war and in gaining independence didn't spare Vietnam from continuing tragedy. Reunification in 1975 was followed by a great deal of vengeance-style bloodletting. Hundreds were murdered, thousands were incarcerated in forced labour re-education camps and many more fled the country as refugees, the majority as boat people.

The sweeping reforms that followed brought a rapid transition to socialism and collectivisation of agriculture in the south. The results of such a hardline command economy were disastrous. A decade after its long-anticipated reunification, almost the entire country was plagued with famine. This dark time, designated as the 'Subsidies Period', is a still-vivid memory for anyone over twenty years old. Tens of thousands more people, including disillusioned northerners who had fought so long and hard for their country and had survived the tough times of the war's aftermath, left to join the Vietnamese diaspora in regional countries and further afield. But in the mid–1980s, trembling on the very brink of economic and social collapse, the Party managed to perform a more or less complete about-turn.

'Doi Moi' is the catchphrase that defines that dramatic rethink and the path that Vietnam has been officially following since 1986. In reality, however, it didn't start to pick up any speed until around 1991. Doi Moi means 'Renovation', and it was intended to revitalise a completely stagnant economy by adopting what was then called 'market socialism'; in other words, opening up the country to foreign investment while at the same time being more tolerant of divergent and critical views from the populace. The program had much in common with Mikhail Gorbachev's Perestroika policy in the Soviet Union, which had been watched, with guarded approval, in Hanoi.

Since 1991 Doi Moi has been an ongoing process, albeit with several large hiccups, particularly during the late 1990s. Major milestones were reached during the 1990s, however, from which there could be no turning back; namely, Vietnam's acceptance as a member of ASEAN — the Association of South-East Asian Nations — and diplomatic recognition by the United States, which had imposed crippling economic embargoes on the country since the 1960s. In 2000 there was the signing of a bilateral trade agreement with the United States, which has proved an economic boon to Vietnam as it moves towards becoming a more modern, democratic society with what it now calls a 'socialist-oriented market economy'.

It was into this new Vietnam that we were about to plunge.

**Central Hanoi, including the Old Town**

*March*

# FIRST IMPRESSIONS

*'A hundred things heard are not worth one thing seen'*

'So now we're going to take you to dinner,' Duong announced. 'You feel okay about going on motorbikes?'

'Sure,' we said without looking at each other, knowing what we were both thinking. We'd seen what Hanoi's traffic was like on the way in from the airport, where we arrived some three months after the initial phone call from AVI. We had also remembered the son of friends of ours who had come very close to dying in a motorbike accident in Vietnam. By climbing onto the back of a motorbike in Hanoi, you immediately become part of the horn-tooting majority. With an estimated ten million motorbikes in Vietnam, mainly Hondas, Suzukis, Yamahas and countless dead-spit replica brands, Vietnam ranks among the top countries in the world in the motorbikes-per-capita stakes. The other thing that happens to you when you slide out into the so-called 'traffic' is that you take your life in your hands. Over thirty people a day are killed in traffic accidents in Vietnam — that's the equivalent of a 747 full of people crashing every ten days.

At first we couldn't believe our eyes. There's really nothing quite like it anywhere else. The impression is of total anarchy and chaos.

*There are an estimated 10 million motorbikes in Vietnam.*

No-one seems to obey traffic signals or lights — what few there are. Motorbikes, cars, even trucks continually drive on the wrong side of the road towards you. At an intersection if you want to turn left from the right-hand side of the road, you simply drive headlong into the oncoming traffic and expect them to make their way around you. And the incredible thing is that they do! What's more, there's no road rage directed at you for cutting across them, because they'll be doing the same thing at the next intersection.

It has been said that Hanoi traffic is symbolic of the Vietnamese psyche. It epitomises their willingness and ability to bend with the wind, so to speak, to give way to obstacles where necessary, let them pass and then emerge to continue on their way.

And no-one wears helmets! The government drafted a law requiring all urban dwellers to wear helmets when riding, but it was never enacted because of a myriad of arguments put up against it by the city residents. (You do see more people in the countryside wearing helmets, however.) On top of that, they ride with whole families, up to five people, including babes in arms, on board.

We had been met a few hours earlier at Hanoi's Noi Ba airport by three students from the Institute for International Relations — Tran Ha Trang, Nguyen Hoang Duong and Tran Quynh Hoa. They gave Trish some flowers and helped us collect up our bags, commenting on how many we had. We didn't tell them there were more arriving in a few days' time! Then we all piled into a minibus for the trip into town to settle into some simple accommodation at their college, where they had been assigned to welcome us to their country with a four-day orientation program.

Waiting for us at the institute was Xavier Nathan, another AVI volunteer, who had taught at the institute for four years. An Indian–Malaysian, he had emigrated to Perth where he had raised a family of four and then, only a few years previously, nursed his wife as she died of cancer. He was, we discovered quickly, a truly gentle man, devoid of ego and full of affection.

Also waiting for us was Nguyen Thi Bao Tam, the dean of the Faculty of Languages, a sassy extrovert with a big smile who had spent six years studying Russian, way out in the boondocks in what was then the Soviet Union. She had also spent a couple of years in Canberra during the time her father was Vietnam's Ambassador to Australia.

'Okay, who's riding with whom?' Hoa asked as we walked downstairs to the institute's parking area, which was full of motorbikes. 'Iain can come with me,' Hoa continued. 'Trish, you go with Trang.' (Vietnamese always call each other by their last name, which is really their given name, and the family name is always placed first.)

To say that we were a bit edgy climbing onto the back of Hoa's and Trang's motorbikes is putting it mildly. But they just chatted away as they drove, one alongside the other, on our way to the restaurant, through all the chaos and tooting of horns, as if nothing untoward was happening.

'That's the American Embassy,' Hoa said as we rode past an uninspiring building on Lang Ha Street with three huge mining trucks parked out in front of it.

'What are those trucks?' Iain shouted above the din of the traffic.

'In case there is any trouble,' he replied.

'Trouble?'

'Maybe a bombing,' he said.

We were four days away from the invasion of Iraq.

At the Bi Doh (Red Pumpkin) Restaurant we enjoyed an excellent meal, our first in Vietnam, and chatted about a range of things, from Tam's experience in Russia and Australia to what we might be doing in our new jobs at the Voice of Vietnam, and what they had planned for us over the next four days of orientation. What we noticed most during the meal was how freely the conversation flowed, and although the company included the dean of the faculty as well as students, an easy egalitarian atmosphere was maintained throughout.

At an introductory session the following morning, Trang set about her task of 'selling' us Vietnam with a will. She presented positive statistics with a tight-lipped earnestness that almost dared us to question her truths. We later suggested to each other that one day she would head up a government department. She also led the lectures on history: 'We overcame the French imperialists, the American aggressors and the Chinese invaders, both ancient and modern'; on culture: 'There are fifty-four ethnic groups. The largest, comprising 84 per cent of the population are the Kinh'. Her tone of voice registered subtle intimation that the rest are pesky ethnic minorities. On religion: 'Freedom of worship is official government policy', and politics ...? Well, almost anything bar cleaning your teeth is a political statement in Vietnam. Or at least in Hanoi.

As we sat, squeezed into the front row of a room full of fixed desk–bench combinations, built for the more-diminutive proportions of local students, we were glad that we'd started the day with an excellent breakfast with Xavier. He had taken us to his favourite spot, at the entrance to the college, where he introduced us to the lady who from 6.00am every day served up hot little French baguettes, sliced open and filled with a small omelette she fried on an open charcoal brazier and in which she sprinkled chopped shallots, sweet peppers and, if you wanted, grated dried meat. Those who asked for it got a little pure MSG sprinkled over the top for a bit of a kick-start to the morning! The whole lot, costing 3000 dong, the equivalent of about 30 cents, was topped off with a flick of fresh coriander: a wholesome and inexpensive meal. And as the three of us squatted at the roadside on Hanoi's ubiquitous tiny blue plastic stools and looked out across one of the city's many mini-lakes, we both knew the city would be easy to like and to live in.

We had our first language lesson and our student trio also gave us a quick tour of the capital's main attractions. Best of all, Trang hospitably invited us to dinner at her grandparents' home. Trang's uncle, Binh, met us in the ground-floor tiled entrance and sat with us in a circle of ornately carved straight-backed wooden chairs while we sipped on beer and soft drinks. Binh is a university-educated businessman who has established his own small-scale IT company. He speaks very adequate English, unlike Grandfather, who came gingerly down the stairs and gestured for us to follow him up into the eating/sleeping/living area where what furniture there was had been moved aside to make room for us to be seated at a simple table which Trang and her school colleagues were loading up with a feast of freshly cooked food, bringing steaming platters from the tiny kitchen across the hallway. We looked in and found Grandmother, pink-faced from the toil of creating this meal on a two-ring gas burner, which was perched precariously on top of a small wooden bench.

She came and sat beside Trish, insisting on piling food onto her plate and watching closely as she took a mouthful, waiting for her to comment on its flavours. Smiling, she took hold of Trish's forearm and, stroking it, she asked the questions that would be asked at least once almost every day in Vietnam: 'Are you married?' 'Do you have children?' 'How old are they?' We came to know of unmarried, childless foreign women and men in Vietnam who created fictional partners and children for themselves rather than suffer the indignity of the shocked response of their interrogator. Happy to hear that Trish had children who would look after her in her old age, she told us, through Trang, that she also had two children, Trang's father and Binh, who shifted uncomfortably on his seat as she explained that he was divorced.

'But,' Trang said, 'my parents were busy people and I was raised by my grandparents.' The three of them beamed at each other in open affection. Trang's whole demeanour softened as she told how her grandfather had sat with her and taught her to read. Not a hint of the political commissar now.

'My grandfather,' she announced with heartbreaking pride, 'is a veteran of the French and the American wars. He's a true patriot.'

At the entrance to the Voice of Vietnam's radio headquarters, the administration offices in Quan Su Street, sits a gigantic old loudspeaker, the mouth of which is close to two metres in diameter. We saw it as we were being shown across the courtyard and up a flight of stairs to a reception room where we would meet our new employers. We learnt later that it was one of the actual speakers that were set up along the northern bank of the Ben Hai River, in what was then known to foreigners as the DMZ, the Demilitarised Zone.

Every day these big speakers and others like it, capable of broadcasting to a distance of 10 kilometres, directed their programming over to the southern bank, urging the opposing South Vietnamese soldiers there to lay down their guns and join the forces in the north. The big speaker sits in VOV's courtyard now as an historical piece, a reminder of those distant and very difficult days.

'And this is Madame Nguyet, Hoang Minh Nguyet, the director of the International Relations Department of Radio the Voice of Vietnam.' We shook hands with a slim, attractive woman in her early forties.

We were standing in the reception room, as a half-dozen or so people filed in. Our first contact with the people we would be working with for the next fourteen months. The introductions continued around the room: Madame Nguyen Thi Hue, a slightly taller and well-built woman, in her fifties, director of the Overseas Service; then a slim, balding man, probably in his forties, with strands of dark hair combed across his head: Nguyen Tien Long, deputy director of the Overseas Service and executive producer of VOV5, the English language service; Madame Nguyen Thi Loc, also slim, with a slightly sad look about her, even when she smiled a polite 'hello', probably fifty-plus, director of the AM English language service.

'We're very happy to have you both here,' Madame Hue said in perfect English. 'Has everything been satisfactory for you over at the institute?'

'Absolutely,' Trish responded. 'They've been very helpful and the students have given us a great introduction to Hanoi.' Cups of green tea were being served as we all sat down on ornately carved chairs, decorated, in mother of pearl, with dragons and phoenixes, both potent symbols from Vietnam's ancient legends and culture of which we would learn more during our stay.

'You know, we've all lived in Australia at one time or another,' Long said with a smile.

'Really?' We were both genuinely surprised.

They all explained their different sojourns in Australia; two as diplomats' wives in Melbourne and Canberra, one as a student in Sydney. Polite conversation continued along these lines for ten minutes or so before turning to the job we were about to take over.

'How soon can you start?' Loc asked. 'Tomorrow?'

We looked at each other and smiled in mild surprise. It was a Tuesday. 'Not really,' Iain replied. 'We want to move into the house we're going to rent.'

Although we hadn't met her, we had arranged to take over the house being rented by the volunteer we were replacing, Nadine Ashton. We had seen photographs of the house, but that was all.

'We can move in on Thursday. We could probably start work on Friday. But we'd like to come in and see the office and meet the rest of the staff. We could do that tomorrow.'

'Tomorrow night we're having a farewell dinner for Nadine,' Long said. 'You're invited to that, of course. You can meet everybody then.'

VOV's radio broadcasting facilities are on Ba Trieu Street, four or five blocks from the headquarters. The English-language section is on the third floor of a six-storey building that also includes French, Russian, Chinese, Lao, Khmer, Japanese, Thai, Indonesian and Spanish language sections.

We arrived there the next day at around 6.30pm, shortly before we were due to head off for dinner with the staff, so we had a brief opportunity to check out the office and meet the members of the English Language Department who would be our daily work companions and Nadine, who was leaving Vietnam the following day.

The dinner was the first of many Vietnamese banquets over the next year or so; 'slap-up' dinners that are organised on the spur of the moment, on almost any excuse, where vast quantities of food and drink are brought in a continuous stream to the table and you stagger home feeling as if you need to hibernate for a month.

The Iraq War erupted on the following day, although we hadn't realised it until we walked past a restaurant and saw people crowded around a TV set broadcasting CNN. We'd been walking in Hanoi's Old Town trying to find sheets and bedcovers, and we looked across the heads of the group to see what had attracted their attention.

We went into the restaurant, ordered coffee and sat there more or less in silence for about an hour and a half watching the opening moves of 'Operation Iraqi Freedom'.

We wondered how they would deal with the war at VOV. It was hard to imagine them being pro-American.

And, on that point, this is probably as good a time as any to explain the set-up at Voice of Vietnam. All broadcasting in Vietnam is government controlled and the government is, of course, communist, one of only four nominally communist countries left in the world; China, North Korea and Cuba being the others. When we took on the job, we knew that this would be a broadcasting experience like nothing we had been through before. Everything tightly controlled, plenty of propaganda to deal with and little chance to influence anything in other directions. Well, that was what we expected. As it turned out, we were both right and wrong. Reasonably right about the first two and wrong about the last one.

Basically, we had been contracted to work two shifts; one from 9.00am until 2.00pm, the other from 2.00pm to 7.00pm, Monday to Friday, plus a few hours on Saturday afternoons. We decided to swap over each week so that we would only have to work the same shift for a week at a time. The main requirement was that of editors, editing the English-language news bulletins and current affairs programming that were being broadcast on VOV's short-wave overseas service, but also, for the most part, working on a network called VOV5, the English language service, which was broadcast in FM in major centres throughout Vietnam.

In addition to this basic editing job, it was hoped that we would be able to 'lift the game' of the local English-speaking Vietnamese reporters working in the department. By this we mean improving, through workshops and coaching, the level of their English pronunciation, their on-air reading and delivery skills, and their comprehension and uptake of modern English idiom and usage.

On our first day, we both worked the afternoon shift together, just to see how everything operated. We were a little surprised when we came in on that Friday afternoon to see CNN and the Gulf War running continuously on the television set at one end of the office. At least they were willing to allow Western coverage of it, we thought. Another TV set at the other end carried Chinese coverage.

On many occasions CNN's coverage was in conflict with the news bulletins we were editing, which, for the main parts came up from the Vietnamese service of VOV, one floor below us, and were translated into English by staff members in our department. But, in general, they were never over the top in condemnation of the American invasion of Iraq. There was nearly always a slight hedging involved. It wasn't until at least six months after the war was officially declared over that one of the members of our department told us of a special meeting of all staff that had been called on the day of the outbreak of hostilities.

A senior spokesperson from the Vietnamese Department of Foreign Affairs apparently came and gathered everyone together to tell them in fairly basic terms: 'The Americans are wrong in this war but we have now signed a new trade agreement with them. We have a lot of American investment coming in and we need their support in our bid to join the World Trade Organization, so our coverage of the Iraq War should ...' etc. etc. We understood.

And so it was that the start of our assignment at VOV coincided not only with the eruption of the Iraq War but also, although we didn't recognise it immediately, with the outbreak of SARS. The severe acute respiratory syndrome had surfaced in Vietnam more or less as we stepped off the plane, but we were so flat out adjusting that we didn't register this. A couple of days after the invasion of Iraq there was a headline in the *Vietnam News*: 'US Boy in Vietnam Contracts Mystery Pneumonia'. But no-one was talking publicly about SARS, least of all in the media and especially not on the English language service of VOV. For a little while authorities closed their eyes and prayed the killer virus would go away. It didn't. It spread with terrifying rapidity.

Subtle and not-so-subtle pressure was exerted from a number of areas to be more forthcoming with information about the virus. This was spearheaded by the World Health Organization's Dr Carlo Urbani, who had been stationed in Hanoi for two years. Dr Urbani had examined the 48-year-old Chinese–American man, the first person in Vietnam, and arguably the world, to fall victim to SARS, who came to be known somewhat callously as 'the index patient' only two days after he was admitted to Hanoi's French Hospital. This unfortunate man lived in Shanghai and had come on a visit to Vietnam, stopping off en route in Hong Kong.

Dr Urbani identified the virus, which was quickly dubbed SARS. By then the 'index patient' had flown back to Hong Kong, where he died, but not before he unwittingly spread the fatal disease, causing an eventual death toll of close to 100 in Hong Kong, and some 700 worldwide, as well as a massive downturn in the city's economy from which it took many months to recover. The government of Vietnam was finally persuaded to come out of its health closet and admit they had a problem. Passengers began to be screened at the airports and the interiors of planes were sprayed with disinfectant.

Initially, these public measures were placebos, instigated mostly in the hope of holding down the mounting sense of panic among a people who have been accustomed to their government attempting to run matters on a need-to-know basis. It was when nursing staff succumbed to the disease at Hanoi's French Hospital, the only truly international-standard hospital in Hanoi, and the institution closed itself down, that proactive measures began to be taken. Those diagnosed with the disease were quarantined along with their families and anyone else with whom they'd had contact. When the international health community reacted favourably to these measures, transparency became the buzzword in Vietnam.

But it was now that SARS took its cruellest victim. On 29 March, at the age of forty-six, Dr Carlo Urbani died while attending a medical conference in Bangkok. He had taken up his position in Hanoi when he was at the peak of a distinguished medical career. He had already lived and worked in demanding situations in Ethiopia, West Africa and Cambodia and in 1999, in recognition of his work, he received the Nobel Peace Prize on behalf of Médecins Sans Frontières.

So now, as the days progressed, it seemed clear that the situation was going to get worse before it got better. People started to pay more attention to food hygiene, washing their hands and giving their chopsticks an extra wipe with a paper serviette before using them. A friend of ours told us of being on a flight from Ho Chi Minh City to Hanoi that was delayed moments before take-off because a man had a coughing fit and was removed from the plane to be examined for SARS. There was an underlying sense of unease in the community.

We watched as a woman of about thirty hauled a bucket of water out of a well. Beside her, in an outdoor communal kitchen, a man squatted in front of a charcoal fire on which an earthenware bowl of noodle soup was brewing. A couple of rats scrabbled among food scraps in the corner of the small open space while, less than a metre away, a mother was scrubbing her naked three-year-old daughter in a tub of cold water. They were people from three different families going about their separate evening chores, and all the while a stream of friendly conversation flowed between them. Closing and locking the steel gate to our front patio, we stepped out into what we would come to call 'our courtyard', smiled and said '*Xin chau*' to the small group as we passed them to continue out through the laneway to the main street.

In some ways, just stepping out of our front door was like stepping back a couple of hundred years in time. We were living in a small Vietnamese village, a *son*, in the middle of the city. The house we had rented in Ly Thuong Kiet Street was opposite a four-

*An outdoor communal kitchen used by several families in our courtyard.*

star hotel, we were a three-minute walk from one of the tallest office and apartment blocks in the city, eight minutes from our office and the studios of VOV and ten minutes from Hoan Kiem Lake, the heart of the city. Yet, when we came in off the street and under an archway, down a small, partly covered lane into the little courtyard where our house was located, we entered a different world, totally inhabited by Vietnamese. Most of them were low-income earners who lived in a small network of lanes that ran back from the street for about 100 metres, with no other exits. The entrance to the courtyard was closed off every evening at about 10.30 by a high iron padlocked gate for which we were given a key.

We were the only non-Vietnamese living in the compound and it was a little embarrassing to us at first that we had this three-storey, three-bedroom house while, immediately to the right of us, a family of seven, including a bedridden woman in her nineties, were living in what was basically one room, about six or seven metres square. We were soon able to work out that we were not the only ones with more than one room to live in, however. There were several other two- or three-storey houses in the complex, all of them rather old or looking old, although they may have been built no more than thirty or forty years ago. These held families of up to six or seven, so that, as close as we could guess, the total population of the compound was around seventy or eighty people.

One day during the first couple of weeks after moving in, Iain strolled into the courtyard and up to the locked iron grille gate to the house, with the key in his hand, only to find the gate and the front door open. Doan Thi Xuan Mai, the maid employed by the former tenant and who had let us know in no uncertain terms that she 'came with the house', was in the kitchen, although it was not the time or the day of the week that she was expected to be working. Mai said something in Vietnamese, which Iain didn't understand, as he walked into the house with a questioning look. She gestured into the sitting room, where a uniformed police officer was just standing up from one of the armchairs.

Police in Vietnam wear a green uniform, a sort of jungle green to olive shade that makes them look very military. Coupled with the fact that their caps have a red band around them, like the army, as well as red collar tabs, you'd be forgiven for thinking they were military personnel.

Iain looked back to Mai, who was standing just behind him, to ask a question.

'He is from the local police office,' she said in her halting English.

Iain turned to the officer, smiled and held out his hand. '*Xin chao*,' he said in what was about the extent of his Vietnamese so far.

'*Xin chao*,' the officer replied, shaking his hand, and continuing with a few sentences in Vietnamese to Mai.

In a brief but convoluted interchange with Mai, half in English, half in sign language, Iain managed to gather that the officer wanted to ask what we were doing in Hanoi and how long we would be here. Over the next ten minutes or so Iain, or rather Mai and Iain, managed to explain what we would be doing at the Voice of Vietnam and that we would be in Hanoi for about a year. Iain showed him the business card of Madame Nguyet, head of VOV's International Relations Department, and suggested he contact her. The officer copied the details and stood up to go, holding out his hand.

'*Cam on ... Xin chao*,' he said, smiling. After a few words with Mai, he left the house and walked out of the courtyard.

As the new kids on the block at VOV, we wanted to tread very lightly, go very slowly and work out the dynamics of the office politics, while establishing what we were expected to do and, more importantly, not to do. However, the situation didn't allow for the luxury of time for any of us to adjust to each other. It was in at the deep end, sink in a sea of cultural gaffes, or swim because you're needed.

On our very first full shifts we were asked to listen to and then comment on the English language and presentation skills of every team member who was on air. Nobody told us of the pecking order, how long each person had worked there or, in what turned out to be the most important factor, to whom each person was related. So it was in, boots and all. Displaying as much tact as possible, we listened to each of them read their scripts, trying not to wince at some of the frightful diatribe (they were reading from the day's news reports), while keeping one eye on the body language of the reader, which we hoped would give a clue as to how they felt about having to read to these new foreigners, and with the other eye checking out the movements around the office to do a guesstimate on the power structure.

We felt immediately that what we needed was a pal. As things developed, it turned out quite naturally that we both seemed to get

**Washing time by the well in our courtyard.**

along best with the newest staff members, the ones who, we discovered later, were on a year's probation. Trish got along best with Huan, who was just twenty-one years old. They clicked. 'It helps,' she said, 'that he laughs at my jokes! I don't mean story jokes, I mean play-on-word jokes, use-of-language jokes.'

Huan had an agile mind and he loved language. His own, as well as English, but also Spanish, as he had only recently returned from six years studying in Cuba, Vietnam's 'fraternal friend' country, where his dad had worked as a counsellor at the Vietnamese Embassy and his mum, in earlier years, had broadcast news about the Vietnam War, beamed across to the American mainland.

'So your mum was a journalist?' Trish had asked him.

'Yes.'

'Is she still broadcasting?'

'Yes.'

'Who does she work for?'

'VOV.'

'Which department?'

'This one.'

'Oh. So which one is your mum?'

'You have to guess!'

She knew then they were going to be friends.

Then there was Thi. Trish called her Tiny Thi for some time because she was very tiny. Then one day Thi asked Trish what she could eat that would help her put on weight and Trish realised she wasn't particularly happy with being so tiny, so she took to calling her Terrific Thi. Her mum, it turned out, had also worked for decades at VOV, for the English Service and then for the Internet Department. She had only recently retired. It took a little while more for us to discover that Thi's mother's brother was married to Madame Hue, which meant that Madame Hue, the head of VOV's Overseas Service, which included the English section and eleven other language departments and who was our day-to-day supervisor, was Terrific Thi's aunt.

So now we'd worked out two things: we would only be told anything — anything at all — on a need-to-know basis, and ... Nepotism Rules. OK.

The final member of the probationary trio was Tram (pronounced Chum). Heavily pregnant, Tram was unrelated to anyone at VOV and able to ask the most personal questions without blinking.

'Do you dye your hair?' was her opening gambit with Trish.

Tram was one of three pregnant women in our team. It also seemed as though half the women in Hanoi were pregnant. In fact, government statistics showed that during the year — that is, the lunar year — there was a 33 per cent spike in the figures for childbirth. A veritable baby boom, and all due to the 'Golden Goat'.

The goat we're talking about is the one in the Vietnamese lunar calendar that made most of this year not just the year of the Goat but of the 'Golden Goat', one that only comes around once every sixty years. It's the combination that results from a formula involving the twelve zodiac animals in the lunar calendar and the five celestial elements: water, fire, wood, metal and earth. Technically, it is the year of the Water Goat, but somehow it's become more widely known as the Golden Goat.

The most important thing about the year of the Golden Goat is that it is eagerly awaited in Vietnam because it's supposed to be a year of extra virility for men and fertility for women. Whatever the truth of that, it resulted in an extra quarter of a million women being with child, way above the regular annual number of pregnancies. All in the hope that their offspring would be more virile, intelligent and successful.

The goat is revered in Vietnam for its sexual capacity. According to a local newspaper, 'The sexual power of one male goat is legendary. It can "satisfy" between thirty and fifty females.' Restaurateurs proclaim the aphrodisiacal qualities of goat's meat, claiming that it can boost a man's performance in the bedroom. They also recommend drinking rice wine distilled for six months in a bottle containing a goat's penis! In our year or so in Vietnam, we did get around to trying quite a few of the national 'delicacies', but definitely not that one!

The CNN correspondent doing a piece to camera in front of Baghdad's main mosque looked more at ease than we suspected he felt. Appearing relaxed in situations like that is something of a learnt trick — madness that appeals to certain hardcore reporters who have established themselves around the world's hot spots as a people apart. He must have known how fragile the success of the invasion by the American troops really was. He would have known about the imminent danger from snipers. One guessed he was living on adrenaline and bitter coffee. But he was there. And so were American troops. You could see them careering about in their tanks.

The invasion, according to VOV, which took the line promulgated by the ubiquitous Iraqi press officer who was seen daily on CNN, was bogged down in the sands, way south. And US troops were coming up against heavy resistance and struggling to hold their own. We also adjusted to the fact that VOV never use the description 'American'. Department Director Madame Hue gave us the pedantic political line: 'America includes Canada, Mexico and Central America and South America.' So instead of 'America', it was always to be 'US'.

'Giang,' Trish addressed one of the senior journalists who had handed her his piece for the news bulletin to check over, 'you see that chap there,' she gestured to the monitor that was carrying the live transmission. 'He's reporting from Baghdad. Those are American troops in Baghdad.'

Giang pursed his lips, but said nothing.

'Of course it is possible that it's just a digitised background,' she said. 'But somehow I doubt it. Don't you?'

A slight nod.

She held up the report he'd just handed her. 'This says the Americans are eating sand 200 kilometres away. It makes us look a bit foolish, don't you think?'

Without pause and without looking at her, Giang said, 'You'll see a big change overnight.'

At that moment the sound of an explosive volley of gunfire erupted from the monitor and Trish watched, mesmerised, live footage of a line of crouching men scurrying along a river bank tearing off their Iraqi army uniforms as they ran, throwing the clothing and their weapons down in an attempt to meld back into the civilian Iraqi population. Trish looked back at Giang, but he had gone.

The next morning's news bulletins on VOV had the American, or rather, US troops, in Baghdad.

It hardly needs to be said that the single most important, iconic and omnipresent figure in Vietnam is Ho Chi Minh. Throughout the whole of our time at VOV, never a day went by when there wasn't some news story, feature article or national celebration of a particular day in which Ho Chi Minh featured prominently. The surprising thing to us, despite all the propaganda we read and edited and were exposed to within the broader community over the course of more than a year, much of it blatantly dogmatic and aimed at perpetuating the myth or creating legends, was that we came away from Vietnam liking the man much more than we could have believed.

One came to the realisation that 'Uncle Ho' — 'uncle' is a universal term of respect and, in some cases, reverence in Vietnam — truly was a statesman of world stature and a visionary. Born in 1890, he led his country through the great military struggles of the second half of the century, first against French colonial rule and then against the Americans in what the West called the 'Vietnam' War, but which the Vietnamese have always called the 'American' War. Ho Chi Minh died in 1969 of lung cancer without seeing the triumph for North Vietnam in the South with its capture of Saigon and the unification of the country in 1975.

We decided we should learn more about him so we started at the end, his end, or really the end of his mortal remains: the huge mausoleum, built to house his body in a glass sarcophagus which was made for Vietnam by the Soviet Union on Hanoi's expansive Ba Dinh Square, the site of one of Ho's greatest days, his declaration of Vietnam's independence, on 2 September 1945. The irony of this great edifice is that Ho stated specifically in his will that he did not want a great tomb or even a big funeral. He asked that he be cremated and that his ashes be divided into three parts, with one lot buried in the North, one in the centre of the country and one in the South. He requested that each urn should be buried on an appropriate hillside and that a simple shelter be built over each, so that travellers could sit in the shade and contemplate. The rulers of Vietnam who took over the reins after Ho's death diverged from his wishes in a big way. The mausoleum, with his body on show to up to 20,000 people a week, plus a huge museum devoted entirely to Ho situated in a large park immediately behind the black marble edifice of the mausoleum, is the result.

On the second weekend after we started work at VOV, we took a cab to Ba Dinh Square and, at a little after 8.00am, joined the already 500-metre-long queue to begin slowly moving towards the tomb. There were very few foreigners in the queue; the vast majority were Vietnamese who appeared to be visitors, many of them clearly poorer people from the countryside, dressed in their Sunday best, with their children. As we approached the entrance, one of the frequent changing of the guard ceremonies took place, with two jackbooted, white-uniformed soldiers, led by a similarly dressed officer, who slow-march goosestepped up to the two soldiers standing guard at the entrance and relieved them from duty to march them back to their barracks. As we entered the mausoleum, other soldier guards kept a close eye on the two lines of people, checking what they might be carrying — all cameras had to be handed in a couple of hundred metres back — and making sure there was no talking. On a wall facing us was a quote in Vietnamese from Ho Chi Minh; a replica of his handwriting in large gold letters. Translated, it read: 'Nothing is more important than independence and freedom'.

We climbed a broad flight of marble stairs, took a turn to the right and then another, straight into the chamber, and there, with his wispy beard and a look of real contentment, lying as if asleep, in a white Mao jacket, with his hands clasped on his chest and a sheet drawn up over half his body, lay Uncle Ho. At least that's what we're all supposed to accept, as is the case with Lenin and Mao. Of course they all could be Madame Tussaud jobs, but at

**The resting place of Ho Chi Minh who ironically said that he didn't want a great tomb or even a big funeral.**

least in Ho's case there's no evidence to support the idea. It's just that he does look a bit waxen. Not surprising, really, if you've been dead for more than thirty years.

As Vietnam reeled from the double whammy of king hits to their economy in the form of the Iraq War and SARS, we got on with the really important things in life, like making the house in the courtyard feel more like home. It was when we filled the tiny upstairs balcony/drying area and the front enclosed patio with greenery that everyone in the courtyard, who up to now had watched our comings and goings with sideways looks, decided that we were going to be good neighbours. Large tropical plants were delivered in several runs by an exceptionally strong and healthy-looking nursery proprietor who, after balancing them on the back of her motorbike for the 10-kilometre run, swung them onto our front patio area with admirable ease. Without inhibition, our neighbours happily became involved in the repotting, positioning and watering procedures and took pleasure in showing us how a new pump-action watering can worked. Having established ourselves and marked our territory, we could now get on with the job at hand.

One of the first descriptive phrases you pick up while living and working in Vietnam is 'Viet Kieu'. It simply means 'Overseas Vietnamese'. It is, however, also a very loaded phrase in that it's generally taken to mean that any individual so described has 'fled the scene' or 'done a runner'. In other words, in either one of two critical periods of Vietnam's recent history, they made the decision to leave their country by any means possible, which invariably meant in some rickety, unseaworthy boat. Viet Kieu in a large percentage of cases meant 'boat people'.

These people were the so-called Vietnamese refugees, and they fell into two categories related to the two periods when they made the decision to leave. The first lot were political refugees, fleeing from the communist takeover of South Vietnam in 1975 and its aftermath. The second wave of people were called economic refugees because they took off during a period of complete economic collapse, which saw famine throughout much of the land during the mid–1980s. These Viet Kieu, or Overseas Vietnamese, number around three million people, of whom about half live in the United States, and a big percentage in Australia. They now constitute a major economic force which the Vietnamese government would very much like to tap. In fact, they have been tapping it with increasing success over the past few years, largely by backflipping on their policy of antagonism towards people who had, in one respect, deserted the ship, and by adopting a new friendly policy of welcoming Viet Kieu back as visitors or permanent residents to their homeland with encouraging offers and incentives to invest their overseas wealth in Vietnam.

Already, apart from any investments in businesses in Vietnam, Overseas Vietnamese remit more than US$2.5 billion each year to relatives, from ninety different countries and territories. In addition, there are some 350,000 Vietnamese who have gone, quite legitimately, to overseas countries; Asian countries such as South Korea and Malaysia, as well as Middle Eastern and European countries; whereas in earlier times the destinations were invariably East Germany, the former USSR, Cuba, Romania and other communist bloc nations. These visits are all on government-sanctioned contracts of up to several years, as foreign workers, who send back an additional US$1.4 billion each year. These people, however, are not regarded as Viet Kieu.

Considerable numbers, around 300,000, of Overseas Vietnamese now visit the country each year and the amount of business investment in Vietnam by Viet Kieu is also growing. In Ho Chi Minh City alone there are over a thousand companies owned by Overseas Vietnamese, with a capital value of almost US$150 million, and throughout the country the level of investments by Viet Kieu is growing by up to US$40 million a year.

But there are still substantial numbers of Vietnamese living overseas who harbour strong feelings of resentment and hostility towards the government in Hanoi. Many families lost everything when the South fell in 1975, while others, who may have been living under communism in the North for many years, found that the strictures of agrarian reform and rigid communist orthodoxy applied to economic management also brought disaster for them and provided sufficient reason to flee. A number of these have formed groups specifically aimed at thwarting any rapprochement between the government in Hanoi and the Viet Kieu.

As a personal observation, it seems to us that those who wish to cling to the past will derive little benefit from the future, while those who have returned to their country, either to visit or stay, and who are now investing there, have found a country which, although it is still nominally communist, is changing rapidly in the direction of greater freedom and democracy, and will provide them with a more dynamic and almost certainly more interesting future.

We had anticipated that living and working in Vietnam would be an enjoyable challenge that would enrich our lives in a number of ways. As it happened, one of the most pleasurable aspects came from our friendship with a remarkable and beautiful young woman, Rebecca Hales. Rebecca has a warm personality, sharp intellect, wide interests and a delightfully wicked sense of irony and humour and, probably most important of all, we share similar values and beliefs.

We had actually met Rebecca at the 'full-immersion' seminar run by AVI during a cold week in Melbourne a few months before we went to Hanoi. The three of us immediately warmed to one another. In Hanoi, she was employed at one of the city's universities to train teachers and at another to teach English communication skills to exceptionally bright science and technology graduates. Right from the start our lives became enmeshed.

Another plus was that for the first time in more than forty years we had no car. Which meant there were no gas, servicing or maintenance bills, and no registration or insurance costs. Also, for the first time, no credit cards. They are accepted in Vietnam, of course, but with everything being so cheap, we never seemed to use cards. And no mobile phone. Which meant no phone calls at intrusive moments. Life became suddenly simpler. Living in the heart of the city meant that we could walk to and from work. And with a flag fall of around 70 Australian cents and no big distances to cover, taxis were a feasible option. On the other hand, emails became de rigeur, especially when the news of SARS was communicated around the world, and it suddenly seemed as though everyone we knew was emailing us with gloom-and-doom stories and both our children were stridently suggesting that it was time, as our son put it, 'to stop playing martyr' and come home.

Not that there was any real chance of that. Although tourists were already striking Asian destinations off their trip lists, we had decided that we weren't going to pack up and head home. After all, Hanoi was a city of four million people. The chances of contracting SARS were infinitesimal unless it really developed into some sort of pandemic, in which case we'd reconsider. However, SARS and the Iraq War certainly captured ours and everyone else's attention over this period, as did another extraordinary story that one feels tempted to say could only happen in Vietnam, although we're sure there are plenty of other countries that could match it.

We didn't find out about it until towards the end of the month as no-one in the office had told us. Perhaps they felt embarrassed, but their former boss, Tran Mai Hanh, the director general of Radio the Voice of Vietnam and one of the highest ranking members of the Communist Party, had been arrested a few months before we arrived. Along with 153 other defendants, he was now facing trial. He was the character with the obviously dyed comb-over haircut we had seen in glossy brochures advertising the Voice of Vietnam Radio network during the few months between the time we accepted the posting to Hanoi and when we actually arrived. He featured in many of the photos, gladhanding people and smiling benevolently over technicians and broadcasters working in studios.

Stories relating to the trial were now dominating the Vietnamese newspapers and television but not the English-language press, which consisted solely of the *Vietnam News*, a government-run English-language newspaper, or on Voice of Vietnam Radio. There were a couple of stories but they were very low-key. Definitely not front-page or bulletin-leading stuff. 'Bias by placement', we decided.

We first picked up on the story through spotting the rather outlandish photos of the defendants, all in loose-fitting pyjama-like outfits of broad black-and-white vertical stripes, which covered the front pages of the several Vietnamese-language papers that were delivered every day to the office. And then, of course, the story was suddenly all on the office TV and everyone was watching it. It was also very noticeable as we walked along any of the streets in the city, that the television sets in shops and stores were all tuned to the live broadcast of the trial.

'Why didn't someone tell us about this before?' we asked Huan.

'We thought you would have known about it.'

And in a sense we should have, but it's a common tendency, it seems, to only pick up on what's happening in a country from the time you arrive there, whereas this had all been building up over the previous year.

Anyway, our guy in this trial, although to us he seemed a pretty big fish, was in reality only one of a number of high-ranking officials, including a vice-minister of public security and a vice national chief prosecutor, who were facing the chop. And that's not just a metaphor for a prison sentence. In Vietnam you can be shot for commercial crimes or corruption. No, the big guy in this one was a real criminal, in *The Godfather* sense. In fact, he was being described variously as Vietnam's 'top crime boss' or Vietnam's 'mafia boss' in all the reports.

Truong Van Cam, better known as Nam Cam, had built up a vast criminal enterprise based in Ho Chi Minh City that included a string of illegal gambling dens, cockfighting rings, drug dealing, extortion, prostitution and sleazy karaoke joints. Hundreds of people, including police, government officials and journalists, were in his pocket. His influence within the Ho Chi Minh City police establishment was so extensive that authorities from other provinces had to be sent to arrest him.

And the trigger for his arrest? A blatant and open murder in which a rival gang-leader was shot as she sat outside a hotel having a drink with women friends in the northern port city of Hai Phong. A hit man appeared out of the dark, shot her in the head and disappeared into the shadows. The woman who was shot, Vu Hoang Dung, was Nam Cam's equivalent in the north. In other words, she was the crime boss of Hai Phong, and obviously, from the long list of government officials arrested in the crackdown that followed her murder, had considerable influence in the capital, Hanoi, just 100 kilometres from Hai Phong.

She and her associates had been making moves to break into the lucrative crime scene in Ho Chi Minh City and, for a time, it seemed as if the Crime King of the south and the Crime Queen of the north might make some sort of a deal to divvy up the crime pickings from the whole country. But the story is that they fell out and, at a birthday party reception thrown by Nam Cam, Dung arranged for a large gift container to be suspended from the ceiling, promising that it contained balloons and party gifts, but when the string was pulled to release the surprises, the guests were showered with live rats covered in excrement. A tall story? Maybe, but the fact is, within days Dung lay dead on the sidewalk at the instigation of Nam Cam.

This dramatic event and the implications of the spreading power of the 'Saigon Mafia', as Nam Cam's cronies were dubbed, sparked the government into action. One arrest led to another and the overlapping webs of influence, corruption and power that Nam Cam and Dung had separately developed was steadily uncovered.

The VOV Director General, Tran Mai Hanh, had been implicated and charged with having on many occasions worked to influence reporting on the Voice of Vietnam of Nam Cam's activities and directing editors to either play down, remove from news bulletins, or give a favourable edge to stories about him. He was also charged with taking huge bribes. With so many defendants, the trial was the biggest criminal proceeding in Vietnam's history and was set to continue for some time, with sentencing not until June. But with charges that included murder, gambling, giving bribes and sheltering criminals, the outlook for Nam Cam, at least, was not good.

'He'll get the death sentence,' Loc murmured, unsmiling.
'What about Tran Mai Hanh?' Iain asked.
'Ah, that's a more complicated question.'

Among the established team members who had been with VOV5 since its inception almost five years previously, the woman Trish found it most easy to strike up a friendship with was Hanh. So much of office life seems to be influenced by the happenstance geography of the placement of desks. The desk we shared as we changed shifts in the early afternoon — a real test of tolerance as we have such different working styles — was jammed up against a pillar on which hung the ubiquitous image of Ho Chi Minh. Hanh's desk hugged the pillar at a right-angle to ours, which meant we could easily converse privately. She was six months pregnant.

During our time in the country it became sadly apparent that pregnancy does not sit well with many Vietnamese women. Time and again we watched as women we knew began their pregnancies looking robust and then with distressing rapidity took on a haunted, strained appearance. Over the months we worked out that this was more than likely due to an underlying low general level of health which, when tested by the usual physical and emotional strains of pregnancy, become worn and threadbare.

Two-thirds of the way through her pregnancy, Hanh looked drawn and tired. The reasons for this became apparent in the increasingly intimate conversations she had with Trish. She appeared to be something of an outsider, by choice. The other senior reporters would josh each other companionably and sometimes not so companionably, calling out to each other across the tops of their computer screens. There was a lot of chat and laughter which never seemed to include Hanh, and when they went off for lunch she rarely joined them. Nor did she join in the girly banter about clothes or household shopping. She had other interests, and once she picked up on the fact that Trish wanted to learn about Vietnamese music and drama, poetry and writing, she was pleased to share her knowledge.

Hanh could readily be described as more serious and studious, perhaps due to her life experience. Whereas the other senior reporters had all studied varying subjects in Hanoi universities, Hanh had been awarded a scholarship to study in the Soviet Union.

'My parents were so pleased,' she told Trish. 'They saw it as an honour.'

That was in 1991. Hanh was part of the last group of Vietnamese students the Soviet Union accepted before it all fell apart.

'The Union was collapsing even as I was leaving home,' she said, 'but there was no turning back. And anyway, I wanted the experience of living abroad.'

As it turned out, it wasn't quite the experience she had anticipated. She attended a university in an industrial town 400 kilometres west of Moscow.

'I was disappointed by what I saw. The Russians had next to nothing. But they still looked down on us, their Vietnamese brothers and sisters, and tried to treat us like poor relatives. They were not hospitable to us at all.'

Hanh lived in a dormitory for foreign students, the majority of them Vietnamese. 'The food was the worst thing,' she said. 'And the cold was almost as bad. We had an allowance, but it was so small it was impossible to eat properly. I couldn't ask my parents for money. Life was difficult enough for them. So a couple of times a year I jumped the train into Moscow, travelling illegally without a ticket because I couldn't afford one, and I'd go to a place I'd been told about by other Vietnamese students where I used what little money I had to buy cheap clothing that I'd take back to sell to other students at a slight profit. I remember one time I made the journey in the winter and I had to sleep out in a Moscow park while I waited for my contact to turn up, and I thought I'd die of the bitter cold in the snow.'

Hanh studied for four years, and after graduating with a degree in Russian, she returned to Hanoi only to find that life had changed so much that her Russian was next to useless. So she began all over again, this time studying English. And now she was married and pregnant.

'You must be very happy after all that,' Trish said to her brightly.

Hanh nodded and said, 'I hope so.'

By the end of March we felt we were beginning to get a handle on things, settling into something of a routine and getting a feel for the personalities and the office politics. However, there was still a wonderful buzz to it. Hanoi is such an interesting and exciting city.

In the office, we were quickly coming to terms with all the unfamiliar names and their pronunciations. Some of them we never got quite right. Vietnamese is a language in which, although they employ the Roman alphabet, they are forced, because of the use of different tones in the spoken language which simply can't be described just with letters, to use accents — five of them. So that with a simple word like *ma* you can have six different meanings: one for the word written without any accent, which means 'ghost' in English and five more — 'mother', 'which', 'tomb', 'horse' or 'rice seedling', just by using the different accents either above or beneath the vowel. This can lead to embarrassing mispronunciations of certain words and, to compound the difficulties, something spelt in a certain way in English is often pronounced in a totally different way in Vietnamese, even without the accents.

For example, the common Vietnamese name Nguyen, which is the equivalent of Smith or Jones in English, is pronounced 'Win'. Tram's name is pronounced 'Chum', and as a general rule any word starting with 'tr' is usually pronounced as if it starts with 'ch'. Hanh's name also got us into trouble throughout the whole time we were there. The closest we can get to its pronunciation is somewhere between 'Hai' and 'Hi' with the ending clipped very short.

To get on top of the names as quickly as possible, Iain went to the rather unusual and initially embarrassing lengths of taking photos of each of the staff members on his digital camera and asking them to say their name into the little microphone on the camera. Everyone took it in very good humour, however, and in fact the photos came in handy later in the year when we set about producing a new brochure for VOV5.

Anyway, by the end of the month we must have been doing something right in the eyes of the Director of the Overseas Service, Madame Hue (pronounced 'Way'), because on the evening of 31 March, she walked across to our desk and put a sheaf of papers in front of Iain.

'This is the fortnightly *Review of the Communist Party of Vietnam*,' she said, with a sort of hopeful smile. 'We'd like you both to edit it.'

# *April*

# PRISONERS, VICTIMS AND HEROES

*'Speak gently to reach the soul'*

At the time of the collapse of communism in Eastern Europe there was widespread destruction of the numerous statues of Lenin in the Soviet Union's client states. But Hanoi's imposing edifice of the lion of Soviet Communism has never had to worry. From atop his pedestal in a leafy park, V.I. Le Nin, as he is designated in Vietnamese, looks confidently across to the entrance of the Vietnamese Army Museum on Dien Bien Phu Street. Designed and sculpted by two Russian artists, he's grim and grey, with his gaze set on the future.

Below him, young couples yearn for more privacy, parents keep an indulgent eye on their ice-cream-eating toddlers and older people play an energetic game of shuttlecock, miraculously hardly rasing a sweat in Hanoi's constant humidity. It seems unlikely that any of them know, or care, that this month sees the one hundred and thirty-third anniversary of the birth of Vladimir Ilich, a figure who for them has probably passed, along with communism, into the realm of historical irrelevancy. This is a fact that the Vietnam leadership faces every day: personal choice and freedom winning out over idealism and dogma. Like the end of a passionate love affair, for many the acceptance that the concept was fatally flawed from its inception leaves an aftertaste of sadness.

Two million people belong to Vietnam's Communist Party. Two million, out of 83 million. By far the vast majority of members reside in the North. Also by far the vast majority are over forty, which in Vietnam is considered to be bordering on elderly. Even so, you cannot just join the Party. You have to be invited. The CPVN leadership must on occasions wake at night in a cold sweat from the nightmare of having a tiger by the tail and the fear that they could be sidelined, as 83 million people clamour for a greater share of the promised and clearly growing prosperity, as well as increasing levels of individual rights. Right now they just manage to keep a lid on it.

No-one is suggesting that a coup, or an overthrow of the government, is imminent, or even likely to happen. It's just that those who hold power in Hanoi have to be even more on their toes than most other politicians worldwide; reading the signs, loosening off a bit there, tightening up a bit here, in order to keep the majority on side. There is only so much that even absolute power can hold in check. In Vietnam, communism is everywhere and nowhere. A chimera. A phantasm. It's what brought the country independence. But it's also brought it close to social and economic collapse on a couple of occasions and held it in stasis for decades.

All these considerations and a plethora more hovered in the background as we attempted to smarten up the writing of the *Communist Party Review*, written supposedly by the Party's intellectual elite and presented to us by Madame Hue. An example:

THE FIGHT AGAINST SIGNS OF PRAGMATIC OPPORTUNISM
IN THE NEW STAGE
In this victorious cause, while the people's confidence in the Party has been increasingly enhanced, there appeared some individuals who have opportunist ideology. Knowing that the

revolutionary trend in Vietnam is irreversible, the opportunist signs are not so extremist to arrogantly distort Marxist-Leninism and Ho Chi Minh's Thought (except reactionary forces). Therefore, opportunism or revisionism on a higher level was non-existent or rarely existed. At a lower level, opportunism is often linked to pragmatism.

And so it would continue, usually for about forty to sixty pages, every fortnight. Our exasperated, sotto-voce expletives as we trawled through page after page of this stuff caused much amusement in the office. Over the months, various members of the staff would reveal the level of their own doubt and even scorn they held for the official word. Gentle scorn, for after all ...

The three senior members of the English Department we had met on our introductory day were, we discovered quite quickly, all members of the Communist Party. We also learnt that they were the *only* Party members. No-one else among the staff apparently showed any interest in membership. They were Madame Hue, Mr Long and Madame Loc, or as they were also more commonly called, Hue, Long and Loc. We're not sure why the women were called 'Madame' and not 'Mrs'; perhaps a carryover from French colonial days.

Both Hue and Loc were due for retirement during the following year. In Vietnam, when a woman reaches fifty-five years of age, retirement is compulsory. For men, it's age sixty. It seemed to us that neither of them was looking forward to it. Hue and Loc — who was director of the English Language AM, or short-wave network — had both spent many years of government service getting to their present positions, either by dint of their own efforts, through their membership of the Party or the influence of their husbands, or by a combination of all three. Long, who was in his forties, still had a long way to go before retirement.

Another woman due for retirement in just a few months was Pham Thi Nam, who we discovered was Huan's mother. She was a short, slightly plump woman with a pleasant, happy disposition, who worked away quietly at her editing, despite the chaos and noise around her in the office, until she had finished a piece and would then come up to either of us, depending on who was there at the time, and say humorously, 'Here comes another of my masterpieces'. In the middle of the day during a quiet period, Nam would open out a folding recliner behind a bank of computers, stretch out, go to sleep and snore gently away, with CNN's coverage of the closing stages — well, what were then *thought* to be the closing stages — of the Iraq War flickering away silently on the TV screen at one end of the room. No matter what one's views of the rights and wrongs of the US invasion of Iraq, it was difficult not to be impressed by the scale of the power used and the speed of the campaign and it was clear to us that the office staff watching it with us through March and April were also amazed.

It's probably best to admit now that in the fifteen months we lived in Hanoi we ate dinner at home no more than perhaps a dozen times. And probably on half those occasions we had home-delivered meals. Why make dinner after finishing work with the 7.00pm news broadcast when the choice of where to eat out is so extensive and inexpensive? But as we still needed to shop for breakfast supplies, we did make frequent visits to our local market, the 1912, named after the date of the commencement of the war against the French, following their reoccupation of Vietnam after World War II: 19 December (1912). The market was just a hop, skip and a jump along from our place.

We could buy everything we needed to sustain life in the 1912, from a sparkly evening top for those whoopee karaoke nights out to little newspaper twists of spices, chosen from an array of delicately perfumed, small colourful pyramids of the freshly ground

*Block ice delivered through the narrow aisles of the 1912 market.*

product. Mind, we did need a strong stomach to run the gauntlet of what could euphemistically be called a 'meat department' that was unlike any we had ever seen in our local Woolworths. Live chickens, chunks of recently butchered larger animals, mostly pigs, swinging from fearsome hooks above wooden slabs appealingly decorated with trotters, tongues, ears and eyes and, in one section, piles of small, skinned and roasted dog carcases.

In Hanoi what you eat follows the rhythm of the year, helping to keep you connected to the earth. Tropical- and temperate-climate fruits, vegetables and fresh spices are all available in inexpensive abundance. Though, of course, whenever we carry our purchases into the office, we are queried about how much we paid and invariably there are tut-tuts about how we have been overcharged. To these naturally thrifty and hard-bargaining housekeepers, we are a dismal failure in the bargaining stakes.

The only area of profligate spending of which they do approve are the flowers that Trish brings into the office. Hanoi is a city of flowers. They are brought into town before dawn, from the huge flower market on the outskirts, and are for sale everywhere; in the markets, on the sidewalks, from the backs of motorcycles and bicycles and from shoulder-slung baskets. Twenty long-stemmed roses, in a range of colours, for 20,000 dong ($2.00). All manner of dramatic exotic tropical blooms and our favourites, the tightly closed lotus blossoms, which open spectacularly over a period of a few days into dinner plate-sized pink or cream flowers. For 50,000 dong ($5.00) you receive armfuls.

Halfway between the 1912 and our courtyard are what remains of the grim walls of Hoa Lo Prison. The French called it Maison Centrale, a direct translation of which is simply 'Central House'. From the moment it was built, in the centre of Hanoi, between 1886 and 1889, to the design of Auguste-Henri Vildieu, the chief government architect in France's colonial administration, Maison Centrale had a forbidding and gloomy air. Before long the local Vietnamese populace had dubbed it 'Hoa Lo', or 'the Hell Hole'. It was designed to hold 450 inmates, but by 1954, in the final days of France's domination of Indochina, it held 2000 Vietnamese prisoners, the majority of whom had been incarcerated on political grounds, sometimes for decades. Many were tortured or guillotined.

Little more than ten years after France's departure from Vietnam and Indochina, the prison began playing host to large numbers of American airmen whose planes had been shot down during bombing raids over Hanoi, the port of Hai Phong and other targets in North Vietnam. These pilots gave the prison its equally well-known name, the 'Hanoi Hilton'. Among the prisoners held there, some of them for six or seven years, was Douglas 'Pete' Petersen, a pilot who bailed out of a burning F4 Phantom in September 1966, and John McCain, who was shot down the following year.

After the release of all the American pilots held in Hoa Lo Prison in 1973, at the time of the American pullout from Vietnam, John

McCain went on to become a US senator and, in 1996, Pete Petersen was named by President Clinton as the United States' first ambassador to the Socialist Republic of Vietnam. He served in Hanoi from 1997 to 2001.

The prison, or rather the museum, as it is now, only occupies a fraction of the entire city block it was originally built on. In the mid–1990s the bulk of it was torn down to make way for the construction of a twin high-rise complex of offices and apartments called Hanoi Towers. The two structures now standing on that piece of real estate provide a stark contrast between the present and the past. And the fact that even a small part of the old prison remains today is due to strong pressure to save at least some of it, which came largely from former prisoners, many of whom were people with influence where it counted.

As the museum was only a few minutes' walk from our house, we had it high on our 'to see' list and, in early April, paid a visit. To say that it is grim is putting it mildly. The tiny barred cells, the leg-irons that clamped prisoners onto the concrete floor of their cells, the instruments of torture all set out on display as you follow the arrows through the three or four main buildings of the museum, leave you with a sense of horror and dread. Then there are the two guillotines, one standing in an outer courtyard, now walled with an impressive but chilling sculptured mural, the other inside, next to fourteen death-row cells and replete with a large wicker basket into which the heads rolled.

The section dealing with the American prisoners of war, nearly all of them pilots or aircrew from almost a thousand US warplanes that were shot down during the bombing of North Vietnam, is at one end of the museum complex and relatively small. It is nonetheless very absorbing, containing as it does relics in the form of flight suits, helmets and various crew paraphernalia, plus many photographs of airmen, either at the point of their capture or in captivity, as well as shots of the huge damage caused by the long-running bombing campaign. There is naturally a degree of pro-

*One of the two French guillotines in Hoa Lo Prison, just a block from our house.*

Vietnamese propaganda, but it's not over the top and not as aggressively anti-American as one might expect.

Also en route between the 1912 and our courtyard and also close to Hoa Loa Prison is Quan Su Pagoda, the most important religious centre for Buddhists in northern Vietnam. Buddha's birthday is a moveable feast celebrated according to the lunar calendar and this year it fell in the middle of April. It was our first experience of the resurgence of religious life in Vietnam since the Party eased off the brakes on large-scale public displays of spiritual life.

During the build-up to Buddha's birthday, the whole block became increasingly busy. The roadside stalls selling incense sticks and bundles of photocopied US$100 notes for burning, together with red cellophane-wrapped sugar pyramids and long-stemmed red roses as altar offerings, doubled and then tripled in number. Shops that specialised in selling religious artefacts were crammed with customers. Lights were strung through the trees and along the edges of the high wall bordering the pagoda and around the entrances so that, at night, the building looked inviting and festive. Crowds built steadily and on the appointed day, when the street was closed to vehicular traffic, the pagoda was one moving mass of happy-looking people.

Every now and again in the crowd there would appear the shaven head, peaceful Buddha-like features and sombre brown robes of a monk or nun. There are 34,000 Buddhist monks and nuns in Vietnam. Many of them attend one of the three Buddhist universities or four Buddhist colleges established around the country, and every year 150 of them are allowed to go abroad to further their religious studies.

This is a huge change from the situation immediately following reunification of the country in 1975, when the triumphant Communist Party, in something of an orgy of anti-religious fervour, closed pagodas, forbade religious teaching and imprisoned many monks and nuns in re-education camps. As the government has eased its stranglehold on almost all aspects of life, however, Buddhism has been allowed to rebloom, albeit still under a watchful eye and firm control.

The Vietnamese celebration of the Christian festival of Easter, this year occurring a few days after Buddha's birthday, was just as much a surprise for us. We had naturally read various criticisms of Vietnam, mainly originating in the United States but occasionally from Europe, on the issue of religious freedom. We decided on Easter Sunday to wander along to St Joseph's Cathedral at the end of Nha Tho Street to see what might or might not be happening there.

The big, square-towered neo-Gothic structure, inaugurated in 1886, fits all the traditions of a medieval European cathedral, with an excellent array of stained-glass windows and an ornate altar. There were large crowds, both outside and inside the cathedral, and fortunately we had arrived some time before the mass was due to start, so we were able to weave our way down one of the side aisles to a position from where we could see a bit of the service. The aisles were packed and we stood, shoulder to shoulder with Vietnamese, young and old, dripping with perspiration in the stifling heat despite the whirring of dozens of fans mounted on the cathedral's columns.

The service, full of the pomp, colour and circumstance of a high mass, was conducted by a man who was, at that time, Vietnam's only surviving cardinal, 83-year-old Pham Dinh Tung. At the end of the service, as he walked down the aisle leading the clergy and choir out into the square and the waiting crowd, the congregation gave him a huge round of applause. The newspapers of the following day showed no pictures of the event, nor any of a service in Ho Chi Minh City. They did, however, have a photograph of the Pope in Rome at Easter.

Estimates of the number of Christians (which in real terms means Catholics) in Vietnam range from six to eight million, but even at the higher figure it's still only 10 per cent of the population — small in the overall religious picture of Vietnam. Christianity did not take off in the same way as it did in the Philippines, largely because it was and is still seen by many as a conqueror's religion, propagated by the former French colonial rulers of Indochina. Christianity's impact on Vietnamese society is, however, disproportionate to its size and ever since the collapse of French rule and the departure of the French after 1954, has been a thorny issue for the communist government, firstly just in northern Vietnam and then, following reunification in 1975, throughout the whole country.

It was the division of the country into two halves as a result of the 1954 Geneva accords that set Christianity and communism at loggerheads in Vietnam. The division was only supposed to last two years, pending nationwide elections to unify the country by the middle of 1956. The elections never took place, of course, but the immediate aftermath of the partitioning of Vietnam saw a huge exodus of refugees moving from the North to the South, almost a million by some estimates, most of whom were Catholics.

This was a time of chaos in which a notorious slogan was put out by the American colonel Edward Lansdale, of the Office of Strategic Services (OSS), who was immortalised in Graham Greene's novel *The Quiet American* as Alden Pyle. The slogan, widely circulated amongst Catholic communities in the North, said, 'The Virgin Mary is going south'.

This exodus coincided with the fact that the communist government in the North entered a period, lasting some years, in which the country was subjected to a strictly doctrinaire form of communism, which included the closure of cathedrals and churches all over the North, polarising the religious scene, more or less forcing it into a Christianity-versus-communism mode and creating considerable tension between the Vatican and Hanoi in the process.

In the past, the government in Hanoi has rejected a number of the Vatican's appointments of cardinals for Vietnam, recognising only three since the end of the war in 1975. In more recent years a lot has been done on both sides to try to re-establish a more stable and rational relationship and in fact, later in the year, a new Vietnamese cardinal *was* permitted to take office. But in the meantime the Vietnamese state permits only a handful of state-sponsored religions to operate and insists on the right to review any appointments, a situation that naturally attracts the attention of civil rights and religious freedom advocates in other countries, notably the United States.

In addition to religious freedom and civil rights, the personal conviction stakes had already shaped up in the early part of April as pretty hard core, what with events marking the anniversary of Lenin's birthday, Buddha's birthday and Christ's death. So there had been plenty of fuel for question-and-answer time in the office. Huan, Thi, Tram and Trish would escape the ever-watchful ears and eyes of the other members of the team and cross to the far side of the large open office. Here, seated around one end of the large conference table, under the pretence that they were practising presentation skills, they would chat about anything and everything.

'Let's go for a good goss,' Tram would suggest, smiling a little self-consciously at the new word she had picked up. They would always take news copy with them, so that if either Mesdames Hue or Loc passed by they could be heard practising their 'L's and 'W's, the two Roman letters that caused the young reporters the most grief. Trish would try to get them to put rhythm and colour into their reading. But mostly it was answering full-on questions like, 'Do you believe in a god?' (Thi) 'Are you a Christian?' (Huan) and 'D'you use mascara?' (Tram). Trish felt on safe ground with the mascara. The rest was pretty tricky.

There were some challenging times, dredging up long put-aside stories and trying to place them in their historical context. And it was fascinating to view from the outside what most people from a Judaic–Christian culture take as read. None of it stands up to much sensible scrutiny. The Vietnamese would flinch at the cruelty of crucifixion and struggle with the concepts of original sin and virgin

*Trish with her favourite flower seller.*

birth but, surprisingly, had no difficulty at all with the notion of the Trinity.

It would be wrong, however, to think that we didn't get around to tackling some of the more professional aspects of our job, like presentation skills. These morning sessions were enjoyable and satisfying and were certainly a relief from the mentally straining job of editing the turgid and repetitive *Communist Party Review*. So whoever had the morning shift would do the readings with Huan, Thi and Tram; that is, if they weren't gossiping. The idea was to try to improve not only their pronunciation of English but also their on-air delivery, to make it less formal and more interesting.

'Read it to me as if you are trying to tell me, me personally, about this particular event or situation,' Iain would say. 'Assume that I know nothing about it and try and make me interested in it.'

And they would read on, or repeat a piece they'd just read.

'Look up at me directly, occasionally,' he would say to them. 'Don't just keep your head down and read from the script. Look at me as if you really are talking to *me* and read it as if you are really keen to impart this information to me.'

And they'd laugh and get into it, or prompt the person reading to look up if he or she wasn't doing so.

'When you go into the studio,' he would say, 'try to imagine that the technician behind the desk, or even the microphone, is the person you're talking to and to whom you're trying to tell this story.'

By the end of a morning's session we felt as if we'd already done a day's mental work but, on the other hand, it was good fun and they really appreciated it. It was important to them because, as the youngest and newest members of VOV5, they were still on probation and only Thi and Huan were given occasional shots at reading on air. Tram, one of the three women in the department who were pregnant, was still not permitted to do any on-air reading. The job of these juniors was mainly confined to translating the Vietnamese versions of local and world news into English, which we would then try to convert into something that was readable and understandable.

Of the other, older members of the English section, Dang Mai Phuong was the third one who was pregnant; about four or five months. Phuong was twenty-nine and had apparently lost a baby through a miscarriage about twelve months previously. She was taller than anyone else in the section and generally had a broad smile. And yet she seemed somewhat aloof and did not really communicate easily with us. She concentrated on doing the translations of her straight news stories and working on the longer current affairs; that is, softer news items that would generally be broadcast in the weekend time slots.

Phuong also co-produced a couple of weekly music programs, which she did separately with two other Westerners who worked outside VOV5 but came in to produce their programs once a week on a freelance basis. We had met one of them, Dan Kirk, a New Zealander, as he spent each morning in an office on the sixth floor of our building, editing VOV's *On-Line News*. He co-hosted his weekly music request program, called *Saturday Jukebox*, with Phuong, but he also performed with a popular mime band called The West Lake Boyz.

Phuong's other joint program was called *Mid-week Music*, which she produced with an exceptionally nice guy, an Australian called Patrick Burke, the director of an American-based HIV/AIDS program called SMARTWork Vietnam, who also happened to be a music buff with a big personal music collection. We would see him every week when he came in to record his program with Phuong and were mightily impressed with his fluent Vietnamese. We were pleased, too, to learn that he had previously been an AVI volunteer and some years ago had become what was known as an 'in-country manager' for Vietnam until taking up his present position.

The current affairs and feature stories on which Phuong seemed to concentrate were also the major concern of Huong, or Dinh Thi Huong, to give her her full name. Huong was a divorcee, something of a rarity in Vietnam, and was raising her eleven-year-old son on her own. Even though she was more or less level with Madame Loc on the VOV5 totem pole, she was never referred to as 'Madame' Huong. She was the producer in charge of FM broadcasting and put a great deal of energy into working up new programs for the weekly *Sunday Show* and other longer current affairs spots. It was clear, however, that there was no love lost between Madame Loc and Huong and we were to witness some incredible spats between the two in the office, unfortunately practically none of which we could understand.

One of the most important, most capable and also most likable members of the staff was Tran Minh Ha, a very attractive 28-year-old woman who was married to a young lawyer, Phong Anh, employed by an international legal firm with its headquarters in Paris. They already had a two-year-old daughter, Nhin. Minh Ha's command of English and her pronunciation and delivery were probably the best in the department, apart from Madame Loc. But her skills as a professional broadcaster were considerably enhanced by a pleasant and amiable disposition and an ability to conduct interviews in English in a relaxed and conversational manner.

The desk and computer station beside Huong was occupied by Nguyen Tam Khoi. Huong was the senior 'non-Party' member of the English language staff but, as we shall shortly see, the balance was about to shift. At twenty-eight, Nguyen Tam Khoi was the second-youngest of the senior group in the department, but he gave off the energy of leadership.

Married, with a four-year-old daughter, Khoi and his wife had met at university in Hanoi where they both studied Russian for six years, only to be caught in the same trap that had enmeshed Hanh on her return from Russia. Times had changed. Fortunately for Khoi, he had studied English as his second language, but his wife had taken Japanese. She continued with this language, spending six months of the time we were at VOV living in Japan to further her qualifications and improve her employment prospects.

Fifteen months younger than Khoi was Do Troung Giang, who had gained his degree in economics and specialised in doing stories on business and finance. Giang, unmarried but under pressure, came and went from the office with a casualness that made you realise he had other interests. He never failed to turn up for office meetings and events, but always just in time. He didn't say much, although when he did it was pertinent and worthwhile, and he slipped away as soon as the meetings were over.

It was Giang who introduced us to the art of frying squid in tape cleaning fluid. Squid was only consumed in the second half of the month, because apparently that was when the creature was free of ink, which, being black, was considered unhealthy by Vietnamese. It could be that we have this fact completely turned around and that it's in the first half of the month when the squid is ink-free. Whichever it is, Giang would regularly turn up with a plate of dried cuttlefish, place it in the shallow metal bowl kept specially for this purpose, pour in a generous amount of the fluid with which old reel-to-reel tapes were cleaned (which one assumes is almost pure alcohol) and take it outside on the little fire-escape stairwell, where he would set it aflame. In this he would give the delicacy a quick basting and bring it back into the office, where we would all stand around chewing at the delicious strips and picking it out from between our teeth. Well, actually, it was like eating salty leather.

Throughout all these activities, going on in both the wider community and in the office, we continued our own personal exploration of the city, in particular the Old Town. This is unquestionably one of Vietnam's great treasures. The fact that it exists at all now, in the twenty-first century, is a marvel in itself and arguably one of the very few good things to come from thirty-five years of warfare against the Japanese, the French and the

Americans, followed by more than a decade of conservative communist economics that kept the country at a standstill.

In retrospect, it was this combination of tragic wars and then a stagnant economy that saved the capital's Old Town from extinction, and it can be fairly said that nothing like it survives anywhere else in South-East Asia and possibly all of Asia — the reason being that no developer was inspired to set his or her sights on changing or developing the Old Town during that period of almost half a century. Fortunately, by the time Vietnam's economy started to pick up speed and entrepreneurs started thinking about how much money they could make by ripping down the crowded and cramped shop-houses in the Old Town, other people, including people in the World Heritage Organisation, had recognised its uniqueness and that it must be saved.

Many folk songs and legends refer to the Old Town as having thirty-six streets. It actually has more, but the figure of thirty-six came from the fact that in the fifteenth century there were thirty-six guilds or trades operating in the quarter and, as a general rule, each guild operated in one particular street. So the streets were named, and many are still named, after the trades that operated there: Silk Street, Tin Street, Silver Street, Basket Street, Salt Street and so on.

Although most of the houses that now stand in the Old Town were built during the nineteenth century, a large proportion of them were built on their fifteenth-century foundations and so retain many of the architectural characteristics of those much older structures. Perhaps the most important of those features revolves around the fact that in those early days, the imperial tax, or what we would call the council or city rates, was calculated not on the overall size of the block or the building on it but the width of the frontage, and so houses were more often than not built to be very narrow, sometimes only two or three metres wide, but very long. These came to be known as 'tube houses'.

The Old Town is not everyone's cup of tea. It's loud and crowded, with motorbikes filling the narrow streets, hawkers and women with conical hats carrying fruit and vegetables, or clothing, or toys, or a multitude of other things for sale. It is also a thriving centre for one of the most controversial aspects of the present Vietnamese economy — piracy. Despite international criticism, threats of legal action and the occasional lawsuit, the copying of almost anything and everything is a major industry in Vietnam. If you wander through the Old Town, you can find pirated versions of more or less any music CD, DVD movie, computer software, photocopied English-language novels and best-selling non-fiction titles, major brandnames in running shoes and sporting goods, well-known fashion labels, luggage and so on, not to mention copied electronic goods such as stereos, TVs and even Japanese motorbikes. Copied versions, many of them from China, are all available in Vietnam.

One slightly offbeat example that flourishes in a number of little shop-houses in the Old Town is the quite amazing art-copying industry. Here you can see rows of artists sitting on stools, painting diligently away at any old master you can think of: the 'Mona Lisa', Monet's 'Irises', heaps of Van Goghs, Degas, Renoirs, Gaugins and so on. And we have to admit that, not only did we find the whole thing fascinating but we were sufficiently impressed with one man's work that on one of our forays into the Old Town, we succumbed and ordered a copy of a Gustav Klimt painting.

Having done so, we wandered down to the Highlands outdoor restaurant by the lake to have a coffee. And, as we sat there feeling vaguely guilty about what we had done, we noted how few tourists we had seen, whereas when we had first arrived in Hanoi, the Old Town and the lakeshore had been crowded with tourists. The reaction by foreign visitors to the SARS epidemic was starting to be felt in Vietnam and for the first time we began seeing people in the streets wearing masks.

In just seven weeks, since it was first diagnosed in Vietnam, five people had died and a further sixty-three had become infected. Not

*Copy artists at work in Hang Trong Street.*

just visitors were running scared. A number of Rebecca's teaching colleagues let her know that they had postponed visits to their home villages and had even decided against socialising at weekends. Rumours were rife.

But gradually, as no new cases were diagnosed, the public's fear receded. When Dr Pascale Brudon, the WHO representative in Vietnam, announced at a press conference towards the end of the month that, 'WHO would like to congratulate Vietnam on being the first country in the world to contain SARS', Vietnamese authorities were justifiably proud. Lives had been saved by a transparency they would perhaps not willingly have chosen. It was a salutary lesson for everyone.

While most members of the VOV5 team were dealing with anxieties about an amorphous threat to their health, Hanh was coping with the very real day-to-day strains on her wellbeing brought about by her pregnancy. She was now in her final trimester and often appeared exhausted. From conversations at their adjoining desks, Trish found out that, even before Hanh started her full and demanding workday at VOV5, she went to her local market and bought meat and vegetables, which she took back home and prepared for the evening meal. When she finished at the office, she rode her motorbike home through the still-extreme heat and, having cooked the food, served it for her husband, her retired mother and father-in-law, with whom she lived, and often for extended family members. She did it, 'Because that's what daughters-in-law do.'

'Even if they are heavily pregnant and have been working all day?'

In response to Trish's indignation, Hanh gave an imperceptible smile. 'My mother-in-law did the same for her husband, when she was a young wife. That's the way it's always been for Vietnamese wives.'

During the short time they'd been building their friendship, Hanh had explained to Trish some of the other constraints of Vietnamese wifedom and motherhood. It was hard at first to fit this travelled, highly educated, professionally qualified woman with someone who was socially subservient to her husband and mother-in-law and who accepted the fact that she would spend her first month as a new mother shut away from the rest of the world as if she were unclean, not allowed to wash her hair or thoroughly cleanse her body.

But if Trish felt cross about women's social position in Vietnam, she was only slightly less annoyed with spending time on what were often vain attempts to make the material that came up for translation from the news department into palatable listening. We would meet at our regular coffee shop for our lunchtime shift-swap debriefing and whichever one of us had worked the morning shift would complain about some particularly appalling pieces of badly written and ill-informed propaganda.

It was with the realisation that we didn't think it would be productive to spend a whole year doing only this editing and rewriting that we started to discuss putting up some other program ideas. Hell of a nerve really, two foreigners thinking that they could just bowl up and get a new radio program on air. But there you go, nothing ventured, nothing gained. So we tossed a few ideas around and decided to get some of them down on paper.

That evening, over dinner, with Rebecca showing her usual stoic tolerance of our invariably nonstop discussion of the day's events at VOV5, we ran our new program ideas past her.

'Go for it,' was her response. 'What have you got to lose?'

The ideas were fairly vague, but we started working on the concept of a half-hour magazine-style program containing a number of different segments dealing with various aspects of life inside and outside Vietnam. We accepted the fact that it would have to be non-controversial. That is, it would need to steer clear of politics and any government policies that might be contentious or attract overseas criticism; for example, religious freedom and civil rights. We also accepted that this would make the program pretty tame, but we had to start somewhere.

The next morning, a Saturday, at around seven o'clock, we took off on a walk with Rebecca over the historic Long Bien Bridge, which spans the Red River but is now used only for pedestrian, cycle and rail traffic. We cheated a bit by taking a taxi to the far side of the bridge, where we alighted and slipped into the stream of pedestrians, cyclists and cyclo-drivers laden with wares, mainly a huge variety of garden vegetables and flowers, who were making their way across the bridge towards the city.

While the scenery from and on the bridge itself is not all that beautiful, it is interesting. The bridge is constructed of steel girders and appears not to be in a wonderfully sound state of repair; in fact we noticed a number of maintenance operations under way at different points as we walked across. Our interest lay more in the history of the bridge than anything else. This was the bridge so repeatedly bombed and just as repeatedly repaired during America's Operation Rolling Thunder, a three-year campaign of bombing North Vietnam. It was built by the French in 1902, and throughout the period of their occupation of Vietnam the bridge was called the Pont Paul Doumer. At the time it was considered a major engineering feat, traversing 1.7 kilometres of the Red River and its shifting sandbanks,to provide the only link between Hanoi and the port city of Hai Phong, 100 kilometres to the east, as well as with much of the rest of northern Vietnam.

It was this fact that attracted American bombers and on 11 August 1967, around 100 tonnes of bombs were dropped on Long Bien Bridge. One bomb demolished the central span in what was an enormous blow to the North Vietnamese. The bridge was reopened for traffic within a couple of months, but it was brought down again within another month and remained a regular target as Operation Rolling Thunder continued. During three years, some 300,000 sorties were flown over North Vietnam, in which over 850,000 tonnes of bombs were dropped, an average of about half a tonne a minute, for the entire period. Long Bien Bridge was eventually rendered useless and remained unrestored for many years after the war was over.

A few days later there was an unexpected visitor to the office, the Australian Ambassador's wife, Lona Thwaites. A Danish-born former journalist, Lona had come into VOV5 to talk about an upcoming activity organised by the Hanoi International Women's Club.

'We're having a dinner in a few days,' she told us during our brief conversation. 'Perhaps you'd like to come.'

The Australian Ambassador's residence in Hanoi is a very attractive French colonial-style building with separate, equally attractive buildings to each side. Negotiations were under way at the time to hand back the lease on these two adjoining buildings which were in need of quite sizeable maintenance work. When the buildings had first been leased from the government back in the 1970s, it was discovered that 127 Vietnamese had been living in just one of them.

The residence is an island of elegant restraint, the main rooms tastefully decorated and hung with Australian art. The dining table had been covered with a starched white tablecloth, locally hand-embroidered in a gold and green wattle design.

Seated at the table were Ambassador Joe Thwaites, the Danish Deputy Head of Mission Mikael Winther and Tran Thi Yen Lan, who was introduced as teaching at the Vietnam National University. On Tran's left and opposite Trish was Jordan Ryan, the United Nations Development Program (UNDP) Resident Representative.

At the other end of the table were Jordan's attractive and talented Chinese wife, Ching, and one of the more interesting icons of present-day Vietnam, Professor Le Van Lan. The conversation was maintained on the polite even keel that such occasions demand. Mikael Winther told Trish he played guitar with an amateur rock group, all of whom were also deputy heads of mission in other embassies. Naturally enough, the group had been dubbed The Deputies. They performed regularly in the Met Pub bar at the heavily renovated Metropole Hotel, now a very popular rendezvous with the younger ex-pat crowd.

Joe Thwaites, who one sensed was not by nature comfortable with superficial socialising, asked about our work at VOV5 and commented that it must be very rewarding to work so closely within the power structure and with Vietnamese colleagues.

Trish elaborated on how the news department had managed to manoeuvre its way through the reporting of SARS and the Iraq

War. She then asked Jordan Ryan what he thought of recent Middle East events. It was, of course, an especially difficult time for anyone from the United States to be out and about in the world and particularly to be answering questions about Iraq. So Jordan, a New Yorker, was having none of that. He deftly steered the conversation elsewhere. We later came to admire the way he handled his role at the UNDP. He was very high profile, always getting a lot of media coverage for what the UNDP was doing in Vietnam, which was plenty, and spread over many areas, both geographical and social. He also had an engaging, dry, self-deprecating sense of humour.

In addition, Jordan had something else rather special going for him: his wife Ching, who helped to keep the conversation bubbling along and not just on lightweight stuff, but important issues such as SARS and the work of the UNDP in Vietnam and in the wider world. She had met Jordan fifteen years previously in her home town of Kunming, in southern China, and since their marriage, had lived in Hanoi, on one of Jordan's previous postings there, and in New York. We were to see quite a bit more of Ching through the year in her capacity as coordinator and organiser of numerous activities related to the United Nations International School (UNIS) in Hanoi, where their eight-year-old daughter was studying.

Professor Le Van Lan was also participating vigorously in the conversation at his end of the table. A professor of history for forty-five years, and now at the Vietnam National University in Hanoi, Le Van Lan impressed almost everyone he met as an incredible character. He was small and bouncy with a thick mop of black hair combed down over his forehead. One of his more engaging features was an extremely infectious smile and laugh, and when we learnt that he ran a successful weekly television quiz show for young people we had no trouble visualising him carrying on in front of the cameras. For a while he talked about the arrest and trial of the Saigon crime boss Nam Cam, plus the incarceration of the Director General of the Voice of Vietnam Radio.

'I knew him well. I knew him well,' Van Lan said. 'It came as a huge surprise to us all.'

Professor Lan has written volumes on the ancient history of the Viet people, tracing it back some 10,000 years, with particular emphasis on archaeology. He is recognised as one of the country's more accomplished archaeologists. He mentioned in passing the legend of Thang Long, the first capital of Vietnam, established in 1010. The story goes that as King Ly Thai To, the first monarch of the Ly dynasty, stepped off his royal barge at the site by the Red River he had chosen for a new capital, he gazed up into the sky and saw a golden dragon flying into the clouds. Taking this as an auspicious sign, the king named his new capital Thang Long, which means 'Rising Dragon', a name due for considerable attention and celebration in Hanoi in 2010, when the city celebrates its one thousandth anniversary. But Professor Lan is not only interested in ancient history; he has played an extraordinary and significant part in the country's more recent history.

'During the American War,' he said with a mischievous smile, 'I was conscripted from the university and directed to devise psychological warfare programs to use against the Americans and the South Vietnamese. They even sent me to the South to operate secretly there for a time.' On learning that we were working with Voice of Vietnam Radio, he mentioned the psychological warfare program carried out by the network during the war, with broadcasts in English directed at American GIs, which were aired twice a day by a woman who became famous, or infamous, depending on which side you were on, and who called herself 'Hanoi Hannah'.

Trish posed a question about the situation in the Middle East to Tran Thi Yen Lan, the attractive teacher seated across the table from her, a woman who was aged perhaps in her mid to late forties.

'I am very bad at politics.' She smiled. 'I am far better at math.'

'Is that what you teach ... math?' Trish asked.

'That and other things,' she replied, telling Trish a little about her work with gifted students from minority groups as Trish began to sense that there were deeper waters there. So she asked, 'Did you always want to teach?'

'Oh yes,' she answered with fervour, and her face, which until then had been perfectly tranquil, became animated with pleasure. 'When I was very small, about three or four, I would line up anything I could find around the village, bits of wood, old cloth, empty rice pots, and put them in rows and pretend to teach them.'

Trish estimated that Lan would have been in her late teens when the American War ended, which meant that her whole childhood had been lived under the constant and heavy shadow of war. 'It must have been very hard,' she prompted, 'for a young girl in those years.'

Lan smiled a trifle sadly and continued talking to Trish as if there was no-one else in the room. It happened to us on other occasions in Vietnam that someone would look you in the eye, draw you to them by the steadfastness of their cool gaze and hold you there while they let go of some searing memory.

Lan was born in a village in the south, one of nine children. The war meant that the entire family moved frequently and she was still only a toddler when her father and brothers left to join the army in the north. She heard no news of any of them until after the war was over, by which time Lan was eighteen and living with distant relatives in Saigon, working while studying to become a teacher. She had found her own way there because both her mother and older sister were dead.

'They were killed by Korean soldiers. They were worse than the Americans,' she said softly but directly. Trish glanced at Jordan, who was sitting beside Lan, but he was engaged in conversation. 'They played with them before they killed them. Both. I was there. I saw it all. Both of them.'

'Played'. Her euphemism for raped. Trish remained still, unable to move her eyes, welling with tears, from Lan's, as the unheard chatter around them continued. The brutal horror of it, expressed in such rational tones and in such banal, civilised surroundings.

Ching's bright laugh from the other end of the table broke the spell.

War, or at least the remembrance of it, was in the air. On 30 April Vietnam would celebrate Total Liberation Day, and for several days beforehand our office in-tray was filled with stories about the build-up to that event back in 1975 and of the men and women who died in the attainment of that final goal, as well as those who are still registered as Missing in Action. The stark statistics are that in the war between the United States and Vietnam, two million Vietnamese died fighting for their country and 500,000 have no known grave. This leaves aside the staggering numbers for Vietnamese civilian deaths and the still-mounting ongoing toll of those affected by Agent Orange and unexploded ordnance that litters the countryside in central Vietnam.

Thirty years after the conclusion of hostilities, national television still broadcasts a weekly program that gives the names and as much detail as possible, including photographs taken in confident youth, of combatants who remain unaccounted for. This, in the hope that some seemingly insignificant detail will trigger a memory and the unhappily wandering soul of somebody's son or daughter will at last be able to come home to find peace in their ancestors' plot. Amazingly, it does happen. It was Nam who, around this time, brought Trish a story she had written about Nguyen Thi Tien.

'As a lieutenant colonel in the Vietnam People's Army,' Nam wrote, 'Tien has spent the last ten years of her life searching for the remains of Vietnamese martyrs.'

Martyr, or *liet* in Vietnamese, is the official description for any Vietnamese combatant who died in action. Working with several of the teams who search for remains, Tien follows every possible lead and has managed to identify the remains of thirty-nine formerly unknown soldiers. Nam's piece on Tien's work, which she carries out with a missionary zeal, included the description of a soldier who had died in battle. 'He was sacrificed by a tree trunk,' Nam had written.

Wanting to give due honour to the soldier, Trish felt she couldn't let his death be broadcast sounding like a parody of some Aztec sacrificial rite, so, a trifle nervously, she approached Nam with the suggestion that she change 'sacrificed' to 'died' and gave her the reason why this would sound better.

Nam drew herself up to her full height, which is about 150 centimetres, fixed Trish with a terrifying glare and informed her, 'The soldier was a hero of the people and heroes of the people do not die, they sacrifice.'

Resisting her intimidatory stance, Trish explained as gently as she could, that, written the way it was, the death would sound farcical to English ears, so perhaps the soldier could instead 'pass away'.

In a slightly mollified tone, Nam explained, 'Only our great men "pass away".'

Then, all of a sudden and so unexpectedly that she caught Trish off-guard, Nam's eyes moistened, her body slackened and, in monotone short sentences she said, 'My father was a hero of the people. He fought against the French. I last saw him when I was two. He never came home. His comrades told us he was shot while they were trying to cross a river. His body was swept away.'

She paused. Trish didn't dare speak. She knew other members of staff were listening and watching. Nam collected herself and continued.

'We have always hoped that villagers found and buried him. We hope that's what happened. That the wild animals didn't get him.'

Trish tried to find words, knowing they would be inadequate, or a gesture of sympathy. Nam cut her short.

'My father was a hero and a great man too, so you can change it to "he passed away". You write it down. I cannot.' She lifted her chin to gesture across the room towards Madame Hue's desk, which was presently, thankfully, unoccupied.

'If you put it in,' Nam said, 'it will stay.'

Trish nodded, not trusting herself to speak. That's how it came about that this unknown soldier who died by a tree trunk and also, by association in Nam's eyes, her dad, Huan's grandad, had 'passed away' and so was elevated to the ranks of Vietnam's great men.

The last day of April in Vietnam is big, very big. Total Liberation Day is one of the most important dates on the calendar and for some people it's *the* most important. It commemorates the day in 1975 that the North Vietnamese army, at the end of the final, short and dramatic military campaign dubbed the Ho Chi Minh Offensive, forced the collapse of almost all resistance on the part of the South Vietnamese army and drove south, with lightning speed, to capture Saigon.

Millions of refugees clogged the roads as they tried to flee the advancing army, which simply bypassed them in its headlong drive on the capital. In the chaos of those final days tens of thousands, hundreds of thousands, of people tried to leave the country, by any means possible. The pictures of them crossing borders on foot, crowding into leaky, overcrowded boats or trying to join the stream of American military aircraft and naval ships that were attempting to evacuate people, were starkly portrayed on television screens across the United States and around the world, right up until the last moments as communist tanks rolled triumphantly into the city.

Ho Chi Minh didn't live to see that final triumph on 30 April 1975, but there's no doubt that, in the minds of Vietnamese all over the country, it was his victory. In the week leading up to the day and on the day itself, Hanoi, already awash with red, purple, pink and yellow blossoming trees, was bedecked with gold-starred red flags, posters and images of Ho. Outdoor stages had been set up at several locations on the streets surrounding Hoan Kiem Lake, where dramatic and brightly costumed traditional and military singing and dancing performances were held every night.

Liberation Day fever was apparent in our courtyard too. Conversations were even more animated as residents went about sticking red flags out of their windows and doorways. The delicate question of what we should do was decided by Mai, who turned up with a sizeable national flag that she propped through the security door to our house. To our left as we looked out into the courtyard was an extended family living in a small and immaculately kept room. Mr Thanh, as we knew him, was perhaps in his sixties and was the only man in the household. He also appeared to hold some position of local authority within the small courtyard community. So it was no surprise to find him hanging a series of large flags above the courtyard entrance. Trish said Mr Thanh reminded her of her own father, with his ever-present cigarette and his smoker's cough. Our courtyard neighbour would greet us with a wave and a smile, without removing the cigarette. His stocky wife, who was also deferred to by other residents, was constantly busy, spending a lot of time with their adult daughter who was cruelly afflicted by a severe spinal deformity.

The children who attended the Sao Mai (Morning Star) kindergarten, in one ground-floor room of a building that was also part of the courtyard complex, of course loved the charged atmosphere. They numbered around forty and crossed through the courtyard in small posses to use the couple of communal toilets, playing tag, keeping out of the way of a number of toiling construction labourers. The children were calling out to each other as they came and went. Now they dawdled for as long as possible to admire the bright colours of the flags, before being shooed back inside the kindergarten by passing adults or called in by their young teacher.

Whenever we appeared on the scene they would surge towards the kindergarten's barred windows shouting in discordant unison, 'Hello, hello, hello', and thrusting their little hands through to shake ours. A small coterie of the more confident ones would attempt to diverge from their visit to the loo, if they spotted us, to give our legs a quick hug.

On the eve of Liberation Day the builders who were involved in renovating the upper floor of one of the courtyard dwellings had a big site clean-up and then something extremely unnerving happened. We woke on the morning of 30 April to complete silence. Because we had a day off work, we lay in and listened to the silence. It made us realise just how much we had adjusted to the constant clamour. Only the family of rats that frolicked around the communal well was seemingly unaware that today, and tomorrow, May Day, were public holidays.

# May
## A PROGRAM PROPOSAL

*'When you throw the javelin you must follow it'*

A good part of our May Day in Hanoi was spent visiting the Temple of Literature, Van Mieu, the nation's first university. Even though the park-like grounds and complex of small, low, traditional-style buildings were busy with other people taking advantage of the national holiday, Van Mieu, on the edge of the French Quarter and fronting onto Quoc Street, was still a place of quiet respite from the hubbub of the surrounding area. The temple was originally constructed in 1070 by another king in the Ly dynasty, King Ly Thanh Tong, to honour Confucius and his disciples, but by 1076 the national university, which trained senior officials for the civil service and which became established as the pinnacle of the Vietnamese educational system, was located within the same compound and the two ideas, Confucianism and education, became forever intertwined.

From then on the benefits of learning and the respect for teachers has been passed down through the generations and still remains a basic tenet of Vietnamese life. It would not be too strong to say that the Vietnamese continue to regard education and educators with total reverence. So it is that Van Mieu has about it an atmosphere similar to that inside a Gothic European cathedral. We walked around among a crowd of visitors all of whom behaved in a most respectful manner. Many of the women wore the *ao dai*, the traditional Vietnamese full-length, figure-hugging split tunic, over wide-legged trousers, either in honour of the temple or the special day, or maybe both.

On each side of the large main courtyard sit row upon row of stone turtles. In East-Asian cosmology the turtle symbolises the universe, with its shell representing the sky and its belly the earth. Each turtle in Van Mieu bears on its back a two-metre-tall stele carved with the names and accomplishments of a *tien si*, or graduate, of the university, the equivalent of a modern PhD, a practice that was initiated in 1442, fifty years before Columbus set sail for the New World. Additional stelae were erected after every examination until 1778 when, due to social upheaval, the practice was discontinued. The Chinese script in which they are written is weathered but still legible.

In translation, one reads, 'Talent is the life source of a nation. A thriving life source strengthens a country; a declining life source threatens it. Thus, among enlightened emperors and princes, there is not one who does not perceive that their most pressing work is nurturing talented individuals, placing confidence in scholars and cultivating the nation's life source.'

The three styles of decoration adorning the tops of the stelae reflect the periods in which they were carved. In traditional Confucianism and Taoism the dragon and the moon reflect the balance between the yin and the yang of the universe and the balance between heaven and earth. Clouds often symbolise knowledge while the phoenix represents the intellect.

Late in the afternoon we decided to take in a performance of what has become a unique Vietnamese cultural icon, the water puppets. Although this relatively old form of traditional entertainment is kept alive now only by its considerable appeal to tourists, it is nonetheless a surprisingly fascinating art. The Municipal Water Puppet Theatre is right on the edge of Hanoi's Old Town, opposite the north-eastern end of Hoan Kiem Lake. Settling into our seats, about three rows back from the 'stage', which is effectively a mini-lake at floor level, with roughly the same surface dimensions as a normal stage, we savoured the welcome effects of the airconditioning after coming in from an oppressively hot afternoon.

Water puppetry in Vietnam, according to most estimates, matches the Temple of Literature in age, being also roughly 1000 years old. Basically, it involves up to a dozen puppeteers, or operators, who stand waist-deep in water, hidden behind a screen or backdrop so that they are not seen by the audience during the performance. From there, they manipulate an amazing variety of puppets, which come out through gaps in the curtains and perform all over the watery 'stage', appearing as if they are walking on water. The purposely opaque water ensures that the complex

*Water puppetry is a uniquely Vietnamese art form which started in the rice paddies of the Red River Delta a thousand years ago.*

underwater mechanisms of poles and controls attached to each puppet are not visible. And, according to tradition, the skills needed to work the puppets have been a closely guarded secret for generations, so audiences are always left wondering how they do it.

Because the concept of water puppetry was not known outside Vietnam for centuries, there is debate about how it originated as an art form. But, as much of the action in the traditional stories revolves around the life of rice farmers, it's generally believed that it was they who first started it. Villagers of the Red River delta developed puppets to tell stories that related to the world they lived in, which was by and large a world of water.

Accompanied by a live band, with drums, gongs, flutes and a bamboo xylophone, plus a singing commentary in Vietnamese but with action that is largely self-explanatory, a huge range of puppets come out to perform. They include farmers, fishermen, children, buffaloes and other farm animals, cats, rats and, of course, mythical creatures like dragons and phoenixes, all taking part in little self-contained scenes that are quite often hilarious and continually captivating. The spell is finally broken at the end, when the puppeteers emerge from behind the big curtain, to the amazement and delight of the crowd.

Perhaps it was a desire for security that motivated Vu Nhat Quynh to work for state radio. He had been with VOV5 since its inception. At thirty-two, he was the oldest in our team, other than members of what we would call the senior management team of Hue, Loc, Long and Huong. That is, apart from Hanh, who was thirteen months older. But she somehow stayed aloof from all the personal and office games. In a society based on Confucian precepts, being the oldest carries considerable clout.

Unlike any of his colleagues, when he joined the group Quynh already had a daughter, who was now seven years old. At university, in addition to English, he had studied Mandarin for five years, so he was a fluent Chinese speaker. After graduating he worked in China for a short time with a fellow university student, assisting him to set up an import–export company. But while his friend stayed in the private sector, perhaps it was family ties that were behind Quynh's decision to become a government employee, or perhaps it had to do with his other standout characteristic: Quynh was a Buddhist.

Most Vietnamese would claim to be Buddhist, but their beliefs are muddied with a complex mix of Confucianism, Taoism and ancestor worship. Quynh had as little of this overlay as it's possible to have and still be Vietnamese. He had studied Buddhism and made ritual daily visits to Quan Su Pagoda. Quynh lived where his family had for generations, in a shop-house in the Old Town, from which his wife ran an up-market tailoring establishment specialising in embroidered silk clothes for women. Her professional skills had made no impression on Quynh, who lived in synthetic tracksuits and flapping sandals. His great passion was soccer, which he followed avidly on the office television. On Saturday afternoons it was a toss-up as to who could scream loudest in support of their teams: Quynh or Madame Hue.

Next down the age chain was 28-year-old Dao Thi Thuy who, following the birth of her daughter, had just returned from four months' paid maternity leave. Thuy broadcast under the alias Linh Chi, which means 'gentle but wise', names she would have liked to call her daughter but couldn't because they were the names of an aunt on her husband's side of the family. So instead, her daughter is Nhi, meaning 'very little'. As with age, the choice and meaning of names is very important in Vietnamese society and in a spin-off from that, aliases are far from unusual. Over his lifetime, Ho Chi Minh, 'Bringer of Light', made use of more than thirty aliases. Madonna and Cat Stevens, eat your heart out.

Thuy was picked, as a specially gifted child, to study Russian and English for four years at university. When she graduated, she spent a further four years with a Singaporean construction company. By the time the job came to an end, she was married and she and her husband — an industrial architect 'who loves his work' — agreed that she should take a job with an SOE, a State Owned Enterprise, because it would offer security and maternity benefits. Like Hanh, Thuy also lived with her in-laws. When we commented that this must offer room for contention on occasions, Thuy laughed and shook her head. 'Not really,' she said. 'They talk. I listen. But I don't take it in.'

It was about this time that we started getting some really torrential rains. It *was* the rainy season, after all, but the strength and density of the downpours was amazing. The sky would darken as tremendous clouds came over in the morning and we'd hear great claps of thunder moving closer and closer. Then we'd look out the office windows to watch the effect on the traffic as the skies opened. What one minute was a road filled with motorbikes streaming in both directions, would suddenly clear, as riders stopped to don plastic capes, some of which were specially designed to fit over and around the handlebars of their bikes. Then the road would gradually start coming to life again, with riders continuing on their way even though the rain was still bucketing down.

On several occasions standing in the shelter of the entrance to VOV and, after waiting too long for an empty cab to come by, Iain would take off his shoes and, carrying them under a $1 plastic cape purchased from a sidewalk vendor, walk home barefoot through water flowing, in some parts, several centimetres deep across the sidewalk. At least the rain was warm but, by the end of a walk home in that drenching rain, he would be just as wet inside the cape … from sweat. Often, on such occasions, he would sit out on the top deck of the house, under cover, cooling off with a beer and just revelling in the sight of the sheets of rain pouring down.

Non-office time, whether in the mornings or afternoons, had been taken up for a couple of weeks with developing our new program idea. The home office, which we'd set up in one of the three bedrooms, complete with a bookcase, a couple of laptops and a printer, as well as phone and internet connections, was now functioning well, so everything progressed smoothly. We were concentrating on putting together the proposal in a form that could be presented to Madame Hue, Long, Madame Loc and Huong very soon.

As it was shaping up '...the program could,' we wrote, 'contain a mix of interviews, scripted commentary on various topics. The interviews would generally be with interesting visitors, local Vietnamese people, or overseas residents who have a story to tell.' Other spots would cover such things as 'What's on in Hanoi?' or in Ho Chi Minh City, Hue, Da Nang etc., and would contain general information about movies, concerts, opera, festivals and visiting performers at various venues. Then there'd be spots dealing with 'Things to Do', 'Where to Go', 'What to Eat', 'What to Buy' and 'Where to Find it All'. There would also be a little information spot called 'Did You Know?' with unusual information about Vietnam, as well as a Business spot that would include an interview — all of this, plus music.

Finally we had it all together; about ten pages, which included a list of contacts at hotels, embassies, foreign corporations and government departments that we had researched, and concluded with the paragraph: 'We realise that this sort of program would be very different from existing or previous VOV broadcast formats, but we feel it would provide an opportunity to present some lighter, brighter listening and, at the same time, move forward, in line with the type of broadcasting that visitors to Vietnam might be used to hearing on their home radios. We feel it would definitely attract listeners and ultimately develop a new and presumably larger audience'.

We printed off four copies of the document, put them in folders addressed with their correct names and titles, complete with the correct Vietnamese accents, took them into the office and gave them to their intended recipients.

The ground-floor entrance to the VOV offices was always a scene from a motorbike enthusiast's dream. Score upon score of bikes came and went all day long as staff changed shifts. Even non-enthusiasts could hardly fail to be enchanted by brandnames such as Dream, Spacy, Wave, Future, Skyway, Majesty, Viva and Jupiter. There was also the Korean or Chinese rip-off version of the Honda Dream, called the Hongda Dream, one called the Weazel, and another with the unfortunate name of the Suzuki Smash, which, surprisingly, is its real name. But what we found even more compelling was the fact that at least half, if not more, of these bikes were the property of women; tiny, delicate creatures who weighed far less than their machines but who flung them around with dexterous ease while making absolutely no fashion concessions to the demands of their vehicles.

The entrance to the undercover parking area was under 24-hour surveillance by a roster of guards and security cameras. The heavy sliding metal bars of the gate could close quickly and motorcyclists were required to dismount outside, at the far edge of the wide pavement, the deep kerb of which still bore the French 'No Parking' edict: *Stationnement Interdit*. This made it necessary for bike riders to manoeuvre their vehicles onto the pavement and wheel them through the gates to where they could find a parking spot. No mean feat, especially in stilettos and tight pants. We were also impressed, if not amazed, at how, when riding their bikes, they managed to press down hard with the slim heels of these shoes on equally small gear levers. In a country where women still bear a very unequal and larger share of the daily burdens, it was a delight to see them zooming along the streets, quite often masked and wearing long gloves to protect their pale skin from wear and tear, very much in charge of at least that one aspect of their life.

Every woman in our department, from Madame Hue, who looked rather like an impressive statue astride her vehicle, to Terrific Thi, who resembled an ethereal fairy on a mechanical moonbeam, rode a motorbike. They expected us to do the same and when we first arrived we did briefly consider it as an option, but the longer we were in Hanoi the more convinced we became that, when dealing with the rigours of the city's traffic, walking was the best choice.

We had now been working at VOV for six weeks and had so far received no pay. It wasn't that we were anxious about the actual money, roughly six million dong (about A$600) that we were owed, but we were interested to know if there was any routine payday and when and how the rest of the staff received their money. So when Trish gave Madame Hue back the latest copy of the *Communist Party Review*, which we had edited, she asked her to explain the wage payment system. Trish immediately picked up on the fact that Hue was a bit embarrassed.

Less than half an hour later Loc strode across the office floor, loomed over Trish as she sat at her desk and, with no preliminaries and in a loud voice, stated, 'You need money, an advance?' She seemed agitated.

Startled, Trish looked up and tried to defuse the situation by speaking in a calm, low tone. 'No,' she said. 'I don't need money. I was just interested to know when everybody gets —'

Loc just continued to talk over Trish in a loud, rather harsh tone. 'Do you need an advance? I believe you need some money.'

Everyone in the office was listening, though they continued to studiously examine their computer screens.

Trish held up a placatory hand, palm out. 'Loc,' she began, still addressing her quietly, 'I just told you I don't —' but when that didn't slow or quieten Loc, she repeated more loudly, 'Loc. Loc.'

Seemingly unable to ease up, Loc continued to hector and Trish felt her gorge rise. She pushed back her chair and rose to her feet, somewhat taller than Loc. 'Loc,' she said, her commanding tone all but drowning Loc out, 'I am not pleading for an advance or a loan. I am simply asking about our salary and when it might be paid. I am not asking for an advance. I am only requesting what is due to me — my wage, having worked here for six weeks. As you are a member of the Communist Party, I would have thought that you, more than others, understand the concept of a fair day's pay for a fair day's work. That is what I am asking for.'

Her statement was greeted by silence. 'Salaries will be paid soon,' Loc finally said. Trish sat back down while Loc quietly explained something about an accounting difficulty. She couldn't take in Loc's words. The adrenaline burst had diffused and she was embarrassed by her outburst. But it worked, because the next morning Trish was told by a smiling Loc to go to the fourth floor to collect her wage. Everyone else in the office was smiling too. They had all been paid.

It was Tram who took it upon herself in their next gossip session to explain to Trish that there was no regular payday for the staff and that quite often monies were delayed for two or even three months. She was amused that Trish found this information shocking and to her question about how could they plan their life, make regular payments on their motorbikes or homes or even be sure they would have enough for necessities like food, she told Trish, 'In Vietnam everyone needs to have a little safety packet. I have two pieces of gold my mother gave me when I got married. I keep them under my mattress.'

Nor, as Trish had feared it might, did her stand-off with Loc seem to have queered our pitch over our proposed program, because that afternoon we were told by Hue that the proposal was now 'at the very top' and it looked hopeful. We had no idea what that really meant, other than that we could be reasonably sure something would happen. We'd just have to wait. In the meantime, we began looking at everything we saw and did in and around Hanoi in a slightly different light, with the prospect of perhaps wanting to mention things in the new program.

So we began to collect information and material on places in the Old Town, restaurants, theatres, pagodas, concerts and so on that we happened to visit. In general, the multitude of museums in Hanoi fitted that category and we enthusiastically prowled through them as the opportunity arose. With the hullabaloo over the forty-ninth anniversary of the Viet Minh victory over the French colonial forces at Dien Bien Phu, we decided to pay a visit to the Army Museum, which lies under the stern gaze of Lenin's statue, in the park across the road.

The main feature of the 10,000-square-metre area in which the museum is located is a huge and historically important 31-metre-tall brick flag tower, built in 1805–12 as part of the ancient Royal Citadel and one of its last few remaining vestiges. Centre stage is a Soviet-built MiG–21 jet, one of the tanks that crashed through the gates of the Presidential Palace in Saigon on 30 April 1975, and a whole courtyard filled with the remnants of crashed American warplanes, including F–111s and B–52s.

The museum itself, spread over two floors in two large buildings, houses thousands of fascinating exhibits tracing Vietnam's long military history, back over a thousand years, to its wars against Chinese invaders. More recent exhibits include two room-sized models of Vietnam's major battles against the French and the Americans, namely Dien Bien Phu in 1954 and the fall of Saigon in 1975. Technically, the battle in Saigon was not fought against the Americans, whose forces had left the country two years earlier, but against the South Vietnamese government, whom they had supported.

We found the story of the fifty-six-day Dien Bien Phu campaign, in which General Vo Nguyen Giap forced the surrender of some

*The wreckage of crashed American B-52 and F-111 bombers at the entrance to Hanoi's Army Museum.*

10,000 French troops and, as a result, the total withdrawal of French forces from Indochina, so fascinating that we resolved to be at the fiftieth anniversary celebrations of the victory at Dien Bien Phu itself, twelve months hence.

Within a week of the news that our program proposal had been up through the hierarchical chain as far as it could go, which meant to the Director General of VOV Radio, we heard that it had been approved. However, according to Huong, even though they liked the whole concept, it was 'a bit too much too soon'. But they'd be happy to settle for the *What's On* segment.

'And,' she said, 'I think it would work well if you could do two or three small spots in the one-hour morning program. It will be rebroadcast several times during the day.'

'The spots?' we asked. 'How long do you want them to be?'

'It depends ... Could you show us some sort of format, and what would go in it?'

We headed back to the drawing board.

In mid-May, Dave Best, a mate of ours from Sydney, and long-time close friend Dick Sheppard turned up in Hanoi. They, as well as a dozen other Australians whom Dave was leading on an organised tour of Vietnam, were the first foreign visitors to our new home. We had drinks with the group before enjoying a relatively expensive fish dinner at the nearby San Ho Restaurant. But we were somewhat disconcerted to find that in just two months we had become so involved in our Hanoi life that they felt more like foreigners than compatriots.

One evening Dave managed to slip away from his responsibilities long enough to join Dick and us on a visit to the Hanoi Jazz Club, an unexpected treat of a place in Hanoi's Old Town, to listen to the owner, Quynh Van Minh, perform with his Red River Band. Jazz, which arrived in a rather sideways manner in Vietnam with black US soldiers in the south, was officially frowned upon by the communist government but developed an underground popularity through records that were smuggled back into the country from former Eastern European countries by Vietnamese students. From his first encounter with jazz in 1968, Minh was hooked and continued to develop his taste for the 'decadent' genre by listening to radio programs broadcast by the BBC and Voice of America. Now, Minh continues to delight visitors to his club, which often showcases international jazz greats, with a mix of classic jazz and his own compositions, many of which are based on the folk songs of the minority H'Mong and Cheo people.

One of the people travelling with Dave's group was a spritely 75-year-old German–Australian woman, Renate Watkinson, who we suggested in the office as possibly being good interview material for VOV5. This time it was Khoi who would do the interview and, while Renate and the tour leader, Dave, both turned out to be interesting interviewees, it was the events surrounding the meeting in their hotel which proved to be more revealing.

Trish had ridden pillion on Khoi's bike to the hotel, chatting away in the casual manner we were coming to accept as the norm in Hanoi traffic.

As they walked up to the reception desk, Trish became aware that Khoi had dropped a few paces behind. The clerk greeted her courteously. She presented a VOV business card, explained that they were there to interview two guests, gave their names and asked him to call through to let them know they were on our way up.

The clerk fumbled with papers on the desk, darting looks at Khoi, who was suddenly preoccupied with his tape recorder. Appearing to come to a decision, he leant sideways and called across to Khoi, who had turned away. He then continued to examine his paperwork.

Trish began to move towards the stairs, thinking Khoi would join her.

'He cannot go to the room,' the clerk suddenly called out in English.

Trish turned and snapped, 'Why not?'

'Vietnamese are not allowed in the rooms.'

There was an awkward silence. Trish walked back to the desk.

'May I please speak with the manager?' She sounded calmer than she felt.

After a long pause the clerk spoke again in Vietnamese to Khoi who, acutely embarrassed, began fumbling for his wallet, from which he produced what appeared to be an identification card. The clerk took the card, rather too briskly, without making eye contact. He waved them brusquely to the stairs. Silently, Khoi and Trish walked upstairs. It was an unexpected incident that brought home the fact that some of Vietnam's new-found freedoms are not as deep as they may appear at first glance.

That particular day, 19 May, was a big one for Khoi for a couple of other reasons. In a special ceremony conducted at VOV's administrative headquarters, four or five blocks away on Quan Su Street, he was inducted into the Communist Party.

On the afternoon shift, Iain was about to settle into a small pile of news scripts in his tray when he noticed Khoi heading out. Instead of his normal jeans and an open-necked shirt, he was wearing a smart pair of pants, a long-sleeved shirt and a tie.

'Going to see the bank manager?' Iain called to him as he passed.

Khoi laughed, but kept walking towards the elevator, without replying.

A little later, Huan told Iain where Khoi was going and what was happening.

'But how did it come about? Has he been interested in joining the Party for long?' Iain asked.

'I don't think so. I think he was asked to join. His parents are both members of the Party, I believe.'

'So there was pressure on him from them to join?'

'Possibly. I'm not sure.'

Khoi returned an hour and a half or so later and there was a round of polite congratulations and handshaking, but one sensed that Khoi had stepped through a sort of magic mirror which somehow separated him from the rest of us. Strange really, looking back on it, as that sense of separateness gradually wore off over the passing weeks and months, with the realisation that being a member of the Party made no difference to Khoi's likable personality or to the way he related to people, particularly to the rest of the staff.

The other important aspect of Khoi's induction into the Party, important or symbolic for him or perhaps for the people doing the inducting, was that 19 May was the one hundred and thirteenth anniversary of the birth of Ho Chi Minh and the place was awash with posters and red flags, most of which hadn't been taken down from the anniversaries at the beginning of the month.

For our part, the occasion and the lead-up to it meant that we had a stream of stories on Uncle Ho and various aspects of his long and amazing life to edit, not only for the news and current affairs programs of VOV5, but also for the *Communist Party Review*. As we've mentioned, the review was a fortnightly publication, of between forty and sixty pages, which unfortunately meant that, just as we were finishing up with one, another lot would start turning up on our desk.

The news and current affairs items for broadcast generally dealt with historical stories and incidents during the thirty years Ho was away from Vietnam in Europe, the United States, the Soviet Union and parts of Asia, ostensibly trying to find a way to liberate Vietnam, or Indochina as it was then, from the yoke of French colonial rule. Whether or not this goal occupied Ho for the entire period may be open to question, but there's no doubt that during the time he was away, he built up a considerable reputation as a very serious revolutionary.

Khoi's big day also happened to have a degree of importance for us. Over the weekend, we had completed a reworked program format for *What's On*, with a list of suggested subjects and items to cover the first few days, and that afternoon we gave copies of the outline to Huong and Long.

Early on the Sunday morning of the following weekend, we took a cab over to pick up Rebecca at Kim Lien pagoda, near her house on West Lake. From there we continued on a few kilometres to the suburb of Quang An and an excellent 50-metre outdoor swimming pool called Sao Mai. Regular swimming was one of the things we missed in Hanoi, not so much for the lack of swimming pools, as there are a number to choose from, but because none were handy to us. Also, because of the nature of the extremely hot climate the water is generally a little too warm to be stimulating and it is, of course, pretty heavily chlorinated. But anything's better than nothing and after doing our obligatory half-kilometre, we did feel a bit more like facing the day.

After a simple breakfast at a lakeside café, we returned for a while to Rebecca's house, which in itself deserves mention on at least how she came to be living there. When she first came to take up her position with Vietnam National University, her flight from Sydney to Hanoi stopped over in Singapore and on the flight from there to Hanoi, she found herself sitting next to a Vietnamese–French woman. During their conversation she learnt that the woman's name was Ea Sola and that she was a dancer and apparently a very well-known choreographer.

'I am living in Paris now,' she told Rebecca. 'But I have a house in Hanoi, which is empty for most of the year. Would you like to rent it?'

The house turned out to be a three-storey building with four bedrooms and four-and-a-half bathrooms on West Lake, the city's most up-market area. The rent that Ea Sola wanted was too high for Rebecca, who explained that AVI would only pay a maximum of US$250 per month per person for rent. But after some initial haggling and the realisation on Ea Sola's part that Rebecca could not go any higher, she agreed that the place could be hers.

The house was not only large and spacious, but was filled with antiques and expensive oriental furniture, like something out of a *Vogue Living* magazine. It seemed as if Rebecca had really fallen on her feet in the accommodation stakes and for much of her stay in Hanoi this was true, except that Ea Sola would keep coming back from Paris for various artistic engagements and contracts and not just want to stay in the house but more or less take it over. She was, after all, in her own words, 'famous'. During these visits, Rebecca often sought refuge in our spare room.

Our own artistic engagements for the rest of the week included attending some of the screenings at the Third European Union Film Festival. Held every other year, the film festival is organised jointly by the EU member states and the EC delegation to Vietnam. One of the organisers we met at the festival, from Sweden, was hopping mad about government bureaucracy and interference, which had nearly scuttled the event.

Every film had first to be scrutinised by the Ministry of Culture and one Swedish film had not passed muster. 'We knew this could happen,' the woman said. 'They rejected the first film we put forward, so we sent in a second one. They said no to that one too. But when they started making negative noises about the third one, I told them, "Enough is enough. If you don't let this one through, we shall not submit another Swedish film and I am sure all the other countries will also withdraw and you will have no European Film Festival." That gave them such a fright that they backed down.'

The film in question was called *The Boy With No Face* and was by far the most thoughtful and powerful film in the festival; a documentary about Hoa, a young Vietnamese boy from the Central Provinces whose face had been all but destroyed by an American phosphorous bomb, a relic of the war. The film is a complex one, involving noble work on the part of various people in raising funds, including a Swedish pastor and an American surgeon, and there are a number of difficult surgical operations before Hoa returns to try to reintegrate into simple village life. It was hard to see any problematic censorship issues there.

When Trish mentioned all this at the office, Giang shrugged. 'There will always be people like that. They have a little bit of power and they want to use it.'

Hanh commented that she didn't enjoy European movies anyway. 'They always show depressing things. There's too much talking, especially in the French ones. And there's not enough action.'

So much for building 'a bridge that can deepen and enhance the mutual understanding of the richness of the cultural heritage of each region', which was how the festival promoted itself.

What with the high-profile European Film Festival happening, the Ministry of Culture and Information must have been pretty pushed, but they weren't so busy they couldn't stage a show of their own. Suddenly, all the local newspapers plus the English-language *Vietnam News* were carrying stories of a big government crackdown on piracy, accompanied by pictures of a road-roller crushing CDs in the street.

'More than 48,000 fake music, video and computer discs and 1200 books have been destroyed in Hanoi, in a purge against piracy,' the *Vietnam News* reported. 'VCDs, DVDs, CDs and CD-ROMS were ground to pieces and then ceremoniously crushed by a road-roller ... the official says of the books destroyed, 210 had "bad content" and 1015 "superstitious" content.' For 'bad' read sexual. For 'superstitious' read religious.

Fair enough. And piracy is an issue that the Vietnamese government has to address, if only for reasons of self-interest, notably its desire to join the World Trade Organization. Widespread piracy and lack of respect for international trademarks would likely prove to be something of a hindrance to its long-anticipated accession to the WTO. But, of course, no aspect of society, especially a poor one that is rapidly changing and developing like Vietnam, is so simple that it doesn't have at least two sides.

Mr Dinh was the other side of piracy. He was Rebecca's find. She had bought a $50 pushbike, on which she braved the hectic traffic, the skin- and lung-clogging fumes and ever-increasing heat, to commute between her home and the three different locations where she taught, sometimes pedalling 15 kilometres a day. Often she would stop off for a break at the Moca Café in the Old Town, and it was outside the Moca Café that Mr Dinh ran his business.

He didn't have a shop, just a patch of pavement. It wasn't until we had negotiated several deals with him that we worked out the boundaries of this area. His patch was invisible, but very exact and established by unofficial arrangement with the local police and his business competitors. Mr Dinh sold photocopied books, most of them for 50,000 dong (A$5). He always had a few under his arm and a ready list of other titles to suggest, which he could very rapidly pull out from his stock, piled just out of sight in a dark alley to the side.

The books Mr Dinh sold, both fiction and nonfiction, by local and overseas writers, were all about Vietnam. Were they banned? It was hard to be sure. Most of them weren't available in the government-run bookstores. Travel guides such as *Lonely Planet* were, but not Duong Thu Huong's brilliant trilogy *Paradise of the Blind*, *Memories of a Pure Spring* and *Novel without a Name*. She still lives in Hanoi, but under an obscure form of house arrest. Nor was Bao Ninh's *Sorrow of War*. It had been a bestseller in the early 1990s, but after the writer had a public dispute with the Party, the book also fell into disfavour.

Mr Dinh did writers and readers a service, keeping in circulation books that would otherwise have dropped from sight, including new titles like American–Vietnamese author Andrew X. Pham's distressingly angry *Catfish and Mandala,* which would later make Quynh cry and which will certainly never be on the high-school reading list in Vietnam. At what point does piracy become a crime? Is it too big a stretch to suggest that by scratching out a niche and supporting himself on the tough streets, Mr Dinh also provides a de facto freedom that doesn't exist in Hanoi's legal book-selling world?

The weather was so hot and humid by now that the short walk from the house to the office would mean arriving totally drenched with sweat. Fortunately informality ruled, and sandals, cotton slacks and a short-sleeved open-necked shirt were standard summer wear for the office. To avoid arriving soaking wet, we opted for taking a *xe om* on really hot days, which for the time being was every day. *Xe om* is the Vietnamese term for a motorbike taxi. And there are *xe oms* on just about every street corner in Hanoi. These are totally unlicensed individuals, always men, who make a fairly meagre living by carting people around on the back of their motorbikes.

Vietnamese generally pay about 1000 to 2000 dong (10 to 20 cents) a kilometre. Westerners invariably pay more, sometimes quite a lot more, but there's a crossover point where it's less expensive for two people to take taxis, which are very cheap in Hanoi. As for our five-minute *xe om* ride to work, we paid 7000 dong (70 cents) to a guy called Hoang, who was very pleased with the arrangement and became our regular *xe om*, jealously guarding his territory. He had a face like he'd run into the back of a bus and, if you didn't know him, you certainly wouldn't have wanted to have met him in a dark alley, but when he smiled, you couldn't help but like him.

Hoang worked his patch during the day. The evening shift was run by a different group of men, but we had our regulars among them too. The women who catered for the patrons of the bar near our home would, with their eagle-sharp vision, see us step out of a cab after an evening out and, knowing our routine, would summon one of the drivers to take Rebecca back to her plush pad. If an outsider tried to muscle in, they received very short shrift from the women, who were accustomed to looking out for their sisters and treated Rebecca like she was one of them and us like we were her parents.

Iain got off the back of Hoang's bike one morning in the last week of May and went up to the office to be met by Long and Huong with the news that the *What's On* program and its amended format had been approved all the way and that they would like it to start going to air on a daily basis from Monday, 2 June. The program would not be live, so they planned to record it on the preceding Friday.

The format we had laid out in our proposal would have the two of us chatting in a conversational style about all sorts of events, happenings, things to do and see in Hanoi, Ho Chi Minh City and wherever else we chose and could dig up sufficient information on to do a short two- to three-minute piece. We say 'chatting' in the sense that it was meant to be casual and informal but, because of the material and the detailed information we had to put over, it would be largely scripted beforehand. There would be three of these spots in each day's program, fitting in with and separated by about eight to ten minutes of other programming. And these spots would be repeated five times during the day and evening.

We were naturally pleased and excited at the prospect, but realised the program, small and inconsequential though it may be, would have a big appetite. We'd been keeping our eyes out for various program 'possibles' and we decided that we could devote at least one spot a week to some of the museums in Hanoi and Ho Chi Minh City.

With that in mind, we visited the National Museum of Vietnamese History which is housed in a beautiful building, well laid out, and with a host of outstanding exhibits. In its sweep across 40,000 years, the few decades of struggle against France and the United States took on their correct perspective.

A few names of places, heroes and dynasties were beginning to register and take shape: Hoa Binh, Au Lac, Dong Son, the Cham dynasty, the Trung sisters, the Ba Trieu rebellion, Co Loa, the Le dynasty, Ly Thai To, Thang Long, Ly Thuong Kiet, Dai Viet, the Trinh and Nguyen lords. Over the year we would become increasingly familiar with them and their iconic importance. We were particularly drawn towards General Tran Hung Dao who, in 1288, tricked the Chinese fleet into following his fleeing army up the Bach Dang River. He then had huge wooden stakes driven into the riverbed behind them, so that when the tide went out and the ships tried to get back to the ocean they found themselves and their ships trapped or impaled and were overrun by Vietnamese warriors. The museum has a large, vivid depiction of this spectacular military triumph and although we would see several other versions in museums and art galleries around the country, this one remains the favourite.

The museum is not vast or in any way overwhelming. The displays are set out on two floors and we felt we took in a good overview in just an afternoon visit, though we went back several times for a more detailed look and for other temporary exhibitions. The building, one of the most dramatic in Hanoi, is located more or less behind the Opera House in the part of Hanoi that was the first to be ceded to France by Vietnamese authorities in 1874. It was used as the residence of the French governor-general and as the French consulate. Painted an ochre yellow and set in a substantial, well-kept garden, it's a prime example of what has come to be known as 'Indochina architecture'. With its elegant octagonal tower and double walls and balconies, which allow perfect ventilation and protection from the strong sun, the pleasing mix of Eastern and Western styles pays tribute to the imagination of its architect, Ernest Hebrard.

Back in the office, Hanh was happy to hear of our positive impressions of the history museum, but we were far less happy to note that Hanh's hands, feet and ankles had become extremely swollen and that she had taken to scratching her arms and neck. She did it a lot and she seemed to do it unconsciously.

Trish was aware that Hanh was making sporadic visits to a medical practitioner and asked if the swelling of her extremities had been noted and if so what had been suggested.

'The doctor says it's common in the last month of pregnancy. He told me to not eat hot foods,' Hanh said. By hot, she meant spicy hot. In Vietnam there is also some superstitious reason for the labelling of foods; for example, some fruits are deemed 'hot' and others 'cold'.

Trish explained to Hanh what basic stuff she knew about fluid retention and its effects. Then she asked gently if she had mentioned her itchiness to the doctor?

'Not really. He was busy. D'you think it's important?'

'I don't know,' Trish admitted. But she came to wish that she had.

Our recording day, Friday, 30 May, dawned but Iain had somehow picked up a bug and felt pretty lousy when we went in to work together after breakfast to record our first program. We had prepared scripts for the following four days, but nobody was sure whether we'd have enough studio time to do them all. There was a long delay before we left the office, but we finally headed off to the studios next door for what was shaping up to be quite an occasion, with Khoi, Minh Ha, Giang, Thuy and Thi all accompanying us.

The studio and its equipment looked old and tired. Very dated Revox tape machines were aligned in a semicircle around the technician, and we sat opposite him in the same room behind two microphones. The tape machines had been a gift from the Australian Broadcasting Corporation twenty years previously, in the first flush of Australia's diplomatic recognition of Vietnam. There was pretty much a party atmosphere as we recorded the first three items for the following Monday, which dealt with the European Film Festival, a temple festival in Ha Tinh Province, and a showing of *Casablanca* at the Green Parrot Film Club which, we advised Ho Chi Min City residents, could be found in the Maya Bar and Nightclub.

And that was it. Studio time, they told us, had run out. We would have to record the rest of next week's programs on Monday. But everybody seemed reasonably happy and it was certainly no problem for us. This was the first time since about 1973 that we had done anything together on air in radio. And it was great!

Iain still wasn't feeling too well and headed home to sleep. He returned to the office at 3.30pm and was surprised to suddenly hear the recorded *What's On* spots being played on the tape-editing machine at the end of the room. It was rather embarrassing for him, as everyone in the office stood around to listen. He cringed a couple of times at small slips that we both had made, but the post-mortem was okay. 'A little too long,' Huong said. 'And a bit too fast with the telephone numbers,' but overall, the playback received a very positive reaction.

As things turned out, that little program would run every day for the twelve months more we stayed in Vietnam and continue with the Vietnamese staff doing it after we left. More importantly for us, it would prove to be not only an entrée into all sorts of fascinating areas of Hanoi's history, culture and society, but a wonderful experience.

# June

## A DEATH

*'Whoever plants the trees, will one day eat the fruit'*

*'Old Macdonald had a farm ee-eye-ee-eye-oh!*
*And on that farm he had a ... PIG ... ee-eye-ee-eye-oh!*
*With a honk-honk here! And a honk-honk there!*
*Here a honk! There a honk! Everywhere a honk-honk!'*

By now, four verses in and having yapped like a dog, miaowed like a cat, and quacked like a duck, we had all the children yelling for more and their parents laughing at our antics. There was a certain freak show value in watching these foreigners making such fools of themselves.

We were at a Saturday morning party held by all VOV staff for their offspring, in the big second-floor meeting room, to celebrate Children's Day, 1 June, in which, one by one, the children stood at the front of the room to give a small performance. Unexpectedly called upon to join in, this was the best number we could think of, but it turned out to be a good choice because once the young ones understood how it worked, they really got into it. We had to choose the animals carefully — no sheep or cows here, and unfortunately Vietnam's ubiquitous water buffalo is a silent beast. As we finished, one of the children came forward and presented us with a little ceramic lucky pig moneybox.

Over the year we came to really get a kick out of these 'mass organisation' events, as they are described by the Party. They occur in an atmosphere of such unsophisticated enjoyment and real camaraderie. All the children in this show were under ten and dressed in their best clothes. Among the performers were Madame Hue's grand-daughter and Huong's son, who sang a confident duet.

Children are treasured in Vietnam. Thirty per cent of the population is under fifteen and wherever you go you see open affection expressed towards them. But, of course, not all of them are as fortunate as the children of VOV staff. There are eight state-run orphanages in Hanoi but their severely limited budgets mean they can only care for a total of less than 850 children, and orphans are often sent back to their home villages to be communally raised. About one-third of the children in these orphanages has a mental or physical disability or suffers from a congenital disease. Their parents often find themselves unable to manage the heavy financial burden of necessary medical care. A disproportionate number are girls.

Then there are the street children — 19,000 in Ho Chi Minh City alone. That's an official government estimate, which probably means there are more. It frequently comes as a surprise to visitors to Hanoi that there is almost no overt begging on the streets, but postcard selling and shoeshining are its tacit form. Throughout the year we wrote stories on scores of fundraisers, from art shows and photographic exhibitions to cyclo races, aimed at raising funds to help children, the most vulnerable members of any society, escape the poverty trap.

Two of the capital's best-known vocational establishments for young people are Hoa Sua and Koto. Hoa Sua is a French-supported NGO. Koto, an acronym for Know One Teach One, is the heart-child of Australian–Vietnamese Jimmy Pham. Both organisations have eighteen-month hospitality and tourism training courses and life-skill classes. They also run catering services as well as good restaurants in Hanoi, which we frequently patronised. The majority of the young people working at Hoa Sua and Koto come from a life on the streets. They are trained in everything from business accountancy and front-of-house skills to bartending and waiting at table through to chefing. Koto has trained more than a hundred boys and girls over the last four years and every one of them has gone on to find full-time, long-term employment, many of them in international five-star restaurants and hotels. Koto and Hoa Sua were naturals for us to cover in the little *What's On* spots we were now doing every day on VOV5, and whenever we had the opportunity to give them a plug, we would do so. We also sought ways to dig as much material as possible out of the Old Town, which was a real mine of fascinating stuff.

Despite the fact that we had rambled our way through quite a bit of the Old Town on our own, there were understandably vast amounts of it — its history, its hidden highlights and stories, offbeat locales, markets and so on — that we hadn't touched upon. To get a slightly more professional approach to absorbing all this information, we decided to go on one of Carol Nelson's short tours of the Old Town. Carol was an Australian resident of Hanoi and a member of a group called Friends of Vietnam Heritage, which was comprised mainly of expatriates interested in preserving aspects of Vietnam's cultural heritage. She had done a huge amount of private research in the Old Town and she volunteered her services to FVH. She had also helped the producers of the film *The Quiet American* to find good locations in the Old Town. We joined her at 7.00 o'clock one morning for the first segment of her tour.

We began in the crowded little street called Hang Bac, which means Silver Street, and while there are still plenty of jewellery stores on Hang Bac, there's a huge variety of other vendors as well. As we negotiated our way around parked motorbikes and throngs of

*Temple gods adorning the tiny Buddhist sanctuary in the Old Town's Hang Bac Street.*

shoppers and shopkeepers, Carol suddenly motioned us into a tiny darkened passageway between two buildings. Around 10 metres in, she turned us right into the entrance of a house, a sort of vestibule, in which three or four people were sitting on stools eating noodles. We stepped past them to climb a flight of stairs and found ourselves in an incredibly ornate Buddhist temple, complete with highly wrought altars, intricately carved, flamboyant statues of venerated figures of ancient legends, and food offerings of mainly fruit laid out on platters on the altars.

'Not many people know about this place,' Carol said, nodding to a shaven-haired monk in brown robes who moved past us, acknowledging her greeting with a nod of his own.

'I'm sure they don't,' we both agreed. 'There's no way you'd spot it from the outside.'

'Well, there is,' Carol said. 'It's just that unless you knew what to look for, you'd walk right by it. It's one of those multicoloured temple flags. And it's hanging by the entrance to the alleyway.'

'And why is it tucked away in here?' Trish asked.

'No reason, it's probably been on this site for generations. And as the pressure of buildings and development began to encroach, it just got squeezed back in here. Nobody wanted to get rid of it, so it just adapted to the changing times.'

Outside again, on a nearby corner we were treated to something even more unexpected and bizarre. It was a shop-house selling tombstones, the kind on which a photograph of the deceased can be photo-chemically etched into the granite. There were sample tombstones set up in front of the shop. The one that caught our eye showed a smiling Britney Spears surrounded by Vietnamese and Chinese funerary script.

Then, one block north to Hang Buom Street we visited another temple, Bach Ma. This temple is only small, but it's one of the most famous and important in Hanoi. It is the most ancient religious structure in the Old Town, dating back more than a thousand years. Bach Ma means 'White Horse', and it was given the name in the ninth century because the king, Ly Thai To, dreamt he saw a white horse emerge from the temple, trace out a rectangular path around the citadel, which was under construction at the time, and return into the temple. The king ordered that the walls of the citadel should be built along the lines of the horse's footprints. The present-day temple contains a white horse, which is brought out and paraded around the streets of the Old Town twice each year for the temple's own festival and the mid-autumn celebrations.

Leaving Carol, we began walking back towards home, along the way soaking up the incredible sights, sounds and smells of the Old Town: women picking through each other's hair, looking for and pulling out any grey hairs, one by one; a small sidewalk café that sold fried chickens to take away. These were tiny chickens, they may even have been some other sort of small bird, we couldn't really tell, because all we could see of them, lined up along the top of a glass cabinet facing out onto the road, were their little clawed legs sticking up out of the top of neatly cut-off Coke cans, or Pepsi cola, or Tiger, Halida or Hanoi beer cans. Takeaway fried chicken, Hanoi-style!

You can be happily trundling along with your life in Hanoi, stimulated by the challenge of an endlessly fascinating culture, when out of the blue, *bang!*, you're pulled to a dead halt by something that makes you reassess and recognise the fact that you are a foreigner. One such jarring moment happened during an early-morning taxi trip we were taking through an outer suburb. The streets were as busy as usual, but then the traffic was forced to slow down, almost to walking pace, by a crowd which had spilled out into the road. We ceased our inconsequential chatter and, drawn by the indefinable air of purpose which the milling mob gave off, stared past them into a small space where two men dressed in the immediately recognisable stripes of prison uniforms, with heads bowed, hands cuffed behind their backs, placards hanging around their necks, stood for all to gawp at on upturned wooden boxes.

In less than ten seconds they were lost to view and we continued on our way. For a few more seconds we were silent, digesting what we had seen. The taxi driver had seen too. In the driving mirror he noticed our shocked expressions. 'Bad men,' he informed us.

Back in the office, and careful not to let the questions sound loaded, Trish asked for an explanation of what we had seen.

Khoi, continuing to run his finger down the list of the week's work schedule, said casually, 'Oh, they would have been caught stealing in the area.'

'Or selling drugs locally,' Minh Ha added without looking up from her computer screen.

'And would they have been arrested by the police and had their day in court?' Trish asked, betrayed by her tone of voice.

They both stopped what they were doing to look at her. Minh Ha spoke patiently, as if to a child. 'They would have been taken to the local police by the person whose shop they robbed, or the parents of a child they tried to sell drugs to. Everyone can read what crimes they committed. They would have been listed on the notice they were wearing. The local People's Committee will decide what happens to them.'

'But that only works at the neighbourhood level and for petty crimes,' Khoi added, imagining that we would find this reassuring.

It was not long after this conversation that convicted Ho Chi Minh City crime boss Nam Cam received the death sentence. No-one in the office was surprised and not one of them had second thoughts about state-endorsed executions. Government figures for state executions are all but impossible to come by, but Amnesty International claims that in 2003 seventy-two people were given the death sentence and nineteen were executed by firing squads in Vietnam. Tran Mai Hanh, the disgraced former Director General of VOV, who had stood trial with the Nam Cam gang, escaped execution but was sentenced to eleven years in prison.

Massive coverage was also given to the trial and subsequent death sentence imposed on the former Director of a Ministry of Agriculture and Rural Development subsidiary, La Thi Kim Oanh. Ms Oanh was accused of embezzling US$4.9 million. Her execution, by firing squad, allowed media debate not over whether or not there should be a death penalty but over whether it should apply to commercial crimes.

Trish took a straw poll around the office.

'Forty-four crimes used to carry the death penalty,' Loc informed her, a trifle tight-lipped, 'and that number has already been reduced to twenty-nine.'

The general consensus was that economic crimes were crimes against the people and anyone who committed them deserved to die. Trish tried discussing this with Huan.

'Do you not execute people in Australia?' he asked with the close-guarded expression Trish was happy to see he wore less and less often when they talked.

She told him no and also that research had shown the death penalty was no deterrent to crime.

'I personally think it's just a legalised form of revenge. It certainly runs counter to Buddhist beliefs,' she said and, for the final unnecessary thrust, added, 'it's not the mark of a civilised society.'

'The United States does it,' Huan retorted sharply.

It was about this time that the government introduced a plan to raise money, a large amount of it. They would sell government bonds to raise several tens of millions of dollars. There was a full-on campaign in the press and on VOV, with reams of material coming across our desk saying how successful the program was. Each morning, there'd be stories about how patriotic individuals and organisations, and particularly government departments, had been by buying X amount of bonds to help the country's economy. The bonds cost a minimum of 100,000 dong (A$10), paid 8 per cent interest and could be redeemed in five years' time. For a while we were impressed at how much employees in different government departments were contributing.

'That's if the reports are true,' we commented as we discussed it one lunchtime.

They were true all right, as we shortly found out when Phuong came round to collect everyone's money for their bonds.

'*You* needn't buy them,' she said. 'It's only for us.'

'But do you have to buy them?' Iain asked. 'I mean, is it compulsory?'

'Oh yes. Just one bond each: 100,000 dong.' That amount represented a significant proportion of their official salary, about 5 per cent.

The government's target was very quickly filled.

Continuing on a financial theme, back in April, when Trish had the emotional conversation with Tran Thi Yen Lan over dinner at the Australian Embassy residence, Lan had mentioned a support group she had organised to help minority girl students attend the university where she taught. Trish phoned her and arranged for her to come around to our place to talk about how the scheme worked.

'It started back in 1994,' Lan told Trish. 'It wasn't possible to live on only what the university paid me. My husband couldn't find work. He had been an army officer but when the war was over there was no job for him. We were desperate to make money, so he went to work in a factory in Eastern Europe. But I begged him to come home. Our daughter needed a father. I needed a husband. The war had already taken too much from my life. Being together was more important than money.

'Then I found additional work interpreting for and tutoring the Italian Ambassador. He was such a kind man. He gave financial help to an elderly Vietnamese man who lived alone in a tiny room. I thought if this man, this foreigner, can do this then so could I, because these were my own people.'

That Italian Ambassador was her first donor and although he moved on to a posting elsewhere, he still sent sponsorship funds on a regular basis. He introduced Lan to other members of Hanoi's international community and so her one-person unofficial NGO was born.

'In the beginning I didn't even have a receipt book. People didn't ask and I didn't want to waste time better spent with students on paperwork. I also didn't want to register as an aid organisation with the government because that also costs money and takes time.'

Lan now had around thirty sponsors, each of whom gave her US$20 a month. She also had a receipt book and a donated older-model computer on which she kept the accounts as well as a list of the students her scheme supports. She took no money for herself and did the work alone, squeezing out the time for it around her full-time teaching schedule and domestic obligations. She talked of this in a matter-of-fact way as if it was the most natural thing in the world to do.

'My students are almost all young women from minority groups,' she told Trish. 'I am like a mother to them. They talk to me about female physical matters. I know they find things difficult. They live four to a room less than half the size of this.' She gestured around our small sitting room. 'They are timid because they come from the provinces, they look different from the majority, they are so poor they can't afford 10,000 dong for a bowl of *pho* for breakfast. Instead, they pay 500 dong for a glass of soy bean. They also feel lonely away from their families.

'So sometimes I need to remind them. I tell them my story. I say, "I had bad luck, I was an orphan too, but if I can do it, so can you. You have parents. You have a government study allowance. You have the support of foreign friends. You have no reason not to do well".'

Listening to her, Trish found it easy to imagine what an inspiration she would be to her students.

'I tell them, "Never, never lie or cheat or try to offer me money for a good mark. But do not be afraid of me. I will always be there for you. To do anything properly in life you need to do it with passion".'

It was partly because the first week in June had presented us with some heavy-duty emotional things to deal with that we felt a sense of relief at the end of the week when we took off on our first major excursion away from Hanoi. We'd planned our weekend trip to the little hill town of Sapa, some 300 kilometres to the north and close to the Chinese border, mainly as an escape from the heat of Hanoi.

We took the sleeper coach on the overnight train from Hanoi, with Rebecca, to the border town of Lao Cai, which is just across the river from the Chinese town of Hekou. Lao Cai was virtually flattened during the Chinese invasion of northern Vietnam in 1979. It's been rebuilt, but remains basically an uninteresting trading town, so at around 7.00am we jumped straight from the train onto a minibus for the climb up into the mountains, some 40 kilometres to Sapa, at an altitude of 1600 metres.

It is spectacular mountain scenery most of the way, with terraced rice paddies, extraordinary in both their beauty and ingenuity, climbing up the steep slopes. The road itself leaves a lot to be desired, but they're working on it. Workers were on the job almost the whole way up and we were surprised to see so many women labourers and also that both men and women were wearing their traditional H'Mong black and indigo clothing together with plastic flip-flops.

In Sapa itself it became patently clear to us that minority groups wear their complex and often beautiful traditional dress because they *want* to, not for tourists or for any other reason. Of course they're interested in tourists as a means of making a living and crowds of young H'Mong women flocked around us, wanting to sell us their handiwork after we stepped off the bus and made our way a couple of hundred metres down the road to the Bamboo Hotel.

After a rest we had a late breakfast at an attractive little restaurant called Baguette et Chocolat, a branch of the French-run Hanoi street-kids restaurant, Hoa Sua. Then we continued along the road leading out of town to wind our way down into the beautiful valley, which is overlooked by the town of Sapa. At the bottom of the valley we crossed a bridge over the fast-flowing Quy Ho River, to wend our way further into the hills on the opposite side, eventually reaching a beautiful waterfall, the Bac, or Silver, waterfall, where for a while we were the only people in what seemed a pristine paradise.

Reaching the outskirts of the town on our return late in the afternoon, we came across a ceremony under way in a small temple on the high side of the road. Inside, we were fascinated to watch a shaman being made up and dressed by a group of women in a glistening, sequined, white satin costume with an elaborate headdress hung with strings of diamantés. The man, in his fifties perhaps, made no move to help in the process. The women turned him around, fussing and doting, until he was all dressed and ready, then they handed him a white feathered fan, with which he began to perform a brief ritual dance to the beat of drums and music from three traditional Vietnamese instruments: a bamboo flute, a two-stringed fiddle called a *dan nhi* featuring a pipe-bowl-shaped sound box, and the slightly bigger *dan ho*, a sound box made from half a coconut. After a short break he was completely rerobed in an incredible electric-blue satin outfit with an equally stunning blue turban. This time, he was handed four lit candles, which he waved around, as if in a trance, watched by a crowd of mainly women, who were seated on the floor and seemed quietly impressed with the whole proceedings. As, indeed, so were we.

For centuries the H'Mong people have combined ancestor worship and animism; the belief that all things have spirits. Shamans perform the role of a conduit between the ordinary people and the world of the spirits or gods. H'Mong women decorate the shaman's clothes with patterns and embroidered symbols to attract friendly spirits and ward off the unfriendly ones, while the shaman's ceremonial performance is believed to help deal with sickness or injury in the community.

Early the following morning, Nguyen Trong Luan, a young man whom the hotel had arranged to take us on a walk, was waiting for us as we finished an early breakfast. He spoke excellent English and proved to be great company and a good conversationalist. As we walked down the road into the valley, in the opposite direction from the way we had gone the previous day, numerous groups of young women passed us on their way up to start another day of hard-sell to visitors.

As we continued our walk down the valley we were hugely impressed with its exceptional beauty. The wooded hills, rising on either side, with small villages dotting its length, gave it something of the appearance of a valley in Europe, the main difference being that the vegetation here was tropical and subtropical rather than temperate. The other major difference is that the villages in this valley are very poor.

For four or five kilometres we walked down a dirt road, which followed the natural descent of the valley, but kept a steady height of a couple of hundred metres above the river that was winding its way along the valley floor. We would pass through magnificent stands of giant green bamboo, some of which were 20 centimetres in diameter. Also, every ten minutes or so, we would be passed by a Russian-built Minsk motorbike, the most popular means of transport in the mountain areas, heading up to Sapa carrying one, two, three and sometimes four family members.

At a small agglomeration of wooden buildings, we turned off the road and began descending a narrow dirt track between rice terraces and open fields of maize, bananas and other smaller crops. Passing several farmhouses, we saw ingenious uses for bamboo, with pieces cut in half lengthwise to bring irrigation water from the numerous streams to farm buildings and surrounding rice paddies. Another throwback to the technology of more ancient times that works perfectly well were water-powered rice-pounding machines. Using a seesaw arrangement with a water bucket on one end and a heavy stone pestle on the other, the bucket is constantly filled by stream water and automatically tipped and emptied as it fills. In the process, the pestle rises and falls into a mortar filled with rice or wheat, which is eventually ground to powder.

We crossed the river on a narrow wooden pedestrian bridge at a picturesque spot and wound our way through alternately farmed and lightly forested country for a kilometre or so to a small H'Mong village called Lao Chai. Because it was Sunday the village school was closed, although the classroom doors were open. The classrooms were a sorry sight: small and grubby, with a few low wooden chairs bearing the words 'UNICEF Japan, Nagano 99'. Each room was divided down the middle by a rattan screen, so, Luan explained, the teacher could take two classes at once. There was a picture of Ho Chi Minh on the wall and a blackboard that could be seen by both classes. That was it. No cupboards of books or teacher aids, no maps; nothing but a few chairs and two or three low tables. The village was without electricity. It was coming, we were told, but no-one was sure when. Most of the houses were of simple bamboo or timber construction with rattan walls, thatched roofs and earthen floors. They contained primitive, open-hearth cooking and outdoor toilet facilities that ranged from deep-pit latrines to sewage run-offs into the passing streams.

A kilometre or so further on we reached Ta Van, which Luan told us was a Dao village. He had arranged for us to visit one of the houses, where we sat down for a cup of tea and some dragon fruit. The house itself and the rest of the village appeared slightly more developed and affluent than the previous village. Its fields and crops were more ordered and some of the houses had tiled roofs and electricity provided by small water-powered turbines. 'Why is there a difference?' Iain asked Luan.

'These people are more involved with the town ... with Sapa,' he replied.

'Involved? How do you mean?'

'In business. They work in jobs there, or they make and trade things that people want there. It is only a small difference in what they do, but over time it makes a big difference.'

We later learnt that, unlike the H'Mong, this involvement would also ensure that they had at least minimal representation on the People's Committee which, in turn, would lead to greater funding in terms of access to health, education and so on. On the return to Sapa we pondered the huge difficulties faced by developing countries like Vietnam in trying to lift their people out of poverty.

Perhaps the heightened altitude had given us a rush of blood to the head because one of the topics for discussion during the day's walk had been the possibility of climbing Mount Fanxipan, the highest peak in Indochina, some time in the future. At 3143 metres, Fanxipan is omnipresent in Sapa, its jungle-clad slopes looming on the opposite side of the valley. Luan enthusiastically encouraged us to give it a try.

'There is a simple campsite halfway up where you can rest overnight. You need to take two men. They would carry your gear and be your guide and cook.' He made it sound so simple. 'I'd be happy to organise it for you.'

Rebecca was more interested in finding out what financial arrangements were made between the hotel, Luan and the people whose homes we had visited during the day. We had paid the hotel US$15 for Luan's services. Without hesitation he told us, 'I am paid US$3 and the families in the village get US$2 between them.'

'So the hotel takes US$10,' Rebecca confirmed, 'for doing nothing.'

During our visits with the villagers that day, Luan had shown a gentle civility. Now he suggested to Rebecca, 'I am still learning my profession.' At twenty-two he had just graduated from a university tourism course, '...so US$3 a day is good money for me. And unless the villagers agreed to receive the hotel's visitors they would get no money. So they are happy too.'

But Rebecca wasn't and as we checked out, she let the hotel manager know that she didn't approve of the grossly unequal division of the spoils.

The man looked back at her, unimpressed. 'The H'Mong don't know what to do with money,' he said. 'They just drink or gamble it away.'

Rebecca was incensed. 'Visitors don't come here to see *you*,' she told him sharply. 'They come to see the minority people ... and the landscape,' she conceded.

On the bus back down to Lao Cai, Rebecca told Luan that she hoped her remarks wouldn't cause him any problems. 'Not at all.' He smiled. 'It's good that you said what you feel. But the hotel people have heard it before and they know that you are only here for just a brief visit.'

As he saw us onto the train he reminded us of our discussion about climbing Mount Fanxipan, suggesting that he would like to organise it for us. 'The end of August would be a good time. I'll keep in touch by email.'

Arriving at Hanoi Station at around 7.00 o'clock the following morning, a Monday, we took a taxi home, had a quick shower and went straight to the office, where our first job was to record the week's *What's On* programs. Fortunately, we had prepared and largely scripted them all during the previous week.

Back in the office the main news was that Long, the Deputy Director of the Overseas Section, would be leaving.

'I'm not leaving VOV,' he explained. 'Just going to another job.'

'A promotion?' Iain asked.

'Not a promotion.' He smiled. 'I am being rotated.'

Iain laughed. 'Oh ... so you're a rotating cadre.'

'Yes, yes, I suppose that's right.' He laughed too.

Rotating cadres had been something of a joke between us ever since we'd started editing the news bulletins and the *Communist Party Review*. The term would come up all the time in the copy.

'What's a rotating cadre?' Iain had asked Loc early on.

'It's giving people a chance to do different jobs ... to gain experience in other fields,' she had explained. 'Usually to jobs that are on the same scale — the same level.'

'Like being moved sideways.'

'I suppose so.'

Long's particular rotation would be putting him in charge of the Training Department of VOV.

'So I hope to be seeing more of you, anyway,' he said.

'Oh?'

'Yes. I'd like to organise some training workshops and it would be good if you could take part.'

'Okay, that'd be fine,' we said casually, without realising what we might be letting ourselves in for.

Our social life in Hanoi began to pick up speed as we crammed in visits to everything that opened and shut to gather material for the *What's On* program. One such opening was an exhibition by Simon Redington, a London-based artist whose work shows how emotionally involved he is with Vietnam. The exhibition was at the up-market Art Vietnam Gallery, owned by Suzanne Lecht, a chic Californian, who has a home in Hanoi. She represents some of the burgeoning numbers of Hanoi's artists who, released from past strictures, are beginning to make a name for themselves overseas. The opening was a good place to meet and mingle with some of these talented people and, looking around the elegant surrounds and the arty crowd, we could easily have thought we were in London or San Francisco.

The exhibition was titled the Ten Courts of the Kings of Hell, and at the core of the display of Simon's dense and complex prints was the Vietnamese version of the Buddhist moral code and its ten courts of justice. Based on the concept of karma and the never-ending cycle of life, death is followed by rebirth which itself is influenced by actions in a previous existence. According to Vietnamese beliefs, the souls of the deceased are not lost forever. Instead, they go to a kind of transitory purgatory named the Ten Regions of Hell. Here, sentence for each type of wrongdoing committed in life is handed out by a judge or king of hell. A guide to Vietnamese religious thought published by the Friends of Vietnam Heritage points out that the concept of hell should not be understood as a permanent state in the underworld, an opposite of heaven, but as a transit chamber for the impartial meting out of justice for human sins.

From the First Court of Tan Quang through to the Tenth Court of Chuyen Juan, Simon's paintings depict each of the ten kings sitting in judgment over the souls of the recently deceased. Souls are taken after physical death to the first tribunal of hell, after crossing the Nai River Bridge that separates the two worlds. They are stripped naked to appear equal to one another before the kings of hell. In the second tribunal, they are brought in front of the Karma Mirror, which reveals each and every deed performed in life, whether good or bad. A pair of scales weighs moral versus immoral behaviour to determine the overall character of the soul under judgment.

In the following tribunals, a range of judgments are shown being meted out in relation to the sins committed. After completing punishment, the spirits are reborn in one of the six planes of existence as described in the tenth tribunal. According to one of the systems of gradation, righteous conduct can lead to rebirth as a king or a mandarin, a rich or noble person, a widow, a spinster, a bachelor or a poor person. Immoral conduct causes rebirth as a bird, an animal, a smaller insect or a crab, a fish and so on. On the way to being reborn, the souls cross another river and are made to drink from its waters to erase any memory of a previous life from their minds.

One place in Hanoi where plenty of people have erased their memories, if only temporarily, is the Spotted Cow. It's a popular watering hole for Australians, New Zealanders and other expatriates, as well as a sprinkling of Vietnamese. As with the exhibition of the Ten Courts of the Kings of Hell, we were attracted to the bar as a possible item for *What's On* because it was one of the more important venues for an ongoing local darts competition. But the other attraction of the Spotted Cow bar was its owner, Vietnam War veteran Bill Maconachie, with whom we had struck up an acquaintance.

'I bought a half share of the bar a couple of years ago, but the bloke who owned the rest of it wanted to get out and move on, so I took the plunge and bought his share also. It's a bit like the United Nations.' Bill grinned. 'There's plenty of Aussies, as you can see, as well as Brits, Americans and Canadians. But what surprised me a bit was the number of Russians, Ukrainians, Swedes, French and heaps of others who come in regularly.

'The darts competition runs most of the year,' he explained. 'The Spotted Cow team competes with teams from other bars in Hanoi, including Jacc's, the Hilton, JJ's Sports Bar, the American Club and others. Then we have a play-off against a similar pub league in Ho Chi Minh City. It's a big affair.'

Bill served with the Australian Air Force in Vietnam in late 1967 and early 1968, working at Saigon's Tan Son Nhut airbase and in Phuc Thuy Province as an aircraft engineer. After Vietnam he served in Malaysia and then, on leaving the air force, he worked in New Guinea for independent airline operators. In the mid–1990s Bill had an opportunity to come back to Vietnam to work as an aircraft engineer with Vietnam Airlines. It was during that time that he realised that he'd found his niche and wanted to stay.

'I love it,' he told us. 'I live only a short distance from the bar. I come to work at about ten or eleven in the morning. I take a cyclo to work every day, because it gives somebody employment. I pay him just about half a day's pay for the ten-minute trip and I sit there in my shorts and T-shirt, rolling along through the traffic thinking to myself, This is it. It doesn't get much better than this.'

One of the aspects of our work that tended to irritate after a while was that we were required to work on Saturday afternoons. One of us was needed for about three or four hours and we decided that by doing the work together we could cut the time in half. There were usually only a few other members of our team working on Saturdays. They would have been dealing with the translation of news and current affairs stories before we came in, so there was generally a bit of a backlog of stories for us to edit when we arrived.

On one particular Saturday afternoon in the middle of June, the line-up was Loc, Giang, Quynh and Hanh, who was now nine months pregnant. Almost as soon as we arrived, however, Hanh left. She didn't look well and gave us a wan smile and a small wave as she waddled heavily to the lift.

'Is she all right?' Trish asked.

'She feels a bit sick,' Giang told us. 'She says she's dizzy.'

There was a slight 'hmmph' from Loc.

The time passed quickly after we sat down on opposite sides of the desk, put our heads down and started working through the pile of stories. When they were finished, Giang and Quynh headed for the studio with the corrected scripts.

It was almost as if Loc had waited until Giang and Quynh had gone for the opportunity to speak.

'They've got it very easy now, these young ones,' she said.

We knew she was talking about Hanh, but asked anyway. 'You mean Hanh?'

'Yes. They're soft now ... weak. They don't know what we've been through. When I was young, we had none of the things they have now. I didn't even have my husband with me. He was in Cuba, and I was here. Now they get four months off work to have their babies!' She paused, shook her head and held her hands out in mock amazement. 'Four months! On basic pay!'

'But she's almost due,' Trish said. 'And she feels sick. It often happens.'

But Loc had already turned and walked back to her desk.

'Hanh's baby has died,' Phuong told us on Monday morning.

We stared at her in horror, hearing the words but not immediately able to process the information. There were other people in the office but, as the shock of the news broke through, we both burst into tears. Phuong was embarrassed but we didn't give a damn.

'What happened?'

'It died inside her.'

Our minds filled with visions of Hanh's baby, on the very verge of life, slipping back into oblivion. Trish wanted to ask more questions but couldn't get the words to form. She needed to escape the awkward silence of the others to be able to sob without restraint. And she was angry. Angry with herself, feeling somehow responsible, that she had failed Hanh and her baby; angry with the other staff who had never really opened their hearts to her as much as they should. She was also angry with a society where women are still expected to kowtow to the wishes of their husbands and parents-in-law, and with the low level of medical care and the lack of quality nutrition.

We escaped to our coffee shop, where we were anonymous. Here, we gathered our emotions and, operating on automatic, we returned to the office where we managed to complete the required program recording. But when we asked more questions our horror and anger only grew.

Hanh had been admitted to hospital on the Saturday evening a few hours after she had left the office saying she felt unwell. When she was examined it was discovered that the baby was already dead in her uterus. More than thirty-six hours later, when we first learnt of the baby's death, that was still the situation, and it was to remain that way for a further thirty-six hours. During all of this time Hanh was sharing a hospital bed with another woman who was awaiting the induction of her dead baby. We also discovered that the ward where she was housed was filled with around twenty beds, each of them occupied by two women.

Up until now we'd had no reason to find out anything about the condition of hospitals or health care in Hanoi, but it was this tragedy for Hanh that brought it home to us with a jolt. Despite all the country's dramatic economic progress and the flood of foreign investment that had produced a veneer of Western-style living, Vietnam was still a *developing* country, a very poor country. Living in a big city like Hanoi could distort that image.

Vietnam has strong ambitions to join the ranks of developed and industrialised nations, particularly those in Asia, like Hong Kong, Singapore, Taiwan and South Korea, but it is starting late and from a very low base; a situation, as we've said, that has been forced on it by decades of war and stagnation caused by economic mismanagement. So its hospitals are not up to the standards of developed countries and a few of its health statistics illustrate that gap. For example, the most common cause of all deaths in Vietnam is pneumonia. Almost 50 per cent of the population do not have access to safe drinking water and over 100,000 new cases of TB are reported each year, 65 per cent of them infectious, making it the fifth most common cause of death. The infant mortality rate, at 31 per 1000 live births, and the maternal mortality rate, at 95 per 100,000 live births, are both higher than those of developed countries. By comparison, infant mortality rates in the United States and Australia are 6.7 per 1000 and 4.8 per 1000 respectively. The lowest in the world are in Japan and Sweden, both of which are under 3.5 per 1000.

But Vietnam is making significant progress in the health field. In 1999 life expectancy was sixty-five for men and seventy for women, producing an average of sixty-seven. These figures are changing dramatically and by 2002, it was sixty-seven for men and seventy-two for women, with an average of sixty-nine. That is higher than in most other Asian countries. When viewed on the basis of average income level, Vietnam's performance in terms of health is much higher than would be expected. More than 90 per cent of all children under one year are fully vaccinated and all children under five have received vaccinations against polio, while 80 per cent of pregnant women receive tetanus vaccinations.

One of the more remarkable aspects of the health system in Vietnam is the prominent role played by traditional medicine, in which some 70 per cent of provinces and cities have traditional medical departments. The main problem, as experienced by Hanh, however, is the shortage of beds in major urban hospitals, a problem that was exacerbated by the fact that because this was the year of the Golden Goat, many more women were pregnant. Vietnam has only one general hospital of international standard. This is the Franco–Vietnamese Hospital, a US$40 million venture privately funded with aid from the Asian Development Bank, which opened its doors in Ho Chi Minh City in early 2003. It has twenty-six wards, 200 beds and nine operating theatres, and is providing state-of-the-art diagnostic services and high-quality medical care through surgical, maternity, cardiology and oncology centres.

The project is seen as part of the government's efforts to develop the private health sector in Vietnam by helping to meet the acute shortage of health-care services. It is also being viewed as something of a pilot model for new hospitals that could be replicated in other parts of the country. None of this, of course, could be of any comfort to Hanh.

For Trish, this was the nadir of our time in Vietnam. She missed her family and friends. She wanted to hug our grandchildren, to feed on their full-of-life-ness. She contacted her sister in Calgary, Alberta, who had specialised in maternity nursing. When she mentioned Hanh's itching skin, which she had sensed at the time was not a good sign, her sister said this was not uncommon in pregnancy, but that her long-distance diagnosis would be that Hanh had probably been suffering from toxemia, the cause of which would now be almost impossible to determine. Trish wished she had been more knowledgeable, or that she had encouraged Hanh more strongly to mention the itching to the doctor.

The 'gossip' team and Trish attempted to negotiate the cultural chasm that had opened between them. This event had underlined how our experiences establish and underpin our view of life's challenges. Trish's focus was on the emotional pain Hanh must be undergoing and the little body who didn't quite manage to gulp a life-breath. Tram, Thi and Huan had also all individually suffered emotional trauma, but their societal values encouraged them to internalise them. Trish felt that they viewed her teary, emotional state as an indulgence.

Almost four days after Hanh's baby died, she went through an induced labour. 'It had been a girl,' Minh Ha told Trish.

'Will she be given any counselling?' Trish asked and then, in response to Minh Ha's inquiring look, 'You know, some help, to assist her with the shock?'

'She's gone to stay with her mother,' Minh Ha said, as if that was the answer to the query. 'And it's been decided that she can take maternity leave.'

'So she won't come back to work until both Tram and Phuong have left to have their babies?'

Minh Ha nodded. It was a relief that at least Hanh would not have to face seeing her pregnant colleagues.

Thi, who was sitting nearby, had overheard. Later in the day she assured Trish in a quiet tone, to console and soothe the breach, 'Hanh'll have another baby.' Then she added, 'And we believe a baby has a soul from the very beginning, before it comes into this world, so the baby who died will have another life at a later stage. Perhaps a happy life, because it will have committed no sin in this one.'

It was not that we wanted to avoid these sometimes intense discussions in the office, more that we simply needed some clear head-space and time to work on *What's On* that made us decide to set up the work space for it at home, rather than staying at VOV all day. We hung a fair-sized corkboard on the wall of our home office on which we began to pin notes setting up the various items for the week's daily programs. Then we'd divide up the stories we'd been researching and, working on two separate laptops, knock them out and print them up several days in advance of the recording date. We quickly finetuned the process so that we would record the programs for Saturday and the following Monday on Friday mornings. There was no *What's On* program on Sundays, and on the Monday morning we would record all the programs for the rest of the week.

It was quite a job finding the story items to fill the program at first, as there were at least three each day, or eighteen in a week. This quickly settled down to a couple of segments each day, or around eleven or twelve stories each week, which was much more manageable, especially as we were doing it in our own time. After we'd been running a couple of weeks, Huong suggested we contact Terry Hartney, who had worked as a volunteer at VOV in the same job but was now a senior member of the Royal Melbourne Institute of Technology's independent university set up in Ho Chi Minh City. Terry agreed to ring us from time to time so that we could record short phone interviews on events or places of interest in and around Saigon. He would be *What's On*'s 'man in Saigon'.

Also, very soon after we started, we suggested that, on two days of the week, as part of the training process, one of the male reporters and one of the female reporters should join whichever one of us was doing the program. This worked quite well and both Huan and Thuy enjoyed the change from their much more formal newsreading.

Living in a city is like being in the belly of a beast. You become intimate with its internal rhythms. This was made more pleasant for us in Hanoi because the capital kept the same hours we enjoy: early to bed and early to rise. Quite often we would wake to the utter silence that cloaked the city in the very early morning and we'd lie in bed listening in anticipation for the evocative hooting of a train to break the spell, as it set off on its journey from the central station just a few blocks away. Usually, though, we'd be jolted awake before dawn by the noisy rattle of a small metal trolley cart juddering over the uneven broken concrete of the courtyard, pushed by a young woman who lived further up in the interior of our compound.

Every morning at the same time, no matter what the weather, she unlocked the big entrance gates and set up her portable kitchen, using ingredients that she had prepared to cook a big steaming pot of *pho*, traditional Vietnamese chicken or beef soup, over a fire made from burning a cylindrical charcoal briquette. By 6.00am her customers were starting to arrive and we could hear the little metal-legged, plastic-topped tables being dragged into position, the miniature blue plastic stools dropped around them and the low murmur of the voices of early breakfasters.

Next the public loudspeaker, attached high up to an electricity pole on the corner of the street outside, would start up at full strength, blaring forth exhortations to be up and about, giving news of local doings and information about various campaigns such as immunisations for preschool children. All this interspersed with screeching music, so distorted it ripped at your eardrums. Throughout the year we planned midnight sabotage attacks with gigantic wire snippers but were too cowardly to ever carry them out.

By the time we had showered and were making breakfast we could hear the happy raised voices of the kindergartners in their room downstairs just inside the courtyard entrance greeting each other with the irrepressible joy of that age and singing their daily rendition of Ho Chi Minh's Five Teachings:

*Love your country and love your fellow countrymen.*
*Study hard and work hard.*
*Be united and disciplined.*
*Be tidy and clean.*
*Be modest, honest and courageous.*

On Mondays, Wednesdays and Fridays, we would also hear Mai rattling her keys in the lock of the outside patio, come to do battle with the gritty layer of grime that settled over everything.

Throughout the day the courtyard was a bit like a village green, in the sense that women hawkers would come through with baskets of fruit, vegetables, meat and cooked delicacies. They brought

**The children of Sao Mai, the little kindergarten adjoining our courtyard.**

shoulder racks of clothing or deep baskets in which they collected discarded cardboard and paper. Other people, mostly men, came on bicycles, with grindstones to sharpen knives, with a fantasy of electrical odds and ends, or with a tangle of metal tubing and pipes. They all had their own individual call, and some added bells or even castanets to attract customers. As dusk came on, the breakfast *pho* maker would wheel out an ancient contraption of heavy metal cogs into which she would feed sticks of sugar cane to produce a gush of sweet juice and, with the day's work over, the entire neighbourhood would gather around her for a refreshing drink and a chat.

During the last week in June we seemed to be focused on our navels, in that many of the stories we were editing dealt with National Media Day, Journalists' Day or, to give it its more correct Vietnamese title, National Revolutionary Press Day. The newspapers, the airwaves and, of course, the *Communist Party Review* were filled with reams of self-congratulatory and critical analyses of the media in Vietnam.

'The media has distinguished itself as a bridge, linking the Party, the state and the people,' Deputy Minister of Culture and Information Nguyen Quy Doan said at a seminar. 'So far, media agencies in Vietnam have done a good job ... as an effective tool which the Party and state can use to disseminate their policies.' We wondered how that would go down in Sydney, or any major Western city really.

However, some stories carried criticism of the way a number of journalists and newspapers were doing their job '... several papers worked outside of their guiding principles and objectives,' one report lamented, '... in order to cater to the tastes of *a majority of readers* and also considered the press to be a normal commodity' (our emphasis).

These stories naturally provoked several interesting discussions with our colleagues, who were quick to point out some of the differences in the way things were reported in the Vietnamese media when compared to the English-language press's only newspapers, the *Saigon Times* and the *Vietnam News*, to which we were exposed. The Vietnamese press seemed to be divided into two groups. The first consisted of three conservative and largely uncritical papers, of which, incidentally, all government offices had to buy a copy each day. These were *The People's Daily (Nhan Dan)*, *The People's Army (Quan Doi Nhan Dan)* and *New Hanoi (Hanoi Moi)*. Then there were the papers that were more critical on most issues: *Youth (Thanh Nien)*, *Vanguard (Tien Phong)*, *Young Age (Tuoi Tre)* and *Labour (Lao Dong)*. Not surprisingly, these newspapers were the most popular, the most colourful, carried the most advertisements, and paid higher salaries to their journalists.

Although we didn't see a great deal of it, censorship of foreign media does occur. For example, very soon after our arrival in Hanoi, we bought a copy of the *International Herald Tribune* to find that two stories inside the paper had been sprayed over with silver paint. The bottom line, we came to appreciate, is that while real press freedom does not exist in Vietnam, it is nonetheless a work in progress, albeit with a number of contradictions. Vietnam's Press Law, first adopted in 1989 at the height of the so-called Doi Moi reforms, brought important gains to local journalists, such as the right to disseminate information obtained through their own sources and limited protection of the confidentiality of those sources. While the law recognised the right of journalists to engage in investigative reporting, it also explicitly stated that the role of the press was to serve as the voice of the Party and the state. The conflict became more acute when local newspapers and journalists, who had been encouraged to expose corruption and mismanagement, found themselves pressured and investigated for doing so.

Foreign journalists in Vietnam for a brief visit apparently meet few difficulties in doing their work, but for foreign correspondents based in Vietnam it's a different story. They are allowed to reside only in Hanoi. Their movements are restricted in that they must advise the Ministry of Culture and Information of any intended journeys outside of Hanoi and, when travelling, are often accompanied by a 'minder'. They also work with the knowledge that their phones and email are almost certainly tapped and their movements monitored.

In what seemed a somewhat contradictory approach, in the light of all the official praise of journalists who toed the Party line, Loc surprised Iain one morning by saying, 'We need you to rewrite the news bulletins.'

He looked at her uncomprehendingly for a moment or two. 'Isn't that what we're doing ... editing the bulletins?'

'No, I mean to fully rewrite them ... completely. We need to free ourselves of the Vietnamese text.'

'But you still want to hang onto phrases like "peaceful evolution"?' Iain said, referring to a previous point of contention.

'Oh,' she said, 'that's different. That means something important to Vietnamese.'

The term 'peaceful evolution' is used in Vietnamese news stories to denote what the government sees as an evil process being promulgated in the Central Highlands, ostensibly by Overseas Vietnamese, aimed at undermining the ethnic minorities. The idea is that by a slow process of inculcating the minorities with anti-government propaganda, and exposing them to 'decadent' Western culture, democracy and human rights issues, they will turn against the regime and either rise up against it or leave the country in sufficient numbers, as in the earlier boat people episodes, to discredit the regime.

'We've been through this before,' Iain said, 'but you have to realise that, in English, "peaceful evolution" nearly always means something *good*. To any English reader, "peaceful evolution" can't be bad.'

'But that's the way it's described in Vietnamese,' she said adamantly.

'Yet you just told me you need to free yourselves from the Vietnamese text.'

'Hmmph.'

# July
## HEROIC MOTHERS

*'When drinking water remember the source'*

'Hey, what's happening here?' Trish asked when she arrived in the office to find the central worktable strewn with piles of fruit and packages wrapped in banana leaf.

'It's party time,' Tram announced.

'With a small P.' Huan smiled as he always did when he did something clever with English.

'But my birthday isn't until November,' Trish joked, settling onto a chair and with a small knife trying to peel rambutans in the attractive and efficient way that Thi was managing.

'It's VOV5's fifth anniversary,' Tram explained.

The party was Huong's idea, even though Loc saw it as a waste of scarce resources. The two of them frequently had ding-dong arguments, invariably about money, the lack of it and the distribution of what there was. During the most recent spat, about bonuses and incentives, all in Vietnamese, of course, we heard the name *What's On* bandied about and felt somewhat uncomfortable. But no-one else did and, as always, work just went on around them.

Despite any subterranean currents, the little birthday bash to celebrate five years of English-language broadcasting went off swimmingly. Hue and Long joined in and eventually even Loc made a conciliatory appearance. Staff from other departments who had done any work for VOV5 during the half decade dropped by. We nibbled our way politely around the edges of glutinous rice patties filled with bits of pork. Giang produced his Cuttlefish à la Cleaning Fluid topped off with rambutans and the polka-dot pulp of the purple-skinned dragon fruit. Minh Ha played music on the tape machine as everybody freshened their palates with swigs of green tea and congratulated themselves on being part of a small but important change in the nation's media. Five years is a long time in Vietnam.

As we were cleaning up, Khoi asked if we could help to produce a new promotional brochure for VOV5. It seemed as if it might be an interesting little project so we sat down for twenty minutes to talk about what sort of thing Khoi, who was apparently going to be in charge of the project, wanted to do and when he wanted it.

In Vietnam 9 July has been designated as Tourism Day, an indication of the importance of the industry in the nation's economy. In 1990 when Vietnam first started to focus on tourism, the country attracted only 250,000 visitors. By 1996 the figure had reached 1.71 million, a sevenfold increase in just six years. In 1997 the Asian financial crisis affected tourist numbers, but there was an unexpectedly quick bounce back and the industry went on to post double-digit growth right through to the September 11 attacks on the United States and the flow-on effects of that tragic event, which marked a change in many aspects of life around the globe.

For Vietnam, some of the effects were positive. One of the upsides of having an authoritarian government is that the country is seen as stable and peaceful which, presently, it certainly is. We always felt safe walking the streets in any part of the city, even after dark. In our time in Vietnam, we knew personally of only two cases of theft from foreigners. One was a bag snatch in Ho Chi Minh City, the other a wallet taken from an insecurely fastened backpack in the early-morning crowd at the Hanoi railway station. Something else that has contributed to the overall success of the tourism industry has been its promotion at overseas fairs in European and Asian cities and in Australia. Most recently, a permanent new information and promotion bureau opened in San Francisco.

In 2003 upwards of two and half million people visited Vietnam. By far the largest number, a million plus, came from China. Almost half a million others came from Western Europe, with nearly the same number coming from Japan and Korea. Also, during the time we were there, visa requirements were lifted on Japanese nationals. Such seemingly unimportant details can make a sizeable difference in where tourists decide to spend their dollar. The country attracted close to 3.5 million visitors in 2005, bringing in more than $US2 billion in much-needed revenue. But even those numbers still leave it as a junior player in the region. For example, Thailand and Malaysia each pull in around 10 million visitors annually.

It was during the first half of July that we found ourselves dealing with small instances of censorship. In general, because the subject matter in our *What's On* segments was relatively inconsequential, the question of censorship didn't arise. The material was all so straightforward, simple and non-political that no-one gave a thought to the need to check the copy before it was broadcast. Then, one morning Hue came across to Iain's desk to tell him that we should not be using the term 'Viet Cong' in our stories.

'I didn't hear it,' she said, '...but Phuong told me that you referred to the Viet Cong in a *What's On* story the other day.'

'Yes,' Iain replied. 'We've done it quite a few times. Is there something wrong?'

The story she was talking about involved a small café in Saigon called the Binh Soup Shop, on Ly Chinh Thang, in District 3. The story goes that, throughout the Vietnam–American war, this little shop was the headquarters of the Viet Cong and much of the planning for Saigon's part in the 1968 Tet Offensive was carried out under the noses of many a GI who sat there eating their excellent noodle soup.

'We don't use the term Viet Cong,' Hue said. 'You should call them "revolutionary fighters" instead.'

'Why?' Iain asked, bewildered. 'What's wrong with Viet Cong? It's a Vietnamese term. Doesn't it simply mean Vietnamese communist? It's what everybody calls them.'

'In the South,' she nodded, '...and in the United States, but not in the North. We never used it. It was a name that was made up by the regime in the South, possibly by President Diem.'

So, no more 'Viet Cong'. And a few days after that it was no more 'Saigon'.

On the occasions when Terry Hartney called in to contribute an item to *What's On*, we would close his piece off with a back-announcement saying, '...that report from Terry Hartney, our man in Saigon'. It had a better ring to it, we thought, than '...our man in Ho Chi Minh City'. But no, that was out too.

'Ho Chi Minh City is the correct name. It has been since 1975,' Madame Hue explained. 'If you are referring to it any time before 1975, it's all right to say Saigon, but after '75 it should be Ho Chi Minh City.'

Then a bit of non-political censorship: the movie *The Exorcist* was to be shown at the Hanoi Press Club one Sunday evening and we ran a little story about it in *What's On*. By this time, Hue had begun checking all our scripts before we recorded them. Perhaps someone higher up had also heard us saying 'Saigon' or 'Viet Cong'. So, *The Exorcist* had to be dropped also. 'It promotes superstition and the Devil,' she explained.

But when she did a final check on one of the news stories that had come across Iain's desk one day dealing with the Vietnam War and changed 'US forces' to 'US aggressors' and the 'Saigon government' to 'puppet regime', Iain took it up with her.

'The Americans may well have been aggressors and the Saigon government at the time may have been puppets,' he pointed out, 'but by continuing to use the same clichéd phrases thirty years after the end of the war, you simply make the bulletin sound even more like propaganda than it is.'

On this occasion she agreed.

He calmed himself a little by sitting down to think about what sort of things might go into the new brochure we'd started working on. An earlier one had several shots of senior staff members and bureaucrats in suits shaking hands, including the previous director general of the Voice of Vietnam, Tran Mai Hanh, who was now serving a long prison sentence. This new brochure, we were determined, would have smiling faces.

Around this time in the office, Trish noticed Tram enviously eyeing a slim, attractive female member of the overseas service Vietnamese staff, whose petite frame was always clad in casual elegance. Tram would watch her as she moved with sinuous grace through her line of vision and then sigh despondently. The birth of her baby was imminent. She looked wan with fatigue. Fluid retention had made her jowly. In the modest manner favoured by Vietnamese women in pregnancy, she wore a loose pinafore-style dress over a short-sleeved T-shirt. Her feet and ankles, though not as swollen as Hanh's had been, were still bloated and she went about in a pair of plastic scuffs. Trish sympathised with how she felt, and although the office was airconditioned, the extreme heat was an added burden whenever she was outside.

'Not long,' Trish tried to console her, 'and you'll be looking like that again.'

'I hope so,' she said and then grimaced. 'The doctor has told me the cord and placenta are wrapped around the baby's neck and that I have to eat hot food to free it.'

Trish's heart sank at such dangerous ignorance.

'Tram, it isn't possible for the placenta to be wrapped around the neck, though that can happen with the umbilical cord. Look at this,' and she did her best to draw a foetus in the uterus, the placenta and the umbilical cord. Trish is no medical expert, just a mum, but she felt she should at least try some explanation of how a baby was nurtured in the womb. From her comments, it was clear Tram had only the sketchiest idea about any of the physical sides of the process.

'I just want it to be over,' she wailed.

Within two days it was. Tram had a caesarian delivery of a healthy baby boy weighing 3.2 kilograms. The relief in the office was palpable. Only one more birth to go: Phuong's baby was due in mid-September.

'Tram obviously didn't sit on the chair,' Huan said in a sly tone, which dared Trish to ask more.

She obliged. 'Which chair is that?'

Huan and Thi were sitting with Trish to read through their *What's On* scripts. Thuy had already found the regular scheduling of *What's On* conflicted with other work so Terrific Thi had taken up the challenge and was proving to be a confident and fast learner.

'The pregnancy chair,' Thi said. 'If you sit in it, you get pregnant, but you always get a girl baby. Everyone who has become a parent in this office, man or woman, has had a daughter. Tram is the first one to have a boy.'

'It's what you call "an old wives' tale", isn't that right?' Huan smiled with the small pleasure of showing off his knowledge of a new English idiom.

Then, as something of non sequitur, he said, 'I would like you to meet my girlfriend.'

We knew she was home on a visit from Cuba, where they had met as students and to where she was returning to continue her studies for another two years.

'It's a long time to wait,' Trish commented sympathetically, immediately realising what a superficial, short-term Western way of looking at things that was. She added quickly, 'But not when you know she's the right person.'

'You will see when you meet her.' He gave a confident smile.

It was time to talk tough again. No pay, no work. Only this time it was the *Communist Party Review* hierarchy that was being recalcitrant, which seemed even more unacceptable than when it had been the government-run radio station that'd used 'financial difficulties' as the excuse for non-payment of salaries.

'Sorry, Hue,' Trish smiled politely as Hue tried handing her another sheaf of close-typed pages. 'We can't do any more editing of the *Review* until we are paid.'

Three hours later Hue sheepishly presented Trish with an envelope bulging with low-denomination notes, as though someone had emptied their piggy bank.

Although editing the *Review* was extremely tedious work, it gave us insights into the mindset of the hierarchy we would otherwise not have had. Strictly speaking, it was 'outside work', not forming part of our job description, and we should have declared the ridiculously small fee to AVI and had it docked from our salary. We didn't and so we became part of the black economy on which Vietnam operates.

Of our team only the newest members, Thi, Tram and Huan, did no outside work. But that was only because they were at the bottom of the pecking order. There was no doubt that, given time, they too would have jobs passed on to them by other staff in the English Language Department.

Salary levels across the board in government offices were completely insufficient to support even a basic lifestyle, let alone the motorbikes and decent clothing everyone now felt was their due. There were two complex grading systems for salaries. The base pay for any civil servant, in every government office, was 295,000 dong (less than A$30) a month. But that figure was only used as a starting point. No-one was actually paid that. Everyone received step-ups, depending on their grade within the system. The basis for starting salary calculations for all staff at VOV was around 550,000 dong (A$55) a month. But then another grading system, which we understood to run from 1 to about 13, came into play, so that lower-paid staff members at VOV5, at either grade 3 or 4, would receive between 1.7 million (A$170) and 2.2 million dong (A$220) a month, still insufficient to survive on in a city.

People who worked for VOV5 were offered translation work, which generally paid a good deal more than could be earned working for the government. Fees for 'outside work' made the difference between barely scraping by and a far-from-flash, but manageable, life. The going rate was US$8 for a page of translation and US$15 an hour for simultaneous translations at, say, conferences or meetings.

Senior members of the staff would disappear for days, sometimes even a week or so, at a time on 'outside work'. Other staff would often be gone for shorter periods of time. Unless it would severely inconvenience the department, approval would generally be given. With everyone understanding each other's needs they would happily cover one another's workloads.

Additional work of a more long-term and official nature was also available from time to time. Several of the staff had attended conferences in different regional countries including Laos, Cambodia, Myanmar and South Korea, as well as overseas training programs in Australia and in Sweden, which has a long-established relationship with VOV. And it was for this type of overseas training that both Giang and Quynh were separately applying during July. Giang asked us for our advice in filling out an application form for a Fulbright scholarship to undertake a masters program in broadcast journalism in the United States. Quynh approached Iain a couple of weeks later to check through an application he was preparing for a one-year secondment to NHK's radio network in Japan.

These developments simply added to the overall texture of daily life at VOV5. For our part we had been caught up for some time in trying to put together a mock-up of the new brochure Khoi wanted to promote the English service of VOV. During the second week in July we brought a copy of it in to the office. The slogan on the front page read, 'English language broadcasts in Vietnam ... ? You've got it!' The brochure unfolded into three pages and, as it opened, you were presented with a colourful spread of smiling faces of all the staff at the bottom of each page.

A month had now passed since the death of Hanh's baby, and on our arrival at the office one Monday morning, all ready to record the week's *What's On* segments, we were told that everyone was going to visit Hanh at her parents' house. About ten of us piled onto motorbikes for the trip out to a suburb called Cong Vi, in the Ba Dinh district of Hanoi. We always felt a little nervous about these impromptu trips without helmets, because of the shocking road accident statistics in Vietnam, but as always, such trips were fascinating, and Hoang Hoa Tham, one of the long streets we followed on our way to see Hanh, is one of Hanoi's more interesting thoroughfares. The street is jam-packed with traffic like most of the city during working hours, but it's lined with an appealing mix of shop-houses selling everything from beautifully carved furniture, exotic caged birds and painting reproductions to tropical plants in numerous nurseries. It also has a reputation as a red-light district, with scores of karaoke bars interspersed along it and Buoi, another long avenue we turned into adjoining Hoang Hoa Tham. Prostitution and brothels are illegal in Vietnam, but karaoke bars have become a convenient cover.

Hanh looked well and was smiling broadly as we arrived at her parents' house, off the main road on a quiet laneway. The house was big; three storeys, with a large and well-kept garden with numerous tropical plants, all behind a high wall, resulting in what was a private retreat from the world outside — just the thing we felt sure Hanh had needed during the past month. We had been alerted to the fact that it was customary on such occasions to give a gift, usually money — '50,000 dong will be okay', Minh Ha had said — so we slipped our contribution into an envelope with those of the others, which was given to Hanh as we arrived.

We crowded into the small living room on the ground floor while tea and savouries were brought in by Hanh's mother. Minh Ha, Thuy and Khoi were sitting on the floor around the low coffee table and after the initial round of polite conversation, began talking about property; the price of flats in Hanoi and so on. We were sitting on the couch opposite them and, naturally couldn't understand the conversation. It was Nam, Huan's mother, sitting between us, who explained.

'Property, property. Flats, Flats. That's all these young people seem to be interested in,' she said.

Hello? We seem to have heard that before somewhere. In fact the endless talk of rising property values over dinner in Sydney restaurants was one of the things we were glad to be missing in Hanoi. There was, of course, another side to it. We were in a country that was emerging from decades of stifling controls on free enterprise and private ownership, and the concept was still relatively new and exciting. What we didn't talk about, however, was the most important thing, at least for Hanh.

The loss of a child, the most tragic blow that can strike a mother, resonates deeply in Vietnamese society. In a country that spent most of the last century fighting wars of independence there are many, many mothers who experienced the grief of outliving their soldier sons and daughters. 'Remembering the source of the water we drink' is a Vietnamese tradition encouraged from a very young age, and in the last week of July we witnessed an intense example of the emotional basis for that adage with War Invalids', Martyrs' and Heroic Mothers' Day.

War Invalids and Martyrs we had anticipated, but Heroic Mothers ... well, that was a step beyond. To be designated a Heroic Mother your only son had to have died at war, or your husband and son, or all your sons. Grief and horror came in hideous gradations.

There were shots of these women on the front pages of all the newspapers, wearing the medals and awards of their dead sons and husbands. Some of them were holding framed photographs of the deceased. Tiny creatures, many of them bent over with years, although it could have been with suffering. Their faces were so wrinkled you could hardly see their eyes and, when you did, you wished you hadn't.

There are 43,000 of these women in Ho Chi Minh City alone. On this special day, each Heroic Mother was presented with an additional 120,000 dong (A$12). All Heroic Mothers are what are called 'policy beneficiaries', numbers of whom are cared for by local government agencies or enterprises, while many live in 'gratitude houses', basic accommodation ranging from one or two rooms, or a small flat to a simple village cottage, provided by the government to needy and deserving widows of soldiers killed in the war. With the natural attrition of the years their numbers are dwindling, and the focus of the day is shifting to war invalids and martyrs and their families. But there is no sign that Vietnam will forget the huge debt it owes to the mothers of those who died to bring independence to their country.

War Invalids', Martyrs' and Heroic Mothers' Day fell on a Sunday, so we decided to use the day to pay our second visit to the war museum, where numerous events were planned in honour of the occasion. The rooms on the ground floor were crowded with men and women in khaki uniforms topped off by outsized caps. The place was awash with red-ribboned medals. Scores of elderly women in black, accompanied by members of younger generations, stood alongside photographs of other Heroic Mothers displayed on the walls.

One that attracted a great deal of interest was of Nguyen Thi Thu, who comes from the central province of Quang Nam, the area so despoiled by wars across a century that it has the highest number of Heroic Mothers. All nine of Nguyen Thi Thu's sons were killed in the Resistance War and at the age of 100, she now lives with her daughter who was injured during the American War. Not a claim to fame anyone would like to make.

The most extraordinary fact was that none of the Vietnamese showed one iota of antagonism towards us, the only foreigners. Quite the opposite. They made gestures of welcome. But we felt like intruders and moved on upstairs to the exhibition that pulls in most visitors because it gives such a graphic depiction of the American War in all its grisly horror, though again the tone is not unwelcoming, simply factual. Even so, the bald facts are so shaming.

There's a phrase that's used quite a lot by politicians, businesspeople, writers and the like, both in Vietnam and elsewhere, which, despite the danger of overuse, is nonetheless true: 'Vietnam is a country, not a war'. And this is a fact that Vietnam would like the rest of the world to take on board. The war is in the past and, for the vast bulk of the Vietnamese, the past is behind them. The future holds an entirely different destiny for Vietnam and that is where they are looking and where they are heading.

At the same time, it's understandable that for those people who went through the war, on both sides, it's a difficult process to push those terrible years and experiences to the back of their minds. Yet increasing numbers of veterans from America and Australia, particularly those who have been traumatised by the experience, are finding that, by visiting Vietnam and meeting with veterans from the other side — that is, soldiers from either the North Vietnamese army or from the Viet Cong guerrilla forces — they have been able to salve some of the mental wounds of war.

A group of Australian veterans of the war in Vietnam came through Hanoi at the time of War Invalids', Martyrs' and Heroic Mothers' Day. In our office, Huong was keen to organise a couple of interviews for the English Service with the visiting veterans and asked us to help arrange a meeting at which she and Khoi could tape them. The group was staying at the Metropole Hotel and, on the morning they were due to leave Hanoi to head south, we went to meet them there.

We were interested in the degree of moderation and understanding both Khoi and Huong showed in their interviews with the veterans, Paul Murphy, Bob Tyrell and Brian MacKenzie. We assumed Khoi and Huong had wanted us there partly because it was uncomfortable territory for them, yet they appeared to be at ease as they endeavoured to draw out some of the motivation behind the need, on the veterans' part, to come back to Vietnam. It was obvious that they understood this need.

As for the three veterans, it also seemed clear that the realisation that Vietnam was a 'country' and no longer a 'war' had come to them a long time ago and that they were now doing all they could to help ameliorate the long-lasting effects on Vietnam of one of the twentieth century's most destructive conflicts.

Also, on the subject of the war, we found, almost as an automatic reaction, that whenever we met or got to know someone of a certain age, we tended to wonder about their experiences during the war; what they coped with, what they might have been through.

Every morning, as we ate our breakfast sitting at our kitchen table, we could see through the screen of tall potted plants on our front patio, a man wearing plastic scuffs, striped pyjama pants and a white singlet, hanging out the washing for his family who lived in one room, at ground level to one side of us. Slow moving, of slight build, a bit of a stoop, and with thinning grey hair, we judged him to be in his late sixties. Doubtless, we imagined, a veteran, and not just of the war but of all that had happened to his country and to his home town over the last seven decades.

For a while we thought that the entire family — him, his wife, who was perhaps twenty years younger, their two student-age children and a trio of others who seemed to make up an extended family — all lived in this one small room. Because of windows left open in the stifling heat it was impossible not to be aware of their intimate living arrangements as we walked into and out of the courtyard. The two almost adult children slept on bunk beds attached as high up on the wall as possible, while still leaving room for them both to work on their computers which they had rigged up so as to be able to squat cross-legged in front of them to study at the end of their bunks.

But over the first few months, we worked out that another member of the family occupied an even smaller room, to one side of the main room and abutting a narrow alley which gave access to other small apartments on upper floors. We learnt that this tiny space was home for our neighbour's elderly, bedridden mother, who we understood was over ninety. Neither room had any facilities other than electricity. Ablutions were taken in the courtyard's communal showers. Cooking was done over a tiny charcoal brazier and the family laundry was done by the grey-haired man, in a battered enamel bowl, down on his thin haunches, beside the well in the corner of the courtyard.

As we crunched our muesli and ate our toast, we could see him using a long stick with a hook on the end to lift up hangers draped with wet clothing and place them on a clothesline that ran alongside the building. There was something particularly moving about the way he meticulously hung the T-shirts, blouses, trousers, even the bras and knickers. He performed this daily chore, which could well have been seen in other places as humiliating, with a gentle grace.

This attitude turned out to be even more astounding to us when we found out that his father, the deceased husband of his now-slowly dying mother, had been the original owner of the entire courtyard area, in which we lived in the largest house while he and his family inhabited the most humble.

When the communists liberated Hanoi in 1954, his father had been 'asked' to 'give' his property to the new government, which used it to help in easing the housing problems created by a sudden influx of people into the city. It was shortly after this 'redistribution' that his father, though still a young man, died and was spared the knowledge that his newly independent country would have to fight a further twenty years before it was truly liberated.

But if you live in Vietnam, you come to believe that there can sometimes be happy endings. Halfway through our year there, the grandson of this former landowner, the son of the war veteran who did the family laundry, was awarded a place in Singapore to study computer engineering for four years and his sister began a degree in English at the University of Foreign Languages in Hanoi.

'Could you stay back later today?' Loc asked us one Saturday afternoon in July. 'We have to wait for the final communiqué of the 8th Plenum.'

Every now and then there would be some political event in the capital, the news coverage of which would require added attention on the part of everybody in the office. For example, the twice-yearly meetings of the National Assembly, the highest legislative body in the land. The Assembly consists of some 500 deputies who are elected every five years under a system of compulsory voting, for which, not surprisingly, there is a 100 per cent turnout. Candidates must be approved by the Party and any opposition parties are prohibited.

At these sessions, in the middle and at the end of the year, the deputies gather for a week or ten days to give their stamp of approval or otherwise, nearly always approval, to decisions and directives made by the Political Bureau of the Party, the 'Politburo'.

In understanding the Vietnamese political set-up, and the power structure, there are four main bodies to consider: the Communist Party, the Presidency, the Government, and the National Assembly.

The Presidency is a separate entity, which used to be a Council of State, or 'Presidium', a sort of collective Presidency made up of around fifteen members, but is now just one person, President Tran Duc Luong, at the time of writing. He and the government, consisting of some two dozen ministries and ministerial-level agencies and led by Prime Minister Phan Van Khai, are all appointed by the National Assembly. The Chairman of the National Assembly, Nguyen Van An, would seem therefore to be in a position of some influence, but it's really the Communist Party, and more particularly the Politburo, which directs the course of the National Assembly and is where the real power resides. Party Secretary General Nong Duc Manh is consequently the most powerful individual figure in Vietnam and the ten- or twelve-person Politburo, which he heads, is the most powerful institution.

The 'plenum' that Loc was talking about, when she asked us to stay back a little later in the afternoon, was not part of the National Assembly meetings, which had been held the previous month, but a gathering of all members of the Communist Party Central Committee, the body which appoints the Politburo.

This Central Committee of the Party consists of about 125 full members and some 50 alternative members who all hold influential positions in different areas of society, including government departments and the armed forces, as well as in provincial and regional councils. For example, the Director General of the Voice of Vietnam is usually a member of the Communist Party Central Committee. The previous incumbent, now languishing in jail, was once a member.

The Central Committee usually meets a couple of times, sometimes only once a year and one of their most important functions is to elect the dozen or so members of the Politburo. However, the closing statement from the 8th Plenum, issued after several days of meetings and which we awaited, late on that Saturday afternoon, brought no dramatic changes or new appointments to the Politburo. As we ripped into the editing process, it seemed there was only the normal Party rhetoric about 'nation building during the country's new stage of development'.

'The building of Socialism and defending Socialist Vietnam are our parallel tasks,' Secretary General Nong Duc Manh had told the plenum. 'It means defending the Party, the state, the people, Socialist rule and the cause of renewal for the sake of the nation,' he added.

'But this is the important part.' Loc smiled, pointing to a paragraph midway down the page. It read, 'The plenum also discussed salary reform for State employees, social insurance and priority social welfare for people who have served the nation.'

The Secretary General had told the meeting that the decision to pay state employees more money 'was an investment in human resources and would encourage workers to boost production and improve the quality of their product'.

'That's what we want to hear,' Loc said. 'A pay rise!'

We both smiled. It's the same the world over.

Another fixture in July was the National Day for the People's Police on 17 July. Not a day for spontaneous celebration, as Vietnam is not really the sort of place where you can step out of line with any sense of complacency. Especially when you read that up to 75 per cent of the nation's police force operate in plain clothes. It's also difficult for anyone living in Vietnam not to hear first-hand accounts of incidents of police corruption, from the lowest traffic policeman, right up to the higher echelons.

The most common form of corruption involves vehicles. Anyone who rides a motorbike is easy pickings. One afternoon one of our team members arrived in the office looking very down-in-the-mouth. She explained that she had been pulled over by a traffic policeman for going through a red light. We'd heard innumerable anecdotes like this in which for a small amount of money, between $2 and $10, the offence was ignored. Sometimes there wasn't even an offence, just a needy police officer. But this time it was different; her motorbike had been impounded for two weeks and to reclaim it she would need to pay a hefty fine.

'How much?' Trish asked.

'Oh, it doesn't matter. I won't be paying it,' she said, going on to explain. 'There would be no point in getting my bike back because it will have been stripped for parts.'

When Trish looked shocked she continued matter-of-factly, 'It was a recent Korean model. The police sell the parts on to traders and replace them with bits from cheap Chinese or Vietnamese copies. That's why it's not worth having a really expensive Japanese bike. You have to pay too much to the police to stop them taking it in.'

'They don't do it to foreigners,' another staff member explained, thinking Trish would find that reassuring.

'Does anyone ever lay a complaint?' she asked, realising immediately how naïve the question sounded.

'To whom?' the former bike owner snorted.

At the very end of July, the Australian Embassy launched a festival of Australian films, to celebrate thirty years of Vietnam–Australia relations. Included was *Mullet*, set in a small coastal fishing town, and *The Man Who Sued God*, in which lightning strikes and sinks the fishing boat/home of the character hilariously played by Billy Connolly.

Ambassador Thwaites was to speak on the festival at a press conference and Trish suggested to Thi that she go along and try to get a short interview with him. It was the first such interview Thi

*Terrific Thi recording her first interview, with Australian Ambassador Joe Thwaites.*

had attempted and Trish went with her for encouragement and support. It turned out to be something of a baptism by fire. In the rushed bunfight these events usually are, Thi omitted bringing the microphone back to her own mouth when asking a question. This habit, which unfortunately seemed to have been adopted by most VOV5 team members, was something we had been trying to persuade them to give up. But Joe Thwaites' responses were interesting and were edited, without Thi's questions, into her piece for *What's On*, which she was pleased with.

The film festival was officially opened by the visiting Australian Foreign Minister, Alexander Downer, at a reception held in the Mirror Room of the Hanoi Opera House attended by, for want of a better word, Hanoi's glitterati.

We had come to really enjoy and appreciate the Opera House through numerous concerts and other performances. It's a truly imposing building, recognised as one of the most beautiful theatres in South-East Asia. Built at a cost of two million francs, between 1901 and 1911, it combines the architecture of the Palais de Tuileries and Opéra de Paris and, like these buildings, it reveals the influence of classical Greek architecture. During the French colonial period its patrons were mostly French officials with a small number of wealthy Vietnamese. Nowadays it is Vietnamese officials and ordinary citizens plus an international mix of music lovers who fill the seats.

While the usual speeches were made we examined the detail of the room and in a corner came across a little typed note taped to a wall mirror below a small, perfectly neat hole. It read, 'Trace of the Winter Battle ... 1946'. Lest we forget.

In addition to launching the Film Festival, Foreign Minister Downer was involved in a number of other official functions, including meetings with his Vietnamese counterpart, Nguyen Dy Nien, and other Vietnamese officials as well as discussing several Australian aid projects under way in the Mekong delta.

On the day of his arrival in Hanoi, shortly after Iain had turned up in the office, Loc asked, somewhat unexpectedly, 'Do you think it would be possible to organise an interview with your Foreign Minister?'

'I'm not sure,' Iain replied. 'I can try. Who will be doing the interview?'

'We'd like you to do it.' She smiled.

'But ...' he was taken aback, 'but we're not accredited as journalists here. I was under the impression that we weren't allowed to do interviews. In any case, wouldn't it be better if one of the staff did it?'

'No, I think he would respond better to you. There will be no problem with you doing it. We can arrange it.'

The interview was relatively simple to organise. It was to be done during a 10- to 15-minute timeslot in his hotel suite on his last day in Hanoi and immediately before his departure for the airport.

The news that the interview had been arranged set a number of unexpected wheels in motion.

'The Vietnamese News Department has sent up a list of questions for you to ask the Minister,' Loc told Iain the following day.

'But I don't need any list,' Iain said. 'I have my own questions to ask.'

'Yes, but they want you to ask *these* ones.' She handed him a slip of paper.

They were pretty straightforward: the significance of Downer's present visit, what he thought of the current investment climate in Vietnam, and the Australian government's future aid plans for Vietnam. Iain didn't argue, as he could easily ask them and throw in a few of his own.

On the day of the interview he suggested to Loc and Huong that, although he would be doing the interview, one of the other reporters, perhaps one of the younger ones, like Huan or Thi, might like to go along with him to get a feel for this type of interview with a visiting foreign politician.

'Oh no,' Loc said. 'It would not be permitted.'

'Why not?'

'We have to have permission from the News Department ... an accreditation label. Nobody here is currently accredited.'

'Okay,' Iain said. 'But surely that's only if you wanted to do the interview. If you just want someone to come along as a guest, surely that's different?'

'Hmm. Perhaps. But whoever went would have to get accreditation from the Australian Embassy.'

'No, no,' Iain insisted. 'I can just tell the people from the embassy, when we arrive at the hotel, that a VOV staffer wanted to come along with me. It won't require any additional accreditation.'

But she was adamant. 'No. Believe me, the security people at the hotel and from the embassy would not let a Vietnamese reporter in, unless he or she had a special pass.'

Iain was reminded of Trish's experience with Khoi a couple of months previously. He just had to let it go and accept that this was one of those weird, paranoid carryovers from the country's more heavy-duty communist past. As it happened, when he turned up at the Melia Hotel for the interview, the embassy people and Downer's staff said they would have welcomed a VOV observer.

After the Minister had thrown some clothes into two suitcases and handed them to an aide to take to his waiting car, he settled into the interview with Iain, which went off quickly and smoothly, with Downer displaying the veteran politician/diplomat's ability to deal instantly with a range of subjects. Iain's question on whether there was any moral obligation attached to Australia's aid program in Vietnam in the light of past events, notably Australia's involvement in the Vietnam War, brought out the diplomat in him.

'No,' he said. 'We build our aid program on the basis of the present and the future, not on the past. But history? No. Life moves on. Circumstances were different in an earlier era and they've changed now ... and we don't dwell on that history.'

Then, as they all took the elevator to the ground floor and his waiting cars, the Minister, who had recognised Iain from a previous life, asked, 'So, what are you actually doing here?'

'We're working at Voice of Vietnam as volunteers, for AVI, Australian Volunteers International,' Iain said.

'Volunteers? Hmm. Good. Yes, that's something I've often thought about doing myself ... maybe when I retire. I won't want to be playing golf.'

Then he turned to Iain and asked, 'Incidentally, who owns Voice of Vietnam?'

# *August*
## SINS OF THE DEAD

*'For the bird its nest, for man his ancestors'*

'**W**hat does ginormous mean?' Huan asked. He often had a list of language questions, many arising from something we had said on air. He got such a charge out of asking Trish something she couldn't explain properly. It became a running joke between them when he caught her flat-footed and she would cop out by saying, 'I'll ask Rebecca.'

Huan had met Rebecca and liked her, but he was concerned that she wasn't married with children.

'It's just a made-up word. A mix of gigantic and enormous. It means it's bigger than *Ben Hur*,' Trish teased him.

'What's Ben Hur?'

'Oh, he was a person and it was a film.'

'An Australian film?'

'No. Like anything that big it was American. But why don't you come along and see an Australian film at the festival? Better still, come with your girlfriend.'

He did and we all watched *Mullet*, which made us squirm a bit with embarrassment. We liked it, but we were both acutely aware that, viewed through Vietnamese eyes, all the men in the film looked like drunken boors, half the women looked like tarts and the entire family appeared dysfunctional in the extreme.

The theatre was packed to the gills (another phrase Trish explained to Huan) with young Vietnamese high-school and university students. The reason, we discovered, was not so much the irresistible allure of Aussie movies, but the fact that Sandra Henderson, the Public Affairs Officer at the Australian Embassy, had come up with the smart idea of each entry ticket being not only free but numbered. Just by filling in your name on the ticket and putting it into a barrel at the theatre entrance, you automatically went into a draw, the prize for which was two Qantas return air tickets to Australia.

We smiled when we saw a few people writing their names on a handful of tickets, dropping them in the barrel and walking out again without bothering to be enchanted by an Australian movie. Even so, the theatre was full for most of the films, but Sandra agreed it was a twist she had not envisaged. It reminded us of one of our favourite stories from Saigon during the time of the American War.

It was election time in the United States and some bright spark at the American Embassy in Saigon had the idea of giving a tangible demonstration of democracy at work. So they took over a storefront on Tu Do, as the main street in Saigon was then called, in which they set up an outsize board on which the voting numbers for the various candidates from the different states and parties were displayed. To the intense gratification and pride of the embassy staff, the window attracted huge numbers of viewers. That was until a staffer thought to mingle amongst the crowd. Whereupon he discovered that someone, perhaps less interested in democracy than in money, was running a tote and that people were betting on the changing numbers!

After watching *Mullet*, we chatted with Huan's girlfriend, Nguyen Hong Hanh, as Huan stood proudly beside her. He had reason to be proud. Apart from being exceptionally attractive,

Hanh was obviously smart, confident, warm and extrovert and, we thought, well worth Huan waiting for her to finish her degree in Cuba and return home permanently.

The next morning he couldn't wait to ask, 'What did you think of her?' and Trish couldn't stop herself from teasing. 'I think she's a ripper sheila!' she said, and added, '*Muy bueno*. Your Cuban connection.' She was rewarded with a beaming smile.

Huan's parents had met in Cuba. His father was working in the Vietnamese Embassy and his mother, Nam, had been a student there with both Hue and Loc. In 1971, at the age of twenty-two, she did her first work in radio on the Cuban overseas service. She participated in regular anti-Vietnam War broadcasts beamed to Florida in both Spanish and English.

'I was the "Hanoi Hannah" of Cuba,' Nam told Iain proudly one day. Hanoi Hannah, as mentioned briefly in the second chapter, was the woman who made daily propaganda broadcasts from Hanoi to the American GIs, during the late 1960s and early 1970s.

The Vietnam we were living in now could hardly be more different from the war-torn country of the early 1970s. There is no better example than present-day Vietnam of the need for peace as a prerequisite for stability, growth and prosperity in any country. Vietnam is still led by a one-party, relatively authoritarian regime, but it is a regime that, touch wood, is becoming more enlightened with every passing year, even every month. It is a country that is thriving on peace.

Now, when at last there is peace, Americans are still coming to Vietnam, though we did notice that of all the numerous nationalities represented in Hanoi, they seem to keep the lowest profile. Many of them admit to being a trifle nervous, at first, about visiting the country, more so perhaps the ones who have blood ties — the American Viet Kieu, or Overseas Vietnamese.

'Do they know immediately you're not a local?' Trish asked Felice Nguyen, an attractive young American Viet Kieu we had met at an event at the Museum of Ethnology.

She laughed and pointed to her cropped hair, coloured a bright red. 'What do you think? Even before I speak any Vietnamese! Back home in New York, we speak Vietnamese, but it's a generation out of date, the language my parents spoke when they left Saigon. Vietnamese can tell which village in which province you are from just by your accent, so I haven't any hope of pretending. Anyway,' she smiled and her elfin features, made even more intriguing by a long jagged scar across one cheek, broke into a wide grin, 'I don't want to. I'm happy with who I am. That's something I've learnt since coming here.'

A recent Columbia University law graduate, Felice was in Hanoi for a year, on a Fulbright scholarship, hoping to discover whether or not she wanted to try to make a career as a writer. With her was another Fulbright scholar, Phan Tai Duong, or, as he called himself, John Phan. A terrifically bright 21-year-old, John was furthering his studies into *Nom*, the Vietnamese idiographic script, which to the Western eye appears all but identical to Chinese writing but which is in fact quite different.

'*Nom* is culturally important from an historical viewpoint,' John told us, 'but only a handful of scholars are still able to read it. It's been all but swamped by the Romanised script, *Quoc Ngu*.'

This script, which was developed by a French Jesuit priest in the seventeenth century, took more than two centuries to gain acceptance, but in the twentieth century it grew in popularity simply because it was so much easier to learn. It also led to a dramatic increase in Vietnam's literacy rate.

The heat in Hanoi continued with relentless ferocity. But at least we slept in airconditioned cool. No-one else in the VOV5 team had the benefit of that relief. So it wasn't surprising that, come the middle of the day, the office resounded to the gentle snores of staff who had collapsed at their desks. Using their folded arms as pillows they put their heads down in an attempt to snatch a few quiet zeds. Those who couldn't quite summon up sleep slumped in front of one of the TV monitors, spooning in food bought from the street stalls opposite our building, while gazing with a soporific blankness at the daily soap. Imagine, if you can, a Chinese version of *Neighbours*, with a voice-over in Vietnamese. The moaning melancholy of the title music set the tone and it was all downhill from there. So much bittersweet sadness. So many farewells. In spite of herself, Trish became attached to some of the characters and she looked forward to this small routine of misery.

All this changed on the day Tran Le Chien from the Overseas Vietnamese Service, a department with which we shared the third floor, approached Trish's desk with Minh Ha, who translated her invitation for us to join an office choir.

We had resolved from the very beginning to say yes to almost everything, even when we didn't know what we were saying yes to. So Trish accepted, on behalf of both of us, and that was the end of slow middays, which were now taken up with rehearsals. To begin with we had no idea what we were going to sing or what we were rehearsing for but, as with everything else, it turned into an intense but fun experience.

'It's the SEA Games song,' Minh Ha told us, handing out the song sheet. The much-anticipated South-East Asian Games were due to be held for the first time in Vietnam in December. As an opportunity to showcase the country it was as important to Vietnam as the 2000 Olympics were for Sydney. We read the lyrics and our hearts sank.

> Hand in hand for happy ness (of) mankind we walk together
> Eastern sun shines up SEA Games Vietnam is expecting for long
> Eager hearts get deep-in emotion all for the Victory
> From your eyes I have the hope the dream I share with you.

*The best that now we try ... future is in our hands*
*All together gloriously Hanoi with SEA Games*
*Tomorrow we believe in ... let's sing out our song*
*This moment we keep in mind for the world of tomorrow!*

'We'll all sing it in English first,' Minh Ha said, 'then we'll sing it in Vietnamese and you can hum,' she said to us. 'Then we'd like Iain to step forward from the line, with Khoi, and sing the English version as a duet. Is that okay?'

'Ummm,' Iain mumbled. 'Couldn't we smooth the translation out a bit? It's terrible. It doesn't make any sense.' He ran his eyes over the lyrics. 'It might be okay in Vietnamese, but in English it sounds silly. Can't we change it?'

'Oh no.' Minh Ha shook her head. 'The music and the words were written by Quang Vinh. He's a very highly respected composer. These are the official words, approved by the Party. We can't change them.'

But that wasn't to be the end of the story.

Meanwhile, more official words kept streaming over our desk from the *Communist Party Review*, which on 5 August celebrated its seventy-third birthday by wallowing in a welter of embarrassingly sycophantic self-congratulations. It was also unwittingly self-revelatory.

'The more the Renovation process, initiated and led by the Party, is expanded in both scope and scale, the higher the requirements for creative and correct application of Marxist-Leninism and Ho Chi Minh Thought to improve Renovation policies.'

For 'creative' read 'multiple backflips, speedy tapdancing and standing on your head' to keep up with the changed world situation.

But the *Review* is nothing if not adaptive. When the theoretical and political organ of the Party first came off the press, it was called *The Red Review* and was founded and headed by Nguyen Ai Quoc. Seventy-three years later it's called *The Communist Party Review* and he's remembered as Ho Chi Minh.

And while we're on the subject of Uncle Ho, the big museum devoted entirely to him, which is located immediately behind his mausoleum on Ba Dinh Square and to which we gave a passing mention in chapter one, opened an interesting temporary exhibition during August. Called 'Nguyen Ai Quoc in Hong Kong', it dealt with the amazing story of Ho's incarceration and trial in Hong Kong in the early 1930s.

Nguyen Ai Quoc, or Nguyen 'The Patriot', was one of Ho Chi Minh's many aliases. In fact the name 'Ho Chi Minh' was also an alias, as the name he was given at his birth on 19 May 1890 was Nguyen Sinh Cung. By the age of forty, when he was in Hong Kong, Nguyen Ai Quoc had spent almost twenty years away from his country, much of it trying to foster revolution in French-governed Indochina. There was a death sentence hanging over his head, imposed, in absentia, by the French colonial authorities for his activities in Europe, the Soviet Union, China and now Hong Kong, where he was a clandestine representative for Indochina of 'Comintern', the organisation founded by Lenin to encourage world revolution.

We went along to the exhibition to check it out for *What's On* and found a fascinating story. Ai Quoc had been tracked down in Hong Kong by French security agents and arrested there by the British colonial authorities at the request of the French on 6 June 1931. France wanted him extradited to Annam, as central Vietnam was then known, where he would undoubtedly have been executed.

There followed a complicated and prolonged legal battle, lasting eighteen months, in which an unlikely and unexpected saviour emerged to take on Ai Quoc's cause. Early in the piece, a British lawyer named Frank Loseby had learnt of the case and, after studying his dossier, went to see Ai Quoc in prison where, following a lengthy conversation with him, he decided to represent his case.

He instituted a writ of habeas corpus in Hong Kong's High Court, forcing a public trial lasting several weeks, in which he challenged the government's deportation order, claiming that the banishment enquiry that led to it had followed improper procedures. The case was eventually lost but, anticipating the judgment, Loseby gave instant notice of an appeal to the Privy Council in London.

In the meantime, Ai Quoc languished in a Hong Kong prison. By the end of 1932, the case was heard by the Privy Council and resolved in Ai Quoc's favour, but he was informed he must leave the British colony within three weeks. After an abortive attempt to go to Singapore, where Ai Quoc was arrested by authorities and returned to prison in Hong Kong, Loseby was quickly able to gain his re-release. But this time the hapless Ai Quoc was given only three days to leave.

Loseby's wife was apparently a close friend of the governor of Hong Kong and she managed to borrow the governor's private launch. Disguised in a wealthy Chinese merchant's gown and headgear, Ai Quoc was spirited after dark to the launch, which headed out amongst the myriad small islands that were part of the colony of Hong Kong. Once outside Hong Kong's territorial waters, it raced after a ship that had just left the colony and was heading for Xiamen, in China. Called on by the governor's launch to stop, in order to take on some important passengers, the captain of the ship obeyed without question. Nguyen Ai Quoc disembarked a couple of days later in Xiamen, a free man.

Ho Chi Minh, when he became President of Vietnam, never forgot Frank Loseby and his wife, and always sent them small gifts and fruit baskets accompanied by cards at Christmas and New Year. In 1960 Ho invited the Losebys to visit Vietnam. They received a hero's welcome and were told by Ho, 'You saved my life.'

Later, in a letter to Ho, Loseby said, 'You say I saved your life. If this is so, then it is the best job I have ever done and the wise should be forever grateful.'

Loseby died during the 1960s and at the big Hong Kong funeral, at which the Loseby family had requested there be no wreaths, one wreath was allowed. It had a silken banner that simply said: 'To Mr Loseby from HCM'.

Death and dying were very much on everyone's mind during the month of August. Vietnamese spirituality rests heavily on the concept of family, which includes not just the living, but also those who have died. Each family is viewed as a temple that holds both the living and the dead. Sacred ties bind members of the same family. Death does not dissolve these bonds but rather strengthens them.

During the year there are many occasions on which offerings are made to the dead but the most important is the fifteenth day of the seventh lunar month, which is designated as the Day for the Pardoning the Sins of the Dead. For us this day would fall on 13 August.

For the Vietnamese, the only difference between the living and the dead is just that they inhabit different worlds. Their needs are the same and so it is hoped that by burning votive offerings for the dead, their loved ones who have passed into another dimension will enjoy at least the same or perhaps even better lives in another world.

Hang Ma Street, in Hanoi's Old Town, is a street like no other in the city. Dependent for business on traditional beliefs, it's the place to shop for votive offerings and was crowded with shoppers for the ten days or so leading up to the festival, with the traders there showing incredible skill and imagination. The offerings are made from delicate coloured paper pasted onto frames of split bamboo. Hanging in the torpid heat were replicas comprising a wish list of everyday objects. There were items of fashionable clothing, up-market sneakers, motorcycles, even complete houses and an array of household utensils and appliances including, believe it or not, flat screen plasma television sets. Which left us wondering what reception is like in the other world. All of them are made of paper and all are to be burnt.

There were also the usual piles of fake Vietnamese dong and US dollar bills which, at this time of the year, are burnt so they can be sent to the dead in order to pay their travelling expenses from and back to the other world. They can also be used by the guilty to bribe the guards to let them visit the world of the living.

One story from VOV5's coverage of the festival was told by Nguyen Thi Van, a 64-year-old widow whose husband had died when he was very young. Van planned, as she had every year since his death, to burn a lot of imitation money and paper clothes for him, in the hope that he would live comfortably in the other world. 'I miss him and don't want him to be lonely,' she said, 'so I will burn some paper warm clothing and,' she added with what we found to be a touching largeness of heart, 'an effigy of a woman to look after him.'

On this special day, besides giving a party for dead relatives, families make up an extra tray of confectionaries, rice soup and fruits, which they place out in the open for the comfort of wandering souls; those who have died but who have no relatives to commemorate the anniversary of their death. This gesture of charity is thought to bring blessings from the souls of the dead, as is the giving of alms.

On 12 August, the day before the main festival for the Day for Pardoning the Sins of the Dead, we received an email from the headquarters of AVI to say that Xavier Nathan, who, as we've mentioned, was also an Australian volunteer and who had met us on the day of our arrival in Hanoi, was critically ill and unconscious in a hospital in Singapore.

We hadn't seen Xavier for more than a month, as he had been on leave in Australia, visiting his son in Perth and a daughter in Sydney. He had told us that, on the way back to Hanoi, he would also visit his other son, who was working as a zoologist at the Singapore Zoo.

For a time, prior to going on leave, Xavier, who was sixty-seven, had been worried that his contract as a volunteer teacher in Vietnam would not be renewed by AVI. However, the Institute for International Relations, where he had been employed for two two-year terms, was keen to have him return, and after some correspondence with AVI, he was told that his contract had been renewed for a further two years.

Xavier, who had nursed his dying wife through a long battle with cancer, had told us that the simple life he had found in Hanoi, living in a tiny bed-sitter attached to the college, was all he wanted or needed from life now.

The news of his illness came as a great shock to us, more so because there was no explanation in the email as to what had happened or what had caused the illness. We emailed back to the AVI office immediately to try to get more details and also a contact address and phone number for his son in Singapore.

A reply came back the following day with the tragic news that Xavier had died in hospital without regaining consciousness and that, for the time being, his son, who was distraught, could not face being in direct contact with Xavier's friends, although he hoped that before long this would change.

'D'you believe in another world for souls?' Thi asked Trish gently. She had told Thi about Xavier dying, how much we had liked him, and what a gentle man he was.

'It would be comforting,' Trish replied wistfully.

'I had a dream about my grandma,' Thi responded, 'my dad's mother. When I told my dad about it, I described the particular blouse and scarf she was wearing. He was amazed and told me that was how she was dressed when she was buried.'

Thi paused for a moment, probably to let that sink in. Trish nodded slowly.

'But I never knew her,' Thi went on. 'She died before I was born.'

That evening, on the way back from work, we stopped at busy Quan Su Pagoda and burnt incense and wads of fake US dollars, joshing each other about sending it on to our dead parents. As the smoke rose for Iain's parents, both of whom had died in the last ten years, we joked that his mother would spend it on a pair of stylish new Feragamo shoes. Trish hoped her mother, who died when she was a child, and her father, who died when she was in her thirties, would use it to go on a sailing cruise. And we sent some on to Brenda, a recent surrogate mother to Trish and our longest-standing friend, who had died just before we came to Hanoi at the age of eighty-five and who, though she was never interested in money, would, we were sure, find a worthy lame-duck cause to give it to.

*An offering in our courtyard for Pardoning the Sins of the Dead.*

We crossed the road and entered our courtyard to find that, in the middle of it, trays had been placed on two stools. These were laden with burning joss, lit candles, bowls of soup, steamed rice, fruit and flowers. No wandering soul would go unwelcome in our courtyard that night.

During this period, Long, who, as we've mentioned, had been made a 'rotating cadre' and was now in charge of training for the whole of Voice of Vietnam Radio, came into the office one morning and sat down next to Iain with a smile on his face ... something of a worry, Iain thought.

'The news workshop we talked about before, we're planning on holding it at the end of the month. Is that all right with you?'

'With me?' Iain responded. 'Workshop? Err ... yes, sure.'

A trifle unsettled, he recalled that, back in June, Long had vaguely mentioned organising workshops for different departments later in the year and that we might like to take part.

'Umm, and what would you like us to do?' Iain asked.

'Just a morning session. About an hour and half.'

'And what's it on?'

'It's on radio production ... the workshop, that is, but we'd like you and Trish to talk about newswriting and editing ... what you're doing here ... as well as something on recording and interview techniques ... any comments or criticisms you might have. Can I leave it with you?'

'Sure,' Iain said unenthusiastically.

As Long left, Iain quickly pushed it to the back of his mind. Although it was only a couple of weeks away, it seemed a long time, and there were other things happening: we were getting ready for our trip to climb Mount Fanxipan and the whole country was gearing up for another celebration, the anniversary of the 1945 August Revolution.

On 14 August 1945 Japan's surrender to the Allied forces came into effect and the Pacific War came to an end. Five days later, on 19 August, Hanoi, the capital of the former French colony of Tonkin, was in the hands of Ho Chi Minh's Viet Minh forces after a bloodless takeover. Anticipating the Japanese surrender, the Viet Minh had left their mountain and jungle retreats in the north, from where they had fought a long resistance war against the Japanese and the Vichy French, and rapidly advanced on the city.

In a bizarre twist, after the Japanese had conquered Indochina in early 1942, they decided to leave the French in control of day-to-day affairs, because of Vichy France's status as a cooperative agent of Nazi Germany, Japan's ally.

Ho Chi Minh's guerrilla campaign against the Japanese and the French was supported by the United States in both men and materiel. American Office of Strategic Services forces had worked with Ho and the Viet Minh in the jungle, providing supplies, equipment and advice for the struggle.

With the Japanese and the French handing over power to Ho's forces, first in Tonkin then in Annam, the central part of Vietnam, and finally in Cochin China — whose borders were roughly equivalent to the later nation of South Vietnam — the way seemed clear for the establishment of an independent, unified country under the leadership of Ho Chi Minh, who was then fifty-five years of age.

But this was not to be. Although, in the weeks that followed, huge crowds circulated through the streets of every city, waving flags and banners and shouting slogans and calling for independence, the major powers — that is, the United States, Britain, France, the Soviet Union and China — had a different agenda and soon British and Chinese forces would be in Vietnam presaging a very different outcome.

The flags still fly all over Vietnam every 19 August, because it represents their first taste of independence, but it would be many years before the dream would finally come true.

'What's the reason for all the flags?' the Western woman having her hair wrapped in foils asked Vu, the owner of the up-market salon Vudoo where Trish went for a regular pedicure. A large gold-starred red flag was draped from his salon's balcony.

'I have no idea,' he waved his hand airily. 'I take no interest in politics. The local Party people come around and tell me, "Put out a flag" and I do.'

'It's the anniversary of the August Revolution,' Trish quietly informed the woman from her chair on the other side of the room and gave a very condensed version of the event.

'You see,' Vu gestured, with both hands this time, 'she knows more about the politics and history of this country than I do. Or than I want to. It's safer that way.'

There were also surprisingly few stories and even less chat about the August Revolution in the VOV5 office. A lot more time and thought was going into rehearsals for the SEA Games song. Iain's low-key suggestion that the English words could be improved had gained more momentum now that there were complaints about them in the Vietnamese-language papers. The journal *Thanh Nien* even went so far as to publish a letter of ridicule from Dang Hoang Doan Trang, a Vietnamese living in New York. The gloves came off and Hanoi's cultural mafia had a very public ding-dong which resulted in the song's composer and lyricist pointing out that he was not responsible for the English translation of the lyrics. That had been done by someone called Bui Nhat Quang.

Three times a week, at lunchtime, a group of about fifteen of us would get together at the far end of the open office and mangle the music, which wasn't as bad as the words, in the stirring, patriotic style that such events demand. Le Chien, the instigator of these rehearsals, had an orchestral recording of it and she'd play it over and over again on a portable tape deck and then she and Minh Ha would shout at each other about how the developing act should be performed.

We still were none the wiser about what it was all for and were having considerable trouble remembering the words, our excuse being that they were somewhat nonsensical and didn't scan. Trish took to handwriting them over and over again, like school lines.

Although it was still more than three months to go before the Games hit town 'our song', as we now referred to it, or at least the professionally recorded version, was being played, before and after news broadcasts and in breaks in television programming.

'I'm getting to quite like it,' Trish confided to Rebecca, who already had a very low regard for Trish's taste in popular music.

Rebecca looked at Trish with disdain. 'Desperate,' she said.

They were sitting in the Moca Café, attempting to replenish their body fluids after sweating through the streets of the Old Town in order to buy a couple of small Australian and Vietnamese flags to carry with us on our climb of Mount Fanxipan, which was fast approaching.

One of the thoughts that flashed through our minds, as heavy hail beat into our faces, lightning flashed and crackled, and thunder rolled around us while we slipped and slithered on the jagged wet rocks of a high and exposed ridgeline, was that if we got zapped by lightning here, our grandchildren would never forgive us.

Without being overly dramatic we knew it was a distinct possibility, because it's common knowledge that sudden fierce electrical summer storms in any mountain range can frizzle people foolish enough to be caught out on high spots.

We were following Rebecca and our guide, Thanh. Behind us was our porter Dao. For an eternity, which lasted probably twenty minutes, the storm raged around us, the air buzzing with static electricity as we stumbled on, all but blinded by the pelting rain, which had turned to sleet. And then, just as quickly as it had come, the storm danced away, leaving us almost too bewildered to be thankful.

Despite this, our venture had begun reasonably well. The previous day, after again taking the overnight train from Hanoi to Lao Cai and the bus on up to Sapa, we had met up with our friend Nguyen Trong Luan, the guide who had taken us on our walk down the valley on our previous visit. He had taken us to the small hotel he had arranged for us there and told us of the plans for Mount Fanxipan. We spent the rest of the day getting our heads around the idea of the climb and organising our gear, with the aim of carrying as little as possible and leaving a clean, dry change of clothes in the small hotel for our return in three days' time.

At 8.00 o'clock the next morning Thanh and Doa, who were to be our guide and porter, picked us up in a jeep, in which we drove north-west for half an hour or so to the Tran Fon Pass at 2100 metres. From here, we had been told, it would take us four or five hours to walk up and down and up again to what Luan had described as our halfway 'sleeping camp', at 2200 metres. But as we got out of the jeep at the pass, we were stopped by an officious chap, armed and dressed in army fatigues, who told us the track was closed and we were forbidden entry.

We suggested to Thanh that he offer a 'present', but Thanh was adamant that this would not be accepted and we had to agree that he was the best judge of the situation. So we bundled ourselves back into the jeep and, under the watchful eye of the 'guard', turned around and headed down the way we'd come, back through Sapa, before heading out north-west again, this time for a further half hour to another entry post.

In Vietnam, atlases and even halfway decent maps fall within the ambit of government disapprobation, so the only map we had for this entire adventure was a mud map sketched by Luan which showed this second entry point as being Sin Chai and that it was at 1800 metres altitude. This meant it was 300 metres below where we had hoped to start out and for a while it seemed that we were not welcome here either.

There was a lot of muttering between Thanh and a couple of men who didn't even appear to be officials. Then, telling us they would be back soon, Thanh and Dao took off with these men in our jeep. When they returned, almost an hour later, by which time the morning had mostly gone, they were all smiles, and without further ado we took off up the mountain. And we really mean *up* and we really mean *mountain*.

We were straight onto a narrow, all-but-invisible track leading up over slippery rocks and muddy clay, closed in on both sides by dense bamboo and treacherously sharp-edged sword grass. The terrain was so steep it was impossible to stand upright and we were forced, on many occasions, into clambering more or less on all fours. In no time we were drenched with sweat and smeared with mud. Every now and then there would be a break in the vegetation and across the dark green of the jungled valley we could see the Tran Fon Pass, still some height above us. Finally Iain was asked not to point to it again or to say one more time, 'That's where we should have started from'. We were all very glad when it finally disappeared from view.

Then came the storm on the ridge. And after that we started heading down, which played havoc with our tired knees and left us with the unhappy awareness that every step down would have to be recaptured if we were to reach the top.

We waded through rivulets and crossed swollen streams on slippery felled tree trunks, until about 4.30pm we eventually arrived at a clearing on sloping ground in which had been erected two large tarpaulin tents built over rough wooden frames. Our 'sleeping place'.

Other climbers were already there: two Norwegians, two Brits and an Australian, all with guides and porters. Iain immediately ascertained that they had come up the shorter route, which made no-one feel any better.

The tent base camp was extremely basic, with just a long wooden bench to lie on. But there were sleeping bags and we immediately took off our soaked clothes, hung them from the tent supports and lay down to rest our battered bodies.

An hour or so later we had revived enough to enjoy an excellent restorative meal of steaming noodles and vegetables brought to us from the other tent by Dao, who seemed completely unfazed by the day's proceedings. We played a few desultory hands of cards by the light of Rebecca's trusty portable reading lamp, but by 7.30 everyone had collapsed asleep to the sound of heavy rain.

The rain continued throughout the night and the floor of our tent turned to mud. Our boots and socks were still sopping wet in the morning, but we put them on in the knowledge that as soon as we left the camp they'd have been wet again anyway. A big hot breakfast of omelette, noodles and fish, plus bananas and tea, was prepared for us in the extraordinarily basic kitchen that had been set up under a tarpaulin by a tree. It went a long way to preparing us for the ordeal ahead, but it has to be said that Rebecca, whose age was definitely on her side in this venture, seemed much more up to the task than we were. In any event, we were ready to go by around 7.30am, but unfortunately were unable to leave until closer to 9.00.

Our guide, Thanh, had somehow hurt his back on the previous day's climb and, after some discussion among the other guides and porters, said he would not be coming. Dao, our porter, would take us. The others who had stayed in the camp overnight had already left by the time we set off, heading *down* instead of up! The rain had stopped and the sky was overcast as we traversed a relatively steep and heavily wooded slope for about twenty minutes, arriving at a small swollen river, which we crossed on a log, while clinging with our hands to a rope strung above it.

Once across the river we looked up in awe at what was basically a vertical wall of jungle. Well, a sixty-degree slope, where our only way up was as if climbing a ladder, by hanging onto the branches, vines and bamboo overhanging and growing beside the track. When the slope eased somewhat, the trail continued up over slippery rocks and muddy clay, but still through dense bamboo and shrubbery.

After about four hours of scrambling, climbing and clinging to handholds of roots and branches, stopping and panting for breath, then edging our way across steep and slippery rock faces, where one false step on a narrow ledge could send you plunging down a vertical slope, we came up onto a rocky outcrop, a small clearing on a peak, about 15 metres square, with a view to the jungled summit of Fanxipan.

But Dao was worried. We had taken much too long. He and Rebecca could have moved ahead faster, but the elderly couple had slowed the pace somewhat. The problem was not so much getting to the summit, but getting back to our camp before dark. The 3143-metre peak of Fanxipan, although now only a couple of hundred metres higher than our position, was also a horizontal distance of about 400 to 500 metres of descending and climbing through the same dense jungle.

Dao estimated that it would take us an hour and a half to get there, arriving around 2.30pm, a five-and-a-half-hour climb. With the sun setting not long after 6.00, even on a bright day a five-hour return trip would have seen us completing the final steep descents to the camp in total darkness. Deciding that discretion was the better part of valour, we pulled out our flags, waved them around for a few photographs and headed back down, arriving at the camp, after a few slippery and painful falls, totally shattered at just on 6.00pm.

The following morning, after sleeping as if in a coma for eleven hours, we set off for the return to Sapa. While the knowledge that we were homeward bound and that a hot shower awaited us in Sapa was a great incentive, the trip down was still nerve-racking and exhausting, with river crossings, a muddy trail, dangerous and slippery rock faces to cross, and quite a few more falls, as we descended the steep track. On one occasion Rebecca slipped and just missed plunging a hundred metres or so over a sheer drop.

Six hours after leaving the camp, we reached the bottom of the mountain where, drenched with sweat, we sat fully clothed in a sparkling stream to cool down. Then we walked through rice paddies and villages, past buffaloes wallowing in deep pools, to a jeep that had been waiting for two hours and which whisked us to the hotel in Sapa, where we had our much-anticipated hot showers.

Less than two hours later we were on a bus to the border town of Lao Cai where, after several cold beers and a good meal, we boarded the overnight train to Hanoi.

Back in Hanoi the following morning, we pampered ourselves with a buffet breakfast at Jacc's, as we discussed our various small injuries. Both of us took unwise amounts of anti-inflammatory tablets over the next few days to ease the aches in joints and muscles. This getting-older business was a challenge!

*Cooling off after our exhausting descent down Mount Fanxipan.*

On the other hand, Rebecca was already booking a month's holiday in Shanghai, where she was meeting up with an Italian photographer she knew. She could easily have run to the top of the mountain and back and we really appreciated the good-humoured tolerance she showed towards us for slowing her down and denying her the opportunity to reach the summit of Indochina's highest peak.

Meanwhile, the pace of work at the office continued unabated, though now, in addition to everyday demands, there were the choir rehearsals and, of course, the fortnightly *Party Review*. Above all there was the rapacious appetite of *What's On* to be fed and then, at the end of the week after our return from Fanxipan, we had to front up to do the news workshop that Long had organised for members of some of the other departments in VOV's overseas service.

These departments were the other-language equivalents to VOV5 in that they broadcast in French, Russian, Mandarin, Japanese, Cambodian, Laotian, etc. on short-wave frequencies. Unlike VOV5, most of them had no local transmissions within Vietnam on FM frequencies.

We had put in a little preparation for the workshop before departing on the Fanxipan trip, leaving the rest of the work to be done in the four days after our return, but fortunately, what Long wanted did not require exhaustive preparation.

'What they need is a pep-up talk …' Long said to us the day before, '… and things that can make their writing more interesting. Also to correct some of the mistakes they are making with the news bulletins.' A tall order really, particularly as it would be coming from outsiders who had only been in the country a few months. We found it difficult to avoid feeling a bit presumptuous. And the workshop was made more complicated by the fact that, while they could all speak another language, whether it was Russian, French, Mandarin or whatever, many of them did not speak English, so we had to do the whole thing through an interpreter.

Anyway we dived in, speaking a bit warily at first and making a few diplomatic comments about how some of the practices adopted by other broadcasting organisations we'd worked with might be of use in Vietnam. Then we started to get into a few areas of criticism, such as in the writing or translating of news stories. Many of the stories we dealt with in our office came with no attribution; that is, something or other is said, or a fact is stated, but the story doesn't tell you who made the statement. We touched briefly on the need for the five Ws and one H — the Who, What, Where, When, Why and How — needed in all news stories, but nothing much on the actual structure of the stories.

We talked about words and phrases that were used too often and about the need to be frugal with the use of superlatives. Much of the communist-angled propaganda would come through with constant repetition of words or phrases like 'glorious tradition', 'triumphant heroes', 'victorious forces' and so on. These were to be avoided or minimised we suggested.

We touched on interview and microphone techniques, as well as on-air presentation, but by 10.30 our spot was over and they moved on to something else.

We had no real idea of how to gauge our impact on the group; in fact we didn't even know if they were people who actually wrote original stories or just translated their language versions from Vietnamese originals. We were left with the feeling that Long had put us through the process as some sort of test.

This was reinforced when he thanked us, with a big smile, at the end of our session, saying, 'Good, good. But I think it needs a longer seminar. We'll have to do some more of this in the future.'

As the last days of August approached, there was an intensifying of activity in the lead-up to yet another anniversary, another big one: Vietnam's National Independence day on 2 September and also the Voice of Vietnam Radio's anniversary, both historically linked to the August Revolution referred to in this chapter.

In fact, the level of hype over the August Revolution only slackened off slightly in the period after 19 August. The ubiquitous propaganda posters all remained up, as new ones were added throughout the city, and the flags were kept flying on public buildings and private shops and houses. But now, as the end of the month approached and Independence Day neared, stages were erected at different locations on the streets around the capital and banners were strung across the streets, as were coloured lights featuring stars and the communist hammer and sickle insignia.

On the last weekend of the month we had spent time on Sunday wandering through parts of the Old Town, where stores were already starting to stock up for another festival, probably the second biggest of the year, the mid-autumn festival, which would come towards the middle of September. After a while though, the temperature and humidity became too oppressive and so, in the afternoon, we headed home to spend some time reading in our one airconditioned room.

Not long after we arrived home, we had a telephone call from Giang. 'The VOV choir is singing in a street concert by Hoan Kiem Lake tonight,' he said. 'I'm singing in it. Would you like to see it?'

For one dreadful moment we thought that by 'VOV choir' he meant the group with whom we had been rehearsing the SEA Games song. But when that moment passed, with some relief we said yes, we'd certainly come along later to watch.

The concert was to be performed on one of the street stages in front of an old colonial building at the corner of Le Thai Tho and Hang Trong streets and a number of seats had been set up in the small triangular park that fronted it. The VOV choir was only one of many different amateur groups from all sorts of businesses and government departments who were presenting a variety of song and dance performances for a large crowd of passers-by who had stopped to watch. These included pedestrian shoppers, people on bikes and motorbikes who parked their vehicles, and some who remained sitting on their motorbikes, taking up a significant part of the roadway in the process and slowing traffic generally.

Giang was the only one in the choir we knew, and when it came on we waved to him a couple of times. Of course, as the singing was all in Vietnamese, we could not understand much of it, but it was clear that it was all patriotic stuff about the revolution and independence, particularly when the other performers came out to do a number of choreographed routines. These were the classic and so often photographed communist-style military and revolutionary dances, with men and women dressed in silken versions of army uniforms waving great red banners and flags as the choir behind them sang what we presumed were stirring nationalistic songs.

Walking home, we talked of how differently Western audiences would have reacted to that sort of performance, compared to a populace that has been conditioned to seeing blatant propaganda on stage. Little did we realise that, within days, we would be able to offer first-hand experience on the matter.

# *September*

# INDEPENDENCE DAY AND FIRST PRIZE

*'Where the Fatherland is there also is found the hero'*

Vietnam can lay claim to at least three Declarations of Independence. The first came in the form of a poem, *Nam Quoc Son Ha* (*The Mountains and the Rivers of the Empire of the South*), which was written by the heroic Vietnamese figure General Ly Thuong Kiet in 1077. The second document, also a poem, is known as the *Binh Ngo Dai Cao, the Proclamation of Victory over Foreign Invaders*. It was penned in 1428 during the Le dynasty by military strategist and writer Nguyen Trai.

It was more than five centuries before the third and, from our present perspective, the most relevant declaration was made by Ho Chi Minh on 2 September 1945 when he addressed a huge crowd in Hanoi's Ba Dinh Square. The audience, estimated at nearly half a million and comprised of militiamen and women, farmers, city dwellers and intellectuals alike, watched curiously as the thin and wiry figure, his wispy beard and receding hair still dark, stepped up to the microphone.

For virtually all of them, he was an unknown quantity. Many had heard of the legendary revolutionary Nguyen Ai Quoc, who had led the Viet Minh forces of resistance in the fight against the Japanese from jungle bases to the north. But practically none of this vast crowd had ever seen him or the man now about to address them, who had just been introduced by the military leader Vo Nguyen Giap as Ho Chi Minh, the 'Bringer of Light'. But the word spread quickly through the vast crowd that the two were one and the same person.

In the two weeks after the Revolution of 19 August 1945, following immediately on the end of World War II, Ho had entered Hanoi and worked feverishly with his revolutionary forces to consolidate their control, not only over the northern capital but also the rest of the country. It was crucial to do so before the Allies, namely the British and Chinese troops, who would deal with both the Japanese and the Vichy French forces, arrived in Indochina. Now he stood before his people to proclaim all of Vietnam independent.

'Dear fellow compatriots ...' he began, as the crowd fell silent. 'All people are created equal. They are endowed by their creator with certain unalienable rights; among these are life, liberty and the pursuit of happiness.' He paused for a moment and then went on. 'This immortal statement appeared in the Declaration of Independence of the United States of America in 1776. In a broader sense it means: all people of the Earth are equal from birth and all peoples have a right to life, fortune and freedom.

'The Declaration of the Rights of Man and the Citizen, promulgated at the time of the French Revolution in 1791, also states: "All People are born free and with equal rights and must always remain free and with equal rights".'

Ho's speech continued for a short period before concluding with a strident assertion of Vietnam's newly won rights: 'Vietnam has the right to enjoy freedom and independence and in fact has become a free and independent country.'

At one stage during his address, he had paused a moment, for maximum impact, and asked: 'My fellow countrymen, have you understood?' and half a million voices thundered back, 'YES!'

Recent research by American scholar and author Lady Borton has revealed an interesting sidelight to Ho's speech: he actually knowingly changed the wording of the US Declaration slightly. The orginal says 'All *men* are created equal ...' In the Vietnamese, Ho used the word for 'people', instead of 'men'. Also, in his opening words, 'Dear fellow compatriots ...' *Hoi dong bao ca nuoc, 'dong bao'* means 'from the same sack of eggs', a reference to Vietnam's ancient legend of the fairy and the dragon, whose union produced 100 eggs, resulting in the first fifty Vietnamese lowlanders and the first fifty highlanders.

Back in the present, Hanoians were busy enjoying the national holiday commemorating that first Independence Day, which this year had fallen on a Tuesday. Mr Thanh, the man in our courtyard who every morning sat on a low stool at the entrance from the street, organising the little food stall that he and his wife operated there, was wearing a white shirt with a tie, for the first time. The streets were filled, as usual, with people going to and fro, but today there was a definite holiday air apparent in everyone.

We went for a late-morning swim at the Sao Mai — Morning Star — pool, a twenty-minute cab ride away in the suburb of Quang An. On the way back, we saw couples and families out in large numbers in swan-shaped pedal boats on the waters of the adjoining Truc Bac Lake. And in Ba Dinh Square, where fifty-eight years previously Ho Chi Minh had delivered his stirring message, a long line of Vietnamese and foreigners queued to enter the great grey edifice that holds his mortal remains.

Meanwhile, celebrations were under way at VOV. Everybody was in their Sunday best. It was party time again and, this time, Party time too: the Voice of Vietnam's fifty-eighth birthday, to be followed by a visit to VOV by Vietnam's President, Tran Duc Luong.

All the men were sporting ties and the women looked elegantly feminine in their *ao dais*. This trick of appearing fragile when really you are as tough as nails is an aspect of female culture Asia-wide which is perhaps particularly appealing. Thi looked positively ethereal in the softest pale pink tunic, delicately embroidered down one side, over white trousers.

The gathering, in the conference room on the second floor, was attended by a number of the usual suspects: diplomats being diplomatic. VOV Director General Vu Van Hien said what was expected, while Australian Ambassador Thwaites managed to avoid clichés and give an upbeat, off-the-cuff performance, getting in a bit of a plug for Australia's long-time, far-sighted commitment to broadcasting in Vietnam.

The guests left and we all went back up one floor and began to rip into the day's news bulletins. Suddenly the place was aswarm with tough-looking characters in plain clothes, carrying what for all the world looked like Geiger counters. Everybody stood aside most respectfully as they pulled open desk drawers and poked around with these machines, going on to scrummage inside the huge box of wastepaper which we had all diligently saved to give, every few weeks, to a gentle-gestured childless woman called Vai, who would resell the paper as a meagre means of supporting herself. Having not said a word, the government security people left, satisfied, apparently, that nothing untoward would occur during the president's visit.

Within half an hour the president and his entourage, including an official photographer, arrived followed by a host of hangers-on. It's hard to blend into a Vietnamese crowd when you are a head taller than everyone else and, in Trish's case, when you have short-cropped blonde hair. But our attempts to stay in the background and make ourselves relatively unnoticeable were to no avail. The president seemed determined to be photographed with us anyway.

The relief when the visit concluded was short-lived.

'You could wear what you have on for the competition performance tomorrow,' Minh Ha suggested to Trish.

***Everybody was dressed in their Sunday best for President Tran Duc Luong's visit to VOV5.***

'What competition performance?'

'We're singing the SEA Games song in the VOV staff concert, on stage at VOV Headquarters. We all have to be there by 8.00am, dressed to perform.'

This was the first we had heard of any competition or public performance and Minh Ha must have noticed our looks of horrified astonishment.

'You'll be there, won't you?' She wanted Trish to confirm.

'Yes, yes. Of course.' She laughed nervously. 'With bells on.'

'I don't know how we get ourselves into this sort of thing,' Iain muttered as we walked past the big wartime loudspeaker, outside the entrance to the Voice of Vietnam's administrative offices on Quan Su Street, a little before eight the following morning.

Iain was wearing a good pair of trousers, a white shirt and tie; it was way too hot to wear a suit or any type of jacket. Around us, scores of other people from different departments of VOV, the majority of whom we had never seen before, but who were also dressed to the nines, many in colourful traditional and ethnic costumes, were making their way up to the third floor.

'Oh my god!' Iain said under his breath as we entered a large auditorium, already partially filled with probably 300 people. The big stage at the far end was decorated with a blue backdrop, with red banners proclaiming the fifty-eighth anniversary of VOV's first broadcast, on 9 September 1945. A golden bust of Ho Chi Minh stood on the left side of the stage, in front of a long red panel affixed with a large gold star, and the whole place was festooned with flowers.

We sought out our office colleagues and soon learnt that our performance was some way down the list and that we would have to wait about an hour. This presented an opportunity to watch the other performances, which consisted of either singing or dancing routines, or a combination of both. They were all extremely colourful, as people had gone to some lengths to devise or prepare different costumes.

From our point of view, as was often the case, we missed quite a bit because of not fully understanding the language, but it was nonetheless a great visual experience.

As our performance involved singing the SEA Games song, in both Vietnamese and English, the women in our group were dressed in costumes representing the national dress of member nations of ASEAN, the Association of South-East Asian Nations, and so we presented a bright and multicoloured display of costumes from Malaysia, Indonesia, Thailand, Laos, Cambodia, Singapore, Myanmar, the Philippines and, of course, Vietnam.

The two of us sort of hummed along during the Vietnamese verses of the song, and then when it came to the English verses, everybody sang in English until it came to four lines, for which Khoi and Iain had to step forward and sing a duet!

By this stage we'd all got over the fact that the words didn't make sense and so we just sang them:

'Eager hearts in deep emotion . . .
. . . all for victory.
In your eyes I see the hope . . .
. . . the dream I share with you.'

At the end of the English version there was a brief non-vocal sequence when we all trundled around the stage waving Vietnamese and ASEAN flags, while we were showered with multi-coloured tinsel. Then a final chorus and it was over.

We came down from the stage, laughing and chatting away to each other.

Minh Ha ran up to us. 'We're in the top ten.' She laughed.

'Really?' Iain said. 'Do we get a certificate?'

'No, but we have to come back tonight for the concert.'

'The concert? I thought this *was* the concert.'

'Oh no. This is just the preliminaries . . . like the SEA Games. It's the heats.'

'You mean we have to do it again?' Iain moaned.

'Yep.'

The morning concert may have been a nerve-racking experience, but our unanticipated success gave us the adrenaline rush to approach the eight o'clock evening show with a touch of hubris. Our team, dressed again in their mixed attire, hung out at the back of the hall watching it completely fill with staff and their families, from grandparents to grandchildren, all of them chattering away in excited anticipation. The numbers were up from the morning so there were probably 500 people in the auditorium. The first performer, Vu Van Hien, the Director General of Voice of Vietnam, sang a solo love song. Hien really got into it and had a pretty good voice too, and the audience showed their appreciation with enthusiastic applause.

He was followed by several group presentations, the best of which was a sextuplet which included Hoang Minh Nguyet, the Director of the International Relations Department, who had been the first to welcome us to VOV six months previously. Minus her spectacles, with her usually constrained hair loose, and wrapped in an artistic approximation of a minority costume, she looked positively beguiling as she moved sinuously around the stage in a carefully choreographed number. More applause.

We didn't think to wonder who was judging the performances, or what were the criteria. By this time we were having fun too.

When it came our turn to perform, it all went off without a hitch again. The music soared, the words flowed, we made the right moves, waved the flags and threw our sparkling tinsel all at the right time. There was even that unplanned something extra special, when a tiny toddler wandered on stage and Trish picked her up in her arms and waved at the audience, who simply lapped it up. There were cheers, calls for an encore and even a few whistles.

Well, of course we won first prize! Fame at last! And money too: 40,000 dong, all of four Australian dollars and, best of all, an Emulation Award, which the next day we hung on the wall in the office. We happily hugged each other and, as the rest of the team roared off on their motorbikes, we walked the short distance home in a daze, stopping off for a self-congratulatory drink at Jacc's, where we boasted inordinately to anyone and everyone at the bar about our success.

A few days later there was a luncheon organised by our office for Huan's mother, Nam, who, having reached the compulsory retiring age of fifty-five, was leaving her position at VOV5. Nam wasn't particularly looking forward to retirement. In Vietnam no-one really wants to stop working that early as it means a sudden drop in income. Government pension arrangements are not all that adequate and, in general, most people need to have some sort of savings, or financial back-up, previously acquired property, or other assets to be able to live with any degree of comfort after retirement.

Also attending the luncheon, from outside our office group, was Madame Nguyet, with whose dance routine at the concert we'd been so impressed. Her attendance at this sort of thing was more a diplomatic gesture towards Nam than anything else, one would suspect, although she had of course known Nam well for some years. Nguyet was sitting opposite Iain.

'I'm going to Australia in a week or so,' she told him out of the blue.

'Oh?' Iain said, with interest. 'What will you be doing?'

'I will be part of a delegation from VOV going for talks with the ABC and Radio Australia.'

Iain's interest level jumped up a few notches immediately. 'Really? What sort of talks?'

'We will be talking about possible joint activities ... support from the ABC and Radio Australia in different areas, like training and programming. Use of some of Radio Australia's English-language programs, for example.'

'Equipment perhaps?' Iain asked, knowing that much of the antiquated equipment in VOV's radio studios had come from the ABC or Radio Australia twenty or so years previously. 'Will you be putting the hard word on them for some new equipment?'

She smiled. 'It would be nice, but I don't think that will be part of the Memorandum of Understanding.'

'So you expect to sign an MOU?'

'Yes, that is really the object of the visit.'

MOUs are often widely described as not worth the paper they are written on and, in this case, we were not even in a position to know what it was to be an 'understanding' of. But if you took a positive spin on things, an MOU between the two broadcasting organisations was, if nothing else, a step in the right direction.

Overnight the shops on the opposite side of the street from our office on Ba Trieu underwent a complete metamorphosis. One day they were selling electric bikes, textbooks or fancy underwear, and seemingly the next all of them were done up in red and gold and were selling *banh trung thu*, or moon cakes. It's as if you went down to your local shops one morning and instead of there being a newsagent, a fruit and vegie shop and a fishmonger, they were all selling the one product, Christmas cake. You can't help being a trifle impressed with what can only be seen as extraordinary levels of adaptability.

Moon cakes are a sweet speciality found throughout Vietnam in mid-autumn, which was the season we were supposed to be experiencing at this time, but which in reality still felt like full-blown summer.

In one popular folk tale, autumn is when the celestial husband and wife, the herd-boy Nguu Lang and the weaving-girl Chuc Nu,

**Banh trung thu: mooncakes are an essential part of Vietnam's celebration of the mid-autumn festival.**

meet. After autumn, they are separated for the rest of the year by the Milky Way. But without question the most outstanding feature of Vietnam's autumn sky is the moon, which is clear and bright and more visible than in any other season. Vietnamese folklore depicts the moon as male — *Ong Trang*, Mr Moon — and to celebrate the mid-autumn festival without moon cakes would be as unthinkable as an American Thanksgiving dinner without turkey.

We found the range to be extensive. Cakes can be savoury or sweet. Or even a mix of both. Hanoi-made cakes often smell of lemon and mandarin-orange and grapefruit. From the South come cakes filled with coconut, taro root, durian fruit, green bean and cocoa or hazelnuts. As the standard of living has improved over recent years, so too has the choice of cakes. Now there are even imported ones; from Malaysia, filled with red beans, lotus seeds and sweet-smelling leaves; from Hong Kong, filled with soybean, white lotus and black bean; and from China, filled with dried sausage, roast lean pork and fish fins, mixed with herbs and spices, particularly ginger.

But really the mid-autumn festival is for children and is all about lanterns and toys. We spent a most exciting evening in Luong Van Can, more popularly known as 'toy street', in Hanoi's Old Town, which was so jam-packed with ecstatic children and their indulgent parents that the police had closed off several streets to motorised traffic.

Everywhere there were lanterns made out of tissue paper or cellophane on bamboo frames in the traditional shape of six-pointed stars, as well as butterflies, rabbits or other animals. We bought a large, quite frighteningly real-looking red cellophane fish whose jaw opened and shut like a monster from the deep. Getting into the spirit, we shopped for collapsible round lanterns adorned with calligraphy and figures in traditional costumes, others decorated with Japanese cartoon characters, plus a string of football-sized versions in a multitude of garish hues, as well as

*Gruesome festival masks for sale in a crowded Old Town night market.*

gruesome masks, tinsel wigs, a sparkling tiara and a politically incorrect mandarin hat with a long queue — a colonial-era pigtail — attached. Of course we paid too much, all up 150,000 dong, or A$15. But hang the expense! We wanted to decorate the bedroom for the upcoming visit of our grandchildren.

Everywhere there were children, wide-eyed with sheer joy, tugging at their parents, nearly all of them in their mid-twenties, happy to be living now in a Vietnam that could afford such luxuries, which they almost certainly would not have enjoyed themselves at the same age.

It was madness really but in the middle of the month we sat over dinner one evening and talked about producing an additional program. It was a seemingly ungovernable old journalists' response to seeing a wealth of stories going to waste. Almost every other day, people cropped up who we knew would make interesting interviews. From France, a World Bank economist and a Nobel Prize laureate in physics. From Russia, the world's first woman cosmonaut. From Australia, a woman doctor working with Sydney's Vietnamese community on HIV/AIDS. From Japan, an eminent ethnologist and a UNESCO Friendship Ambassador. From Germany a world-class architect and city planner, and from the United States a group of specialist physicians making their annual visit, as part of Operation Smile, to fix cleft palates and other oral deformities in young children. Then there were the visiting musicians, conductors, singers, dancers, painters, film-makers and writers. The list was endless. And that didn't take into account all the brilliant local talent. It got our journalistic juices going. But there was also the matter of hours in the day.

'What about,' Trish suggested, 'we talk to Madame Hue about the style of program we could do for them and when she says yes, which I'm sure she will, we say we'd like to do it instead of doing the *Communist Party Review*?'

But we would have to find someone else to edit the *Review*.

'I think Marie,' the Melbourne woman who ran The Bookworm, the only English-language bookshop in town, 'might be willing to take it on.'

So it was agreed and a few days later Trish gave Hue a positive spiel about the new program idea. We had already settled on a name for it: *Personally Speaking*.

Her response was immediately enthusiastic. Trouble was, that when Trish suggested that, in order to have the time necessary to do the program we would like to ask Marie to edit the *Review*, Hue said, 'I'm sure you could manage to do both.'

The following morning, Huong came across to Iain's desk with what he had come to recognise as a dangerous smile on her face. He expected it to be something about our suggestion for *Personally Speaking*. Instead, she said, 'We would like to do a one-hour special on Australia's aid to Vietnam.'

Iain nodded slowly, collecting his wits, in order to deal with something unexpected. By now we'd come to realise that 'we would like to do ...' should be read as 'we would like *you* to do ...'

'Uh-huh,' Iain nodded again, cautiously. 'Aid?'

'Yes, Australia gives a lot of aid in big projects ... like the A$90 million My Thuan Bridge across the Mekong River, building schools, working against malaria and dengue in the villages ... That sort of thing.'

There was almost certainly some political motivation, Iain thought, in doing a one-hour radio special on Australia's aid program. Perhaps a little buttering up of the local people involved, in the hope of increased largesse in the future. Anybody's guess.

'When would this be?' he asked.

'It'll be for the *Sunday Show* in the first week of November.'

'And who will be doing it?'

'We'd like you and Minh Ha to host it together,' she said. 'Giang and I will record some additional interviews.'

'Just aid?' Iain asked. 'What about trade and investment? There's a lot of trade and business going on between Vietnam and Australia now. Don't you think it should take a look at some of that also?'

'Hmm. Yes, perhaps. We'll see how it develops. Can you get some information on aid ... umm, and trade ... And do you think the ambassador would take part?'

'I don't know,' Iain said, thinking back to the interview with Alexander Downer, 'but I can ask.'

He sat back down at his desk and thought about it for twenty minutes or so, making a list of different people to contact and how they might fit into the program, but as there was about six weeks before it would go to air, he put it to one side for a few days.

It was during that short hiatus that Loc came across to tell him that, 'VOV has signed the MOU with the ABC and Radio Australia.'

'What was the MOU about?' Iain asked.

'I don't know yet,' she said.

The following day, Phuong, whose pregnancy was now full term, did not come in to work.

'The baby is due any moment,' Thi told us. And within a couple of days we heard that she had had a little girl. There was great relief all round, as Phuong, like Hanh three months earlier, had miscarried and lost a baby during the previous year. Phuong was now the last of the three pregnancies in the office to have come to fruition, although only two had done so with a happy result.

It was not long after this that it was apparently deemed acceptable to visit Tram and to see her baby, which was now just on a month old. We never did get a sensible explanation of the Vietnamese custom of not visiting the mother and newborn child until at least a month after the birth. We assumed that it was because of the traditional acceptance that the baby might not survive the first month. Anyway, one evening we were told in the office that everyone was going to see Tram and her baby the following morning.

As with our trip to visit Hanh, we all piled onto motorcycles, both of us riding pillion, and took off through the traffic to Tram's flat which was out along busy Lang Ha Street in the Dong Da district, on the western side of Hanoi.

Though not in a very attractive building, the apartment was reasonably modern and comfortable and was something of which Tram was very proud.

'My husband bought this place all on his own,' she told us at one point during the fairly chaotic visit, in which at least a dozen people crammed into the flat, alternately nibbling on small cakes and sipping green tea and 'oohing' and 'aahing' over her little boy, who sported a shock of thick black hair and lay on the bed throughout the proceedings, sound asleep.

'He had no help from his parents,' Tram continued. 'He's done it all by himself.'

Her husband, who was at the office at the time, was a salesman and, although successful at what he did, apparently paid the same sort of price his Western counterparts did.

'He works very hard,' Tram told us. 'There is a lot of stress.'

That afternoon, following a call from Sandra Henderson at the Australian Embassy, we took a cab with Huan back out to the western side of the city again to meet the young Vietnamese girl who had won first prize from the tickets to the Australian Film Festival, held four months previously. The winner was only now being announced, as they apparently had to go through some long procedure to ascertain whether he or she would be allowed by the Vietnamese authorities to travel to Australia and back, which was part of the first prize.

Huong told Huan to go out and do the interview with the teenage girl, who came from the port city of Hai Phong, about 100 kilometres fom Hanoi. It was Huan's first recorded interview and he was nervous, not only about doing the interview, but also about going to the Australian Embassy, so we came along just to provide a bit of moral support.

The girl, who was accompanied by her parents, was also nervous, as they sat in a small, but quiet reception area of the embassy. We stood to one side as Huan began. He was somewhat embarrassed and awkward to begin with, but perceiving that the girl was also nervous seemed to help and he improved as the interview progressed. Again, because of not holding the microphone close enough to his own mouth on several occasions, his questions were at too low a level to be used, but he asked the right ones and got some reasonable answers, with the end result that his first interview was used in part as a small grab in the news bulletin and in a slightly longer excerpt in *What's On*.

It was a relatively small thing, but a big step for Huan, and in the cab on the way back to the office he was beaming.

There really was no reason for Huan to have been diffident. His use and understanding of English was among the best in the group of people at VOV5, all the more surprising because of the time he'd spent in Cuba mastering Spanish as a second language. Now, although his English was excellent, he was avid to perfect it even more.

And he was not the only one. Around the world some 350 million people speak English as their first language and a further two billion speak it as their second language. This total, of over 2.3 billion people, actually surpasses the numbers who speak Mandarin as either a first or second language and the numbers are growing dramatically all the time, with many tens of millions wanting to speak English and paying good money to learn to do so.

Living in Vietnam, we became very aware of just how fortunate we are to have English as our first language. All foundation members of the team at VOV5 had started off studying Russian as their second language, apart from Quynh who, with perhaps an even more far-sighted view of the future, studied Chinese. Sudden changes in the world political situation then made it necessary for them to grapple with English. It seemed that every Vietnamese we knew was either already studying English, or planned to study it as soon as possible.

Hanging out with Rebecca often meant meeting her professional colleagues, all of whom use those acronyms so beloved of the pedagogic profession. TESOL, we quickly discovered, stands for Teaching English to Speakers of Other Languages and IELTS translates as International English Language Testing System. To gain admission to an overseas university, whether taking its study courses from Vietnam or attending in person, like the 3000 Vietnamese students at present studying in Australia, it is imperative to achieve a set standard under IELTS.

The result of all this clamour to master the mysteries of the English language is a proliferation of language schools and teachers supposedly with TESOL qualifications and professing to offer a quick, painless and inexpensive route to getting the right IELTS score. If every person we met was learning English, then every second person we met was teaching it. We met so many 'teachers' that we would tease Rebecca by saying anybody could do her job and she would often retort by suggesting, 'If all else fails you could always get a job teaching English.'

*Hanoi's old East Gate, the only remaining entrance to the original Hanoi citadel.*

*The main north-south train line runs through the heart of Hanoi.*

*A sidewalk barber plying his trade beside Hanoi's Thu Le Lake.*

*A lunchtime nap in Hanoi's summer heat.*

*Catching up with the news on a quiet Saturday morning in the park.*

*Sidewalk motorcycle repair shops can be found almost anywhere in Hanoi.*

*Street hawkers come in from out of town daily to sell everything from pots and pans to brassieres.*

*Balloon and trinket sellers out in force on the edge of Old Town.*

*Paper lanterns festoon scores of shops in the Old Town during the mid-autumn festival.*

*In spring the streets of Hanoi come alive with the fragrance and colour of blossoming trees.*

*There are no parking meters in Hanoi ... yet.*

*One of the myriad fresh food markets on the sidewalks of Hanoi.*

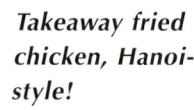

*Takeaway fried chicken, Hanoi-style!*

*A fast-food outlet and its ubiquitous blue stools in a Hanoi side street.*

Above: *Most Hanoians probably don't need billboards to tell them where they're going.*

Right: *Flags displayed in the streets for Total Liberation Day (30 April).*

*Hanoi is a city of flowers. A huge array of fresh, inexpensive blooms flood the city every day.*

*Women from the provinces on a visit to the Temple of Literature.*

*Eighty-three-year-old Cardinal Pham Dinh Tung conducts the Easter mass in Hanoi's St Joseph's Cathedral.*

*Easter crowds outside St Joseph's testify to a resurgence in Christianity, since the easing of government restrictions on religious worship.*

*Dancers perform a patriotic routine in an open-air stage on one of Hanoi's streets in the lead-up to Independence Day (2 September).*

*VOV staff throw a party to celebrate the fifth birthday of the English-language service.*

*Shaman performing a ritual with candles in a small temple outside Sapa.*

Left: *A young Red Dao woman brings her basket load of embroidery and handicrafts into the Sapa market.*

Below: *H'mong seamstresses hard at work in Sapa's indoor market.*

*Rebecca surrounded by H'Mong girls in the Sapa market.*

*Ornate temple figures adorn one of the two remaining pagodas of the ancient Vietnamese capital of Hoa Lu.*

*Part of the ancient Perfume Pagoda complex, 60 kilometres southwest of Hanoi.*

*Hill tribeswomen from mountain villages surrounding Dien Bien Phu.*

Colourful headdresses highlight the costumes of hill tribeswomen in Dien Bien Phu market.

Veterans wait for a bus in the rain after celebrating the fiftieth anniversary of the victory at Dien Bien Phu.

*A veteran of the historic 1954 rout of French forces at Dien Bien Phu, which had a profound impact on colonialism worldwide.*

# October

# OZ AID AND TRADE

*'Poverty fetters wisdom'*

'It's good to have you back.' Huan gave his slow, warm smile.

'It's good to be back,' Trish told him and meant it.

We'd had a wonderful twelve-day holiday with our grandchildren and their parents. In addition to introducing them to the exotic excitement of Hanoi we took a two-day boat trip out on Ha Long Bay as well as treating ourselves to a few days in the beautiful little town of Hoi An. This former port, halfway down the eastern coastline of Vietnam, is becoming hugely popular as a World Heritage-listed site and as a tourist destination. We promised ourselves we would return to spend more time there. Just these few days had made us realise how much more of Vietnam we wanted to see and enjoy.

The heat had only abated slightly towards the end of their stay, but the visit had been a success and, as we waved them off at the airport, Trish asked our grandson if he'd enjoyed his holiday. He nodded and then said, 'But we didn't get to see the dead man.'

It took her a few seconds to work out what he meant.

'Ah, Uncle Ho. No. Sorry about that. He'd gone on holiday.'

'Nana!' he said reprovingly, as if she was telling an unacceptable fib, and went through the airport gate, with hardly a backward glance at the oldies, laden down with boy treasure and already anticipating the thrill of life's next adventure.

We'd picked up on local customs enough by now to know that whenever you returned to the office from a trip away — whether it was moonlighting, working or holidaying — you brought a small gift of food. An admirable social gesture, which, for us, underlined the importance the Vietnamese attach to sharing. So we had brought in a couple of packets of Tim Tams that we had been pleasantly surprised to find one day on the shelves of our local supermarket, and we all sat around the big office table nibbling them and sipping green tea. They showed a genuine interest in what we had done and, after we had answered their questions for a while, we caught up with their news. We felt welcomed like family, which seemed to bring home the fact that we were already halfway through our time with them.

The day after our return to work, 10 October, was Vietnam's 'Double Tenth', the forty-ninth anniversary of the second Liberation of Hanoi and, once again, the gold-starred red flags and banners were everywhere.

This was the day, some five months after the crushing defeat of French military forces at Dien Bien Phu, in May 1954, when Ho Chi Minh's Viet Minh forces once again left their jungle and mountain redoubts to enter and claim the capital as their own. A repeat, in many ways, of the 1945 story which saw the Viet Minh make a triumphant entry into Hanoi at the end of World War II.

That, as we mentioned, led to Ho's Declaration of Independence and a brief period — about eighteen months — of Vietnamese rule over their own land. It was a frustrating period, troubled and disrupted by the French, before France eventually reasserted control over all of Indochina, with the French General Jacques Leclerc entering Saigon uttering the words, 'We have come to reclaim our inheritance.'

Then, after eight years of guerrilla war, France had eventually been massively defeated on the battlefield of Dien Bien Phu, the surrender coming one day before the scheduled opening of peace talks in Geneva, which were aimed at finding a resolution to the long-running conflict.

The talks involved delegates from France, Great Britain, the Soviet Union, China, the United States and the Democratic Republic of Vietnam (DRV), as well as representatives of the former Bao Dai Imperial government of Annam and the Royal Governments, by then officially referred to as the Associated States of Laos and Cambodia.

If Ho Chi Minh's representatives at the talks had felt that they were on the cusp of achieving real independence and unification of Vietnam, their hopes were crushed, not just by the major Western nations, who feared the spread of communism in the region but, to the dismay of Vietnam, by its supposed allies, the two giant communist powers of China and the Soviet Union. Both countries effectively helped to pull the rug out from under the DRV.

Beijing's representative, Zhou Enlai, and the Soviet's Vyasheslav Molotov had both warned the Vietnamese that they would not support a continuation of a ground war. Fearing direct intervention by the United States, they also blocked the establishment of a new Indochinese Federation of Vietnam, Laos and Cambodia, which could be expected to quickly become a communist federation.

Additionally, and — in the light of history — tragically, they also backed the idea of dividing Vietnam into two zones, northern and southern, with plans to hold national elections within two years to unify the country. Zhou Enlai assured the chief Vietnamese delegate, future Prime Minister Pham Van Dong, who was not keen on the compromise, that it was a small price to pay for the withdrawal of the French.

Shortly after the conclusion of the conference, John Foster Dulles, the US Secretary of State, ominously told a press conference that the United States would now begin the task of aiding the development of non-communist states in Laos, Cambodia and South Vietnam.

On 9 October 1954 French troops rolled out of Hanoi and across the Paul Doumer Bridge — the same Long Bien Bridge we had walked across in April — on their way to sail for home from the port city of Hai Phong.

So while Vietnam now celebrates the Liberation of Hanoi one day after that French departure, there was actually little for them to celebrate and millions of lives would be lost in the war with the United States and the southern regime which was soon to follow.

'Will many people be interested in this?' Madame Hue queried our *What's On* story, announcing the launch of the Rugby World Cup and a rundown of the venues around the country where it would be telecast.

'I'm not that madly interested personally,' Trish told her, 'but it seems that worldwide about a billion people are.' So the story stayed in.

It fell to Joe Thwaites, as Ambassador of Australia, the country hosting the series, to launch the telecasts on giant screens both indoors and outdoors at the Hilton Hotel. Hanoi's expatriate community turned out in force for the event ... and the free food. Jacc's, Al Fresco, the Spotted Cow, all owned and run by Australians, carried telecasts and ran totes along with Dakshin, a vegetarian Indian restaurant in the Old Town, whose south Indian owner also telecast Test matches and sent his son to be educated in Canada. Ho Chi Minh City had a similar number of telecast venues.

Light-hearted displays of nationalism were the order of the day. One brave Scot went so far as to wear his kilt. As we threaded our way through the capacity crowd, we picked up regional English dialects vying with Irish brogue, French, Italian, Canadian, Russian and of course Australian but, oops, look at that face. When the young man with the extremely broad Aussie accent turned, we saw he had a face as Vietnamese as Huan's. We introduced ourselves.

Nguyen Dinh Thien grew up in Sydney, where his parents had finally settled after leaving South Vietnam as a result of the American War. Qualified as an architect at the University of New South Wales, he was working with his father, who had returned to Vietnam several years earlier and established a company called VABIS, Vietnam Australia Building Industry Services.

It was obvious from the way he talked that the company was very busy and, from later conversations with other people, we found that they had been responsible in large part for the building of the relatively new Australian diplomatic compound.

When Trish asked him in which country he felt most at home, he answered without hesitation.

'When I'm here, I am Vietnamese. When I'm in Australia, I'm Australian. I'm a lucky man.'

While Thien's story is one example of successful foreign investment in Vietnam, he and his father did have a significant advantage in being of Vietnamese origin and speaking the language. Nevertheless, direct investment by complete foreigners or foreign companies has been going through the roof over the past few years. Foreign investment generally was a constant feature of the news stories that came across our desk every day. There was always a story or two which dealt with the President, the Prime Minister or the Party Leader exhorting a particular sector to do more to encourage foreign investment in certain areas, or to lift their game in order to meet annual growth targets of 10, sometimes 15 per cent.

Early in the month, Franz Xaver Augustin, the Director of the Goethe Institute in Hanoi, whom we had met while attending some of the cultural functions at the Institute, called Iain on his mobile phone with an unusual request. He sounded a little stressed.

'You know we have all the choir members for the Frankfurt Music Academy arriving to sing at the Opera House in little more than a week?'

'Yes,' Iain responded.

In fact we had been looking forward to what promised to be an amazing performance of the classic choral work *Carmina Burana*. The performance would involve a choir of over 200 members, plus the orchestra of the Vietnam National Opera and Ballet and the Hanoi Conservatory. One hundred and twenty members of the choir were German singers from the Frankfurter Singakadamie and were due to arrive in Hanoi in a couple of days.

'I've run into a big problem,' Franz Xaver went on. 'A couple of the hotels they are booked into have now told me they don't have sufficient rooms. And a few of the singers don't have enough money to pay for their accommodation.'

'So you need some extra rooms?'

'Right.'

Iain told him we'd be happy to provide a room for one of his choir members, which was how it came about that Mechtilde Weisner, a bright young woman in her early twenties, turned up at our house and introduced herself before settling into a demanding schedule of rehearsals for two big performances within the week.

*Carmina Burana*, composed by Carl Orff in 1937, is now recognised as one of the most powerful and challenging musical works of the twentieth century. Based on a collection of medieval songs and lyrics discovered some 200 years ago, Orff's work is a scenic cantata in twenty-five movements, with parts for soprano, tenor and baritone soloists, a boys' choir, a full choir and an orchestra.

To combine Western and Vietnamese singers in the one performance was a huge challenge for American conductor Linda

Horowitz, who had led the Frankfurter Singakademie for four years, and for the Vietnamese performers themselves.

'Some singers don't even have any concept of the piece,' Pham Hong Hai, head of the Vietnam Opera and Ballet Art Department, said at one stage during the rehearsals. 'It has taken a lot of effort to practise the singing styles for a 25-movement piece that is written in Latin, German and Italian.'

And to top off the organisational and rehearsal problems, there was a last-minute drama with a somewhat recalcitrant Ministry of Culture, which wanted to scrap the big *Carmina Burana* banner outside the Opera House and a huge one at the back of the stage, because they included a depiction of a fifteenth-century nude by Hieronymous Bosch. You would have had to examine it with a telescope to recognise it as a nude, but the ministry wanted them taken down. Xaver argued for three hours before finally convincing them that this medieval art wasn't really going to get anyone's hormones pumping.

The irony of the situation was that, on the day of the concert, Hanoi's English-language newspaper, *Vietnam News*, carried a page-three story about the Asia–Pacific Hair Olympics in Manila, which featured a photograph of a totally naked female model, whose body was painted to look as if she had clothes on. Apparently, no problem for Hanoi's morals police. Either that, or they didn't even realise she had no clothes on!

Sufficient to say the performance of *Carmina Burana* was a triumph, with continuous standing ovations for Linda Horowitz, the orchestra and the combined choirs who performed four encores.

During the period of the rehearsals for *Carmina Burana*, Vietnam observed yet another International Day. Its importance, though remote from the German and Vietnamese singers, the musicians of the Opera and Ballet Theatre orchestra — and indeed from most city or urban dwellers — was nonetheless of great significance to the majority of Vietnamese, who live in rural areas and earn their living from agriculture.

The International Day observed on 17 October was known as HEPA, an acronym for Hunger Eradication and Poverty Alleviation, and, in Vietnam, at least, there is reason for some commendation for past and current achievements in this field. At the time of the launching of the Doi Moi renovation process in 1987, average per capita income in Vietnam was around US$170 a year and poverty was widespread, particularly outside of the cities.

One of several reasons for this was the dominance of communist-style central planning mechanisms, which provided little opportunity for people to generate or increase their income. The government at the time, it seemed, knew how to plan and run a war, but didn't know how to benefit from peace, at least at an economic level.

The Doi Moi process moved dramatically to change that situation by providing an economic reform package to master the crisis of the 1980s — which had seen widespread food shortages and hunger — but more fundamentally to overcome poverty and develop the country.

According to World Bank studies, the overall poverty level in Vietnam fell from well over 70 per cent in the mid–1980s to 58 per cent in 1993 and to 37 per cent in 1998. By 2003, it was down to 9.5 per cent with predictions that it would be under 5 per cent by 2010.

But figures can be deceptive: earning more than $1 a day puts a person above the poverty line. And the reality is that many Vietnamese are still very poor, with many just hovering above the line. They remain very vulnerable, susceptible to floods, poor sanitary conditions and sickness, which could easily push them back into poverty at any given moment.

In addition, there are significant differences between the overall, or national, poverty levels and the poverty levels of the country or rural areas, which are significantly higher. The city figures, which are generally lower, tend to bring the overall figures down a notch or two and make them look better.

Nevertheless, there's no denying the impressive achievements, which coincidentally have produced a significant rise in per capita annual income. From the figure of US$170 in 1987, it had grown to just over US$400 annually by the period we were working with VOV and, at the time of writing, it's reported to be pushing US$500 a year, with urban levels at around $1500 a year.

During October, a 'new' member of staff arrived on the scene at VOV5. However, he was new only to us. Nguyen Hong Ngan, the 26-year-old son of Madame Hue, had worked in the English section of VOV for several years, but for the past twelve months had been in England, studying at the University of Leicester. Without any fuss, he slotted straight back into the office routine as if he'd never been away.

It took us a while to get to know him properly and to find out, for example, that he had a wife and daughter, who had remained in Hanoi while he had been away. He was easy enough to get along with, but we never seemed to achieve quite the same level of friendship and camaraderie that we had with most of the other staffers.

Ngan's return would have have relieved some of the potential pressure on staff numbers had Giang been successful with his application for a Fulbright scholarship and Quynh with his own efforts to spend a year working with NHK in Japan. But, in mid-September Giang received the unwelcome news that he had not been accepted, while Quynh's negative response came a couple of weeks later. However, both were asked to reapply in the future.

Shortly after Ngan's return to the office, in the third week of October, it was time for another baby visit — this time to see

Phuong and her month-old daughter. It was also the occasion for another hair-raising pillion ride through Hanoi's traffic. Not that we didn't frequently take a *xe om* to ride to and from work on super-hot days, but that was only a matter of four blocks along Ly Thuong Kiet Street, usually taking less than five minutes. When we rode off on these 'baby visits', it invariably involved a much longer ride through Hanoi's hazardous traffic. What made these rides more complicated and, one would have thought, even more perilous, was that there would usually be seven or eight, maybe more, motorbikes in our convoy and not everyone knew exactly where they were going. They would quite often ride three abreast, chatting away as they rode — as most Hanoians do. We do concede though, that we never saw any of our crowd using a mobile phone while riding through the traffic — as most Hanoians do!

Phuong's parents' house was tricky to reach. The last bit of the twenty-minute ride was down narrow alleyways, crowded with street vendors selling all sorts of meat, fish and vegetables.

The house, like many Vietnamese residences on these congested streets, was a surprise in that it was elegantly furnished in an oriental manner, with dark, intricately carved wooden furniture on which we all sat while we took turns nursing the baby. Phuong's baby, like Tram's, also had a shock of black hair and slept through the whole proceedings, as we ate lychees and watermelon and drank glasses of tea.

On the way back to the office, we paid more attention to the street stalls we had passed on the way in, after being told by Giang and Khoi that this was one of the ubiquitous 'frog' markets of Hanoi. Iain stopped to take photographs of fish and meat being sold right next to metal-workshops, where, literally within a metre or so of the fish or meat tables, men were arc-welding brackets and hinges.

'Why are they called "frog" markets?' we asked Giang.

'Because they are illegal. The police allow them to stay for a while because they perform a service, or because the police are paid

*Meat laid out on a butcher's stall next to metalworkers in one of Hanoi's 'frog' markets.*

off. But at some stage, if there is a crackdown on the market, it just "hops", like a frog, to another site somewhere else, often quite nearby.'

One of the few good things about getting older — at least in theory — is that it's supposed to bring you more respect. We know that's a bit of a joke in Western countries, but in Vietnam the concept is still alive and well, and in fact it's probably carried a bit too far. There was slightly more attention paid to the question in the latter half of October when Iain's birthday came around.

The pecking order in any Vietnamese group of people, whether it's a family, an office group or whatever, is nearly always established, at a very basic level, simply by the age of the persons involved. To Westerners, one of the most bizarre aspects of the Vietnamese language — a really ungraspable aspect until you become quite accomplished in it — is the fact that, in place of personal pronouns like 'you', 'me', 'he', 'she' and 'they', Vietnamese use a bewildering array of almost thirty different words, which vary depending on age, sex, social position, level of intimacy and whether it's a close or a distant relationship. And they change if the level of intimacy changes.

All this is a sort of a spin-off from the Confucian ideals of respect for your elders. For example, to say 'you' when speaking politely to another person, you would say *'ong'* if you were talking to a married man, a grandfather, or someone older than you, but you would say *'ba'* if the conversation was with a married woman or a grandmother ... also older than you. If you were talking informally to a person roughly the same age as yourself, you would say *'anh'*, and *'chi'* if it was an informal conversation with an older lady. If, on the other hand, you were talking politely to a single lady, a female teacher or an aunt, you should say *'co'*, whereas an informal 'you' to a younger person or sibling would be *'em'*. The popular travel guide *Lonely Planet* warns, however, that one should be careful about referring to a younger female as *'em'*, 'especially in front of her partner, because they might suspect that you are in love with her ... if not necessarily her lover!'

The term 'Uncle' for Ho Chi Minh is simply used as a universal sign of respect and admiration and variations on it are used across the societal spectrum. For instance, on occasions we became 'Bac Iain' and 'Bac Trish'; that is, Uncle Iain and Aunt Trish. The terms for uncle and aunt become the same word, *'bac'*, if you are older than the parents of your dialogue partner.

Anyway, on birthdays it was the accepted practice that the birthday boy or girl brought in various goodies to the office for everybody to enjoy. So, instead of the usual Vietnamese cakes and sweets, Iain went to an excellent little French patisserie and bought a stack of small cakes and tarts, as well as a big French-style apple pie, which we all got stuck into at lunchtime.

Whatever we did in Vietnam invariably turned out to have unexpected twists and dimensions. So it was with our visit to the important and historic temple, the Perfume Pagoda. This was another excursion with the Friends of Vietnam Heritage, the educational group whose wide range of activities was always planned in close collaboration with Vietnamese scholars, local experts and museums.

At seven in the morning, we boarded a private bus outside the Hotel Nikko for a two-and-a-half-hour trip through the heavy traffic of industrial suburbs and then over rutted roads, through a string of small villages. At Duc Pier, we clambered aboard a shallow-draught, metal-bottomed skiff, squatted on a low plank and tried, nervously at first, not to move about too much as a woman confidently plied us for an hour along the Yen River as it flowed between steep limestone crags.

Before we began the climb, we spent some time looking around the sizeable and impressive lower Thien Tru Pagoda, and listening to a swag of information about Buddhism and Buddhism in Vietnam from the FVH guide.

Trying to digest it all, we sat in the pagoda's shady grounds and, to give ourselves stamina for the climb, we were eating our packed lunch when we were joined by a couple who introduced themselves casually as Bob and Pam Gordon. Robert Gordon, it turned out, was the new British Ambassador to Vietnam. Friendly and well travelled, they had just completed a four-year stint at the embassy in Myanmar. We started an animated conversation with them, and our friendship developed and deepened over the coming months.

The four-kilometre climb up was really just a matter of following a boulder path, though we were glad it was dry, because it wouldn't be much fun in the wet when the path underfoot would be slippery with mud. A new high-tech cable car system is planned, but unless you are disabled, it could well take the point out of making the pilgrimage.

We were also glad that we went when we did and had the mountain more or less to ourselves. From the end of January through to early April every year, the track is crammed with hundreds of thousands of Buddhist pilgrims who come from all over the country. They process up the track, visiting the smaller pagodas that cling to the edge and all of which are well worth a visit. The aim is to reach Hong Dich Dong, the Grotto of the Perfumed Vestige, which is hidden from view in a gigantic cave at the peak. The big stone statue of Bodhisattva Kwan Yin is at the far end of the cave, splendid in the candle-lit gloom, among the natural stalactites and stalagmites.

Having made it to the top, we staggered back down, balanced ourselves in the skiff for the return trip through *Lord of the Rings* scenery and clambered back on the bus.

During October, a fair amount of Iain's spare time went into pulling the upcoming program on Australian Trade and Aid into some sort of shape. The plan was for Minh Ha and him to be co-presenters, joined by three other participants in a program that would be recorded in the studio, as if it were live, on 30 October, a Thursday, but would not be broadcast until the following Sunday.

The three participants would be the Australian ambassador, Joe Thwaites; Andrew Rowell, in charge of the Australian aid organisation AusAID; and Paul Fairhead, Chairman of the Australian Chamber of Commerce in Vietnam. In addition there would be three other participants who would be recorded separately, with their edited interviews played into the main program as it was recorded. These three would be Tim Gauci, the

Senior Trade Commissioner and Director of AusTrade; Alistair Briscombe, who acted as project manager for a highly effective program to combat dengue fever in Vietnam, implemented by an Australian NGO called the Foundation for the Peoples of Asia and the Pacific; and Dr Vu Sinh Nam, of Vietnam's National Institute for Hygiene and Epidemiology, one of the main partners in the project.

Iain met with both Alistair Briscombe and Dr Vu Sinh Nam, but it was arranged that Giang would go out to their offices off Lang Ha Street to record interviews with them during the week before the main program was recorded. Also during that week, we arranged for Huong to record an interview with Trade Commissioner Tim Gauci at his office in the Australian Embassy.

Tim Gauci is a forty-something businessman turned diplomat. He headed up the Australian telecommunication giant Telstra's foray into Vietnam, which not only revolutionised Vietnam's primitive telephone system over a period of about five years, but remains the Telstra company's single most profitable overseas investment. When the job was finished he stayed on in Hanoi with his wife and children and has now spent more than a decade in the capital.

Iain went along with Huong when she did the interview, just as an observer, but also to make sure we got the sort of responses that would fit in with the shape of the program. Everything went well and, with Giang's interviews also on tape, we were basically ready for recording on the last Thursday in the month. In the studio the program, which was simply called a 'Vietnam/Australia Special' as part of the Sunday Feature hour, was recorded with Minh Ha's opening comments highlighting the fact that this was the thirtieth anniversary of diplomatic relations between Australia and Vietnam. Joe Thwaites provided an overview of the present relationship between the two countries, also pointing to other important areas of cooperation outside of aid and trade, in the fields of education, defence, police and anti-terrorism work and in cultural exchanges.

Paul Fairhead described the changes in Vietnam since he first began living in the country in the early 1990s as phenomenal. 'Any country that doubles its wealth and halves its poverty rate in such a short period is phenomenal. Another big change we see is colour,' he said. 'In 1991 everyone wore green, there were no cars and hardly any motorbikes ... now it's all colour.'

He spoke of how the business climate had improved dramatically for investors since the first entry into Vietnam by major businesses like ANZ banking, Foster's Breweries, BHP Steel and Telstra Communications in the 1990s. He said, however, that major investments should now be concentrating in the area of knowledge-based services, such as the IT and computer industries, and that more needed to be done by the government of Vietnam in providing a comfortable environment for investors in their negotiations to establish businesses in the country.

'What do you think of the level of transparency in government negotiations that exists here now?' Minh Ha asked him.

'What transparency?' Paul replied.

Oops, Iain thought. This is the sort of thing we want. All eyes were now focused on Paul.

'There's no real transparency,' he went on. 'At least not at the level that's needed. The government might say they have done major things to improve the level of transparency and to provide a level playing field for investors, but it's got a long way to go yet.'

He made a couple more comments along the same lines and then diplomatically reinforced his earlier comments on how much progress *had* been made since 1991, when 'there was no understanding at all of what was involved in business or investment'.

The program moved on when Minh Ha changed the subject to aid, but Iain made a mental note to talk to her about making sure the comments stayed in.

On the aid side, Andrew Rowell talked about the shift in Australian government policy with regard to aid to Vietnam, to concentrate more on rural and industrial development projects such as the My Thuan Bridge in the Mekong delta and governance in the form of helping Vietnam develop legal and financial systems that fit with those of the rest of the world and could help it along the path to membership of the World Trade Organization.

The recorded pieces with Alistair Briscombe and Professor Vu Sinh Nam told the impressive story of a world first in the use of biological controls. A microscopic creature called misocyclops was introduced into water supply and storage systems to virtually eradicate the larvae of the dengue mosquito in seven northern provinces where the Australian-funded aid project operated.

As Minh Ha and Iain parted with the Australian trio at the end of the session, Iain asked Minh Ha, 'The piece on transparency, from Paul Fairhead. You're going to leave that in, aren't you?'

'Yes,' she said. 'Definitely.'

## *November*

## AN OFFICE BLOW-UP

*'A man without education is like an uncut gem'*

That Sunday morning, as we ate breakfast, we tuned in to 105.5FM to listen, with a certain nervous anticipation, to the early-morning broadcast of the Aid and Trade program recorded a few days earlier. Iain was concerned that it would be chopped around in some way to accommodate the political requirements of whoever, or whatever government ministry, it had been done to please. Recalling that Huong had initially wanted it to only cover aid to Vietnam but not trade, he was under no illusion that there was not an ulterior motive for the program.

Cynical? Maybe, but we must admit that we were relieved to hear that Minh Ha had left in Paul Fairhead's criticism of the lack of transparency in government dealings with foreign investors. We both thought it showed that they were willing to let at least a little bit of criticism of the government go through. The program would be repeated four more times during the day and the evening.

'It'll be interesting to see if Minh Ha gets any backlash over it,' Iain said.

On Monday morning, we were both in the office, as usual, to

record the next four days of *What's On*, so we both made a point of complimenting Minh Ha on the fact that the piece had been left in.

To a Western reader, it may seem a bit over the top to be going on about such a small thing, but Vietnam — particularly North Vietnam — has had fifty years under communism, where anything that is critical of the government is out, so any small step is considered progress. In recent years, of course, the whole process of renovation, Doi Moi, has brought tremendous changes in the area of freedom of expression, so that what Vietnam is like now is virtually unrecognisable when compared to the Vietnam of only a few years ago. In the early 1990s, for example, local residents could not be seen even talking to a foreigner in the street without feeling uncomfortable and, on occasions, coming under some scrutiny.

The hangover effect from that fear of government disapproval was obviously still in play at VOV as, when we made the comment to Minh Ha, she looked at us in an odd way and said, 'You heard the early-morning program, did you?'

'That's right.'

'Well, we had to take it out of the later broadcasts.'

'You mean you chopped it out after the first one went to air?' Iain asked incredulously. 'Who told you to do it?' He knew she wouldn't have done it willingly.

She nodded in the direction of Hue's desk, but Hue was not there.

He felt a surge of anger and disappointment. This was something important. It was something that was symptomatic of what was a flawed system.

An hour later, after having recorded our programs, Iain returned from the studio building to the office and went straight over to Hue. She looked defensive.

'Why did you tell Minh Ha to take out the piece about transparency from the Sunday program?' he asked.

'It was only a small bit that came out,' she replied. 'It was not important.'

'If it wasn't important,' Iain responded, somewhat heatedly, 'then why bother to take it out?'

Hue looked at Iain in surprise. This was a side of him she hadn't seen.

'I understand it was critical of the government,' she said, 'and we wanted the program to be positive.'

'It *was* positive! That piece was only a very small negative. The overall program was positive. But from what you just said, it seems you didn't even hear the program. So what made you tell Minh Ha to take it out?'

'Loc said she thought it was too provocative.'

'Loc?' Iain looked back across the floor to Loc at her desk. 'Provocative?! It was simply advocating what the government has been proclaiming for ages, that there needs to be transparency in operations with foreign investors.' He charged across to Loc.

'What was wrong with that comment about transparency? It was important that it should stay in.'

'It was only a few sentences,' Loc replied with a tight smile. 'It did not give the right picture.'

'The right picture? It was a comment from someone who is dealing with the government all the time and is confronted with this lack of transparency. It may not be the right picture from the government's point of view, but it's probably an accurate one. And transparency is what the government says it wants to promote in dealings with investors. Isn't this what Doi Moi is all about?' He knew he was getting a bit carried away, but what the hell. 'What you've done is a betrayal of Doi Moi.'

Loc looked at him, surprised too. 'It may be,' she said. 'But we need to travel slowly.'

'If you travel this slowly,' Iain snapped, 'you'll never get there.'

He marched away to his desk and sat down to rip into some of the news bulletins that had piled up. A half-hour or so later, when he'd calmed down, he went separately to Hue and Loc and apologised for being so aggressive. Hue smiled somewhat enigmatically and said it was nothing. Loc also smiled, but tried to pick up where the conversation had left off and convince Iain that she had done the right thing — but he had already accepted it as par for the course and was ready to forget all about it.

Other less-heated conversations were also going on in the office, sparked by the fact that we planned to attend a quiz night and dinner run by the Australian Embassy. Each table at the event was to be given a subject — such as history, geography, sport — and the teams from each table had to choose a name and dress in a costume relating to their subject. We were a bit nonplussed to have been given the topic 'War and Religion', so we took 'Power and Glory' as the name of our team and then racked our minds to think of appropriate fancy dress. Iain had a highly decorated purple cardboard Bishop's mitre made in the Old Town and planned to wear it along with a camouflage uniform. Rebecca suggested that she and Trish wear Buddhist robes, bags and prayer beads, bought from a stall alongside Quan Su Pagoda, topped by smart Vietnamese army officer's caps.

The VOV5 team watched with growing interest as these pieces of dress accumulated and listened in some puzzlement as we tried to explain the whys and hows of the upcoming quiz. It was instructive to note that because none of them had any formal religious education, such religious trappings held no undertone of significance.

It wasn't until we went to purchase some toy weaponry, with which to top off our outfits, that we ran into problems. No shop in Hang Can Street sold toy guns and we couldn't help noticing that when Iain described, with suitable gestures and noises, what it was we wanted to buy, the shopkeepers all looked nervous and tried to move us on.

'You can't buy toy guns in Vietnam,' Thuy told us, putting Trish's red-banded officer's cap on at a jaunty angle and laughing at her reflection in the office wall mirror.

Khoi explained. 'The government banned the sale of them a few years back because there were some incidents of injuries from air rifles and also from groups of boys lying in wait and firing paint pellets at passers-by, often women.'

So, in one generation, the nation had gone from the requirement for everyone to be ready to fight for their country to the banning of even imitation weaponry.

Thuy plopped Trish's officer's cap on top of Khoi's thick hair and took pretend aim at him.

But though they both laughed, we all knew that if the call came to serve there would be no joking then. All student-age Vietnamese are required to spend one month a year in national service. This is quite often not just military training, but more usually involves heavy labour on roads and other infrastructure, often in remote areas.

'Young people enjoy it,' Khoi said. 'It's a great way for them to spend time together away from the confines of their family.'

There is a paper requirement for every member of the community to keep up their military training on an annual basis. In fact this is far from rigorously enforced. But again there is an indefinable but nonetheless ever-present feeling that, if push came to shove, there would be no hesitation in defending the country.

Something of a running joke developed between us all that whenever we managed, barely, to kick-start a piece of terminally tired equipment to life, or cobble together a piece of news for the main bulletin even while the headlines were already going to air, someone would intone, 'That's how we won the war.'

We came to realise, however, that for them it wasn't a joke. It was a truth.

The Power and Glory team, by the way, came second on Quiz Night, pipped at the post by the 'Sports' team, who were all dressed like the mascot for the SEA Games, a yellow, somewhat anthropomorphic water buffalo.

At a more serious level, there were other military developments in the air at this time, in Washington, with the first-ever visit of a Vietnamese defence minister to the Pentagon since the end of the Vietnam War in 1975. In a historic and symbolic meeting, the Vietnamese Defence Minister Pham Van Tra held discussions with US Defence Secretary Donald Rumsfeld and Air Force General Richard Meyers, Chairman of the Joint Chiefs of Staff, over a working lunch.

The meeting was described as 'a final burying of the hatchet' by once-bitter enemies, who are now enjoying a greatly improved political relationship, as well as dramatically increasing economic ties.

Tra, who fought against the United States during the war, discussed regional security, the global war on terror and future military ties with the American defence officials. Some two million Vietnamese military personnel and civilians died during the conflict, which also claimed 58,000 American lives. During the past decade the United States has been able to negotiate special arrangements with the Vietnamese government to conduct searches for and the recovery of the remains of MIAs, American troops described as missing in action. So far some 700 have been accounted for, with more than 1800 still listed as missing. The number of Vietnamese soldiers still missing is in the hundreds of thousands.

Tra also raised the issue of unexploded ordnance: American bombs and shells left over from the war, which continue to maim and kill dozens of people each year. In addition, he asked for help in dealing with the after-effects of Agent Orange, the powerful defoliant used by American forces to clear swaths of jungle during the conflict. The long-lasting residue of the chemical has been linked to diabetes, cancer, birth defects and other illnesses.

The United States, for its part, wants cooperation with Vietnam in promoting security and stability in this part of Asia, where terrorism has become a growing problem.

Until recent years Vietnam has felt a degree of isolation from this issue, but the Bali bombing, the Marriott Hotel explosion and the attack on the Australian Embassy in Djakarta, the capture of Jemaah Islamiyah terrorist Hambali in Thailand, and the appearance of radicals linked to Jemaah Islamiyah in Thailand and neighbouring Cambodia have reinforced the view in Vietnam that fundamentalist Islamic terrorism is closer to home than was previously thought.

For two decades after the withdrawal of American troops from Vietnam, the United States imposed crippling economic sanctions on Vietnam. President Clinton lifted them in 1994 and established diplomatic relations with Hanoi the following year as well as signing a bilateral trade pact that took effect in 2001.

A few weeks prior to Tra's visit to Washington, US and Vietnamese officials signed agreements providing for direct flights between Vietnam and the United States and, as a further symbol of American–Vietnamese defence cooperation, the Pentagon announced plans for the groundbreaking friendly visit by an American frigate, the USS *Vandegrift*, and its crew of 200 sailors to Ho Chi Minh City later in the month. How the wheel turns.

And, as the wheel turned, along came another birthday. This one for Trish. Rebecca gave her a beautiful little carved buffalo-horn compass; a bit of a tease really because she is as deficient in orientation skills as Trish is. Then we indulged in a slap-up lunch at the Hilton Hotel where the Czech band the Dr Jazz Trio was performing as part of a jazz festival.

It was the country's third European Jazz Festival and concerts were given every night of the week, featuring musicians from

Denmark, Belgium, France, Norway, Sweden and Switzerland. They were joined by local bands in a freewheeling example of the power of music to break through language and culture barriers.

And, also for Trish's birthday, we paid a visit to an Aladdin's cave of a shop filled with embroidered, bejewelled and sequined handbags, all of them imagined up by a young woman named Christina Yu. Trish didn't need to be told twice to choose one of her splendid pieces as a birthday present.

We had taken note of Christina early on in our time in Hanoi. She is hard to miss, even in a city with so many exceptionally interesting residents, and Trish had made it her business to meet her. Being over-the-top attractive makes it difficult for Christina not to be noticed when she enters a room. It also helps that she has a warm, extrovert personality and laughs a lot. Which is probably why her handbags are happy and why she is such a successful business operator. Her designs sell worldwide and she employs up to a thousand people. Quite something for a 37-year-old Hong Kong-born lawyer.

'My legal training was good mental discipline, which has helped me in my business life,' she told Trish when she interviewed her for a piece for *Personally Speaking*. They sat in Christina's top-floor office in a bright yellow building which serves as her design studio, business headquarters and salesroom, surrounded by her designs, all of them unusual shapes, colours and patterns embellished with an eclectic mix of materials: lace, sequins, fake fur, glass buttons, even photographs.

For her own top-of-the-range trademark, Ipa-nima, Christina produces two collections a year. She also manufactures rather more mundane designs on a large scale and under their label for around half-a-dozen of the more important retail chain outlets in the United States and Europe. Less than 20 per cent of her handbags are sold through retail outlets in Hanoi and Ho Chi Minh City. She happily admits that, even when she was working as a lawyer in Hong Kong, she was moonlighting in the fashion industry. 'I've been attracted to it since I was a very small child, but it wasn't considered a legitimate career.'

So why move from freewheeling, madly capitalist Hong Kong to set up a business in a Vietnam which is still struggling to loose itself from the restraints of a government-controlled economy?

Christina's laugh was infectious. 'I enjoy a challenge and running a business in Hanoi is challenging, though it's a bit easier now than when I started almost ten years ago. We've all learnt a lot — me, the government and the work force.'

Was it hard finding workers who could learn the skills required and who she could trust to produce the high quality she demands?

Another laugh. 'Look at me. Chinese? Right! But what you can't see is Catholic. Which means I belong to the world's two largest diaspora. I'm a Maryknoll girl. So when I wanted to find people to work for me, I went to the church for advice. They put me in touch with people in a village about four hours south of here, in Nam Dinh Province, where most people are Catholic and a large number are Chinese-Vietnamese. We all of us know where we're coming from. I visit the factory about once a week. Most of the workers are women. The conditions are hygienic and there's absolutely no child labour. They get a fair wage and take holidays on Saints' Days. They work hard and are proud of the quality they produce. It's a team effort.'

'What about competition?' Trish asked. 'And piracy of your designs?'

'The Asian financial crisis of a few years back cleared out a lot of the cowboys.' She laughed. 'There's a lot more realism and a deeper understanding of what's required now. Among those of us who have survived, there's a comradeship. You develop close friendships very quickly under these conditions.'

Tien Long, the former 2IC in our department who was 'rotated' sideways to become head of staff training, dropped by our office during the following week and once again raised the subject of a seminar on news-gathering. It had been back in August that he had first mentioned it, more or less in passing. Now he was a little more definite about timing.

'I'm thinking about holding it in the new year, probably around March,' he said. But he was not very clear about what part we might have to play in it.

'You might like to talk about modern newswriting,' he went on, 'also broadcast and interview techniques, that sort of thing.'

Once again the vagueness of the whole thing, plus the fact that it was at least four months away, gave the impression that there was no real urgency. But Long wasn't letting us off the hook.

'I wonder if, in the meantime, you could prepare a report,' he said, 'on methods of staff training and areas in which we could improve the writing and interviewing techniques we use here?'

'A report? Staff training? You mean here, in the English section?' Iain asked.

'Yes, but also any ideas you might have about training of reporters in general, that I could translate into Vietnamese.'

'Ah well, I guess so. When do you want it?'

'Oh, no hurry. When you've got time.'

Mmm. Well, we talked it through and started putting something together a few days later. However, it quickly began to dive out of control, so that it had little to do with staff training or techniques and became more of a 'View of the Future for VOV5', in which we delved into the whole concept and importance of English-language broadcasting in a developing country like Vietnam.

Apart from the obvious countries in the region where English is widely used — like India, Singapore, Malaysia, Hong Kong and the Philippines, which have had radio and television broadcasting in English for many years — other countries in Asia have introduced or stepped up their AM and FM radio transmissions in English, notably Indonesia, China and Thailand.

As we've mentioned, some two billion people around the world speak English competently, either as a first or second language and, with many millions more wanting to learn, there is a great need for professional-standard English-language broadcasting in many countries. At least, that was the point we made in the paper we prepared.

We argued for a significant expansion in English-language broadcasting. At the present time, VOV5 (the English service), in addition to its short-wave transmissions overseas, shared the 105.5FM frequency with four other languages, French, Russian, Chinese and Japanese. Admittedly it had the lion's share of the time, with five rebroadcasts and updates daily, but, we stressed, the idea of changing languages throughout the day made for major difficulties in creating continuity and building a loyal audience. It would also pose difficulties in developing any commercial opportunities for an English-language network, one of the steps apparently favoured by the government as a means of paying for the operation of VOV5.

Consequently, we plugged, as a first step, for the allocation of a separate frequency, dedicated to English-language broadcasting. We tried to point out the benefits of improved, entertaining and informative broadcasting in English. It would, for example, generate an increased awareness among Vietnamese listeners of their part in a globalised world. But more importantly, it would also signify to Vietnam's international trading partners, aid providers, the World Trade Organization, and a host of other international bodies that the country was continuing to embrace the concepts of freedom of speech and expression that go hand in hand with a modern, democratic society. This, in turn, would benefit Vietnam in its relations with other nations.

Feeling a bit as if we'd been up on a soapbox for most of the document, we did include a bit of what Long had originally asked for in the last few pages with some thoughts on our views on news and current affairs reporting and writing, journalistic style, presentation and on-air techniques, as well as interview methodologies.

Although it had been a bit of slog, by the time we'd finished it and handed it to Long, bearing the grandiloquent title 'VOV5 — A View of the Future', we felt quite pleased with it. We may not have, if we'd realised how effectively we'd locked ourselves into a commitment further down the track.

It was around this time, during the second week in November, that the media, including our VOV radio bulletins, were suddenly filled with news of a sensational archaeological discovery in the heart of Hanoi, actually right next to Ba Dinh Square and the site of Ho Chi Minh's mausoleum. Archaeologists announced that they had uncovered the ruins of the ancient citadel of Thang Long, dating back over 1300 years, and described the find as the most important in Vietnamese history.

No mention was made at the time of when the discovery was made, but it soon emerged that it had actually occurred almost a year previously, in December 2002, when workers preparing a huge area for the proposed new National Assembly Building and a convention centre started to uncover vast amounts of historical artefacts. Apparently this was followed by a long period of debate between government officials, who wanted to press on with plans for the new buildings, the army, who owned the site, and archaeologists and others in the government who saw sound reasons for preserving the area, not the least of which was that it could prove to be a major tourist drawcard for Hanoi.

It's worth noting that the site is only a small part of a huge chunk of army-owned real estate right in the heart of the city to which there is no access for the general public. Vietnam never puts on the big displays of military might like those of the former Soviet Union, China and North Korea. But if they ever wanted to wheel out the tanks, this is almost certainly where they'd come from.

Fortunately, in the case of the archaeological site, the preservationists won the day, but it's a telling comment on the government's control of the media that not a word leaked out during those eleven months, despite the fact that the archaeological work continued apace in an area the size of two football fields between some of the busiest roads in Hanoi.

Tantalising photographs of some of the artefacts that had been uncovered were published in the press, the most beautiful of which were huge, ornately decorated terracotta dragons and phoenixes that had apparently been used as roof decorations for the Imperial Palace and had been retrieved from the clay-like soil virtually intact. Tens of thousands of tiles and bricks, as well as cannons, swords, spears, arrows, coins and jewels, household items and ornaments made from a variety of metals had also been uncovered in the process.

Tong Trung Tin, deputy director of the Institute of Archaeology and chairman of the committee overseeing the excavation of the site, said the significance of the finds could not be overestimated. 'The value of the excavated relics and vestiges cannot be measured in terms of Vietnamese dong, or dollars,' he said. 'They are priceless assets of the nation.'

The ruins have been identified as part of the citadel occupied by the Ly, Tran and Le dynasties, more than 1300 years ago, not long before Thang Long, the ancient capital of the Viet people, was established on the same site by King Ly Thai To in the year 1010.

According to legend, the king had ordered that a fortress and the citadel called Dai La that existed there be developed into a new capital. When he stepped off his royal barge to visit the site, he spied a golden dragon flying into the clouds. Taking this as an auspicious sign, the king named the spot and his grand city-to-be Thang Long, or Rising Dragon, 'a metropolis where men and wealth from the four corners of the world could gather and prosper'.

From a historical point of view, the discovery had come at a perfect time. Hanoi was taking the first steps in planning large-scale celebrations of the one thousandth anniversary of the founding of

*A brilliant terracotta dragon's head, one of thousands of artefacts excavated from the newly discovered Thang Long archaeological site in central Hanoi.*

Thang Long in the year 2010. Prior to this discovery, the only proof of the existence of the earlier citadel had been in the form of ancient writings and documents. Now, these meticulously crafted and magnificent relics provided clear evidence of a prosperous society, a vibrant culture and centuries of continuous occupation.

The excavation site covered some 16,000 square metres, but the archaeologists estimated that it probably extended for up to 150 hectares underneath the surrounding buildings of Hanoi. We were keen to see the diggings, but were told that no-one was allowed to visit just yet. We hoped that it would be possible soon.

That Friday, as we were getting ready to leave Hanoi for the weekend, Trish was hit by a motorbike ... and it wasn't even Friday the thirteenth. But it took the wind right out of her sails, quite literally. *Whumpff!* She heard, as well as felt, the air leave her lungs. It was completely her fault. She did what she had been told never to do. She changed direction mid-street and, by doing so, stepped into the path of a fast-moving motorbike. It happened in a nanosecond. The rider caught her with his elbow, she thought, hard on the breastbone. Winded, she fell forward into the side of a parked taxi, rendered speechless for once. The motorbike had wobbled precariously for a second or two after hitting her, before straightening up and disappearing into the morning rush-hour traffic. It could so easily have been far worse. A few millimetres either way and it would have been flesh and bone impacting on hard metal and both the rider and Trish would have had a very different morning.

She managed to record our *What's On* spots, but then the shock set in and she needed to lie down for an hour or so. Heavy doses of Ibuprofen rendered the constant pain manageable, but after a couple of weeks she had to agree with Rebecca, who had kept admonishing her that it would be more mature to visit a medical practitioner.

She did and was told, 'Nothing broken, just bruised. It'll take a week or so for the pain to ease.'

But then, the doctor was half our age, so we doubled her anticipated recovery time, because that's what happens as the years pass. It was in fact six weeks before Trish could get a full night's drug-free rest. And we doubt the motorbike rider's elbow felt too good for a while either.

During our time in Hanoi two freelance contributors to VOV5 had minor prangs. One Saturday night Dan Kirk was riding his Minsk and collided on a main road with two young women sharing an unlit bicycle. He was unhurt but gallantly accompanied the duo to hospital where he saw so many horrific sights, many as the result of traffic accidents, that he was still in need of a major debrief on Monday morning. The women had only superficial injuries and a small payment to their family sufficed.

On another Saturday, we came across a shaken Patrick Burke limping along with his battle-scarred motorbike, having just been in a scuffle with a woman rider who careered out — without looking, as was the usual practice in Hanoi — from a petrol station and collected him. Huan was also run into one lunchtime by a rider running a red light, another all-too-common occurrence.

These were all minor incidents but the death of the head of the Radio Listeners' Department of Voice of Vietnam, Tran Trong Truy, was a far more sobering event. Again, it was another rider charging across a red light who scuttled him one Sunday lunchtime. His mother, riding pillion, was thrown clear and was unhurt. But he hit the tarmac with his head, which was crushed like an eggshell.

Even following that event we couldn't have a sensible conversation about the recklessness of driving without a helmet. 'Too hot' and 'too restricting' were the most commonly cited excuses. In the meantime, we were both even more careful when crossing Hanoi streets.

At least a couple of times during the year AVI, the aid organisation that sent us to Vietnam, held what it called 'an in-country meeting' of as many of its volunteers as it could get together. This was often quite a difficult procedure as many of them were working in the field and operating in fairly remote places. It was also complicated by the fact that some were in the south, others in the central highlands and the rest in the north of the country, so getting everybody together at one time could be quite expensive.

We had been to a dinner with other AVI volunteers in Hanoi a couple of weeks after our arrival there but nothing formal had been arranged since. Now we were advised that Scott Rankin, the acting In-country Manager for Vietnam, would be coming up from Melbourne to direct a three-day workshop with all of the AVI people working in various parts of Vietnam. Rebecca was asked to come up with suggestions as to where to hold it and queried our thoughts.

'Ha Long Bay,' we both said. 'We can have it on a boat on Ha Long Bay. We can go swimming ... maybe we can even go kayaking.'

Rebecca required no convincing. In fact, it was her unspoken preference before she mentioned it to us. However, the emailed suggestion to Melbourne that we organise kayaks for part of the trip fell on rather fallow ground. 'This is meant to be a *working* workshop,' came the reply. 'Kayaks are not really part of the formula.'

After some rather barbed comments about 'all work and no play makes Jack a dull boy' and that a couple of hours' kayaking out of three days wasn't much to ask, Rebecca won approval to organise a boat to take ten AVI people out into Ha Long Bay the weekend.

We left for the trip late on the same morning that Trish had been hit by the motorbike. For a while, as we were recording *What's On* that morning, we thought we might have to drop out, but with the pain subsiding and the lure of the trip on Ha Long Bay present, we met up with the rest of the crowd at the Tamarind Café to take the bus. By early afternoon we had boarded the *Hai Au*, a large timber vessel purpose-built in a style not unlike an oversize Chinese junk, but fitted out with a dozen comfortable cabins, each with small bathrooms, and were sailing off into the bay.

Ha Long Bay, which we had previously visited with our son and his family during early October, is one of the most extraordinary sites in Vietnam. A unique geological feature and recognised as one of the great natural wonders of the world, it has not only become a tourist magnet, but has been listed by UNESCO as an important World Heritage site.

More than 3000 steep and often jungle-clad islands rise from the emerald waters of the Bac Bo Gulf, which covers an area of some 1500 square kilometres to the north-east of Hanoi. The islands are filled with grottos created by the wind and the waves, as well as countless large caves.

We had met two or three of the other AVI volunteers, apart from Rebecca, previously, and now, as Ha Long City slipped lower on the horizon and we sailed between the stunning craggy islands of the bay, we sat around on deck having a beer and getting to know each other.

They were a good mob and we felt proud to be a couple of them. We don't mean puffed-up proud: we mean honoured to be on the team, none of whom were puffed up. We sometimes think it would be easier to introduce yourself as a cross-dressing bank manager than to say you are a volunteer. 'Aid worker' is probably more socially acceptable — 'volunteer' sometimes carries the implication of Christian do-gooder, which throws some people. Aid workers are not quite so challenging.

Our experience has been that, in general, people react in one of two ways when it transpires that you are a volunteer. If you are young, the assumption is that you can't get a 'proper' job and that you are just filling in time until you can. If you are at the other end of the age spectrum, it's thought that you are just filling in time before you die. And whatever your age, it's taken as read that you have a hidden agenda and that anyway, 'you're *only* a volunteer'. So it was good to spend time with a few kindred souls, not to have to dissemble or explain, but instead to be taken at face value and to share experiences without restraints. We came away from the weekend feeling that it's at this hands-on level that the world can strive for healing.

There was Beverly Wickham, a nursing sister based in Ho Chi Minh City, who was helping to run a clinic for people with HIV/AIDS. She was working with the Red Cross there, disseminating information to at-risk people — especially prostitutes and detainees in re-education camps — about HIV prevention strategies. Her task was made increasingly difficult by the fact that some in the government have considered both AIDS and prostitution as 'social evils' brought into Vietnam from the morally bankrupt West. Prostitutes and people with AIDS, according to them, are not really worth investing time or money in. She was a widow and a grandmother and Vietnam was the fourth country in which she had worked as a volunteer, having previously spent several years in Cambodia, the Solomon Islands and East Timor.

Then there was Sebastian Buckingham, an agricultural scientist, about to be married, but who had brought along scores of photographs not of his bride-to-be but of cardamom bushes. And not only the plantation of bushes, close to the Chinese border, but of the whole planting and harvesting process from go to whoa and who explained in endearingly enthusiastic detail how, living rough in the bush, he had built up the skills of the local farmers to such a level of sustainability that they could now make a living from selling the spice into the voracious and enormous market of Vietnam's northern neighbour.

Jo Maloney, an appealingly loose-limbed practitioner of yoga, was working as a community development adviser with the Forestry Science Institute of Vietnam, also in the field and particularly with women. She had some funny–sad stories around the issue of the government and NGOs trying to break the tragic cycle of poverty by encouraging the purchase of inappropriate farm animals.

David Payne was the young Australian director of the Centre for Non-Government Organisations in Vietnam. Technically, he was not an AVI volunteer as he was paid a reasonable salary by the Centre and we think AVI paid his medical insurance and airfares. It was a sort of half-and-half deal. David, a sincere and thoughtful Christian from Sydney, was responsible for co-ordinating the 514 non-governmental organisations from twenty-six nations and territories worldwide that operate in Vietnam. All up, they have funded more than 1600 programs across the country with a total disbursement of some US$700 million. So, in one sense David could fairly be described as the CEO of a multimillion dollar, multinational company.

He was also dating Ly, an attractive Indian-educated Vietnamese girl whom we had met at a Mexican music night some months previously, where we'd seen her dancing a mean tango and salsa. We suggested he do something about firming the arrangement up and tying the knot 'before some other lucky bugger grabs her'. We took some personal pleasure when he announced the engagement a few weeks later, although he was still being a bit cagey about setting a date for the actual marriage.

Then, of course, there was Rebecca Hales, teacher extraordinaire, who let rip with her dissatisfaction at the way the administrator of the university where she was employed also ran her own private teaching institution. Rebecca had been sent, under the auspices of AVI, ostensibly to train teachers to teach, but she found herself manoeuvred into teaching at the administrator's institution, as well as giving private lessons to individual students who, it had to be assumed, had paid the administrator for the favour.

'I'm not being used in the way I should be,' she complained to Scott. 'She is just getting a teacher for free and I don't think AVI should replace me when I leave.'

Scott made a note of her comments.

John Sampson and Alison Hetherington were two other volunteers who had been less than impressed with the way their journalistic skills were used by the *Vietnam News*, the English-language daily newspaper. They had arrived to find that the company employed a number of other foreigners as subeditors and that again, like Rebecca, they felt the company was just using AVI to get two free staff. So they had renegotiated their contracts, both with AVI and the *Vietnam News*, accordingly. John felt particularly pleased with doing his bit for sustainable development by more or less single-handedly creating, producing and establishing a regular weekend magazine for the newspaper. He had some pretty amusing stories to tell of his stand-up battles with the editor over censorship and other professional issues.

The business side of the trip on Ha Long Bay took the form of sort of round-table discussions in which Scott Rankin firstly spent some time explaining a number of rather dramatic developments within AVI in Australia, before listening, in turn, to the positives and negatives in the experiences of individual AVI members in Vietnam, plus how they saw the future of their particular jobs and of AVI's role in the country.

Most of the AVI volunteers, including ourselves, had become aware that there was a certain amount of turmoil being experienced within the parent body back home. We had heard indirectly that branch offices were being closed down and that several people had lost their jobs or been offered redundancy packages. But no-one from the organisation had been in touch with any of the volunteers in Vietnam to provide an official rundown of what was happening and most of us felt not only as if we were being left out of the loop but also somewhat annoyed about it.

As Scott explained it, AVI had come under significant pressure from its main source of funding, AusAID, to cut back on its infrastructure of offices and staff within Australia, which was seen as being too top-heavy in the break-up of resources and their use, both in Australia and overseas. In addition, it appeared that the program of providing upwards of 800 volunteers for service in 70 countries abroad would not automatically belong to AVI, as it had for the past 50 years, during which time it had sent some 6000 volunteers abroad. Instead, AVI would now have to bid for the right to run the program. Apparently the harsh reality of bottom-line economics had struck and AusAID was interested now in seeing what each overseas position could achieve in the area of poverty reduction, one of the major UN millennium goals. When all this was made clear, most of us appreciated AVI's difficulties, but still felt that, as the people on the ground, we should have at least been kept informed.

Fortunately, nearly everybody's individual experiences in Vietnam came out as positive, certainly from the point of view of the impact of the experience on the persons themselves. However, looking at the other side of the coin — that is, the impact of the volunteer on their particular work environment — sometimes revealed difficulties, either in the form of unexpected bureaucratic or official hindrance, or the frustration, in some circumstances, of being a woman, particularly in rural areas, taking on what was perceived to be a man's role.

During a three-hour break between the morning and afternoon sessions on Saturday, half the group took off in the two-person kayaks that we'd arranged. It proved to be a great experience. Leaving our mother ship anchored in a small cove, we headed off across the deep, calm waters, around the corner of a steep and craggy islet into a maze of other similar formations and broad channels. It was easy to imagine getting lost if one was on a longer journey, as the land and seascape appeared so similar at every turn.

The whole area is full of amazing places. We saw a low granite archway in one of the larger islands, which had light coming through from the other side. We paddled towards it and had to lower our heads for about 20 metres before emerging into a beautiful lagoon, surrounded at every point by steep, rocky and forested slopes. Re-emerging, we continued on what turned out to be a long circular sweep through the islands that eventually brought us back to the boat. On the way, we passed tiny, isolated beaches, but also two or three small protected bays where groups of fish farmers lived on floating platforms, from which nets hung and where they raised a variety of ocean fish for sale in the mainland markets.

On the way back to Ha Long City on the Sunday we stopped briefly at Cat Ba Island, the largest of some 3000 islands in Ha Long Bay and one of the very few that is inhabited. Cat Ba itself, half of which has been declared a national park, has a small number of tiny fishing villages and a fast-growing town that is generally crowded with tourists. But, as there is much more to see and do on the island, including seeing the endangered Cat Ba langur, one of the ten most endangered primates in the world, we put it on the list for a return visit.

Back in the office on the Monday we found that Tram had returned from her four months' maternity leave, in crotch-hugging pants and very high-heeled, pointy-toed boots. Happily strutting her engorged breasts she asked Trish to check whether one was slung higher than the other in her bra, a factor which, prior to her breastfeeding, would have been impossible to register.

'They're looking great. The whole of you is looking great,' Trish assured her. And she was: blooming, rounded, softened, lovely. Motherhood obviously agreed with her.

'My husband bought me these boots,' she boasted, 'as a thank-you for giving him a son. We have a live-in nanny now so it's important that I stay looking good.' She paused and smiled. 'I don't want to end up at your age looking like you do.'

Dear Tram! Such a way with words!

'Tram, mate,' Trish responded a little sharply, 'if you manage to get to my age having produced two children and then having two grandchildren and your husband still wants to make love to you (except she put it more explicitly than that), you'll be a lucky woman.' Trish gave her a big hug and they both laughed.

Then Tram showed off the photographs of her four-month-old bonnie baby and asked for help in filling in her *Anne Geddes Baby Book*, which we were amazed to find was the genuine article, not a photocopied version. There was a space for putting in some of the newspaper headlines which had appeared around the world on the day of her son's birth. 'My husband looked some up on the internet but they were all about war and killing. Horrible. Will you please find me something happy?'

Difficult.

Later in the day Iain was checking news stories as they came across our desk and was startled to find one which opened, *'Israeli terrorists today killed fifteen Pakistanis as they left a mosque in Karachi.'* He let out a little yelp and everyone looked up.

'Who did this one?' he waved the offending item in the air, 'about the Israeli terrorists in Pakistan?'

Blooming, bosomy Tram laid claim. So Iain asked her to show him the original Vietnamese version and the mistake was easily explained. I and S are the first two letters of Israeli but also of Islamic.

'You could have ignited World War III if this had gone to air,' Iain joked, 'or at the very least a diplomatic incident.'

Completely unabashed Tram sat with Iain as he drew a mud map of the present Middle East. The 1967 edition of the *Phillips School Atlas*, which was all the office had, showed the old Israel with the West Bank still as part of Jordan and the Gaza Strip as part of Egypt. He gave her a bit of a rundown on the current political situation in the area and how it had developed, including such basics as the fact that Israel is a country, while Islam is a faith.

'But I think her mind was more on G-strings and frilly knickers to keep her husband happy than on the complexities of world politics,' Iain told an amused Rebecca over dinner that evening.

'Perhaps this is the real reason why AusAID are questioning our impact as volunteers,' Rebecca suggested.

During November, education had been one of the main focuses of government attention, with the issue of millions of dollars' worth of Government Education Bonds. As with the other issue of government bonds earlier in the year, the general public, as well as government and non-government institutions and businesses, were encouraged to buy the bonds to help the government's drive to improve educational facilities across the country. As before, the bonds were 100,000 dong each, paying 8 per cent interest, with a maturity date of ten years, and everybody in the office and in every government department was expected to buy at least one. So we bought one each, in the anticipation of more than doubling our money to US$15 by the year 2013!

But it was Teachers' Day, on 20 November, when education was really in the spotlight, a day which resulted in extraordinary displays of recognition, on the part of the populace in general but students in particular, for the role played by their teachers in the education process. Teachers all over the country were honoured and fêted and given flowers or gifts by their students, in a genuine display of respect and affection that one would never see in a Western country.

There were two large secondary schools very close to our office and on Teachers' Day the streets were crowded with teenage students, a high percentage of whom rode their own motorbikes, bringing flowers and gifts for their teachers.

Rebecca found to her surprise and pleasure that she was showered with small gifts and flowers. Some of the more money-savvy students had even presented her with flowers a couple of days before the actual day — in anticipation of the price increase on Teachers' Day. The price of flowers triples on the actual day, they had told her proudly.

Vietnam, like most Asian countries, places a great deal of importance on education and pushes it as one of the main stepping-stones in its campaign to transform itself in the next two decades from being an agrarian economy into an industrialised and knowledge-based society that can compete on an equal basis in the wider world.

At present, the literacy rate in Vietnam is well over 90 per cent, one of the highest in Asia. But it wasn't always like that. In fact when Ho Chi Minh came to power for the first time in 1945, after the defeat of the Japanese at the end of World War II, it was exactly the opposite, with an estimated 90 per cent of the Vietnamese people illiterate, a damning indictment of the educational policies of the former French colonial government. A decree was issued requiring that all Vietnamese learn to read and write the national script, *Quoc Ngu*, within one year. Mass education programs were set up to provide training for students ranging in age from the very young to the elderly, with children teaching parents and spouses teaching each other. By the autumn of the following year more than two million additional people had attained a reasonable standard of literacy.

Now there are around 720,000 teachers in 34,000 schools across the country. Some 22 million pupils attend primary and secondary schools, about eight million people have attained some form of tertiary qualification, about 18 per cent of the workforce are university graduates and 21,000 have either an MA or a PhD.

About 15,000 Vietnamese students a year study abroad, 3000 of them in Australia. But in a move to boost the skill levels of young people at an even faster rate, Vietnam is permitting foreign schools to set up operations in the country for the first time. The first 100 per cent foreign-owned university is the campus of the Royal Melbourne Institute of Technology (RMIT), which was established in Ho Chi Minh City in 2002.

The attraction of institutions like RMIT is the cost; for a three-year bachelor degree course in applied science in the field of information technology and multimedia, a student will pay around US$8000, much less than if he or she is studying in the United States or Australia.

Nanci Griffith is an American country music icon who has recorded over twenty-five albums, one of the best-known of which is *Travelling Through This Part of You*, which was inspired by her visits to Vietnam. During her third visit to Hanoi, for a series of concerts, Trish arranged an interview with Nanci at the Hanoi office of the Vietnam Veterans Foundation of America, during which Nanci spoke of the things that brought her back to Vietnam.

'I come back here because Vietnam changed America forever. It changed our view of our society and our politicians. It changed the way we looked at the world and the way the world looked at us. It changed the way we looked at ourselves. It changed us all forever.'

She paused. Trish waited.

'My former husband is a Vietnam vet. *Travelling Through This Part of You* was written for him.' Another pause. 'He came home as an addict. Like so many of them did.'

Nanci's eyes filled with tears and her shoulders slumped.

While drug addiction amongst former GIs is one of the sad and unfortunate legacies of America's involvement in Vietnam, one of the most tragic after-effects of the war, from the Vietnamese point of view, is the uncounted number of landmines and unexploded ordnance (UXO) that still lie undiscovered throughout the country.

In the three decades since the end of the conflict, thousands of people have been killed and tens of thousands injured by landmines and unexploded bombs and shells. Almost every week a story would come across our desk of someone, often a child or a teenager, killed or maimed in the areas most affected in central Vietnam.

Despite ongoing programs organised by the Vietnamese government, through the Ministry of Defence and British and American NGOs, to clear explosives from areas of land, the remaining problem is not only vast but will require bucketloads of money and years of painstaking work to overcome. One of the hardest-hit areas is Quang Tri Province in central Vietnam, which covers territory on both sides of the former Demilitarised Zone (DMZ), which divided North and South Vietnam. This was one of the most heavily fought-over areas in the country, particularly during the period from the early 1960s to the American withdrawal in 1973. In late 1967 and early 1968 fierce battles raged along Route 9, which cuts east–west across the province. American air power was used extensively over the whole area and Quang Tri City, the provincial capital, was reduced to rubble. The US navy also shelled areas of the province near the coast and a network of electronic sensors, minefields and firebases called the 'MacNamara Line', stretching from the coast to the Lao border, was established.

The end result was to leave Quang Tri as the province most heavily infested with mines and UXOs in the whole country. A survey has shown that more than 50 per cent of all families have been affected in their home environment by landmines or UXOs. Twenty-two per cent have had family members injured, while 16 per cent have had their land rendered unusable because of landmine or UXO contamination.

A recent study was funded by the Vietnam Veterans Memorial Fund to produce an in-depth look at one small area around Trieu Phong, a rice-farming community in the central part of Quang Tri Province where many of the villagers are missing one or more limbs. The study found that 1270 people from this one district had been either killed or wounded since 1975. Nearly half the victims were between the ages of sixteen and thirty and 80 per cent of them were men.

Compounding the tragedy was the fact that almost 10 per cent of the incidents involved poor people scavenging for ordnance to sell as scrap metal. Thirty-two-year-old Phan Xuan Quang, quoted in the survey, says he's lost many friends this way, but he has to do it to earn extra money. As a farmer he earns less than $70 a year, but he can earn up to 200,000 dong, or about US$13, for each bomb he digs up, as scrap metal.

Since 1999, the British Mines Advisory Group (MAG) has helped to clear mines and unexploded ordnance from thirty-four communes in just two small districts of Quang Tri Province. They cleared 2190 landmines and 19,650 bombs, shells and other unexploded weapons in the process, which gives some idea of the size of the problem.

Apart from the personal tragedies and grief incurred in the continuing story of death and injury from this grim residue of war, there is also the huge impact caused by the loss of arable land, which diminishes the productivity of significant parts of the country, inhibiting development activity and preventing people from climbing above the levels of poverty that have plagued Vietnam during decades of colonial rule and devastating wars.

A book that highlights many of the various tragedies that have beset Vietnam in the wake of the war with the United States is Andrew X. Pham's *Catfish and Mandala*.

'What's this about?' Quynh asked, picking up a copy Trish had carelessly left on top of our desk. We say carelessly because we were invariably careful enough to put 'sensitive material' — which a photocopied book, unavailable through regular outlets, certainly was — out of sight in a desk drawer.

Quynh began to leaf through the slightly smudged pages. 'It's the story of a Vietnamese–American, a Viet Kieu,' Trish replied, using the faintly pejorative Vietnamese terminology, 'who returns to his homeland in an attempt to discover who he is, to reconcile his history with his present.' Ignoring her soppy psychobabble, Quynh continued to skim.

'Can I borrow it to read?' he asked and when Trish paused he added, 'I'll give it back.'

Embarrassed that he might have mistaken her hesitation for anxiety that he wouldn't return the book, Trish quickly stammered, 'I think, perhaps … umm, the book is not sort of … umm, available, here. You know, in bookshops.' Quynh made no response. 'And it's not a very happy book,' she added pathetically, 'but please, do, borrow it.'

To say that *Catfish and Mandala* is 'not a very happy book' is a gross understatement. That would be because, in addition to being a very unhappy man, Andrew X. Pham is also chock-full of anger.

His book seethes and boils with these emotions. Even though these are understandable responses to what he and his family have endured, the result is not pleasant reading. For example, an early chapter gives a confronting description of his father's knife-edge scrabble for existence in the Minh Luong prison and labour camp. He had been incarcerated there after his entire family as well as 300 other people who were heading for the coast, hoping to flee the country, were trapped outside the southern port city of Rach Gia by a Viet Cong road barricade.

It was a quiet news days and there were only a couple of other people in the office. Several of them were off, moonlighting no doubt. Within half an hour Quynh was back and Trish looked up to find him leaning against the square supporting pillar beside her desk and hidden from sight of the others, tears coursing silently down his slim face.

She looked down again, unsure how to react.

'I had no idea,' Quynh spoke softly. He held the borrowed book in his limp hand. 'I have always wondered, and never been able to understand, why they hated us so much. I have never known that we did such things.'

Trish knew he was referring to the description of the extreme mental and physical torture Pham Van Thong, the author's father, had been subjected to in the re-education camp.

She could find nothing to say and, after a little while, Quynh collected himself and went back to his desk, taking the book with him.

In the decades since it ended, the war between Vietnam and America has come to be recognised as far more complex than many, perhaps the majority, of Americans understood it to be. The same, we came to think, could probably be said of the majority of Vietnamese.

Historians now see it in part as a religious war. John F. Kennedy, the first Catholic President of the United States of America, and the enormously powerful Catholic lobby were almost certainly partially blinded in their visceral support for South Vietnam's President Ngo Dinh Diem, a staunch Catholic who'd received his religious training in a seminary in the United States.

With the benefit of hindsight, it may now also be seen as largely a civil war. Northerners and Southerners had always been as different from one another as the proverbial chalk and cheese. The difference in their experiences, stretching way back across the centuries, meant that they were more like cousins than siblings. The concept of a united Vietnam was in large part an intellectual construct. But the North had its way. That is now a given.

It's been suggested in recent years that what both Northerners and Southerners alike should do now is begin to be honest with themselves about the darker truths of the conflict. The thinking is that they have to do this, because a lie or a denial is fallow ground in which nothing deeply good can grow and so, unless they do so, they won't be able to truly move forward. Perhaps, with nations it's the same as with individuals; a sign of courage and maturity to say, 'Sorry.'

## A FUNERAL AND A WEDDING

*'An elephant obtained, one demands the fairies'*

World AIDS Day, on 1 December, was marked in Hanoi by a documentary photo exhibition opened at the Press Club by the Vice Minister of Health, Professor Pham Manh Hung, and attended by UNDP Resident Representative Jordan Ryan and representatives from the sizeable number of international NGOs working in-country in the AIDS area, including our friend Patrick Burke. He looked only slightly less stressed than he had before a recent holiday in Australia.

'I'm learning not to drive myself so hard,' he assured us.

We doubted that, feeling that it would be next to impossible to avoid being consumed by your job if you worked in the area of HIV/AIDS. This is especially so in the many parts of the world, including Vietnam, where government policy stereotypically links the disease to 'social evils' (code for drug abuse and prostitution).

A survey of 200 workers in Vietnam, carried out by the UN's International Labour Organisation (ILO), has revealed that 70 per cent believed their companies should not employ HIV/AIDS carriers, while 62.5 per cent said infected people should be isolated in separate work units. Dr Le Bach Duong, a consultant to the ILO, reported that 'there are even opinions that infected people deserved their fate and should be dismissed from their job, separated or controlled'. RoseMarie Greve, ILO Vietnam director, commented that with such treatment, 'their fundamental right to equal treatment would be violated'.

Reactions like this are of course based on ignorance and fear, emotions that are perhaps more understandable in a country which has for so long been closed to the wider world and in which the hard scrabble for a basic living may go some way to hardening people's hearts towards those who they judge to have strayed off the unrelentingly straight and narrow path. HIV/AIDS, we had frequently been told, was still all too often seen as a 'Western disease' imported by foreigners. This view was tacitly encouraged by a government that was only too happy to let the major burden of work and spending in the area be carried out by foreign NGOs.

Vietnam's Ministry of Health estimated that there were more than 160,000 HIV carriers at the end of 2002. Independent experts, however, say the figure could be as high as 300,000 and growing at the rate of forty new cases every day. While it is true that intravenous drug use remains the primary cause of transmission in Vietnam, infections by sexual contact are on the rise and are showing up with an increasing frequency among women and younger Vietnamese.

RoseMarie Greve points out that 'non-discrimination is not only the right thing to do, it simply is good business. Educating workers about HIV and AIDS will help avoid costly workplace conflict. In a supportive workplace workers may be more willing to learn about HIV/AIDS and to get voluntarily tested.'

There are no quick, easy, sure-fire ways of dealing with the deadly epidemic, but an exhibition of captioned photographs, such as the one presented on World AIDS Day, certainly helps in the areas of public education and consciousness raising. The shots showed HIV-positive people, some of them with AIDS, in their daily lives, with their families, friends and work colleagues. They were extremely raw. Perhaps the most touching, taken just a few days previously, showed a couple getting married. The bridegroom was HIV-positive. He and his wife, holding hands, were in the audience. It would be hard to overestimate the courage of this public act and it was heart-warming to notice how many people approached them to offer their congratulations.

But perhaps the most significant display was made by the Vice Minister of Health, Professor Pham Manh Hung, when at the close of the formal speeches he announced that one of the HIV-positive attendees was celebrating his birthday and, calling him forward, presented the very young man with a bouquet of flowers and gave him a warm embrace.

In addition to the publicity and activities attached to World AIDS Day, the first few days of December seemed pretty full for several other reasons. The whole country was building up to the opening of the SEA Games in a few days' time. There were activities and stories dealing with the International Day of the Disabled, and Ron Marchant, an Australian we had met a month or so earlier, was back in town to oversee a revolutionary change in Vietnam's currency. But perhaps most interesting, from our point of view, was the impending arrival in town of a couple of senior executives from Australia's largest commercial broadcasting organisation, Austereo. They were apparently coming for talks with VOV about commercial radio opportunities in Vietnam.

Hello! A commercial radio network in Vietnam? To say our ears pricked up is putting it mildly.

We had learnt of the upcoming visit a few days previously on VOV's internal grapevine and, seeking to find out a little more, contacted the senior Australian trade official in Vietnam, Tim Gauci. Tim was surprised to hear of the Austereo visit, but after a couple of phone calls to Australia, quickly confirmed it and set up a meeting with the two men, Peter Harvie, the chairman of Austereo, and George Chapman, director of Austereo's highly successful broadcasting operations in Malaysia.

The day before their arrival, we had lunch with Tim at the upmarket Vine Restaurant, in Tay Ho district on the northern side of West Lake. Tim was interested in getting a little more of a background to the existing set-up at Voice of Vietnam from a grassroots level and perhaps sounding us out on some of the individuals and personalities in the hierarchy, as well as their policies. In other words, picking our brains. That was okay. We didn't mind and said as much. If we could do anything to help in the process, we'd be happy to.

As a result we joined Tim, Harvie and George for dinner the following evening at the Wild Rice Restaurant and learnt quite a bit more about the project.

'This is just a preliminary visit,' Peter explained. 'It's come as a result of the short visit to Australia in September by the group from Voice of Vietnam.'

'We thought the visit had been only to talk to the ABC and Radio Australia,' Iain said, 'to sign an MOU.'

'It was initially,' Peter responded. 'And at the time, we knew nothing of it. It had nothing to do with us. But apparently Hien, the VOV Director General, or one of the others in the group asked Russell Balding, Managing Director of the ABC, or Jean Gabriel Manguy, head of Radio Australia, how they could commercialise the operation at VOV. "You're talking to the wrong people," they had said. "We are completely non-commercial. You should be talking to Austero." So they got in touch with us and we had a brief meeting in Melbourne before they all flew back to Hanoi.'

'Were they wanting to commercialise the whole operation … everything?' we asked.

'Well, it was fairly broadly put. It's the Vietnamese-language channels they're talking about. They wanted suggestions. And what we said was that we might be interested in setting up a completely separate "Easy Listening" channel along the lines of Triple M, or the Today FM programming in Australia. And we pointed to what we'd done in Malaysia and in Greece, and in the United Kingdom, but we stressed that it shouldn't be a part of the VOV structure and we would need to be able to run the thing ourselves.'

'Wow!' Iain said. 'You'd have thought that would have been the end of it. What did they say?'

The concept of any communist government, particularly the Vietnamese government, which has total control of all of its media — and above all, its electronic media — ceding *any* degree of control to any outside organisation, let alone one from another country, was a bit difficult to take on board.

'Well, the good thing is that they didn't back off,' Peter said. 'I think they appreciated the fact that we would be fairly non-controversial and non-political and that any news components in the mix could originate from them.'

George nodded. 'They wanted us to put together a proposition, a business plan that would give them an idea of how it would all operate ... how we could make money and they could make money out of the whole thing. Obviously, it's not going to happen immediately. We've got a rough outline for them and it's probably going to take a few visits to sort it out, but this is the beginning.'

'Once we get the details sorted out in principle,' Peter put in, 'we could go ahead, but we're not going to put a lot of money in unless we can do some pretty thorough surveys. We'd want to know what the audience is and what it could be, the possible advertising revenue and so on, and that's going to take a bit of groundwork. But if they don't measure up to our expectations, it'll be us opting out, not them.'

We left them that evening with our wishes of good luck and the exciting feeling that broadcasting in Vietnam could well be in for some big changes.

At the time of our prize-winning effort at singing the English version of the SEA Games song we'd hardly thought about the Games themselves. But now they had arrived and the song could be heard issuing from radio and television sets in shops and houses at all times of the day. You couldn't walk down any street without hearing it at some stage or other and it also resounded around our courtyard from morning to evening like some sort of delirious mantra.

We remember seeing a little girl singing it aloud to herself as she sat on the footpath playing with her doll, while her mother squatted beside a coal burner, cooking up noodles for sale to passers-by. We gave the little girl the surprise of her life by walking up to her and singing along with her in English. At first she looked amazed and apprehensive that a couple of 'foreign devils' would come up to her and do such a thing. Then she smiled and laughed and so did her mother.

The Games themselves were a watershed event for Vietnam. It was immensely important to the government to prove to its neighbours and to the wider world that it could run such a high-profile, complex international event as these Games. It was to be a showcase of Vietnam's new, open and increasingly democratic society that required a considerable relaxation in rules and regulations across a wide range of activities, not least of which were those involving the media and freedom of the press.

There had been a considerable amount of tub-thumping on the part of the Vietnamese media about how many medals they were going to win and how well the Games had been organised and would be run. With more than 5000 athletes competing in over 400 events in thirty-two different sports, at venues across the country, the Games were not exactly Olympian in scale but they did present an enormous organisational task for Vietnam.

Some 40,000 spectators packed Hanoi's My Dinh Stadium to see the spectacular opening ceremony begin with the arrival, from the darkened sky above, of twelve parachutists carrying first the SEA Games flag, followed by the flags of the eleven South-East

Asian countries competing: Brunei, Cambodia, East Timor, Indonesia, Laos, Malaysia, Myanmar, the Philippines, Singapore, Thailand and Vietnam.

But it was the people in the streets who seemed to be enjoying the Games most. They really let their hair down. It had begun the night before the official opening ceremony when a preliminary match in the soccer program was played between Vietnam and Indonesia. When Vietnam won, Hanoi, and we presume all of Vietnam, went crazy. When we came out from having dinner with Peter Harvie and George Chapman of Austereo, the streets had been jam-packed with people on motorbikes carrying huge gold-starred red Vietnamese flags as they roared up and down, shouting and singing.

The following day, the opening day, the chaos in the streets was even greater. Not having tickets to the opening ceremony, we had gone to an exhibition at the Goethe Institute. Upon leaving, we had found the bedlam in the streets made it impossible to get a cab or any other form of transportation. The only alternative was to walk home amid the happy, chanting throngs of pedestrians and motorcyclists. They rotated rattles, banged drums, blew whistles and did wheelies on their motorbikes, all the time watched benevolently, and somewhat nervously, by khaki-clad policemen. The word was out that they all had to be off the streets by midnight. We didn't stay up to see if they complied, but consoled ourselves that, in terms of visual entertainment, the walk home had been almost as good as going to the opening ceremony.

Vietnam–Australia relations experienced a minor blip in early December when Australian public broadcaster SBS suspended television re-broadcasts of news programs produced by VOV-TV. We'd been loosely following the kerfuffle which had erupted in October when the multicultural network first put the half-hour program *Thoi Su* to air as part of its 'World Watch' series.

We hardly watched any local television programming in Hanoi, largely because it is so dire unless you enjoy men in army uniforms crooning against painted backdrops of peach blossoms. So we hadn't seen *Thoi Su* and didn't even know it if was produced specifically for an overseas Vietnamese market or if it was part of the local programming schedule. Madame Hue had told us a couple of months previously, with a little touch of pride, about its anticipated broadcast by SBS. She made no further comment as on-line news started to filter through that *Thoi Su* had caused something of a ruckus. Then a couple of stories came across our desk about 8000 people demonstrating outside the Sydney headquarters of SBS, demanding that the show be dropped.

Now that Tram had returned to work, our gossip sessions were back to full strength and Trish found herself struggling to explain why and how, if Australia was such a free and democratic country, a broadcaster could be pressured into dropping a program.

'Well that's exactly why,' she said. 'It's because it is democratic that people are free to have their say, and big corporations like SBS have to take notice.'

Their expressions all showed that they did not comprehend this totally alien concept.

Huan asked, 'What did the demonstrators not like?'

Suddenly the penny dropped. What the VOV5 news stories had completely failed to mention, and what our colleagues in the office had also not grasped, was that the demonstrators were all *Vietnamese*-Australians. And, when Trish explained that they *were* Vietnamese, they still didn't get it. In fact it seemed to make it even more incomprehensible. So she elaborated and tried explaining that almost all these people were refugees from the South, who had suffered physically and mentally at the time of reunification. Many of them had been imprisoned in re-education camps and all of them had risked their lives to flee Vietnam on an uncertain journey during which they faced further hardships and dangers. A large percentage of them had also had to endure incarceration in refugee camps before they finally made it to Australia. There, they had to struggle to begin their lives all over again, in a very foreign and not always too welcoming country, where they were often dismissively labelled as 'boat people'.

They looked at Trish blankly, totally unaware of this history.

'They saw the television program as biased propaganda for a political system which harmed them,' Trish said, quoting a sentence from an Agence France Press piece she had taken off the internet and read to them. They were the comments of Tien Nguyen, president of the Vietnamese community in Sydney, who claimed that the program *Thoi Su* created 'psychological damage in people who had fled their homeland to escape the communists and caused many to experience post-traumatic stress disorder'.

Trish did her best to explain that, although Vietnam has been changing and evolving over time, in the minds of many of the people who left the country it remained frozen some time back in the 1970s. Particularly for these Viet Kieu living in Australia, their idea of Vietnam is remembered as a place of terror, grief and fear. So their distrust of the current government understandably remains high and their reactions against the television program were based on past experiences, rather than those of the present.

However, if Vietnam's relations with Australia were put under a slight degree of strain over the SBS affair, they took a big step forward with the United States during early December, when a landmark agreement was signed to provide direct air services between the two countries. The five-year aviation agreement allows airlines of both countries to provide flights between Hanoi and Ho Chi Minh City and several major US cities, including Los Angeles, San Francisco, Seattle and Chicago, as well as unlimited code-sharing arrangements. Initially, the Vietnamese carrier would be just Vietnam Airlines, while both United Airlines and Continental would be the two American carriers granted access to Vietnam.

For twenty years the United States maintained sanctions against the Vietnam government, which inhibited direct travel between the two countries. After diplomatic recognition in 1995 and the bilateral trade agreement in 2002, trade, commerce and travel have escalated rapidly. One of the offshoots of the negotiations leading to the aviation agreement was the scrapping of what was known as the 'dual fare system' by which foreigners were charged more than Vietnamese for tickets on the same internal flights. For example, a Vietnamese would pay US$87 for the popular flight between Hanoi and Ho Chi Minh City, while a foreigner would be required to pay US$106. The new arrangements, apparently linked to the international aviation agreement, eliminated any discrimination, with both foreigners and locals now paying a compromise price of US$96.

Life was very full for us now. There was hardly an evening that wasn't accounted for but, just occasionally, we yearned to veg out. Slumping in front of the telly wasn't really an option, due to the quality of the programs, so we were delighted when we heard rumours that a new cinema, showing English-language and foreign films, was going to open in Hanoi.

It transpired that it was a private venture developed by Gerry Hermann, an American we had met briefly at the exhibition at the Goethe Institute on the night of the opening of the SEA Games. Gerry has had a career as a film writer in Hollywood, spent some time working in Australia, established a financially rewarding advertising business in Ho Chi Minh City and says he is now happy to spend the rest of his life in Hanoi which he loves with a passion. The guidelines under which Gerry had to operate his new venture demanded that he run a not-for-profit cinema club, showing classic movies. It was to be called the Hanoi Cinematheque and would operate from a central location.

We were keen for him to get it up and running, but because of the delicacy of his relations with various government departments, he made us promise not to mention its imminent opening on *What's On*.

Huu Ngoc, who is regarded as something of a national treasure, announces, with a touch of whimsy, that 1000 + 1000 + 900 + 80 + 30 = 1 is a succinct formula for describing Vietnam's history and he can do it all, in an entertaining and informative manner, in just forty-five minutes, in any one of five languages. Oh and by the way, he's in his mid-eighties.

Huu Ngoc is a writer, journalist, translator and researcher on culture. Whenever anyone asks him what task he is working on at present, he gives the same enigmatic answer: 'Import and export... dealing strictly in culture.' We had also become regular readers of his 'Cultural Snapshots' column, published every weekend in the *Vietnam News*, and were delighted by Lona Thwaites' invitation to join her for one of his always packed talks.

At 8.00am Huu Ngoc gallantly met us in the lobby of the Sun Way Hotel. Despite his age he disdained the elevator and led us, in a spritely manner, up two flights of stairs to one of the hotel's meeting rooms where a group of American 'travellers' — as distinct from tourists — were engrossed in watching a video documentary about Huu Ngoc, his life and work.

These people, mostly professionals in their fifties and sixties, emanated the confidence that comes with affluence and the inherent knowledge of your county's global status as a superpower. Yet Huu Ngoc, physically fragile and rheumy-eyed with age, metaphorically loomed over them, an intellectual giant. The years had not dimmed his mental or verbal skills and, in a dazzling display of wit, charm and extensive knowledge, he mesmerised them with the breadth of his understanding of world politics. Stitching it all together like a piece of beautiful lacework, he left them with no misunderstandings about the dense and turbulent history of his people.

Jotting out his equation on the large sheets of white paper hanging beside him and flipping them over with a flamboyance that belied his birdlike proportions, he performed his spellbinding wizardry at such a pace that his audience was hard pushed to keep up. Not once did he falter or slow, deftly using his mastery of Russian, French, German, English and Vietnamese to weave his way across the centuries and through the comings and goings of would-be conquerors.

'My equation,' he warned us, 'is only a very approximate periodisation, a rough rounding off of the dates to help make recall easier.'

We paid attention. After announcing each figure in the equation he expanded on his remarks.

'One thousand: for 1000 years before Christ ... the formative period for the Vietnamese national identity. Civilisation of the Viets in the Red River basin. Bronze Age.

'Plus 1000: 179 BC–AD 938. Chinese domination. Numerous insurrections.

'Plus 900: from 938 to 1858: 900 years of national independence. National dynasties. Territorial expansion to the south. Relations with China: cultural influence and resistance to invasion.

'Plus 80: from 1862 to 1945: 80 years of French colonisation. The first French conquests date from 1858. French–Japanese occupation from 1940 to 1945.

'Plus 30: from 1945 to 1975. Wars of independence and revolution. War of Resistance to the French: 1945 to 1954, ending with victory at Dien Bien Phu. War of Resistance to the Americans: 1965 to 1975, ending with the fall of Saigon.

'All of this,' Huu Ngoc dramatically turned the big pages he had scribbled on backwards one by one over each other, 'all of this adds up to one.' He circled the figure he had drawn in the middle of a blank page. 'One nation. Vietnam.'

We, chastened products of a mere 200-year history, grappled with this thought. Huu Ngoc went on to finish his overview with a brief round-up of efforts since 1975 to overcome social and economic crises up to the point of the introduction of Doi Moi, the politics of renovation, which began in 1986.

We were to meet Huu Ngoc on several more occasions and even be given the honour of hosting a joint talk with him. With each meeting, and as we learnt more and more of his personal history, our respect for him grew.

Huu Ngoc's history talk had been on a Tuesday morning and, as it happened, that particular December day also held some historical significance for large numbers of Vietnamese, but for a couple of very different reasons — although admittedly neither was of quite the same degree of importance as the events portrayed to us by Huu Ngoc.

The first was a Thanksgiving Mass held at Notre Dame Cathedral in Ho Chi Minh City and attended by thousands of the southern city's Catholic community. Its significance was due to the fact that it was held by the new 'younger' Vietnamese cardinal, 69-year-old Jean-Baptiste Pham Minh Man, who had been appointed by the Vatican in September. He had initially been rejected earlier in the year by the communist government in Hanoi, which has been at loggerheads with the Vatican for years, but his appointment was eventually approved.

The nod from Hanoi signalled a certain warming of ties with the Vatican, although there were no diplomatic relations between the two. Catholicism, which was spread in Vietnam by the French, had long been viewed with suspicion by the communist government, because of its links with the former colonial power.

Vietnam, with some eight million Catholics — about 10 per cent of the population — holds the second-largest Catholic community in Asia after the Philippines. The government recognises six religions, but reserves the right to review any appointments. Cardinal Man's appointment was the first to be approved in ten years.

Wearing his scarlet cap and robes, Man was handed a floral garland as he entered the cathedral for the two-hour service amid the chiming of bells and thunderous applause.

There was also thunderous applause — and then some — for the other major event on that Tuesday which, once again, we seemed to get caught up in. We're talking about the semifinal SEA Games soccer match between Vietnam and Malaysia, which Vietnam won in thrilling fashion, 4–3.

We had been at a fundraising Christmas dinner held by the Australian Chamber of Commerce and, having watched some of the final moments on the Hilton Hotel's big TV screen, attempted to make our way home. If we'd thought that the exuberance and chaos in the streets on the occasion of the two previous Vietnamese victories couldn't be exceeded, we were wrong ... in spades. It was just impossible for any vehicle to move from the hotel or anywhere in the streets. Hanoi was gridlocked. Tens of thousands of people thronged the sidewalks and the streets themselves, so that the only way to get from A to B was to walk and somehow thread your way through the yelling and chanting crowds. At one point it took us close to five minutes just to cross a street, being stuck in the middle for most of it.

Everybody was either waving a huge Vietnamese flag or wearing a scarlet headband bearing the slogan '*Vietnam Vo Dich*' (Vietnam the Champions) — or both. As a matter of discretion and simple commonsense, we bought headbands and wore them as we walked home, to the obvious delight of the throngs in the street. We didn't want anyone to think we might have been supporting Malaysia in this particular contest.

Gridlock in the streets was not the only result of the SEA Games soccer matches. Quynh and Madame Hue, both soccer tragics, became glued to the office TV monitors for every match of the competition and both looked distinctly seedy when they came into the office the day after Vietnam's big semifinal win.

At one point during the morning, Huong, somewhat self-consciously, slid her chair alongside Trish to whisper, 'I'm leaving!'

Trish must have looked as though she was about to make a loud exclamation, because Huong put her finger to her lips.

'The others don't know yet. I have to be careful. For various reasons. I'm sure you understand.' (Trish didn't. But would shortly.) What she immediately did understand was that this would deal a heavy and negative blow to the dynamics of the VOV5 team. We were a cohesive group and Huong, the oldest by a decade and more, had been its leader since the English FM service had been established five years before. But she was not a member of the Party and we knew this meant she had progressed as far as she was likely to up the pyramid of power.

'Where are you going?' Trish managed to ask.

Huong shook her head. 'I can't say yet. You know why. You've been here long enough.'

When Trish remained looking bewildered, she gave a small smile and said, 'Later,' before sliding her chair off to another workstation. After only a moment she was back and whispered in a conspiratorial tone, 'Don't mention any of this to anyone else,' adding, 'only Iain,' before moving away again.

Trish was still trying to digest Huong's momentous news and imagining the impact it would have when she received a second body blow, this time from Minh Ha. She had gone across to Minh Ha's desk to check details of a story she had written. As she stood up to go Minh Ha said, 'By the way, I've applied for a job at National Public Radio.'

Trish sat back down, hard. Surprised, yet not surprised. In fact, we had intended to mention the job to her.

'It was advertised in the *Vietnam News*,' she said.

We had seen the ad. It was for a local assistant to help a correspondent open up a new bureau for the American public radio network. We had immediately thought Minh Ha would be ideal for the job. Smart. Sassy. It would be a great opportunity for her to extend her professional life and develop her career.

'My husband's not too happy. My dad's not either.' Her father, a veteran of the American War, worked in the administration department of VOV. 'But I have to think of my own future. I know

I won't go anywhere here.' She too was not a Party member. 'Please don't tell anyone. They can make it very difficult.'

Winded, Trish nodded and walked back to her desk.

Returning home that evening, after a dinner with Rebecca at which we talked nonstop about our suddenly imploding office, we spotted a notice, outlined in black, stuck to the wall at the entrance of the short alleyway that led into our courtyard. From having seen others around the city, on numerous occasions, we knew it was a funeral notice. Someone in our courtyard had died. Looking more closely, it was easy to work out that it was the elderly woman, Pham Thi Nhuong, who had lived with six other members of her family in the two small rooms next to our house. The date of her birth was shown on the notice and we quickly calculated that she was ninety-eight years old!

Nhuong was the matriarch of the family that, prior to independence, had once owned the entire courtyard and whatever other homes that had existed in it at the time. We had known that she was ailing and bedridden in this tiny dwelling, but we had never seen her. Now she was dead, and the notice, we assumed, gave details of the funeral arrangements. Iain took a digital photo of the poster, intending to ask Huan to translate it for us the following morning.

However, before we left together in the morning for our Friday recording session, the doorbell rang and, on coming downstairs, we found the old woman's grand-daughter, red-faced and teary-eyed, waiting to talk to us. We had spoken briefly to her before. Her name was Vinh Hang, an attractive twenty-year-old who had just started a degree course at the Hanoi University of Foreign Languages.

We immediately told her how sorry we were to hear of her grandmother's death.

'Yes,' she said, holding back her tears, 'the funeral will be tomorrow. We want to tell you that we would like to put a tent up in the courtyard today.' She pointed behind her to some workmen already laying out metal poles. 'We need to have a ceremony here. We hope it is all right with you.'

'Of course it is,' we both said almost simultaneously.

Later, at the office, we learnt that the marquee was an established and almost essential part of the ritual for many funerals. It was there that relatives and friends would gather throughout the day to eat and drink, somewhat in the manner of a Western wake, and where they would also burn joss sticks and make small donations in red envelopes to the family of the deceased.

'You can also visit and take part in the ceremony,' Huong told us, as we discussed it in the office that morning. 'You must take some joss sticks and an envelope.'

'How much should we put in the envelope?' Iain asked.

'About 100,000 dong' (A$10), she said. 'That is the usual amount.'

At midday we returned home from the office to find the marquee occupying virtually the whole courtyard, almost blocking off our front entrance. We edged past the opening of the tent, in which around thirty people were sitting at long tables laden with food.

'Please, will you have something to eat?' Vinh Hang asked.

'Thank you,' we said, 'but we really just want to pay our respects to your grandmother.' Hang, who was still clearly devastated by her loss, led us into their small rooms, where we placed our envelope with others on a table and stuck three joss sticks in a sand-filled bronze urn filled with already burning sticks. We had been told by Huong that we must be sure to burn an *uneven* number of sticks. 'It is bad luck to give an even number at a funeral,' she had warned.

At around 1.00pm on the following day we arrived at the parlour on Phung Hung Street where the funeral ceremony was already under way. On the footpath outside we met Mai, who was well known to all the courtyard residents. She had asked us if we would like to attend the funeral.

Up the steps and past the broad columns framing the entrance, we found ourselves in a high-ceilinged room with an ornately tiled floor, hung with wooden and silk Chinese-style lanterns and bedecked with red and gold silk banners lamenting the passing of Pham Thi Nhuong. A large horizontal banner bearing her name in gold letters on a brown background hung, with a photograph of her as a middle-aged woman, in an ornately carved wooden frame, against a backdrop of maroon velvet curtains.

Below was an altar on which were two large blue ceramic vases and two tall red candles. In front of this, a huge bronze urn, topped with a dragon, stood at the head of the red and gold coffin in which she lay.

A succession of speakers, some reading from prepared notes, whose words had been relayed by a loudspeaker system to those outside, came to the end of their speeches and almost immediately a wailing sound arose from four musicians, one playing a long, wide-mouthed, recorder-like wind instrument, two others on single-stringed instruments and another banging a drum slung across his shoulder. As the sound built, we joined a queue of people and were announced as mourners, along with the others that filed past the casket, gazing for a moment through the small glass panel that revealed the old lady's calm white face, the skin drawn tight over her almost skeletal features.

Turning around the head of the coffin, we followed the line as they gave their commiserations to a row of a dozen or so close relatives standing to one side and all wearing white bands, symbolising death and mourning, tied tightly around their heads. At the head of the reception line was the dead woman's son, the elderly, grey-haired man we would see hanging up the washing each day. At the end was a distraught Vinh Hang. We held her hand briefly and murmured our condolences before moving outside.

Shortly afterwards Vinh Hang, now openly weeping, and followed by the four musicians, led a procession from the building towards the hearse, a converted minibus, which would carry her grandmother to the cemetery. When the coffin was slid into the back of the vehicle, it began to move off slowly down the street, followed by walking mourners. On the dashboard of the bus, Pham Thi Nhuong's photograph faced outwards towards the road, while inside, next to the driver, one of the family's close friends from the courtyard sat throwing tiny oblong red paper packets from the window. These, we were told as we watched the bus disappear around a corner, symbolised packets of money and were to assuage the ghosts along the way.

The bus drove back to park for a few minutes in the roadway outside our courtyard. The musician playing the wind instrument alighted from the bus and, continuing his playing, walked into the courtyard where he was led into their tiny flat by the woman's elderly son and other members of the immediate family. Walking around inside the two rooms for a minute or so, the musician kept playing, going through the motions of collecting up the spirits associated with the departed woman, and led them out, like the Pied Piper of Hamelin — all the while watched by twenty wide-eyed children from the courtyard kindergarten — to the bus, where it was intended they should join the old woman's mortal remains on their way to the grave.

Another funeral, of sorts, occurred that evening. At least that's what the sombre atmosphere felt like among the gigantic crowds that had gathered in the streets when Vietnam lost in a very closely fought soccer final against Thailand.

The score was 1–0 in Thailand's favour right through until the last five minutes, when Vietnam's captain scored an equaliser and the home crowd went berserk. The game went into penalty overtime, fifteen minutes each way, during which everyone alternated between holding their breath and screaming themselves hoarse.

In the end, with no score during the penalty overtime, it came down to that worst-case scenario, a sudden death kick-off, which the Thais won.

Trish too was disappointed. She was not immune to fantasising about a fairytale ending. Poor, socialist Vietnam, Doi Moi-ing their way to victory over wealthy, capitalist Thailand. At least that was the dream ... showing the world, or at least the region, that they were now a force to be reckoned with. Sport as national honour and all that.

So at first Trish was sympathetic with people in our office and tried brightening them up by telling them that Thailand was a top-class team and had always been expected to win, and that Vietnam, as the underdogs, had given them a good run for their money. But when the mournful faces and detailed autopsies of play continued she rather rapidly ran out of patience and pointed out that it was only a game.

The following day, a Saturday, presented a fantastic opportunity for us to join a group that was being shown over the newly uncovered Thang Long archeological site outlined in the last chapter. This was the first time that any foreigners had been allowed to view the area.

We only made the group by the skin of our teeth and by stretching the truth a little. The visit had been arranged by the Friends of Vietnam Heritage group, with whom we'd made several other excursions, but on this occasion the emailed notice we received two weeks prior to the event specified quite clearly 'No journalists allowed'.

We quickly pointed out in our return email requesting to join the group that we were not journalists and that our visas plainly stated

'Editors/Radio Programmers'. It was a fine point but, after several more emails, it was agreed that we could join the group so long as we didn't write anything about it. As these words are written now, more than a year after the event, we feel we can be let off the hook.

Anyway, it did turn out to be a fascinating and inspiring morning. The group, consisting of about twenty Westerners, many of them foreign business or embassy people, met on the huge excavation site which sits on Hoang Dieu Street, a main thoroughfare right next to the impressive monument to the Unknown Soldier. The site is totally invisible to the general public behind a two-metre-high concrete wall that has been augmented by another metre or so of steel-framed fencing.

The Deputy Director of the Institute of Archeology, Tong Trung Tin, led us over an incredible landscape, littered still with half-buried, half-exposed artefacts, speaking all the while in Vietnamese, which was interpreted in English by an architectural scholar using a loudhailer. Much of the material had been left in place because the whole site was still a work-in-progress, so we could see big, magnificently worked terracotta pieces lying exactly where they had been for centuries.

According to Trung Tin, the oldest finds which they've unearthed date back to the seventh century and are witness to the highly developed state of Vietnamese architecture under the feudal lords of the Ly, Tran and Le dynasties. As he walked and we followed, he pointed out and explained how the soil strata revealed the varying socioeconomic layers of the historic Thang Long Citadel.

Some of the subterranean layers in the excavated area, along with many unearthed vestiges and artefacts, clearly indicate three distinct cultural layers. The deepest one, at a depth of 3 to 4.2 metres, contains vestiges from the pre-Thang Long period, dating from the seventh to ninth centuries. The middle layer, at a depth of 1.9 to 0.9 metres, yielded objects from the Dinh-Le tenth-century period and the Ly-Tran fourteenth-century period. The next layer includes

*Skeletons found in the Thang Long archaeological site: at least one showed evidence of a blow to the head.*

vestiges from the Le period between the fifteenth and eighteenth centuries, while in the uppermost level they found some shallow pits containing articles from the nineteenth-century Nguyen era.

Among these multicultural layers, hundreds of architectural relics were discovered around pillar bases, along with architectural foundations and ponds. There are also remnants of drainage and sewerage systems, plus several wells and gravesites in which were found skeletons of people who had apparently been executed. It appeared that the individuals had died with their hands bound, and with at least one of them killed by a blow to the head.

But apart from the slightly macabre aspect of those findings, it was apparent to us that the Thang Long citadel site could well rank as one of the greatest archaeological discoveries in the world in recent years. It's a bit like the Forum suddenly being uncovered in Rome. There's little doubt that it is the most important archaeological find in Vietnamese history.

Later in that week there was a 'soft' opening of the Hanoi Cinematheque, on a trial-run basis. There were only ninety seats, but they were deep and comfortable and the place was luxuriously carpeted with dark blue walls and recessed lighting. Behind the automatically opening curtain was a big screen that, as Gerry pointed out proudly, 'uses state-of-the-art technology and the most highly reflective screen material in the world'. The projection room was all fitted out and ready to go.

'It's all digital,' Gerry explained. 'No film projection at all, just DVDs projected on the big screen. But not any of these cheap pirated ones,' he insisted, 'only the proper legal ones. I'm getting them all from Singapore.'

The film was a full-length feature movie, a fascinating new Chinese film called *Together*. What made the film doubly interesting was the fact that, while the story was about the trials and tribulations and family dramas of a young violin prodigy from the Chinese provinces trying to make his way in the cut-and-thrust musical world of the capital, the teenage actor who played the central role and was himself something of a prodigy might be coming to Hanoi to perform with the Vietnam Symphony Orchestra.

'There's a bit of negotiating to do,' Gerry explained to the audience before the screening, 'but we're hoping we can pull it off in a couple of months.'

On its 'trial' night, the theatre had a full house of just on a hundred patrons, some of whom were sitting in the aisles, and all of whom gave the film a big 'thumbs up'.

The showing had been free and on an invitation-only basis, as Gerry had not yet been able to get full approval from the Ministry of Culture to open the cinema for public viewings.

'I'm still a bit worried,' he said, 'that the approval hasn't come through. It's been months since the formal application went in and I've already been working on it for several years. It's only in recent months that we've been able to settle on this property as the location. The ministry is okay about it on the surface, but I haven't got written approval yet. Everybody says, "Oh, don't worry, it'll come through, and even if it doesn't come immediately, they've given the nod so far; they won't pull the plug." '

Gerry's confidence and enthusiasm and the high quality of the project — he'd put around US$400,000 into it so far — enthused everyone who had come into contact with it. But there was a long way to go and, as we were to see, as time passed, Gerry's project would provide a sobering insight into the unfathomable and sometimes irrational machinations of the Vietnamese government when it came to dealing with and being 'transparent' in the handling of foreign investments in Vietnam.

Ho Chi Minh in the Uncle Ho portrait for which he became famous worldwide — wispy beard and hair, benign expression but always those startlingly intense eyes — graces every denomination of banknote issued in Vietnam. In mid-December, those notes were set for a radical alteration. We had known about the move since early November when we met the man behind the change, Ron Marchant, a senior executive of the Australian company Securency that produces the polymer notes used in Australia and several other countries.

When the government decided to release some details to the press ahead of the official date for the release of the new currency, a small frisson of financial anxiety ran through the always gossip-prone capital. To avoid a potentially dangerous escalation of these fears, the release date was then brought forward by a few days and the deputy governor of the State Bank of Vietnam made a public statement that the exchange rate for the dong against the US dollar was under control and that the bank 'is able to act to stabilise the market, if that is necessary'.

Vietnam has really only had just over a decade of social and financial stability and the public's memories of famine, struggle and hardship are all too recent and harsh for them to have any mental comfort zone. Even more than in nations with a longer history of stability, there is a quite understandable fear of any change. They are forever on their guard and alert for any negative signs.

Three new polymer banknotes were released to the cautious public who were assured that they would make life harder, but only for counterfeiters. Replaced was the 50,000 dong note, the most widely forged denomination. We'd been the unwitting recipients of a couple of these forgeries: once in our pay packet from the VOV paymaster and, even more unexpectedly, once over the counter at the ANZ bank. They were pretty good efforts; apparently it's the paper and lack of a watermark which give them away. We kept one as a souvenir of our gullibility. The 100,000 dong, equivalent to roughly A$10 and until then the largest denomination, was also replaced, and the third note, a totally new one, was to the value of 500,000 dong, A$50, evidently a sign that there was more money in circulation and that the economy was doing okay. Naturally they all still carried a picture of Uncle Ho.

In addition to being a deterrent to counterfeiters, another reason for the introduction of polymer notes was that they have a considerably longer lifespan than paper money, especially in the humid heat of Vietnam. This was also given as one of the reasons for the reintroduction of coins for 200, 1000 and 5000 dong, which had been shelved in 1985 because of spiralling inflation.

Members of the VOV5 team were amused rather than impressed by Iain's demonstration of the durability of the new banknotes, in which he took a somewhat excessive national pride, attempting to tear one in half, then crumpling it hard in his fist and releasing it with the air of a magician. We refrained from pointing out that they would stand up to a turn in the washing machine rather better than the paper versions, because we knew better than to imagine that these thrifty souls would be careless enough to leave notes in a pocket.

But there was another surprise in store for us when they all wanted Iain to exchange his brand-new notes for their limp, tired equivalents. When he didn't have enough to cover everyone, they asked him to please get more.

'You can get them yourselves,' he pointed out. 'All you have to do is go to the bank.'

'None of us have bank accounts,' Khoi responded.

We tried not to appear as surprised as we were, although of course we shouldn't have been.

'You don't need a bank account in order to change your notes for the new ones,' Iain assured them, then, seeing their obvious disappointment, added, 'but I will go and get some more.'

Despite these diversions, morale in the office continued at a low ebb, firstly over the impending departure of Huong — everyone now knew she was going, but still didn't know where — and Minh Ha's application for a job with the American NPR bureau, which was still pending. This was not widely known in the office so it didn't come into the overall picture, but the issue of low salary levels was still a sore point with everyone. Also, some of the details surrounding Huong's proposed departure had come into the open and contributed to the depressed feelings all round. It seems that although Huong had worked for the Voice of Vietnam for more than twenty years, and paid into a government fund — the equivalent of a superannuation fund in the West — during that period, it now emerged that she may not receive any of her entitlement.

'It all depends on whether they *want* to pay you or not,' she told us rather glumly. 'If they don't like the fact that you're leaving, they can refuse to pay it.'

She didn't say who 'they' were, just that it was somebody well up the food chain in VOV who apparently would make the decision.

'But surely,' Iain said, 'if you've paid into the fund over the years, there must be some guarantee that you'll get it back when you leave?'

'Not if they don't want you to leave, or if you go somewhere they don't approve of.'

'Approve of? It's got nothing to do with them what you want to do,' Iain said. 'Have they said this to you?'

'They've said they are examining my application to leave. And that I may get part of my entitlement, or may not. I have to go for more interviews. I don't know what's going to happen. But I've made up my mind. I have to make the change for my son ... he's going to high school in a couple of years.'

'Can you tell us where you're going yet?' we asked.

Huong smiled. 'Not yet. Soon.'

If the powers that be at VOV were having trouble showing much Christmas spirit towards Huong, we were also having trouble getting into the mood. The tempting thought had occurred that we could have a Christmas-free year, but somehow or other it always manages to ensnare and when Rebecca, who feels similarly ambivalent about the festival, had a two-metre live pine tree delivered to our house as a Christmas tree, we decided to jump into the whole process once again and had fun decorating it, much to Mai's amusement.

'Happy Christmas,' Huan said to Trish, a little self-consciously, as he prepared to leave the office on Christmas Eve.

She smiled in appreciation of his gesture and asked him, 'What is Christmas?'

'It's the day Christians celebrate the birth of Jesus, isn't it?'

Others, overhearing their conversation, came to join in. Minh Ha, Huong, Giang and Tram all described it as a Westerner's holiday at which Santa Claus came with presents. Khoi, Hanh and Thi, like Huan, knew that it was celebration of the birth of Jesus Christ.

'I think it's what you make of it,' Huan added sagely.

Giang had taken to turning up in the office wearing a Santa hat, which had become such a must-have fun accessory that on our taxi ride across town to a party at Rebecca's West Lake home on Christmas Eve we were surrounded by a sea of red hats with white pom-poms worn by individuals, couples and entire families on motorbikes, all taking advantage of the occasion to enjoy a secular celebration of their own.

Along the causeway road dividing West Lake from Truc Bac Lake, numerous stalls had been set up with an assortment of luridly coloured cardboard Santas, sleighs, reindeer and painted snow scenes, against which excited small children were having their photographs taken. Equally startling was the papier-mâché rendition of a corpulent Father Christmas, wearing a conical straw hat and sitting in his sleigh, which was being pulled by a water buffalo, the whole of which sat above the entrance portico of the Metropole Hotel, where we went the following day for our hang-the-expense Christmas dinner.

Christmas, although not a national holiday in Vietnam, nevertheless provided an opportunity for us to take some time off. By pulling out all stops, we had been able to put together enough material in advance to record six days' programming for *What's On* and put them all on tape on Christmas Eve, which was a Wednesday. This, along with the fact that we still had a couple of days' leave due to us, meant we could take the Thursday and Friday as well as the weekend off.

So, still recovering from our overindulgence at Christmas dinner, Rebecca joined us early on the Friday morning, Boxing Day, as we took off in a car provided for us by VOV for a three-day trip to see some of the attractions around Ninh Binh, some 90 kilometres to the south-east of Hanoi.

Rebecca is one of those people unfortunate enough to have been born either on Christmas Day or the day before or after. In her case it was the latter. So, fully aware that most people who have grown up with this 'impediment' are sometimes unhappy that the two events are usually rolled into one, we had some separate small presents for her birthday, which she opened in the car as we trundled southward along the crowded two-lane road to Ninh Binh.

Ninh Binh Province, which supports almost a million people, is considered the southern gateway to the Red River delta. The township itself, sitting on the northern border of the province, is uninspiring, but in recent years several of the surrounding features within the province have transformed Ninh Binh into a significant tourist destination.

But, although we took off almost immediately after we'd checked into the Thuy Anh Hotel to explore some of the province's attractions, it turned out that the hotel owner, his daughter and some of the 1000 guests they were preparing to entertain over the next two days to celebrate his daughter's wedding proved just as interesting as the tourist destinations.

We met the owner, Tong Anh De, more or less immediately we arrived, as there was a huge marquee being erected outside the front entrance of the hotel, and he was standing there supervising its erection. Handing each of us his bright-red visiting card, he proudly introduced his beautiful young daughter, who was standing beside him watching the proceedings, and, with an apology for any inconvenience it might cause, explained that they were preparing for two receptions for his daughter's wedding: one on the following day, a Saturday and the day of the wedding, the other on the Sunday morning.

'Each reception,' he beamed, 'will be for 500 people ... all from around here.' He waved his arms expansively.

We learnt more of the stories behind the big bash on our return from the afternoon's jaunt to two of the province's major tourist sites, Tam Coc and Hoa Lu. At Tam Coc, a spritely 75-year-old woman with a splendid sunrise smile, who used her feet to paddle the oars, bicycle-fashion, rowed us through some breathtaking scenery in what is known as Vietnam's Ha Long Bay of the rice fields. Huge limestone rock formations jut vertically from the green paddies as a backdrop to the journey, which takes you into and out of three large flooded caves.

Not far from Tam Coc is Hoa Lu, the ancient capital of Vietnam in the period from 968 to 1010, when the Vietnamese shook off a thousand years of Chinese domination to become the nation of Dai Co Viet. What still stands are two much-restored, but beautiful pagodas dedicated to King Dinh Tien Hoang and King Le Dai Hanh.

Returning to the hotel for dinner that evening, we found the preparations continuing at fever pitch. Not so frantically, however, that the owner, Anh De, could not take time to talk to us. We had stopped in the foyer to examine some of the photographs around the walls showing various personalities, politicians and dignitaries visiting the hotel and invariably shaking hands with him.

'My hotel was used by the athletes in the SEA Games,' he told us. 'Some of the events were held at the stadium here and, because the hotel has been upgraded to two-star level, they chose to stay here.'

'How long have you had the hotel?' Trish asked.

He threw his head back, smiling. 'Ahh. It's a long story.'

He paused for a moment to shout at some waiters who were carrying bottles of wine, telling them where to place them on temporary bar tables that were being set up in a big central hall.

'You see, I left Vietnam many years ago, to work in Bulgaria. I come from a small village outside of Ninh Binh. My family were very poor … we were a farming family. I went to Bulgaria with other Vietnamese workers to take up jobs as labourers, or at whatever work was available.'

'What did you do there?' we asked.

'I did many things, but most of the time I worked in factories … on the production line, you call it. I stayed there for nine years, saving money, before I came back home … here to Ninh Binh.'

'But surely, you couldn't have saved enough money to buy this hotel?'

He laughed. 'Oh no. There was nothing here. I bought just the land and built a small hotel with only four rooms. Then, after a while, I was able to build some more storeys on it, so that it had sixteen rooms and it was like that for some time until, two or three years ago, I used the rest of the land to put up this new building, six floors high, with forty rooms.'

And the hotel, though only rating two stars, was very impressive: clean, well laid out, well furnished, with comfortable en-suite rooms. Not bad for a boy from the bush. And it was all his relatives and friends and then some who were coming for the wedding and the follow-up reception. We weren't sure how the guest list was to be divided, but it seemed that closer relatives and friends, plus the higher-profile, more important personages and business contacts would be attending on the morrow, with all of the people from the surrounding countryside and villages, either of close, or distant acquaintance, attending on the Sunday morning.

On the Saturday, we drove 45 kilometres to the north-eastern corner of the province to spend most of the day in the Cuc Phuong National Park, Vietnam's first and one of its most important national parks. Covering 22,000 hectares of primary tropical forest, it is home to an enormous variety of rare species of flora and fauna, the vestiges of prehistoric cave dwellers, many kilometres of beautiful walking trails and a fascinating centre devoted to the rescue of endangered primates, mainly various species of gibbon and langur monkeys.

By the time we returned to the hotel, the wedding and most of the festivities were over, with only a few very inebriated guests remaining. We had a quiet dinner, played some cards and then retired. But, on coming downstairs for breakfast the following day, we found hundreds of people already seated at rows of tables, getting stuck into their food, as well as bottles of wine and beer ... at 8.30 in the morning!

These were definitely the 'B List' invitees; all men at some tables and all women at others. Many of the men wore those Russian-style fur hats, with the earflaps down, and sat with toothpicks in their mouths, smoking, shovelling down the food, knocking back the liquor, talking loudly and obviously having a great time celebrating the home-town boy's success.

At one point, while we were having our breakfast at a table in one corner, we noticed that quite a crowd of village women had developed around the glass-fronted elevator and there was a lot of 'oohing' and 'aahing'. But nobody seemed to know how to open the doors. It was then that we realised that the women had never seen an elevator. So Iain went across and pressed the button and the doors slid apart, to a peal of laughter and more 'oohs' and 'aahs', but the women wouldn't get in. So he stepped into the lift to show them it was safe and gestured to them to join him, which they did, laughing all the while, until the lift was so full the doors couldn't close. So a few had to get out.

Then he pressed the button for the top floor — the sixth — and off they went, with them all laughing and shouting loudly to one another. When the lift stopped at the top, they all piled out, but decided they'd prefer to walk back down the stairs, so Iain took the elevator back down and brought up another laughing crowd of them.

'It was wonderful,' Iain said when he returned to the table. 'They were so excited. I couldn't help feeling envious of them ...

*Excited village women crowded into the lift in Ninh Binh's new Thuy Anh Hotel. They had never seen an elevator before.*

being so excited by something that we've all become so blasé about.'

There was a childlike wonder that we, who have used lifts and escalators all our lives, no longer have. It seemed something of a loss in us.

The atmosphere in the office on our return from Ninh Binh was dismal. The general feeling was that, though Huong's imminent departure may not actually scuttle the ship, it would certainly cause it to have a heavy list. Huong, who had still not made public where she was going to be working, though there were rumours that it was at a foreign embassy, continued in her usual way to talk brightly and loudly and to laugh a lot, putting a brave face on what we all knew was her anxiety that she would not receive her financial payout. Loc sat at her desk, enigmatic and silent, Madame Hue remained aloof, while Khoi looked increasingly anxious, as the others huddled in little gangs and whispered a lot.

Energised by our brief holiday and determined to counteract this atmosphere of doom and gloom, Trish arrived for her afternoon–evening shift with armfuls of flowers, which immediately seemed to lift everybody's spirits. The search through cupboards for vases, followed by the clearing of spaces to put them, spontaneously sparked off a massive clean-up and, for an hour and more, the office turned into a scene of noisy activity.

Cloths and brooms were wielded; books and files were moved and restacked. We stood on chairs to dust top shelves. Greeting cards from listeners around the world were placed on display and we hung a series of emulation awards, which had been left lying about in a neglected stack.

Then Minh Ha suggested that we take over Long's vacated desk, which had been unused since he had left to be rotated months previously. At first we resisted the idea because the desk was at the far end of the office and, by slightly distancing ourselves from the rest of the team, it might also appear as if we were assuming some added status. We wanted to remain part of the group and not be seen as supervisors. But, once mooted, the idea was taken up by everyone else, especially when Khoi pointed out that it staked a claim for VOV5 to a bit of extra floor space.

With whoops of loud laughter (Loc had by now left the office for the day) the office furniture was shoved and lugged into new inclusive positions, so that we weren't left in isolation, then we all stood back and admired the results, which we agreed were a considerable improvement. It seemed to make the ambience less austere and office-like, more welcoming and homey. Emboldened by this positive response, Trish decided to paint the tired-looking coffee table a glossy black.

A day or so later, at a farewell luncheon for Huong, she finally revealed where she was going to work. It was to be at the Swedish Embassy as a personal assistant to the ambassador.

She was nervous about the move. 'I'll miss you all,' she said as she gestured around the table. 'But it's an opportunity I can't afford to turn down. In the end each person is responsible for themselves, no matter what the government says.'

That same 'socialist' government had waited until the day she left before finally agreeing that it would return to Huong the money she had paid in over twenty years to the employees' support fund.

It was one evening around this time that Trish returned home from work and more or less collapsed, felled by what she at first thought was a dose of the flu, but which, over the next day or so, progressed to bronchitis and finally a frightening bout of pneumonia.

# *January*

## TET — CONFIDENCE IN HUMANITY

*'New spirits fear old ones!'*

Dr Bob was not a happy man. In fact he was near to incoherent and apoplectic with rage, and Trish's consultation turned into such a major debrief for him that it almost took her mind off how stupendously lousy her pneumonia-infected lungs felt.

The good doctor, an imposingly tall man, had flung open the door to his room with such force to usher out his previous clients that it had twanged on its hinges. Staff behind the desk picked up non-ringing phones or studiously studied blank-faced computer screens while the line-up of patients, including Trish, became instantly engrossed in the waiting room's dismal choice of old magazines. Four people — a woman, two men and a teenage boy — reeled out through the surgery's glass doors into the chaos of the streets. The doctor, his countenance dark with anger, watched like a guard dog seeing off intruders, then slammed his door shut.

When, five minutes later, his nurse indicated that Trish should go in, she gave him what she hoped was a calming smile. The Australian medico's initial expletives were unprintable. After some minutes, during which time Trish sat opposite him, stifling her coughs, they had moderated to 'bunch of bloody corrupt little deadshits'.

It transpired that the woman and one of the men were the parents of the teenage boy for whom they were trying to elicit positive medical reports that were necessary for him to gain acceptance at a university in the United Kingdom.

'They've already been in here with phoney X-rays,' Dr Bob said. When Trish looked puzzled he explained. 'They're both doctors. They know the boy has TB and that would preclude him from going, so somehow they produced X-rays of someone else's lungs and tried to pass them off as his.'

Before Trish had time to drop her jaw in amazement, he went on: 'Today they brought in the results of compulsory blood tests, which would also show he has TB, but of course once again it was someone else's blood they'd had tested.'

'But,' Trish stammered, 'as they are both doctors and if they know he has TB, surely they know he will get even sicker if he goes to England to study, instead of getting treatment for his disease?'

'Oh the bastards don't care about that. Although maybe they think that if they get him there, on a clean sheet, he'll be able to get free treatment on the National Health. Who knows? They obviously don't care about him infecting 10,000 other students.' His anger drove him to exaggerate, though it is a fact that 145,000 new cases of TB are reported annually in Vietnam and 65 per cent of all cases are of the highly infectious strain.

'I hate having to do these sorts of examinations and tests,' — he all but ground his teeth — 'but it's part and parcel of the contract we have with the government which allows us to operate here. We're compelled to do them for free and to be fully and finally responsible for the results. If he goes to England and infects others, the buck stops here.' He stabbed his finger at his own chest. 'End of business. No more insurance. Off the medical register. Whole kit and caboodle. But do these bastards care? No. Not one whit. They think I'm stupid. Worse still, they think they can buy me.'

'Buy you?'

'Yes, that's why they brought the other little deadshit with them this time. Said he was a relative. But I was too quick for them. I ordered them out before they had time to offer me a bribe. If they'd tried that and it failed, their "relative" would suddenly turn out to be a tame police officer whom they'd paid off and who would then falsely charge me with having asked for money in return for accepting their phoney X-rays and blood tests. It's all happened before, with others. But so far I've been quick enough to spot the trap. You've got to keep on your toes here.'

He slumped back in his chair, his anger drained.

'Well, at least you've stopped them,' Trish said and the doctor looked at her with the pity reserved for idiots.

'They didn't scrabble up this far to give in that easily. They'll go on until they find some other way. They'll forge papers. Pay people off. They won't give up.' He pushed his glasses down his nose to glance over the top of them at her medical history, 'Now, what can we do for you today, eh?'

Although the bronchitis and pneumonia Trish had been diagnosed with laid her low for several days, the antibiotics and physiotherapy she was undergoing gradually started to take effect and she felt up to emerging one evening to take in a movie at the Hanoi Cinematheque, which was now finally open for business on a full-time basis. We had joined up as members, along with a throng of people — both Vietnamese and expatriate — which soon ran into the hundreds and before long was over a thousand.

Membership cost 100,000 dong (A$10) and Gerry Hermann was keen to stress that tickets could only be bought on production of the membership card. 'I don't want to make a wrong step here,' he said. 'We still haven't got the official green light, but unofficially we've had the word that it's all right to go ahead.'

Mmm, we both thought, bit of a worry. Not the sort of risk we'd like to be taking with US$400,000. Anyway, the first string of movies released for showing were several of the great early Charlie Chaplin films, as well as other famous vintage classics.

What now made the whole Cinematheque set-up even more interesting and attractive was that, in the courtyard where it was established, Gerry had opened a great little bar, with tables arranged around and underneath a huge tree that presented a welcoming atmosphere for a pre-movie drink or something to eat.

Just when everyone thought Vietnam had recovered from SARS, along came Avian Flu and the TV news and papers were again full of shots of masked people in protective clothing. Only this time they were spraying sacks full of chicken carcasses being shovelled into lime-filled pits. Almost 12 per cent of the country's stock, 38.3 million chickens, were killed across the nation.

As with SARS, it turned out that the disease had first appeared in China, again spreading quickly to other countries in South-East Asia and, though this time it was less of an immediate threat to humans, low levels of hygiene made it possible for people who handled infected birds, including children, to develop deadly symptoms. Within the first few weeks, fourteen people had died—nearly all children or young people.

The great fear was that the H5N1 strain of the flu virus could swap genes with a human flu virus, enabling a deadly new mutation to spread between people at an unstoppable rate. Many health workers believe this is not a case of *if*, but *when*, and are certain that a worldwide pandemic is inevitable, with the equally predictable consequence of striking hardest and with the greatest impact in the world's poorer nations. Fortunately its time had not yet come.

But the outbreak still struck a severe blow to the economy, an economy without the depth to be able to withstand too much of such punishment. So many times, in so many various ways, in Vietnam we were reminded of how little gas there is in the reserve tank.

Hanoi's rumour mill was soon cranked up to full bore with stories that H5N1 had been wiping out chickens since the middle of the previous year, but had not been officially reported. Or perhaps it had been, but had been ignored, for fear of its impact on the SEA Games.

Just as likely was that individual Vietnamese farmers whose animals had died did not report the fact to local commune officials because of the absence of any insurance or other compensation schemes. Reporting of sick animals is voluntary and relies on a sense of social responsibility. Village bureaucrats are poorly paid and may well ask for a handout to visit a farmer's small-scale backyard poultry business from which he only just manages to make a hand-to-mouth living.

So it goes on up the loosely knit social, political and health food chain to the toothless hydrahead: the United Nations Food and Agricultural Organization, the World Organization for Animal Health, and the UN's World Health Organization which, apart from having little history of cooperation, have absolutely no legal power to force individual governments to comply with recommended measures for detecting and dealing with such outbreaks.

As the epidemic spread and community fears grew, small measures were introduced. Live chickens, which had been routinely slaughtered in far-from-hygienic conditions were no longer permitted to be brought within the city limits. Gradually the sale of raw chicken meat was banned and — surprise, surprise — the price of beef and fish skyrocketed. Chicken disappeared from menus. Even eggs became unavailable.

But there were no such health and safety regulations at work in our courtyard, where the cockerel continued his early-morning vocals, spared the knife until the soon-to-be-upon-us traditional New Year festival of Tet, when he was silenced beside the communal well.

Tet was in the air. It's hard to overemphasise the importance this traditional New Year holiday holds for the Vietnamese. It's like Christmas, New Year's Day, Easter, the Melbourne Cup, the Football Grand Final and everyone's birthday all rolled together with a sprinkle of Anzac Day and Australia Day thrown in for good measure. Although the Lunar New Year is observed throughout East Asia, each country celebrates it in its own way, in conformity with its own national psyche and cultural conditions. In Vietnam, Tet is a festival of communion, purity, renewal and universal peace.

Occurring, as it does, somewhere in the last ten days of January or the first twenty days of February, more or less halfway between the winter solstice and the spring equinox, it remains first and foremost a festival of communion with nature. All Vietnamese, including those who live in big cities like Hanoi and Ho Chi Minh City, retain strong emotional ties to the land, to the cycle of the crops and to village life.

The first intimation we had in our commune, or *son*, that Tet was imminent was when Mai arrived for one of her regular thrice-weekly morning clean-ups and began planting out a bed of yellow chrysanthemums, a plant which, in the office later that day, Terrific Thi explained the Vietnamese consider noble because it can withstand cold weather and also because its leaves remain attached to the branches after they die. Trish mulled over her words and realised there was some symbolism here. It was, she understood, something to do with the nuanced layers of the relationship the Vietnamese believe exists between living people and their ancestors.

Then, as if on a signal, a forest of trees started to stream into the city. In whichever direction you looked, there were motorbikes with a potted or bagged cumquat tree riding passenger. Dozens, then scores, then hundreds, so that eventually it seemed a rarity to spot a motorbike without a cumquat tree on the back. The shiny dark green leaves and the small, bright, orange-coloured fruit generally towered above the rider who invariably wore the smile of someone who has once again managed to survive another year and was participating in a celebration of that fact. Not infrequently the tree nestled carefully between the driver and his passenger, more often than not a man and his wife. Sometimes a child would also be there on the bike, squatting at the front, between Dad's arms which were gripping the handlebars, again all of them smiling contentedly as they transported the symbol of the new year to their home.

Both cumquat tree and peach blossom branches are essential for every family at Tet. The peach blossoms are required because, according to ancient legend, a branch of it will protect the household against evil devils while the three genii, who traditionally

**Bringing home the cumquat tree at Tet: a symbol of fertility and life.**

protect people against the devils throughout the year, are away in heaven at year's end, reporting to the Celestial Lord.

The cumquat trees are a symbol of fertility and the cycle of life, and orchards all over Hanoi have nurtured tens of thousands of these trees throughout the year so that they come into a very specialised form of fruiting just the week or so before Tet. They must be perfectly shaped, a bit like a Christmas tree; they must have blossoms, symbolising birth; green fruit, denoting youth; ripe fruit, symbolising adulthood; and a few over-ripe fruit for old age.

Two days later we found ourselves the proud owners of a cumquat tree, when Mai turned up and began unloading one from her motorbike for us.

In the week before Tet, the woman from whom Trish usually bought flowers was joined on her patch outside the 1912 market by an elderly woman who squatted on a little blue stool surrounded by piles of plastic bags, which she proffered to passers-by. Trish crouched down beside her to have a look at what it was she had for sale and she emptied the contents of a bag for her to examine. All beautifully handmade from bright tissue and gold paper, there were, in miniature, three coronets, three pairs of boots with turned-up toes, three capes and a carp. Trish had no idea what they were for or what they represented but she bought a couple of sets and took them along to the office, where she was sure Terrific Thi, who over the months had become her mentor in matters spiritual, would be able to explain.

'They represent Tao Quan, the Kitchen God,' she told Trish, as always pleased that she had taken an interest. 'On the twenty-third day of the twelfth moon he goes up to heaven to give the Jade Emperor a detailed report on the behaviour of each member of the household. He's most usually represented as a single male, but is actually three people: two gods and one goddess.'

Three-in-one, one-in-three... where had that been heard before! But Trish didn't mention that to Thi, who continued: 'In the kitchen they take the form of the three stones on which the kitchen pot rests. The idea is that they watch over the family, protecting and controlling it. There is a beautiful legend about these kitchen gods.'

'Beautiful but unhappy no doubt,' Trish teased Thi, with whom she had often talked about the deep vein of sadness which appeared to run through all Vietnamese legends and folklore and which seemed to carry on even into their present-day TV soaps.

Thi nodded and, as they lined up the hats, capes and boots on the desk she told it to her. It seems that once upon a time there was a husband and a wife called Trong Cao and Thi Nhi who, although they had been married many years, had no children. The unhappiness this caused turned to bitter quarrels, but when Trong Cao became violent, Thi Nhi decided enough was enough and left. She travelled some distance to another district where she eventually married again to a loving, kind chap called Pham Lang.

Trong Cao, who deeply regretted how he had behaved towards Thi Nhi and was unable to forget her, decided to search for his lost wife. Over time he ran out of funds and was reduced to begging for alms. Ragged, poor, and all but blind from illnesses brought on by his hard travels, he eventually turned up at Thi Nhi's new home one day, after her new husband Pham Lang had gone to work in the fields. Because of his physical deterioration, Trong Cao didn't know Thi Nhi, but she recognised him and gave him money as well as a good wholesome meal, after which he stretched out on the mat and fell deep asleep. Wanting to avoid possibly embarrassing questions from her new husband, Thi Nhi wrapped Trong Cao up in the mat, took him out into the courtyard and covered him with straw.

When Pham Lang came home from the fields, he set fire to the pile of straw to make ash for fertiliser. By the time Thi Nhi realised what was happening, it was too late and, distraught with remorse, she threw herself onto the blaze, whereupon an amazed Pham Lang, who loved Thi Nhi so deeply he didn't want to live without her, did the same and the three of them were consumed together.

When she had finished the tale Trish commented, 'That wasn't just sad, Thi, that was terrible.'

'I know.' She smiled. 'But it has something of a happy ending because the Jade Emperor was so moved by their story he made the three of them into the three Kitchen Gods and every year, in the week before Tet, people try to persuade the trio to make a favourable report by preparing a farewell meal for them and offering votive gifts and a carp,' she picked up the paper fish and made swimming motions, 'on which the gods ride to heaven. After the ceremony, the fish must be released into a river or lake.'

Trish left the charming little paper outfits set up on the desk and, later in the day, when no-one else was around, Loc, who had overheard Thi's storytelling, made a point of coming over to Trish's desk where, picking up one little boot, she muttered, 'Superstition. Superstition.'

With Tet only a few days away, Minh Ha had at last heard back from the American NPR bureau chief about her job application, which unfortunately was not successful. It had been narrowed down to two, but another woman had got the job. The news was a disappointment to her and she was understandably low for a couple of days, but as Tet approached, everyone seemed to be all of abuzz if for no other reason than that it meant they would have at least five days' holiday.

This was going to require a considerable amount of pre-recording of many of the programs that would normally be put to air, either live or recorded a day or two before they were broadcast. This degree of prerecording would almost certainly not have happened in any major Western radio organisation, other than some FM music networks, but we weren't complaining, as it meant that we too would have five or six days off, which we had not been expecting.

A range of traditional foods began to appear on the large table in the centre of our office, among them the unique *banh chung*, a kind of cake made with sticky rice stuffed with beans and pieces of fat pork and all wrapped up in coconut leaves. Our landlord also suddenly appeared at the house one morning with a large *banh chung*, and then sat down to watch us as we opened it, with us making polite comments and going through the process of eating some with him despite the fact that it really didn't appeal to our tastebuds very much at all.

'But, you know,' Giang said to us in the office later, 'the *banh chung* they make now is not like it used to be.'

We both smiled at this, coming from Giang, who was not yet twenty-seven years old.

'When my grandmother used to make it, it would take many hours and it would go on long into the night ... and all the family would take part ... in stirring the big boiling pot and adding the different ingredients. It was all part of the ritual and festive feeling of Tet. Now, it's all become much more commercialised and the *banh chung* you buy in the shops is not as nice.'

Hmm. It seemed we'd heard that somewhere before too.

But still, there was no doubt about the festive feeling all around — much more pronounced, of course, than at Christmas. Then on the day before everyone broke for the Tet holiday, Khoi assembled the staff for a little proclamation. Not a serious one, in the sense of any formality, but it was clear that it was important to him.

'After Tet,' he said, 'we're going to reorganise the office. We're going to have a comprehensive revolution.'

The real emphasis at Tet is family. It's a festival of communion for the members of the same family and village. It's also a festival of the communion of the living with the dead. The transitory world of the living celebrates under the benevolent gaze of the ancestors, who are invited back from the other world during ceremonies to mark the move from the old year to the new.

In the days leading up to Tet, tombs are given a big spruce up and those who died for national independence are remembered. In each village their memorials are sites of collective pilgrimage.

A plate piled with five types of fruit sits on the altar of every Vietnamese home over Tet. Five because in Asian mythology the world is made of five elements: metal, wood, water, fire and earth. The choice of fruits varies across the country, but always includes a hand of green bananas, and the idea is to make the arrangement a perfect match of form and colour as evidence of refined taste.

On the eve of Tet, at dusk, the floor is given a final clean, to sweep out the last remnants of the year and any bad luck which may be left over, making sure not to sweep out the fairy of good fortune. Then the door is closed and people either involve themselves and their family in whatever ritual practices they follow or they pay a visit their local pagoda.

There are also set customs which accompany the celebrations of the first day of the new year, revolving around who your visitors should be and in what order they should arrive. The first visitors of the new year, so tradition holds, bring all their baggage with them. So, if they are healthy and wealthy, that's what you'll be throughout the coming year. But if they are not, that's your bad luck.

All these little titbits of information we had picked up from members of the VOV5 team, who were always happy to tell us more than we could possibly take in. What we were left with was the feeling that the complexities of Tet and what it means to the Vietnamese is not something that can be imbibed in one experience.

On the other hand, what the word Tet still means to numerous foreigners, as well as to many Vietnamese, particularly the inhabitants of the former imperial city of Hue, was something we were not about to bring up for discussion with the others in the office. The 1968 Tet Offensive, as it came to be known, was probably the first time many Westerners had even heard of the festival, which then went down as one of the bloodiest and most brutal events in the whole Vietnam–American war. The surprise mass attack, on the eve of Tet, was marked by uprisings in over a hundred towns and cities across the entire south of the country, including Saigon where, in a dramatic suicide attack, Viet Cong commandoes took over the courtyard of the American Embassy.

About 1000 American soldiers were killed during the Tet Offensive, as well as 2000 troops of the South Vietnamese army. The North gave up more than ten times that number. Approximately 32,000 of their fighters died. With the exception of Hue, the North only held these southern towns for three or four days at most, which meant that in purely military terms the Americans could claim to have won. But the event, which was seen by a stunned American public on nightly television reports, was a massive blow to the credibility of the US generals and, by association, the then US President, Richard Nixon. It took another five years, and many thousands more lives, before America withdrew, but essentially the 1968 Tet Offensive was the beginning of the end of the American War.

This year's Tet also provided an opportunity for the Hanoi government to demonstrate, quite dramatically, the reversal of its policies of previous years of unfriendliness and antagonism towards the hundreds of thousands of Vietnamese, the Viet Kieu, who had fled the country at the end of the war and later, during the economic crises of the 1980s.

For several years now, the policy had been to try to create a friendly and receptive climate for Viet Kieu to return to their homeland, either as visitors or residents, and to invest some of the huge reservoirs of foreign funds they have built up over the years through developing successful businesses in their adopted countries. Direct remittances alone, from Overseas Vietnamese to relatives and friends, are approaching US$3 billion annually.

Almost 200,000 Viet Kieu now return home specifically for the Tet Lunar New Year celebrations. This year, at a lavish government reception held in Hanoi for 500 high-profile overseas Vietnamese,

State President Tran Duc Luong made a point of stressing the dramatic changes taking place and called on countrymen living overseas, even those who may have been former political foes, to return and see the new Vietnam.

We took advantage of the six-day Tet holiday to catch our breath and have a bit of a clean-up of the paperwork that seems to silently sprout like fungus in all the corners of one's life. Once we got the bit between our teeth, we decided now was the time to move our *What's On* files and the corkboard on which we regularly pinned up plans for a week's programming into the office as part of easing it over to Huan and Thi, before our all-too-rapidly approaching time to leave.

Trish also took in her laptop computer with the plan to work on the program during regular office hours, in the hope of that giving us more time at home to put in to *Personally Speaking*, which was under dire threat of boiling dry on the back burner, through lack of hours in the day.

While in the office, she decided to take advantage of the total absence of anyone else to paint a timber desk with the same glossy black paint with which she had coated the coffee table. The non-essential furniture in the office — that is a settee, two armchairs, a coffee table and a desk — were all from what was designated the 'subsidies period'. Utilitarian in design, they were produced in government-run factories and for the 1970s and most of the '80s were the only furniture available. Even so, economic conditions were so constrained that it was necessary to 'qualify', to fulfil certain criteria, before you could have one of these pieces. For example, the requirements for ownership of an armchair, made from timber slats with deep maroon-coloured plastic-covered cushions, included a specified number of people in the family being over sixty years of age.

Naturally enough, human nature being what it is, these reminders of austerity, although you still see them in all government departments and many homes, tend to be superannuated as soon as financially possible. In fifty years they will have become collector's items. But that was not a concept we tried explaining to our Vietnamese colleagues who later showed evident pleasure at the shiny new appearance of the desk. 'It's undergone renovation,' we joked. 'It's the Doi Moi desk.'

The following day, as a result of an earlier invitation, we went to visit Tran Thi Yen Lan, the woman we had met at the Australian Embassy dinner not long after our arrival in Hanoi. It was she who had told of seeing her mother and sister raped and murdered by Korean soldiers during the Vietnam War and who now ran a program helping disadvantaged minority students find the funds to study the teaching of English, a program which has led to her being described as a 'one-woman NGO'.

For the Vietnamese, Tet is a time of nonstop visiting, dressing up in one's best clothes and calling on friends and relatives. In addition to the importance and the possibility of either good or bad luck implied by the person who is the first visitor on New Year's Day, everything one does during the first three days of Tet symbolises and forecasts actions during the coming twelve months. People try to avoid anger and using bad language. Mothers and daughters-in-law make friends and children promise to be good. According to the inspirational Huu Ngoc, Tet is meant to bring a message of confidence in humanity, as well as redemption, hope and optimism.

Lan lived with her husband and daughter in a small one-room apartment about two kilometres from us. The apartment, on the ground floor, was minuscule, with a kitchen, measuring not more than two square metres, the first room you entered. And it was in here that Lan had somehow prepared an amazing spread of cooked pies, spring rolls, various rice dishes and other Vietnamese specialties for the dozen or so Westerners who were crammed into the only other room in the flat, a bed-sitting room, which itself was only four square metres and contained a bed, a dresser, a table and two chairs, with no room between any of them.

Joe and Lona Thwaites, their two daughters, Anna and Julia, and a cousin were crowded onto the bed, one member of a Danish family of five stood, while the rest shared part of the bed and one chair.

We talked a bit about Lan's work, about Tet and a range of other things as Lan and her daughter shuttled back and forth to the kitchen, bringing new items of food to the table.

Although she was not well off, even in the remotest sense (as a salaried lecturer at the University of Foreign Studies, she was paid somewhere between 1.2 million and 1.5 million dong, or A$120 to A$150 per month), it was with a sense of pride that she had organised this little get-together for Tet and we could only hope that some of the symbolism implied by the visit of someone like the Australian ambassador would work in her favour during the rest of the year.

From Lan's place we moved on to keep a second Tet appointment, this time at the home of Minh Ha's parents. Though not affluent in a Western context, by comparison to Lan's humble and modest circumstances they were positively wealthy.

Most importantly, the three-storey house on Nguyen Khang Road, in the western suburb of Cau Giay, was their own. Minh Ha's and her brother's motorbikes were both parked, in the fashion of Hanoi, in the lobby. Although we didn't see the rest of the house, the ground floor was spacious and well furnished with the ornately carved dark wooden furniture so popular throughout Vietnam and other parts of Asia. We were greeted by Minh Ha and her husband, introduced to her mother, who immediately laid out an impressive spread of sweetmeats and Vietnamese delicacies, and then her father, who offered us either green tea or a dangerous form of

Vietnamese firewater, the name of which Iain missed ... but not the burning punch in his chest that came with the first swallow.

Minh Ha's mother was a maths teacher, while her father held an administrative position at the head office of Voice of Vietnam. He was joined a short while later, at the low table around which we all sat, by his brother, Minh Ha's uncle, who struck us as being a bit of a lad. He had obviously already sampled a few tots of the firewater Iain had just tried and was keen for someone to keep him company while he tossed back a few more. He thrust another one at Iain, laughing and saying something unintelligible in Vietnamese. Iain's never been much good when peer group pressure comes into play and clearly this was one of those times when, at least in his view, he was required to demonstrate his ... well, who knows what? ... by joining the uncle in drinking loads of the hazardous stuff. Mind you, after he'd forced a few down, it apparently started to warm the cockles of his heart. And with the weather outside freezing cold, he started to think it might do him some good.

But fortunately the uncle's mother, Minh Ha's grandmother, came downstairs and interrupted the proceedings by calling him away to do some odd job. Iain switched to tea and soon, after lots of laughter, we said our goodbyes and headed home.

There, within half an hour, we answered the doorbell to greet Huan and Thi, who were out making Tet social calls. It may seem only a relatively small thing, but we were more than delighted that Huan and Thi had come, as it showed a measure of self-confidence on their part to just turn up, with no prior arrangement. In the West, it would be quite acceptable and would generally pass without much notice. In Vietnam, however, it is normally not done. You don't just arrive at somebody's house, especially a Westerner's house, without being invited. As we've pointed out, a little more than a dozen years ago Vietnamese weren't allowed to talk with foreigners in the street, let alone visit their homes, so we took it as a compliment that they had done so.

On the morning of our return to work at the end of the Tet holiday break, we were amazed to find slightly inebriated people wandering from floor to floor congratulating each other and wishing everyone a happy Lunar New Year. People we'd never seen in our section before would arrive from other departments, surprisingly juiced up for nine o'clock in the morning, to carry on for five or ten minutes before moving on to another location.

Also, during the first day or so after our return from Tet, Khoi voiced his concern about the future of VOV5. Much of it was due to the knowledge that, within the year, both Hue and Loc would be retiring and the weight of responsibility would shift inexorably in his direction. In a much more immediate sense, he was to pick up where Huong had left off, after her departure to work for the Swedish Embassy. Although, in theory, he and Minh Ha would share the responsibility for the program work that Huong had been doing, Minh Ha had been a bit preoccupied with the possibility of a move to the private sector in the form of the job with the American public broadcaster, NPR. Although it had not eventuated, it still left Khoi as the man on the spot, picking up most of the pieces.

Iain tried to allay his doubts by talking positively about future changes.

'The whole society here is changing so rapidly,' he said, 'and the radio set-up in Vietnam will be part of it.' He referred to what was happening with Austereo on the commercial side of broadcasting. 'If that comes off and they get a commercial station up and running in Vietnam ... even though it will initially be just in Vietnamese ... if it is successful, the impact will be very big. The spill-over effect will almost certainly show up in English-language broadcasting and the whole scene will be revolutionised and people here will be in a prime position.'

Iain knew that he was stretching a long bow and may well have been raising false hopes, but the possibility *was* there. It was just that it might take a long time — perhaps too long for these young people to wait.

It would be wrong to say that Khoi was depressed; he was still keen to launch his 'comprehensive revolution', which now looked as if it would not come until the beginning of February, but we thought he was just recognising the size of the job before him.

However, Thi provided one very positive sign for the new year, by presenting a couple of *What's On* pieces that she had researched and written on her own. Prior to this, the pieces had been researched and written by either one of us. Now, with our departure from VOV and Vietnam little more than three months away, we were beginning to set things up for Huan and Thi to take over.

And they were both good pieces, very much in the relaxed, conversational style we were hoping to develop in their writing. Huan followed a day later with two of his own, and from then on they began to write all of their own spots for *What's On*, which we recorded with them.

On the last day of a Tet-filled month, we flew out of Hanoi to spend a weekend in Dien Bien Phu.

The sky was clear as the plane dropped steadily down into the valley and, looking at the surrounding hills and the sprawling town below, it was all but impossible to imagine this as the scene of one of the most pivotal battles of the twentieth century.

The picture of thousands of men toiling up the jungled slopes on the far side of those hills, as they hauled huge artillery pieces into place through tangled forests and over a previously trackless terrain, was a difficult one to formulate in the mind's eye. And yet that is what happened. And when they were finally in position, they were overlooking the valley of Dien Bien Phu, in which close to

15,000 French troops, entrenched in a highly fortified encampment, were preparing to fight the decisive battle of the Indochina War — although they didn't recognise it as such at the time.

Iain doesn't really think of himself as fanatical, but there was no doubt that he was being somewhat obsessive in organising this trip to Dien Bien Phu at the end of January, just to make sure we would be able to return there, three months later on 7 May. This was the date of the upcoming celebrations of the fiftieth anniversary of the battle that effectively ended French colonial rule in Indochina, and influenced the development and outcome of struggles against colonialism right around the world.

Iain was convinced, after fractured and frustrating telephone calls to several hotels, twice using a Vietnamese interpreter, that the only way we could really be sure of getting a hotel room — on an occasion when the town would be swollen with over 100,000 visitors trying to fit into less than 1000 hotel rooms — was to actually go there in advance, pick the hotel, pay for the rooms and the return flights and have the actual tickets and hotel receipts in his hand.

Anyway, here we were in Dien Bien Phu, just 300 kilometres from Hanoi, for the weekend. Booking in at the Muong Thanh Hotel, we asked if they had a map of the town so that we could locate some of the more important sites relating to the battle. Nothing. 'Just walk down the main street,' we were told by the manager, 'and you'll eventually come to Hill A–1, the cemetery, and the museum.'

Hill A–1 was one of a number of small hills around the township and the airstrip that had been turned into defensive positions, where the French had dug in with trenches and tunnels and which had been heavily fortified. They were marked on the war map of Dien Bien Phu by the French as A–1, A–2, B–3, C–2, etc., but the French commander on the ground, Colonel Christian Marie Ferdinand de la Croix de Castries, gave them women's names like Eliane, Dominique, Anne Marie, Huguette, Claudine. Three more were reputedly named after his current mistresses: Gabrielle, Beatrice and Isabelle.

At Eliane, or hill A–1, right on the main street, we climbed a thinly forested slope, where workmen were refurbishing and concreting old trenches and laying barbed wire to re-create the entanglements that covered the hill at the time of the battle, right to the top where we gazed into an enormous crater caused when the Viet Minh had exploded one tonne of TNT deep beneath the French position, in a secret tunnel which they had dug during the preceding days.

Beside A–1 is the impressive and, in its own sad way, beautiful cemetery dedicated to the estimated 10,000 Vietnamese soldiers who died in the campaign and which contains, in hundreds of unmarked graves, the remains of those that were recovered from the field of battle.

The museum was closed for renovation, but nearby we crossed over the small Nam Oum River via the Muong Thanh Bridge, another important site in the course of the battle, where the French artillery commander, distressed at having failed in his prediction to be able to wipe out any Viet Minh artillery piece as soon as it fired upon the French, put a pistol to his forehead and pulled the trigger.

A short distance beyond we came to the major icon of Dien Bien Phu, which is known simply as 'de Castries' bunker'. It's a low, curved, reinforced steel roof over a deeply dug underground post, from which the French commander, who was by then a general, had directed his side of the conflict. It was here, after the Viet Minh had stormed through the French defences to capture the bunker, that General de Castries signed the surrender on behalf of some 10,000 French soldiers.

A few hundred metres south of the bunker is the only memorial in Dien Bien Phu to the estimated 3000 French soldiers who died during the campaign. It is a small white obelisk, about 3.5 metres high in an enclosure of some 10 or 15 square metres. It was erected in 1994, not by the French government, but by one man, a former commando from the French Foreign Legion, who had fought defending the southern outpost of Isabelle.

It simply says:

*Aux officiers et soldats*
*de l'armee Française*
*Morts à*
*Dien Bien Phu*

'To the officers and soldiers
of the French army
who died at
Dien Bien Phu'

## February

# A VISIT TO LUAN'S VILLAGE

*'A single drop of blood is worth a pond of water'*

February witnessed a huge lift in spirits at VOV5. Perhaps some of it was due to the change of years from Golden Goat to Monkey, but mostly it came from the leadership qualities shown by Nguyen Tam Khoi. Cometh the time cometh the man, and Khoi stepped up to the mark in an impressive manner. At the first self-criticism/weekly office meeting of the month he presented his 'comprehensive revolution'.

Just before we'd flown off to Dien Bien Phu, Trish had had a sleepless night during which she'd nutted out a small strategy of her own. She had approached Khoi about it with a degree of diffidence because we were, after all, outsiders who had only the barest inkling of what this group of people had struggled through to reach this point in their personal lives and careers. He received her ideas with enthusiasm and, we thought, not just out of politeness but because he saw the suggestions as positive. But he wanted Trish to actually present them to the others, which is how she found herself in the embarrassing position of standing up at the team meeting in front of a whiteboard on which she had tried to soften her suggestions by making light of them.

We had also attempted to curry approval by bringing with us fresh bread and a large jar of cumquat jam we had made from the fruit of the tree that Mai had given us for Tet. It was an absolute winner and definitely helped in gaining acceptance for the ideas, but Trish still had to serve them her plan.

HOUSEKEEPING. She pointed to the first heading and went on to suggest that we should all, except, of course, Madame Hue and perhaps Madame Loc, be on a weekly roster to clean and maintain tidiness in the office. She suggested that whoever was responsible for housekeeping should also bring in some flowers. She volunteered to be first on the housekeeping roster and added that, from now until the time we left, she would enjoy continuing to bring in the flowers because they gave her such pleasure. The staff all responded positively to the idea and agreed that keeping the office looking good made it a more pleasurable place in which to work.

CORPORATE CULTURE. Here Trish stepped into a murky world towards which we have a rather ambivalent attitude, and came up with an idea with which we were not 100 per cent comfortable but which we felt fitted in with their structured society.

'I think we should vote for an Employee of the Month.' Trish cringed as she said it, but they loved it.

'Vote!'

'Yes!'

Better still, 'A secret ballot,' she insisted.

'Yes! Yes!'

'How much do you win?' Of course it was Tram who asked.

'You win the esteem of your peers,' Trish told her prissily and, with a grin, added, 'and you get to choose where to have an office lunch and, perhaps, the rest of the team pays your share of the meal.'

The third heading read I ♥ VOV5 at which Minh Ha immediately narrowed her eyes and said, 'I love VOV5.'

Madame Loc muttered, 'Yes, yes,' in agreement as Trish pointed out to them, with as many jokey references as she could muster, that, while they were in the very enviable position of working in a job which enabled them to polish up skills in written and spoken English, which in turn gave them a continually increasing commercial value outside of their paid employment, their first and highest commitment should remain with VOV5.

'Absolutely,' Loc insisted. 'That is the most important point.' The others shifted in their chairs.

'But employment,' Trish said pointedly, 'is a two-way street. You owe the employer your loyalty and hard work but in return your employer owes you loyalty, support and a decent wage.'

With that Trish reached the fourth and final heading: DOI MOI STRIKES AGAIN. 'Renovation,' she was sweating now, 'is the buzz word and I think VOV5 could do with some. Changes are needed. The government goes for five-year plans and I reckon we,' — she purposely used the inclusive pronoun — 'need a five-year plan with the aim that within that period of time the English Service of Voice of Vietnam will have an all English language service on air twenty-four hours a day. It's something to aim for.'

At that she dismissed herself and we left Khoi to take the stage and present his schemes.

We hadn't stayed to hear Khoi's comprehensive revolution, because these weekly staff self-criticism meetings never included us. However, Khoi had explained to us what he wanted to do and when we returned to the office, Huan told us of the generally favourable reaction to it from the rest of the staff.

It was a pretty basic five-point plan, but it had the potential to make a difference.

First on the list was BETTER TEAMWORK. Khoi wanted them to work on a new approach to the news bulletins, with more realistic and presumably less propagandist news that would include at least two reportage items; that is, recorded pieces — possibly on location — by reporters, each week.

Second was PLANNING. Everybody needed to start thinking further ahead when planning and developing programs and program ideas.

Third was PROMOTION. He wanted the English service of VOV to be promoted more widely within the community, both English-speaking and Vietnamese.

Fourth, EXPANDED RELATIONS with other departments. That is, increased cooperation with the different language sections, including the main Vietnamese News Department.

And finally, STAFF. He made a strong point to both Mesdames Loc and Hue that at least two or three extra staff would be needed.

Although things had improved noticeably for the three youngest members of the staff, Thi, Tram and Huan, during the ten months we had been at VOV, they were still technically on probation and were still treated by the rest of the staff as such, as junior members.

'You should be firm with them,' Khoi said on one occasion in the first week of February, referring to the fact that they had now started writing scripts for *What's On*. 'You should make sure they have them done for you on time.'

'They *are* getting them done,' we said, 'and they're not too bad either.'

Tram had also contributed one script, which was okay, after a little editing, but, as she had not yet been allowed on air to read any of the news bulletins or current affairs programs, there was correspondingly little chance for her to do any *What's On* segments. Nevertheless, we let Khoi and Loc know that she was willing and improving steadily.

This sort of comment by us became doubly important in Tram's case because, in this same week, Loc had told Tram that her salary was being reduced until such time as she could bring her on-air presentation skills up to scratch. Not that there was any *actual* on-air presentation work being done by Tram, but Loc would take her in for regular sessions of reading news bulletins aloud and would often be quite disparaging and dismissive in her comments.

This all tended to make Tram diffident and anxious. It was clear that she had a constant struggle to balance her salary with the day-to-day needs of a family and an infant son and any doubts about her position at VOV only tended to make her more uneasy.

'I want to buy the best powdered milk for my boy,' she said to Trish on one occasion. 'Do you think Chinese milk is as good as American powdered milk?'

'It's a long time since I've had to buy it.' Trish laughed. 'And in those days there was no Chinese powdered milk being sold, so I don't know anything about it. I suppose it's cheaper, is it?'

'Yes,' Tram replied.

'Hmm. Well, cheaper and better don't necessarily go together. Maybe you're better to stick with the more expensive one and perhaps give the Chinese one a try now and then.'

Tram laughed and gave Trish a friendly push. 'You don't know, so you take the easy way out.'

At it turned out Trish's 'easy way out' was the right way to go. A couple of months later a huge scandal over fake Chinese baby milk formulae was exposed and several Chinese milk manufacturers were arrested. Tram had fortunately opted for the more expensive milk, despite the fact that her position at VOV was generally a more difficult one than that of most of the others, as there was no element of nepotism involved in her position, which was more than could be said for the majority of the staff. This had also proved a problem for her at a previous job she held at the *Vietnam News*.

'I left,' she told Trish, 'as I knew I would never be able to progress there, because I didn't know anyone high up enough.'

Australia Day was swamped by events of another kind, but was finally celebrated at the end of the first week in February with a big outdoor bash at the American Club, a venue chosen, we were told, because it had more space and easier access for the general public, but probably also because there were fewer security issues. Wrong date, wrong place. Yet it still managed to be a very Aussie event with beer and a barbecue, and the drawing of raffle tickets and door prizes, after which, it was noticeable, the majority of Vietnamese guests left. It was, however, a bitterly cold evening. We stayed on for a while trying to warm up by dancing to loud music provided by a group we believed was called The Attachés, but later found out was the Friendly Fire Rock Band. It was a multinational group of musos who, in their other lives, were all defence attachés from various embassies around town.

It was an interesting line-up: Colonel Eddy Krisapong from the Thai army on bass; Colonel Steve Ball, US army, on guitar; Colonel Naoki Tuomi, Japanese army, on drums; Colonel Volodymyr Kruglov from the Ukranian army, vocals and guitar; and Group Captain Paul McLeod, Australian air force, on vocals and keyboard.

'I don't think that gig was one of our best performances,' Paul told us later. 'The sound mixing was all wrong. We had no keyboard sound to the main speakers, and the harmony vocals drowned out the main vocals. But we had fun anyway!'

And so did we although we do remember thinking it was just as well their friendly fire was confined to musical instruments rather than anything more deadly.

During this week, in early February, two close American friends from San Diego, Sally and Mike, came to stay with us in Hanoi. We had asked them to buy and bring with them a large, concise version of the *Times World Atlas*. This was to be our departure present for the staff of VOV5. The little 36-year-old *Philips School Atlas* in the office was falling apart and had long since passed its use-by date. We hadn't been too sure though about Sally and Mike's prospects of getting the new one in. We had been told on several occasions that atlases were on the list of proscribed books, which attracted the attention of customs people, and in the past had been banned.

Fortunately, it came through with them with no trouble and we put it aside to await the right time for us to present it to the office.

Although it was not something that came up for discussion with our visitors, a significant development in US–Vietnam relations occurred during that same week, when three Vietnamese victims of the defoliant Agent Orange took the unprecedented step of filing a suit against the American companies that had produced the toxic chemical that was used by American forces during the war.

Between 1962 and 1971, American C–130 Hercules aircraft sprayed upwards of 100 million litres of Agent Orange over Vietnamese forests where they believed communist troops might be hiding. Almost a third of southern Vietnam was razed by the defoliant, which contains TCCD, a powerful dioxin strain that, according to the World Health Organization, 'when it enters the human body, is there to stay due to its uncanny ability to dissolve in fats and to its rock-solid chemical stability'.

Washed by rain into valleys, wells, ponds and rice fields, the TCCD polluted drinking water in much of the South. At the time of the aerial sprayings, it is believed there were anywhere between two and five million people directly or indirectly affected. Even now, more than three decades after the war, an estimated one million people in Vietnam are victims of the dioxin, including second- and third-generation victims. But the Hanoi government has never formally asked for compensation for them.

Vietnam and the United States held a joint scientific conference in 2002 on Agent Orange and its effects and a study released the following year found that very high levels of dioxin continue to be found in food samples in Vietnam.

Many American veterans as well as Vietnamese victims have blamed the defoliant for a variety of illnesses, including cancer, diabetes, spina bifida and birth defects. But the US government has all along insisted that there is no direct evidence linking dioxin with illness. Nevertheless, some 10,000 American veterans of the war receive disability benefits from the government that are related to exposure to Agent Orange.

The lawsuit, against ten American companies, including Dow Chemical and Monsanto, two of the primary producers of Agent Orange, was brought by the Vietnam Association of Victims of Agent Orange. The three people who are the subject of the claim were a man, Nguyen Van Quy, and two women, Duong Quynh Hoa and Nguyen Thi Phi. Quy has cancer and has two children with birth defects. Hoa has breast cancer and high levels of dioxin in her blood, while Phi has suffered four miscarriages.

But they are only the tip of the iceberg. And one unexpected tragedy is that, although the spraying was confined to central and southern areas, provinces in the far north, like Thai Binh, not far from Hanoi, find they must deal with thousands of cases. These are the result of soldiers returning from the South, to find, years later, that not only do they themselves develop cancers and a range of illnesses, but their children and their children's children suffer limb and facial deformities, mental retardation and other abnormalities.

Thai Binh Province alone has some 20,000 first-, second- and third-generation victims.

One Monday morning in mid-February, we arrived in the office to learn that Terrific Thi's grandmother had died and that all the staff were going to attend her funeral. Not only the staff of VOV5, but large numbers from many other departments too. This was because Thi's paternal grandmother was also Madame Hue's mother-in-law; that is, the mother of Hue's husband, who was 2IC of the Chinese-language section of VOV.

The head of the section was based in China, which meant that in reality Hue's husband was in day-to-day command of what was almost certainly seen by the government as the most important and sensitive department in VOV's overseas broadcast set-up. He would be a member of the Party, and a senior member at that.

In death as in life and in the world of power politics, one assumes it's good to be seen in the right place at the right time. So it was that Thi's granny was given a very big funeral.

The word had obviously gone out beforehand, because all the men in the office were in ties and jackets and the women, never flash dressers by any stretch of the imagination, were even more modestly attired than usual. We took off in a convoy of motorbikes, stopping briefly at our place for us to put on appropriate attire, then on to the large funeral reception hall which we later found out was the special building established for funerals of high-ranking government and military officials.

At the entrance to the expansive car park, which was filled with scores and scores of motorbikes, everyone was given a little strip of black tape to stick onto their clothing and three joss sticks. A smaller parking area was totally filled with chauffeured vehicles. The stepped approaches to the main reception hall were lined with dozens of flat oval floral tributes, each emblazoned with a black sash bearing the name of the mourners: individuals, families, community associations, government departments.

All the side-rooms were crowded with men and women, either in military uniforms or dark clothing. In a rare display of social sensitivity, Tram had opted to stay back with the motorbikes, gesturing at her bum-hugging pale-coloured pantsuit as the reason. At that moment we liked her more than ever.

We wrote our names in the condolence book, lit our joss sticks and joined the long queue that moved slowly forward to circle the body of Thi's grandmother, which lay in an ornate coffin on a raised dais before a wall, on which hung a red silk cloth emblazoned with her full name. As with the funeral for the old lady in our courtyard, the lid of the coffin had a small glass window through which we glanced down at the shrivelled features of Thi's granny, waxen pale in death. The shock was how much like Thi she looked.

We knew from conversations with Thi that her grandmother had been bedridden, incontinent and suffering from what sounded like Alzheimer's disease for a considerable time. Death was more than likely a blessed relief for her, as well as for her immediate family, who had cared for her at home until her end, so it wasn't as though there was immense grief at her passing; instead, a deep sadness and a reflection about the changes, at national and international levels, which she had seen across almost a century of life.

Born in China, her arranged marriage to a man who eventually became a judge under the French colonial system had lasted many decades. They had four children, all of whom had survived, with varying degrees of personal success. In her long life, she had experienced the end of the French colonial period, the routing of the Americans, the economic and social upheavals of the establishment of a communist state and now the opening up of her country and its fast gallop into globalisation. We were pleased for her that, for whatever reason, she was having this big send-off. She deserved it.

On the far side of the coffin, we proceeded along the line of close family mourners — all of them wearing white headbands — hands together, bowing slightly in respect and bowing a little lower at Thi, who had inherited her grandmother's world and, we felt sure, her survival genes.

A Vietnamese experience of a quite different nature, but no less absorbing, came to us almost out of the blue at the end of the week, when we had an unexpected but very welcome email from our friend from Sapa, Nguyen Trong Luan, who had organised our trip up Mount Fanxipan.

It was not entirely unexpected because he had mentioned back in September, when we had made the climb, that he would like us and Rebecca to visit his home village, Thon Luu Xa, to the south of Hanoi, at some time in the future. And now was a good time, apparently. He would be back from Sapa, where he had been continuing his work as a guide, for a brief period to help his parents with the harvest and asked if we would like to meet them and see the place where he had grown up.

We naturally accepted and it was arranged that we should meet up with Luan at our place in Hanoi on a Sunday, and take a hired vehicle and driver that we would organise for the trip south into Ha Tay Province.

Luan arrived on time, about midday, and we set off, loaded with gifts of flowers and fruit. The village was hardly any distance away at all, about 20 kilometres, and probably should really be classified as an outer suburb of Hanoi, but despite the nature of the city and the inexorable urban sprawl that was occurring, somehow these 'suburbs' retained the nature and appearance of villages.

The main road we were travelling on remained continually crowded with motorbikes and small trucks, even as it narrowed down to two lanes, with occasional rice paddies appearing between the never-ending roadside distribution of shop-houses, stalls, small factories, pottery kilns, cafés and so on.

And then, at Luan's direction, we turned left onto a minor surfaced road, running between rice paddies, which quickly became a lane that wound its way through more and more closely packed dwellings, which, in turn, became high brick walls. We stopped at an even narrower lane leading off to the right, wide enough only for two people or a bicycle to follow.

Leaving the vehicle, we followed Luan and, accompanied almost immediately by a crowd of laughing and yelling children who were amazed and delighted to see three foreigners in their village, we made our way down the maze of narrow alleys to his home. It was a low brick dwelling with a tiled roof and a small verandah facing out onto a yard.

The house, though substantial in construction, was simple as far as facilities were concerned. It had an outdoor kitchen under a tiled roof, but without walls, where the cooking was done on a charcoal-burning brazier. Water came from a well and there was an outdoor toilet, which was flushed with water from a bucket. Immediately next to it was a small pigsty occupied by a huge sow. Where the sewage flow went, we weren't quite sure.

Inside, the main room, though small, was dominated by a large, carved wooden altar set against the centre of the back wall and adorned with burning candles and fruit offerings. Long tables and chairs were placed at either end of the room. There was a small bedroom leading off one end of this main room.

His parents, both only in their fifties we imagined, greeted us with smiles. They spoke no English, so Luan translated everything for us.

A ginger cat and three kittens played on the verandah, while a dog of indeterminate breed paid close and slightly nervous attention to a cuddly round ball of fur that was her seventeen-day-old pup, as we took turns at holding it in our arms.

We explained, through Luan, what we were doing in Vietnam and talked about how we had met in Sapa, naturally with some complimentary comments about Luan as a guide, at which his parents both nodded appreciatively. They were proud of the fact that he was the first in the family and one of very few in the village to speak English.

We also met Luan's sister-in-law and her young daughter and, after taking some group photographs, were led off by Luan on a walk through the alleyways again to visit the local village temple. Its intricately carved adornments and interior decorations were little different from the many other temples and pagodas we had visited since arriving in Hanoi, but the smallness and intimacy of this little village pagoda gave it a particular charm.

A tiny, wrinkled old woman, wrapped in brown robes, with a black woollen beanie and a brown scarf around her head because

*An elderly Buddhist nun in the temple at Thon Luu Xao, Luan's home village. She had been there since she was a child.*

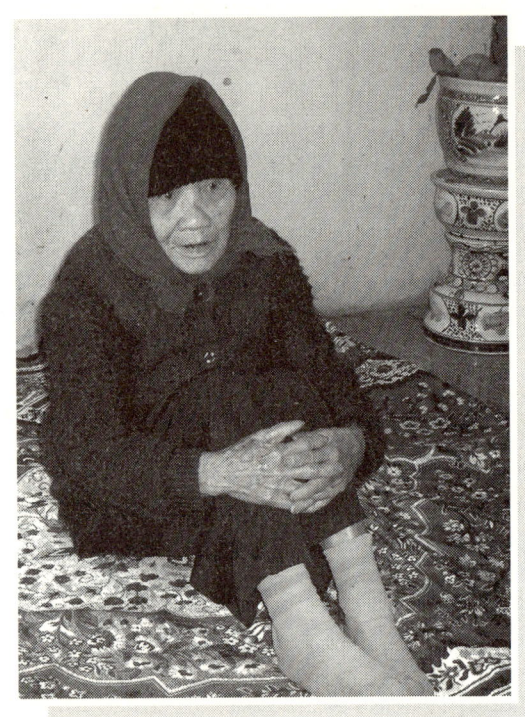

of the cold, sat on a carpet in front of the altar. Her rheumy eyes glistened as she flashed us a smile of blackened teeth when Luan introduced us.

It was always fascinating for us to see older women with these discoloured teeth, which they had purposely painted many years ago. It was done with a dye made from plants and insects to produce a look which, in the fashion of the time, was considered to be very attractive, although there is also a suggestion that it was done to prevent tooth decay.

'She is a nun,' Luan explained. 'Over ninety years old.'

'How long has she been here?' Iain asked.

Luan passed on the question in Vietnamese and the old lady replied.

'Since she was a teenager,' he told us.

We sat and talked, through Luan as interpreter, for about a quarter of an hour, asking her about the changes she had seen and about the village during the war. Then, after making a small donation towards the major renovations to the temple's exterior structure, we moved on.

We had known, almost as soon as we had received Luan's email inviting us to come to his village, that it would not only be an opportunity not be missed but also a rare privilege for us to be taken into a world we would not otherwise have been able to see. Luan's family, the temple and this little old nun confirmed it for us. And there was more to come.

After a brief respite back at his parents' home, where we drank green tea, we followed Luan, again accompanied by a gaggle of noisily exuberant children, threading through the narrow alleys, passing numerous homes. There were the obviously more affluent dwellings in which extended families lived in small houses scattered around a central courtyard, as well as the simpler single-family ones. What was most noticeable was how much building work was under way and also how the entire village was so well kept and clean. We were very conscious that what we were seeing was an aspect of the 'real' Vietnam, not a photo opportunity.

The village turned abruptly into rice paddies. We straggled along the tops of the dykes taking in the vista of a soft grey winter landscape framed by a few scraggly-limbed eucalypts. The rice had been fairly recently harvested so the water in the little enclosed plots reflected the dull sky.

Only young boys had followed us this far and now, shouting and yelling, they scrambled off the main dyke and, whooping with laughter, climbed onto the low walls of a family grave marooned in a larger than usual flooded paddy. There they postured and gesticulated, demanding that Iain take a group photo, after which they splashed back to him to check out how it looked on the playback.

'My grandparents, the four of them, are buried over there,' Luan pointed to where, not far off, there was another cluster of walled graves.

*Children from Luan's village clambered on a family grave to celebrate life among the dead.*

There was about the scene the sort of serenity which eats into the soul and for which people yearn with a desperate homesickness when they find themselves in places of more exotic and immediately accessible beauty. The ties that bind. We understood why Luan loved to come home. Why he would be content to be buried alongside his parents and grandparents. The dead among the living. Across Vietnam there are thousands of villages like this. Home, in the most deeply meaningful of ways, to millions of Vietnamese.

On the far side of the village we visited the market where laughing women were selling unnameable slabs of meat at stalls set up around the large village pond. We peered through the barred gates of the communal house where, Luan explained, important annual festivals and special meetings were held. On the way back to his home Luan took us to his sister-in-law's place where we smiled and gestured our way through meetings with very elderly relatives and very young relatives, and drank more green tea.

At dinner, for which Luan's mother and daughter-in-law had gone to the trouble of making us vegetarian food, we were joined by Luan's brother who worked nearby in a timber yard and workshop. 'My dad works there too,' Luan told us, 'in the period between harvesting and planting.' Also joining us was Luan's best mate, who was the same age, but already married with a small son. Very smartly turned out, he spoke good English and told us he worked in a local restaurant owned by his family.

Throughout the meal they were all most anxious that we felt welcome and comfortable, which would have been easier if Luan's mother and sister-in-law had joined us instead of eating their food from bowls while squatting around the cooking brazier. But there was no hope of that; the women were more at ease leaving the social niceties to their menfolk.

It had been a wonderful day. All we could hope, as we took our leave, was that as honoured guests we had come up to their expectations.

Luan wanted to give us all a lift back, right into Hanoi, on motorbikes driven by his father, brother and his friend. But we were most insistent that a lift to the local bus station was as much as we wanted. It actually turned out to be rather more than we wanted! It was dark and none of the bikes had adequate lighting. The narrow road was one continuous stream of speeding traffic, including trucks and buses. And it was a lot further to the bus stop than we wanted it to be.

But we arrived, safe, though shaken, to await the bus, which came shortly afterwards. It was about half-an-hour's drive into town and, just as we were getting off the bus, Iain's mobile rang. It was Luan, just wanting to check that we had reached home safely.

On our return to work, something else came at us out of the blue. This time it was from Khoi. He had been offered the chance to apply for a scholarship to study radio journalism for a year in Sweden. As seemed to be the practice now, he came to us to ask our opinion before making it known within the rest of the department.

The problem with dealing with this sort of situation, from our point of view, was that we naturally tended towards thinking that any overseas experience of the type being offered to Khoi was an opportunity that should be grabbed with both hands. But this one involved Khoi. Khoi, who was developing into the key figure in the department. Khoi, who had just introduced his 'comprehensive revolution', with all his new plans for the future of the English service of VOV. Now he could suddenly be whisked away for a year, at a time when he was most needed. And yet ... and yet?

'When did you find out about this scholarship?' Iain asked.

'Over the weekend. Huong told me about it. It's through the Swedish Embassy.'

'It's very difficult to give advice on things like this,' Iain said. 'I would normally say go for it, but, the way things are here now ...' He looked around the room. 'Would you take the family?' he asked.

'No. We couldn't afford it. They pay for only one person.'

'So your wife would look after your daughter. Would she continue to work?'

Iain thought of the fact that Khoi — well, actually he and his parents — were presently looking after their three-year-old daughter while his wife was in Japan for six months studying Japanese.

'Oh yes. She would look after Phuong Linh ... with my parents' help, of course.'

Periods of long separation, even for young couples, was something that seemed to be taken with a great degree of equanimity in Vietnam. From poor labouring families, from which a husband or son might leave for a prolonged period overseas as a 'foreign worker' in South Korea, Japan, or some Middle Eastern country, to — for want of a better word — the more fortunate intellectual elite, where, as in Khoi's case, a husband may be required to be away from home for a year or more, it was simply accepted as something that was necessary.

We talked about Khoi's dilemna over coffee at the Tonkin Café around the corner. And, while we both agreed it would have a considerable impact on the department, it was something he had to go for. And we told him so.

Madame Loc's intitial reaction to the suggestion was simply that he could *not* go and that someone else in the department could apply.

When this was passed on to Huong at the Swedish Embassy, she replied, with some satisfaction, that the offer was not open to just anyone. If Khoi could not apply, then no-one else in the English Department would be considered. Touché.

In Hanoi, as in many other Asian capitals, karaoke has developed into code for prostitution. There is one short interconnecting alley in the Old Town which is lined with small brothels advertising themselves as karaoke clubs and another row of similar businesses operating along the well-known two-kilometre stretch of road in the inner suburbs.

Prostitution is not legal in Vietnam and one can only suppose that the authorities turn a tolerant eye to such obvious lawbreaking, just so long as it stays within acceptable limits. But in February some incident or other must have wound them up too tight, because they suddenly twanged unstrung and the media was full of reports about government closures of karaoke establishments and threats that karaoke was to be totally banned.

Well, it seemed it was one thing to ban the sale of toy guns, but quite another to forbid people — that is, legitimate karaoke fans —

the right to make fools of themselves by warbling in public. While people didn't exactly take to the streets in their thousands, the press — more so the Vietnamese-language papers and most notably those marketed for the fifteen-to-thirty age demographic — was inundated with letters from outraged citizens, all of them pointing out that while a proportion of karaoke clubs were fronts for 'antisocial elements' and 'dirty behaviour', by far the majority were straight-up-and-down places where people could go to let off steam and have good clean fun. That was surprising enough, taking into account the strictures of an autocratic regime, but what was even more amazing was that the authorities backed down. Perhaps, after all, it had been just a political tactic to pacify the moral majority and to remind the brothel owners to stay within certain unstated boundaries.

Whatever the motivation, it didn't change our antipathy towards actually participating in a karaoke session. It was something for which we had carefully managed to be unavailable whenever it had been suggested. But, as we were soon to discover, our assiduous avoidance of karaoke would soon all come to nothing.

We had received an invitation to visit her home from Thuy, a woman who worked on the fifth floor and was responsible for the day-to-day administration of our office building — everything from loo paper to topping up the caddy of green tea. Thuy, we were to discover, was a fanatical ballroom dancer. And we mean fanatical. She and her husband danced every day, a fact which was apparent in the elegant and graceful way she moved about the office.

On a Saturday afternoon in the latter half of the month, in response to her invitation, we turned up at their house, way out in the southern suburbs with a couple of other people from the office. It was so newly built that it fronted onto a dirt road and, as with our visit to Luan's village, we soon realised it was a privilege to have been asked. She showed us around her small two-up, two-down brick home with as much pride as a society matron, laying out her splendid dancing gowns for our appreciation, offering us beer and whisky as well as slices of sweet potato and nuts.

Then we were led out of the house and around the corner to another house in the next street, where we were introduced to a couple who were perhaps in their fifties, both of them dressed to dance. Ooops! we thought. Their house was identical, except that a large extension, which we were shown into, and which had a corrugated-iron roof, was lined with mirrored walls. Music from a CD player was turned up and suddenly we both found ourselves dancing; Trish in the arms of Thuy's husband and being waltzed around the space while Iain, realising what was expected of him, shuffled Thuy about. When the music stopped, we swapped partners. In no time our shirts were wet through, while our poised Vietnamese partners remained cool.

Then, to give us an opportunity to stop sweating we were taken back into the main sitting room, set down in front of a big TV monitor, given a microphone each and expected to sing in time with the moving words. On the karaoke screen a couple of Westerners, the woman in an almost-no-dress dress, danced against bizarre Disneyesque backdrops. By now numerous neighbours and friends had come by to watch the foreigners perform. We must have been a great disappointment to them because our singing was even less accomplished than our dancing and made us sweat just as much. If there wasn't already a law against it, there should have been.

'Had I been born Chinese, I would have been a calligrapher, not a painter,' is a remark attributed to the legendary Spanish artist Pablo Picasso, which perhaps goes some way towards illustrating the international allure of an art which is unique to Asian cultures. In the wan hope of grasping a little more about the cultural importance of the art ourselves, we went, one bitterly cold Saturday morning, to a talk on calligraphy organised by the Friends of

Vietnam Heritage at the Temple of Literature, the site of Vietnam's oldest university.

In Vietnam, calligraphy faded away during the French colonial period and remained low on the agenda during the initial revolutionary period when other issues, like having enough to eat and surviving through the fighting, were of more importance. Its quite apparent resurgence now is one more sign that the standard of living across the country is on an upward curve.

*Shu Fa*, or calligraphy, was one of the four basic skills and disciplines demanded of the Chinese literati. The others are *Hua*, or painting; the playing of the *Qin*, a stringed musical instrument; and mastery of *Qi*, a strategic boardgame. But it is calligraphy that is regarded as the most abstract and sublime form of art in Chinese culture and is often thought to be the most revealing of one's personality.

There were three speakers at our little session, all with the same surname: Nguyen.

Quang Thang gave a necessarily very brief history. 'During the imperial era,' he explained, 'calligraphy was used as an important criterion for selection of executives for the court. Calligraphic strokes are permanent, demanding careful planning and confident execution, and these are also the skills necessary in governance. But in calligraphy, while one has to conform to the defined structure of the word, the expression can be extremely creative, and the ability to bring the human touch of imagination to faceless laws and regulations was acknowledged as a virtue.'

There were smiles and small murmurs of understanding amongst those listening, in some of whom the comments seemed to have struck a chord.

Quang Thang moved aside for Van Anh, who then gave us a rundown of the deceptively simple-looking tools of the calligrapher's art, holding up implements as he went.

Brushes, he told us, 'could be soft when made from goat hair, stiff when made from wolf hair, or a soft–stiff combination made from both goat and rabbit hair. The history of the Chinese brush,' he paused, 'can be traced back at least 6000 years.' He smiled with the impact this fact had and continued with the ink stick, invented a mere 3000 years ago. 'Again,' Van Anh explained, 'there are three major categories. Ones made from pine-soot, glue, medicinal material and spices. Ones made from tung-oil, sesame oil and rapeseed oil. And ones made from a mixture of the ingredients of both.'

Taking us through a bewildering variety of papers, he then spoke of the ink slab, or stone, on which the ink is prepared and of which examples have been found dating back 7000 years made of materials as widely disparate as porcelain, jade, silver, iron and copper.

As we were left reeling from all this information, the third member of the scholarly trio, Quang Duy, informed us that all this was of little value unless the calligrapher held the correct posture while seated, which he now demonstrated. 'Body erect, feet evenly and firmly on the ground. Fix your eyes on the spot where you intend to write. Eyes and tip of brush should be thirty centimetres apart.'

It sounded for all the world like a callisthenics class.

'Your whole body should feel natural. Do not pay undue attention to your posture or your body will become stiff or rigid. If you write characters larger than ten centimetres you will need to stand up to write.' Showing us how to hold the brush and how to use the wrist of one hand to support the writing of the other, he made it appear deceptively easy. But somehow we knew we would never be calligraphists.

The three men then took requests for some instant calligraphy and, after Iain told Quang Duy that we were about to celebrate forty years together, with a flourish of the brush he stroked the characters for 'Your Life. My Life. Forty Years. Your Love. My Love'. Plus the tiny symbol which we both had tattooed, palm side, at the base of our middle fingers on our right hands decades before tattoos became *de rigueur*.

One morning, after Trish had settled down at her desk, Huan strolled over with a smile on his face to present her with of a couple of jumping frogs, which he'd cleverly made from folded cardboard. By pressing lightly on the back of the cardboard creature and then releasing your finger, the frog would jump. Trish wanted to give him a thankyou hug, but restrained herself and instead gave the make-believe frogs stick-on bulging eyes and challenged Huan to a few frog-leaping competitions ... all of which he won with ease.

'You know,' he said, trying for a matter-of-fact tone as their toys leapfrogged across the desk, 'it's almost a year since we met ... '

'... and fell into our happy friendship.' Trish smiled.

'It wasn't altogether happy for me.' He gave her an anxious glance and added quickly, 'Because the others,' he inclined his head slightly in the direction of the busy team members, 'didn't like it that we got along so well and they told me so. They told me I was behaving arrogantly.'

Trish's frog leapt clear off the end of the desk. 'I'm really sorry,' she said quietly. 'Sorry to have caused you trouble.'

Huan picked up her frog. 'You need not be.' It was his turn to smile. 'It was worth it. I have learnt a lot from you ... not just about broadcasting.'

She nodded, not trusting herself to speak.

'Like, "What's this bloody crap?" ' His handsome features split into a broad grin and he laughed at his own audacity as he walked back to his desk.

Trish had lined up Huan's frogs in her in-tray and was trying not to laugh out loud over Tram's latest piece describing British Prime Minister Tony Blair as someone 'cooking up weapons of mass destruction', when Minh Ha sat down in front of her. She'd been off sick for a few days and still looked peaked and tired. Trish asked her how she was feeling.

'Better, but still a bit dizzy. For a couple of days I couldn't even sit up. It's happened before. Twice. No-one seems to have any idea what it can be.'

They chatted for a while during which time Trish established that it was a herbalist, not a medical practitioner, Minh Ha had been consulting. Knowing that her husband had a well-paid position with a French law firm, which most likely gave him and his family medical coverage, Trish tentatively suggested that perhaps a check-up at the French Hospital wouldn't go astray. Minh Ha agreed.

But Trish sensed that her health wasn't all Minh Ha had come to talk about and, whether it was just coincidence that the conversation came so shortly after the chat she'd had with Huan or because she felt it was the appropriate time, Trish had no idea, but as she fiddled with Huan's toy frogs, Minh Ha said, 'It's been good for Huan that you two get along so well.'

'It's been good for me too,' Trish managed to squeeze in before Minh Ha rushed on, speaking as though this was something she wished to get off her chest.

'We didn't think so at first. We thought he shouldn't be so forward, so pushy. Being new and the youngest, as he was, we felt he should know his place and stay in it. That's the Vietnamese way. But we were wrong.'

Trish gave a small nod but remained silent, aware that this was a huge admission for Minh Ha to make, and the fact that she felt comfortable enough to do so was a measure of the ease and confidence she had in the relationship between the two of them.

'We have all learnt a lot from his willingness to take the risk,' she concluded.

Later that afternoon, Long dropped by, as he sometimes did, to have a talk with Madame Hue; no doubt about how the training section to which he had been rotated was coming along. On his way out, he detoured past Trish's desk, which had originally been his place in the office.

He, too, found Huan's frogs irresistible and was perhaps motivated by the realisation that our time with VOV5 was coming to an end. As he played with the paper creatures he said, 'I am still hoping you and Iain can participate in a seminar for us.' When Trish responded positively, he added, 'Next month.'

'Who else would be involved?' she asked naïvely.

'I'm not sure yet. But if we ran it across a few days, VOV staff from other provinces could attend.'

'And what would you want us to talk about?'

'Modern News Writing and Dissemination,' he said, in grand capitals, and Trish got the first inkling of what we had let ourselves in for.

Nguyen Quang produces and hosts a science program for children and young people in another branch of the Vietnamese media, television. It's broadcast weekly on VOV-TV2, one of the country's five government-run TV networks. But, although it's a standout program and he puts a great deal of time and effort into it, it's really only a sideline or a hobby for him. His real job, which has occupied him for several years, is as an engineering consultant to the Australian company Connell Wagner, which took part in the construction of the huge Pha Lai coal-fired power plant in Hai Duong Province, about 70 kilometres north-east of Hanoi.

He also happens to be an Australian citizen — and, in some people's eyes, is a Viet Kieu who has returned to live and work in his original homeland.

Quang had been keen to meet us because of our earlier involvement with the *Beyond 2000* science program for TV, which we had helped to found and which had been distributed in almost 100 countries worldwide.

'I watched it regularly in Australia,' he told us when we met up at Jacc's.

We talked a little about his TV program and would learn more of it later, but Quang's personal story was more interesting. He came from a desperately poor farming family in the south, but somehow his family was able to support him through high school. On one occasion, not long after he had finished his schooling, he was sent to visit a relative in the Mekong delta.

'I was at a friend's house one day, when his father said to me, "You have very good grades at school. Why don't you continue your studies overseas?" I told him that my family was very poor and we could not afford it.

'So this man, the father of my friend, just got on the phone to someone in Saigon who was looking for students to apply for Colombo Plan scholarships. I submitted an application and, even though it was two months late, I was accepted.'

Quang didn't say so, but obviously he must have been pretty bright. This was in 1971, at the height of the Vietnam War. Shortly afterwards, at the age of nineteen, Quang left for Australia, where he stayed for another twenty years. By the time he had finished his university studies and post-graduate work as an electrical engineer, the war was over and the situation in Vietnam had become such that he would almost certainly have been shuffled into a re-education camp had he returned. He married an Australian woman, took out citizenship and had a daughter.

'In the early '90s, when my marriage broke up, I had the opportunity to come back here with Connell Wagner to work on this big hydro-electric project, so I took it.'

He now runs a successful engineering consulting firm and owns a seven-storey office and apartment building in Hanoi.

'I married again,' he said, 'and we now have two small sons. But I know I was very lucky to leave Vietnam when I did.'

He paused for a moment, sipped on his drink and continued, 'I also know I was lucky to come back to Vietnam in the way that I did. But it's sad for me to see what has happened to some of my old friends in Saigon.'

'In what way? Do you still see them?' Iain asked.

'Yes, about once a year. We have a reunion. It's so depressing. Some are rich but others are extremely poor, selling lottery tickets on the street or working as cyclo drivers for one or two dollars a day. But the saddest is one of my classmates who, also when he was just nineteen, not long after I left for Australia, was pushed into the ARVN (the South Vietnamese army) and went into Intelligence.'

Quang's voice lowered slightly and we leant forward.

'He told me that he interrogated and tortured people … and often killed them.'

'My God,' Iain whispered. 'He told you this?'

Quang nodded. 'At the end of the war, he spent almost fifteen years in a re-education camp, but somehow his crimes were never uncovered and, in the late 1980s, he managed by some means to escape from Vietnam and get to the United States. I have visited him there, in Orange County. That's when he told me. It was horrible.'

'What is he doing there?' Iain asked.

'He drives a delivery truck. But he has become an alcoholic. Whenever he is not at work, he is drunk. He is plagued by the guilt of what he has done. He told me stories of the people he had murdered and of the look in their eyes as he killed them. I couldn't stay. It was terrible.'

Walking home from Jacc's, we were silent for a time, and then spoke gloomily of how many horrible stories we had heard and read of the brutalities on both sides of the war in those days and how often it is that one's life and the direction it takes can turn on a dime.

Part of Trish's four-point plan which she had outlined for the office at the beginning of the month was for the staff to elect an employee of the month. We have to admit that, initially, we worried about the plan, as it sounded a bit like a scaled-down version of McDonald's or KFC-type razzamatazz, but when the time came, on the last

Friday of the month, Trish cut up fourteen pieces of paper, handed them out to everyone and told them with a smile, 'This is democracy at work. Put your votes in the biscuit tin on my desk.'

They took to it with good humour, or perhaps they were just humouring her. But everybody was keen to know the result, and when the biscuit tin was opened later it was good that she was able to announce an unambiguous decision. There were a couple of votes for us, a couple for each of two other members and three single votes for other members of the staff but, with five votes, there was a clear majority for Khoi.

Over the weekend, Iain did a little fiddling on the computer, drew up a page that looked a bit like a certificate and headed it up in big coloured letters with: 'VOV5 English Service Employee of the Month February 2004'.

Underneath was a coloured photograph of Khoi, culled from the shots taken for the brochure some months previously, beneath which he added some quotes from the voting slips where they gave reasons for their selection. It read:

Chosen by his colleagues for his ...

'Sense of responsibility, hard work and ideas to improve the program ...'

'For stepping up to the mark and grasping the nettle ...'

'For good communication with others, and good performance in his own work ...'

We bought a small A4-size frame and on Monday morning hung it up on the wall in a prominent place, beneath the photograph of Ho Chi Minh.

Everybody loved it.

# March

## WOMEN'S DAY

*'One must chew when eating and reflect when speaking'*

'How do you celebrate International Women's Day in Australia?' Terrific Thi asked, twirling one of the single long-stemmed red roses that had just been gallantly presented to every female VOV staffer by a roaming band of grinning male employees.

Trish chickened out of mentioning the lesbians who celebrate the day in Sydney by holding a get-together in Hyde Park, openly declaring their sexuality and demanding legal recognition of same-sex marriages.

Women in Vietnam have traditionally been described as 'holding up half the sky' and 8 March is a big national day with paeans of praise hitting the headlines, as well as the television and radio airwaves. And this seems more than appropriate in Vietnam. If it were not for the almost one million female guerrillas who fought against French colonial forces in the 1950s, or the 40 per cent of the Viet Cong regional commanders who were women during the American War, there would more than likely be no nation there to hold national days. Other than the Soviet Union, no country comes close to having had that percentage of their women in direct combat roles. It is perhaps possible to say that it was women who tipped the balance towards victory in the war.

Even in peacetime, women everywhere can be said to hold up quite a bit more than half the sky. It was apparent from observation and from intimate conversations with women, both in our team at VOV5 and elsewhere, that women still carry the majority of the inevitable and seemingly unchanging daily burdens which come with a family and domestic life.

It starts at birth. Throughout Asia, boy babies are still preferred. When we were informed by one member of staff that Hanh's full-term, stillborn baby was 'only a girl', we were shocked. When Trish was told the same thing by two more, she was just angry. When she snapped back that the sex of the child was determined by the father, she was regarded with looks of total disbelief.

'Ten girls are not equal to the testicle of one boy,' runs a well-known Vietnamese proverb.

Girl babies make up a disproportionate number of the cross-border trafficking in human lives which goes on with China, in an obscene attempt to make up for the large numbers of female foetuses which are aborted as an unanticipated side-effect of China's one-child policy.

In Vietnam, abortion is so freely and widely available that it's close to being regarded as a form of birth control. Sex education at school is minimal, although it is at least given to both girls and boys.

Such ignorance only adds to the already inherent dangers of pregnancy, and birthing is a high-risk event due to insufficient availability of medical care. Tram told us during her pregnancy, 'I have to find 500,000 dong (A$50) to pay a doctor, in advance, before he will agree to take me as his patient and I will have to promise to pay him a further 500,000 when I give birth.' This was a government-employed doctor in a government-run hospital. As it turned out, Tram had a caesarean section for which she had to pay a kickback of a million dong, or about A$100.

Social attitudes bordering on the barbaric, added to a lack of knowledge, make the first few months of mothering a dangerous period for both mother and baby. The baby is heavily swaddled, even in Hanoi's stifling heat and humidity, while the mother, by tradition, is sequestered away as if impure during a period known as *buon de*, when she does not wash any part of her body for up to a month. But on the positive side of the ledger, this is the only time in her married life when a woman gains a brief respite from the venomous demands of being a daughter-in-law.

All women work in Vietnam. The rural poor and the urban strugglers. The money they earn is a necessity, not a luxury. It's not a matter of choice. Government employees are the fortunate ones. They get four months' maternity leave paid at their base level salary.

When they return to work it's the women who take on the responsibility of finding a carer for their child. 'I pay 300,000 dong (A$30) a month to a village woman,' Minh Ha explained. 'That's quite a lot out of my salary.'

Many of the women who seek domestic work in the cities are fleeing insupportable situations, mostly domestic abuse, which is as common in Vietnam as it is elsewhere. The difference is that it is not openly discussed, nor are there social support mechanisms for violated women.

As for abused girl children, the figures for which would no doubt be similar to those worldwide, to date that is simply a bridge too far. All of which, and more, adds up to the fact that Vietnam's women have a long path ahead to true emancipation, let alone equality.

But it was still great to see the markets and streets overflowing with gorgeous blooms in the build-up to Women's Day, even though of course, in the spirit of a market economy, it meant the price of flowers trebled. It was also great to learn that Hanh was pregnant again, which gave Trish an excuse to give her a superabundant bouquet of exotic flowers, a hug, and to tell her she was very brave.

She demurred. 'Not at all,' she shrugged. 'I had no choice.'

One of the more extraordinary and also influential non-Vietnamese women in Hanoi is the American writer and long-time resident Lady Borton. Amongst many other initiatives undertaken by her to help ease the relationship between the Western world and an emerging Vietnam, particularly in the field of foreign investment, is a thirty-page publication called *To Be Sure*, which has become an essential guidebook for individuals and companies interested in investing in Vietnam.

Densely researched and collated with the help and contributions of more than a hundred Vietnamese and expatriate colleagues, *To Be Sure* has proved to be an invaluable source of information on the customs, policies, prejudices, attitudes, work relationships and practices, cultural traditions, government regulations and much more that a foreigner can expect to have to deal with in Vietnam. In areas such as establishing a company, opening a branch office, investing in a Vietnamese organisation, setting up a partnership, or just importing goods from Vietnam, there is a huge amount to learn that is not immediately apparent to foreigners.

Understanding 'yes, yes' and listening for 'no' are just two of the basic lessons. 'Expatriates all too often incorrectly assume "yes, yes" means agreement, but the phrase is only meant to indicate "I'm listening",' Lady Borton points out in *To Be Sure*. Equally confusing can be the fact that Vietnamese rarely say 'no' in business dealings, as a refusal causes loss of face. Instead, Lady says, 'Vietnamese usually say "No" indirectly through expressions such as "It's complicated", "It's a little difficult", "It's not the right time", or "There's a problem ..."'

The latter part of the publication is devoted to ten very useful and practical 'Principles for Working with Vietnam', which include such things as listening and communicating in a Vietnamese way; hiring the best possible Vietnamese staff; requiring transparency in accounting and program records; and enforcing a clear policy on such things as commissions, kickbacks and gifts.

Our introduction to some of the wisdoms of this little publication coincided with the second visit to Hanoi of George Chapman, the senior executive from Austereo whom we'd met in December. George was accompanied on this occasion by two young Austereo executives: Ben Taylor, a 'number-cruncher' from Austereo in Adelaide, and Roshni Ananda, on the business development side of Austereo's highly successful Malaysian commercial radio venture.

'We're here to put the business plan to them,' George explained as we sat down to dinner at La Place, a small but popular restaurant facing out onto the square in front of St Joseph's Cathedral. 'We've been working on it for the past few months, since the meetings here before Christmas. Nothing is set in concrete, by any means, but this is where we try to show them how the whole thing could work, how it's worked in other places, what's required to set it up and so on. We're due for our first meeting tomorrow.'

We mentioned Lady Borton's guidelines for investors, *To Be Sure*, and told them a bit about it.

'I'd like to see it,' George said with considerable interest. 'That sort of advice is always handy.'

The following morning, we dropped a copy around to his hotel in the hope that it might be of some use.

Two days later, dining at Cha Ca La Vong, the no-menu, one-dish fish restaurant on Cha Ca Street in the Old Town, George, Ben and Roshni seemed upbeat.

'To be honest, I don't know whether *To Be Sure* made any difference,' George told us. 'It's not something you can put into practice in a big way so early, although I was listening for the Yeses and Noes, and at least we're now onto first base. They want to go ahead and, at this stage, it looks as if they're going to pick up most of the tab for the infrastructure.'

'Will that affect the profit split?' Iain asked.

'Oh yes, naturally. But the plus is we don't have to put out all that cash upfront. You can't have it both ways, I suppose. But the good thing is they're talking about having it up and running by next Christmas.'

'Is that possible?' we asked.

George shrugged and raised his eyebrows.

It was one of those meetings you walk into feeling fine, knowing what to expect and reasonably confident about what's going to be discussed and your contribution to it, and then walk out feeling as if a bag of wheat or something equally heavy has suddenly been dumped on your back. You stagger out thinking, how did that happen?

This was a morning meeting that Long had told us about the previous week. It would be with the head of the News Department of VOV; that is, the head of the organisation's Vietnamese-language News Department for all of Vietnam — someone we'd had nothing to do with during the whole time we'd been in Hanoi. After taking the elevator to the third floor of the building next door, we were ushered into a room, where we and two other people — Le Nghiem, a senior journalist from the Vietnamese-language *Nhan Dan* newspaper, and a female journalist, Ly Thai Phuong, from the Economic Department of the Voice of Vietnam — as well as Long, would meet with the News Director to discuss the upcoming seminar that Long had been organising and in which we had been asked to participate.

Participate? Hello? Within no time at all we sensed that the word for 'participate' must have quite a different meaning in Vietnamese.

Dao Nguyen, the head of the News Department, sat back at his desk examining files and going through papers, while we all arranged ourselves around a table adjoining the front of his desk.

He paid no attention to or even acknowledged any of us. Long began speaking, in Vietnamese, by giving a rundown on how he saw the seminar proceeding, day by day. The director looked up, but said nothing. We felt rather uncomfortable.

Long continued speaking. From time to time, he gestured to us. Dao Nguyen nodded and said a few things, unsmilingly. Long went on, occasionally translating some of it into English. The other participants made comments, part of which were also translated for us, but through it all, Iain recalls feeling the growing sensation of a huge void forming in the pit of his stomach, along with the realisation that we were not going to be just 'participants' in this six-hours-a-day, five-day seminar. We were it!

We shook hands with the director, thanked him for the warmth of his welcome and friendly approach, and staggered out into the muggy warmth of the street, completely stunned.

Over coffee, we sort of slid into crisis mode. The seminar, to be attended by forty reporters from VOV offices all over Vietnam, was just ten days away. We had both felt okay about doing a couple of talks as *part* of a seminar, but we were equally aware that to do the whole thing would require a hell of a lot more preparation than we had done so far. And Long wanted some sort of outline of what we were going to do in two days' time!

Iain headed home to the laptop to do what he could there to get it all under way. Entering our courtyard, he found the whole area in a state of chaos. A single-storey house at one end of one of the narrow lanes leading off the courtyard was being demolished, and the rubble, bricks, broken concrete, timber beams, doors, tiles and so on were piled up in front of our house and front door. As he watched, sweating labourers, wearing rubber sandals and carrying huge loads on their backs and heads, ferried the material from the demolition site to the middle of the courtyard.

'What are they going to do here?' he asked one of our neighbours.

'New house. New house … big one.'

*Our neighbours lived in a small network of laneways that ran back from the street.*

The area that had been occupied by the original, and quite simple single-storey house would not have been more than about 50 square metres (say, 10 metres by 5 or 6 metres) so the only way the building could be made 'big' would be by going up.

'How high?' Iain asked.

'Four, maybe five storeys,' was the reply.

In the middle of March Mr Dinh disappeared. Living in Hanoi it's inevitable that you develop relationships with people who just barely manage to survive by scurrying between the interstices of life going on around them. Mr Dinh, from whom we bought photocopied books, was one such person. There was also Hoang, the *xe-om* driver, as well as the elderly cyclo or pedicab operator, both of whom earned perhaps three or four dollars a day. Much further down the economic ladder were Vuong and Bac, the shoeshine lads and, at the very edge of crisis, an elderly woman with an enormous smile and a twisted body, who begged.

Over time we became acquainted with each other's routines and habits, so much so that on several occasions Hoang appeared unexpectedly beside Trish as she was walking in some distant part of the city and insisted on giving her a ride home. Once she even went with him when she didn't want to, because she didn't have the language to explain this and because she didn't want him to have made a fruitless trip to pick her up. On another occasion she saw the old lady with the ruined spine hobbling around so far from her usual patch that they greeted each other like friends who unexpectedly run into each other at an international airport.

With his finely honed street smarts, Mr Dinh had quickly worked out that Trish was a dead cert buyer for any book about any aspect of Vietnam and that she made regular calls at his sidewalk 'shop', so he invariably had some new book to offer her. When, on one visit, he was absent, she was not immediately worried. But when she dropped by again a few days later and he still was not there, she sensed there was a problem. After discreetly asking around, she found that he had been jailed.

It seemed that he had managed to fall foul of the police to whom he gave a small regular 'present' so they might turn a blind eye to his business, which he operated illegally from a crack in the wall of Nha Tho Street in the Old Town because he couldn't afford to buy a vendor's licence. Or perhaps it was part of the relentless vendetta with other similar salespeople in the area. According to Mr Dinh, he had a permit to sell, but only in a very limited area. When he stepped outside that area just for a moment, to sell a book to a passing tourist, he got caught. It was also not unusual to see a small squad of heavy-handed police who cruised around in open trucks, confiscating any wares which spilled out of the shops onto the pavements.

It's a fact of life in Vietnam that unless you have the correct permit you cannot live and work legally in the capital. Every adult

Vietnamese must carry an identity card with them at all times. The card states their legal home address. To move either between villages or towns, or even to travel, requires permits, which in turn invariably requires money.

If he'd had the money, Trish was told, Mr Dinh could have paid to avoid being incarcerated or, failing that, at least to have something like decent food and living space once he was inside. As it was, he served his three weeks in appalling conditions. 'It was very cold, with no light and just a little daily rice,' he told us when he reappeared, looking frighteningly gaunt and stricken. And, 'Ten men in a room about this big.' His gesture indicated the size of an average Western bathroom. But with limited education and skills, Mr Dinh could see no option other than resuming his former tough life on the street.

If the increased availability of previously inaccessible literature represented one example of significant change in government attitudes towards the media and the arts, films were another, even though all cinema product continued to come under the heavy scrutiny of the Ministry of Culture and the censor — whoever, or whatever, group of people that might be.

Gerry Hermann's Hanoi Cinematheque seemed, on the other hand, to be somehow avoiding the heavy hand of officialdom as it continued to screen English-language films that had not been given wide release; several, apparently, without the government's official stamp of approval — that is, having been passed by the censors.

'I still can't get anyone to give us the official nod,' Gerry told us in desperation one day, as we sat enjoying a beer in the outdoor bar area before a screening of one of his films. 'We keep asking the Ministry. In fact I've told them I will give it all to them and I'll just run it for them, if they like. But no-one is prepared to move on it and say we've got an official licence to run it.'

'So it's a big risk to just keep showing films, isn't it?' Iain commented.

'It sure is. But I've got no choice. It's started up now and we've already got a really big membership, including something like forty different ambassadors. It's working. But my official partners, the Hanoi Film Club, are not pushing hard enough. They should be the ones that do all the lobbying. I'd rather the actual Ministry took over their role as partners really and then we'd have some legitimacy for the whole thing.'

One of the important things about the Cinematheque was that, in addition to the Western and other international films screened there, it had quickly become a venue for showing important films that were either produced by Vietnamese, or were about Vietnam. *Nostalgia for the Countryside* by acclaimed Vietnamese director Dang Nhat Minh, shown in March, was one of the former: a powerful and poetic film which examined the dramas and traumas of life in a rural Vietnamese village. Though considered controversial at the time of its release, it nevertheless got the nod from the Ministry and won international acclaim as a masterpiece.

A couple of other films by American producers were also controversial, though for different reasons, and were not available for general release. Notably, *Hearts and Minds* and *Regret to Inform*, two very different but equally moving documentary-style movies about the Vietnam War.

*Hearts and Minds*, a 1975 Academy Award-winning documentary by Peter Davis that, at the time of its release, had been described as 'probing the depths of what was a still-open wound', was shown separately at the Cinematheque to members of the Friends of Vietnam Heritage. Without the aid of a narrator, the movie alternated between eminent talking heads, including several American presidents and war commanders, plus graphic stock footage and testimony from war veterans, to present a dense weaving of sound and image that all combined to confirm the futility of war.

*Regret to Inform* was the incredibly touching documentary film made by American war widow Barbara Sonneborn, whose husband went to Vietnam on 1 January 1968 only to be killed eight weeks later. On her twenty-fourth birthday she received an official a letter, beginning: 'We regret to inform you ...'

Twenty years later she decided to begin the long process of trying to make a film about the anguish she had suffered, as well as that undergone by widows on both sides of the conflict. The film merges stories about the war — often tragic, often heroic stories of loss, survival and healing — experienced by the wives of men who fought for either North or South Vietnam, or in the American forces.

Another film, *Vietnam: The Next Generation*, introduced on-stage, again for an audience from Friends of Vietnam Heritage, by its producer, American documentary maker Sandy Northrop, tracked the lives of six young Vietnamese, part of the postwar generation that never knew the war and now seizing opportunities unimaginable in their parents' time.

All of these films seemed to resonate more deeply, simply through seeing them in the country where it had all happened.

'The first thing you must do is set the rules, clearly and concisely. Write them on the whiteboard outside the meeting room and tell them that if they break them they will be expelled from the seminar,' Nguyen Tien Long instructed us.

Rules? We felt we'd failed already, before the course on Modern News Writing had even begun. The forty people who were scheduled to attend from Ho Chi Minh City, the Delta, Danang, Hue and Hai Phong, as well as Hanoi, were all VOV radio journalists, professionals, the majority of whom no doubt, being twenty-something, were also married and with children. Hardly a bunch of kindergartners who would appreciate us wagging a finger at them. But nor were they the indulged products of liberal Western democratic traditions in education and Long insisted it was what was expected.

8.30am, start. 10.00am, coffee and cigarette break. That's another difference to take into consideration. Smoking is a far more socially acceptable habit in Vietnam. 12.30pm, break for lunch for two hours, siesta in the heat of the day and to give time for mothers to either breastfeed their babies or shop at the market. Finish the day punctually at 4.30pm, because VOV is a government department. No smoking in the meeting and also no chatting.

Seated around the large table in the conference room, they looked so keen and eager, as if they thought we had all the answers. Beside us at the head of the table sat Le Nghiem from *Nhan Dan* ('The People') newspaper, whose endearing manner we immediately warmed to. To one side, Dao Nguyen, head of News and Current Affairs, the inscrutable and brusque-mannered man in whose office we had first realised this seminar was going to rest on our shoulders. We introduced ourselves and gave a very brief run-down of our experience. Dao Thi Thuy, from our English-language team at VOV5, began the massive task of translating as we went.

Iain had done by far the lion's share of the nitty-gritty of getting the contents of the seminar down on paper and going through it with Long, which meant he had skipped shifts during the pulling together of the stories for the current week's *What's On* programming. In ten days of hard yakka, we'd managed to get it into some sort of shape.

Saying you want to be told is one thing; being told is quite another. Conscious that we were engaged in something of a highwire tightrope act, for which nobody was willing to set the parameters and in which our only safety net was the knowledge that we had another home to go to, we leapt in, boots and all, pausing only to make a passing apology in advance for the fact that 'Western journalists often seem pushy and abrasive in Vietnamese eyes and we hope that what we say here does not leave you with that impression, but we would hope that there are things you can take from our talks that will be of value to you.'

It was all pretty simple, basic stuff. But some of these people, working as journalists for the national broadcaster, had never had any professional training. It was a skill they were picking up on the job, so we began by discussing the difference between news and current affairs and moved on to sources of news and how to gather it, giving examples as we went along and getting them to evaluate pieces for news bulletins, as well as softer stories.

On the second day we spoke about the principles of news-writing, centred around the essential story elements of Who, What, Where, When, Why and How. In their assignments they had to examine four *Vietnam News* stories and four VOV news stories, assess whether they contained these elements and if not, rewrite them. Then we moved on to story structure: the lead, the back-up lead, the lead quote, the essential paragraph and so on.

Le Nghiem spoke about how all this applied to *Nhan Dan* and Thuy did a sterling job of translating back and forth.

By the time we broke for lunch on the second day we felt we were going well enough to leave them with a teaser for the afternoon session. 'We're going to discuss how to recognise bias in the news,' Iain announced. 'Bias through selection and omission, bias through placement, bias by headline, bias through use of names and titles, and bias by choice of words.'

Oops! Dao Nguyen, head of News and Current Affairs, who appeared to have dozed like a lizard in the sunshine throughout the sessions, blinked slowly.

Not that we really felt there was anyone keeping a watchful eye over what we said or did in a political sense. Actually it turned out to be quite the contrary. As we continued, it became apparent that they truly did want us to spell out how radio journalism was done in the rest of the world ... no holds barred.

So, in the section dealing with bias, Iain latched onto a news story, buried on page five of the English-language newspaper, dealing with a 35-year-old man who had developed a system of underground filter chambers connected to a backyard lead-smelting furnace that would save the local people in a village not far to the south of Hanoi from lead poisoning. It wasn't until halfway through the story that you read that, in the cottage industry operating there, 600 households were melting down forty tonnes of lead waste every day and that hundreds of kilograms of lead dust were being poured into the air daily. Five hundred people were suffering from respiratory diseases and twenty-five children had been born with lead poisoning, birth defects or brain disorders.

'This is a classic example of bias by placement,' Iain said. 'It's a newspaper story, but it happens in radio stories also, when a story is buried at the end of a bulletin. This story should have been on page one!' he declared. 'In the West, a story like this would spark a national outcry. Everybody, from local councils and regional administrations, to the national government would be called to task.'

But, in addition to the story's placement in the newspaper, the structure of the story itself showed bias — bias clearly aimed at directing the public's attention away from the real issue. 'The real story here is not that the man invented some device that could ameliorate the problems,' Iain pointed out, 'but that hundreds, probably thousands of people's lives are being put at risk, on a daily basis.'

On the third day, we began to deal with the more practical and fun areas, involving the use of tape recorders. We began by launching into some of the theoretical stuff around recorded interviews: the difference between news, current affairs, features, documentary interviews, the 'stand-up' and or 'on-site' reporter's piece, and finally the vox pop.

They spent the morning on exercises built around formulating lists of questions for the different types of interviews with hypothetical people we had chosen. They also had to interview each other on different subjects.

But what they were really all waiting for — although some of them were dreading it — were the vox pops. After explaining the Latin origin and that it meant the 'voice of the people', we divided everybody into six groups of six or seven, giving each group a portable recorder and instructions to go out into the streets close by the office to seek answers to a couple of simple questions.

'You must just walk up to anyone you see ... complete strangers ... and ask them the question,' Iain said. 'Don't get into long conversations. Each person in the group should try to get answers from at least three people, then hand the mike over to one of your colleagues. You only want quick, thirty-second responses,' he insisted. 'And, when it's all put together and cut down, we're looking for about two minutes from each group.'

So, we all headed out into Ba Trieu Street and branched off in different directions. Well, they just loved it. Some were a bit shy, others went for it with a vengeance. After finishing their recordings, they had to come back with the material and, on the next day, edit it all down into some sort of coherent shape. There was laughter and joking as they returned to the seminar rooms as, for most of them, it was the first time they had ever done anything like it.

The last day and a half of the seminar were devoted to practical work on programs they had to prepare, based on the elements — including the interviews and vox pops — that had been covered during the course, plus music. Sitting in the studio listening to the end results, as each team compiled their material in a simulated live broadcast, we felt a combination of relief, at having got through what had become a bigger job than we had anticipated, and satisfaction that it had, according to Long and the taciturn News Director, Dao Nguyen, gone off very well. This was confirmed in a way, we guess, when he stood up at the end of the seminar and instructed his reporters to 'do exactly what the two Australian journalists have told you to do'.

It had been at the Australian Embassy residence, almost a year previously, that we had met Professor Le Van Lan, one of Vietnam's best-known scholars of the country's history. But we became aware during the year that he was much more widely known for his extremely successful weekly television quiz show for children than for his vast knowledge of history and archaeology. Nevertheless, it was around history — very ancient history — that our next meeting revolved.

It's not really surprising that Vietnamese people have a strong sense of history. It's dealt them some pretty awkward hands over the years. What is surprising though, is that *ancient* history seems to be so strongly remembered, emphasised and understood, even amongst young people, for many of whom the more recent colonial wars with the French and the American War are drifting into the realms of obscurity and irrelevance.

Somehow the historic battles of Ly Thuong Kiet and Tran Hung Dao against what are euphemistically called either the northern feudalists or the northern invaders (in both cases read 'Chinese'), are remembered and celebrated with almost as much fervour as the more recent victories against modern enemies. Any of the young staff at VOV, for instance, could readily reel off for us the details of the legendary union of Lac Long Quan, the Herculean son of a dragon, and the fairy Au Co, which resulted in the birth of the Vietnamese people.

This all became very relevant to us towards the end of March, when we decided to join a group of people led by Professor Le Van Lan to visit the temple of the Hung kings, about 100 kilometres north-west of Hanoi. The Hung kings were a dynasty of seventeen successive rulers, who followed the first magical offspring of the fairy and the dragon.

'Lac Long Quan means Dragon King of the "Lac" country,' Professor Lan explained to us as we climbed the several hundred steps leading up the densely forested sides of Nghia Linh mountain to reach the temple of the last Hung king. 'But at the time of his

*Professor Le Van Lan tells the story of the Dragon and the Fairy who gave birth to the Viet people.*

meeting with Au Co, he had transformed himself into a handsome prince.' (Of course.)

'After they had been together for a time,' the professor continued, 'Au Co, the fairy, became pregnant and eventually gave birth to a sac containing 100 eggs, which hatched to produce 100 children. Later, Lac Long led fifty of the children down to the coast and Au Co took the other fifty up to the mountains.'

Van Lan paused on the steps to catch his breath. 'It's good for us to do this trip now,' he said, 'because next week, during the annual festival of the Hung kings, one of the most important in Vietnam, there will be thousands of people on this path every day for at least ten days.

'As Lac Long left for the coast,' Lan continued, 'he said to Au Co, "I am of the dragon race and you are immortal. We cannot live together. Let us divide the country between us and rule it jointly." And that is what they did, creating, in the process, the Viet People.'

Soon we reached Den Thuong, the High Temple, below which, on one side of the hill, is the tomb of the eighteenth Hung king. 'It's empty,' Professor Lan told us with a smile. 'In fact there may never have been anyone in it. Because no-one knows the date of his actual rule. It's back in the time of legends ... even before the time of Christ. It's more of a memorial than an actual tomb.'

Standing in front of the steps of the High Temple, we were reminded of a famous photograph of Ho Chi Minh seated on these same steps in 1962 amid a group of admiring young soldiers. He had made the pilgrimage up to the temple at the age of seventy-two and it had been a struggle. But, he had insisted to those around him, 'Once you start, you must go on to the end.' On another pilgrimage, eight years earlier, he had stood at the temple before a different group of soldiers, not long after the victory at Dien Bien Phu, and delivered a similar message: 'The Hung kings established our country. It is up to us to keep it.'

Our tour, which had included a visit to the Hung Kings History Museum at the foot of the mountain, plus three other temples at different levels on the hillside, had been memorably enlivened by the diminutive professor's running commentary. 'Even though the story is shrouded in myth and fantasy,' he concluded, 'it's a well-established archaeological fact that, by the end of the first millennium BC, a distinct civilisation had blossomed in this part of the world.'

Every night now our courtyard was a scene of frenzied activity. The demolished house had been removed and materials for the new house were being delivered. Due to the restricted hours during which trucks could do this, bricks, sand and gravel all had to be brought in after seven in the evening.

We would return from our adventures, usually about 10.30pm, to find that we had to surmount an obstacle course of loose material in order to reach our outside gate. Wearing plastic sandals and work pyjamas, with the women also wearing cone-shaped hats, at least a dozen people toiled back and forth from trucks parked in the street outside, through the narrow entrance alley and into the courtyard, bearing on their heads large, shallow rattan trays, heaped to overflowing with sand and gravel. They must have made hundreds of trips every night, their path dimly illuminated by low-wattage nightlights on the surrounding buildings.

For the most part they worked in silence, saving all their energy for the task at hand, but when we turned up, the men would put on a bit of entertainment for us, staggering under their loads and assisting us, in the manner of Versailles courtiers, across the corrugated tin pathways they had set up, all the time laughing.

Often in the mornings we would wake to the sound of one of them lightly singing, always some sweet melancholy piece — no doubt a song of love unrequited or a soldier's farewell to his

*A young labourer at work on the new building under construction in our courtyard.*

sweetheart as he goes off to defend the fatherland from yet another invasion. We would go out on our top balcony and look down to find the courtyard either empty of material, which had already been moved further into the interior of the village to the building site, or to find it neatly stacked and covered with tarpaulins with the surrounding area swept spotlessly clean.

One very early morning we were dragged from our sleep by the sound of shouts and manic shovelling and stepped out onto the balcony to find that we'd been hit by a torrential tropical storm. The rain, though still heavy, was easing and all of the workmen had thrown plastic raincoats or, failing that, plastic sheeting, over their undershorts and were sieving the sand out of the gravel, which had been washed together into one enormous sodden pile.

Each day, before heading off to the office or starting work at home, we would make a visit to the site of the new house for a tyre-kicking inspection. The owner and the building foreman took great pleasure in showing us what progress had been made. All achieved with one small, much abused and wheezing cement mixer, erratic timber and bamboo scaffolding, a handful of buckets and a lot of backbreaking manual labour.

By the end of March, they were working towards laying the slab for the third floor; putting in the steel reinforcing rods and side ties. In the middle of the day, at the height of the mounting heat and humidity, they took a two-hour siesta, flopped out like rag dolls in any piece of shade they could find. Following a full afternoon's labouring, they soaped up and washed off at the courtyard's corner well, modestly leaving on their undergarments, joking as they emptied pails of water over each other's wiry bodies. Then there was just time for an evening meal, cooked in the communal kitchen and eaten perched on the ubiquitous tiny blue plastic stools, before the evening deliveries got under way and the routine began all over again.

At some time during the night they must have rested up on the wooden bunks in the one tiny room set aside for them behind the well and the kitchen, but it surely was an exhausting cycle of labour.

In the office, we were now reminded almost daily of the fact that there was little more than a month before we were due to finish up at VOV. Theoretically the one-year term should have ended on 20 March, but both Madame Hue and Madame Loc, as well as Khoi, had been asking us to stay longer, so we had extended the term until the end of April. This arrangement also fitted in with our plans to be in Dien Bien Phu for the fiftieth anniversary celebrations of the victory there, on 7 May.

Although the daily requirement for two or three *What's On* stories only represented a relatively small amount of the overall daily workload, the pressure for developing and writing up the necessary segments was now shifting fairly solidly onto Huan and Thi and everyone could see and appreciate that these two, the youngest members of the department, were taking on the extra responsibility with a will. Between them, they were researching, writing and voicing at least five or six of the thirteen or fourteen pieces needed each week, which left the two of us doing only a little more.

However, Khoi's comprehensive revolution was facing a problem in that, not only would the department be severely impacted if he was selected to go on the training course in Sweden, but it now appeared, once again, as if Minh Ha might be leaving temporarily, this time to do a six-month training course in Singapore.

And things were looking more difficult for the department in another sense, as we learnt from successive emails that AVI was continuing to have trouble in finding replacement volunteers to fill our positions when we left. Ideally the replacements were intended to be in place about a week or so before we finished up, so there could be some sort of briefing, but this was now in doubt. We began to feel even more uncomfortable about walking away from VOV5, virtually leaving them in the lurch to cope as best they could.

The slightly anxious mood in the office was lightened considerably on the last day of the month, when Trish got out the biscuit tin and, stepping into the role of electoral officer again, handed out slips of paper, making sure everyone voted for the Employee of the Month.

When the vote was counted, Huan was elected the winner, by a sizeable majority, and we admit we found it impossible to contain our pleasure. He had come such a long way in a year, both professionally and personally.

*April*

# A COURTYARD PARTY

*'A gift from the heart is valuable'*

So long as Ho Nguyet Co keeps a gem in her throat, which she has done for 1000 years, she remains a woman with extraordinary strength and magical powers. Without the gem, she not only loses those powers, but is doomed to resume her previous incarnation as a fox. Losing her good sense one day, Nguyet Co falls in love and, during lovemaking, is tricked into surrendering the gem to her lover.

A cautionary tale. A moral fable. And a traditional Tuong play.

We were delighted when the opportunity arose on the first day of the month, April Fools' Day, to see a performance by the National Tuong Theatre of Vietnam that was accompanied by an explanatory introductory talk in English. Once again, it was one of the excellent cultural events regularly organised by the Friends of Vietnam Heritage group.

Tuong was founded in twelfth-century Vietnam and reached its popularity zenith in the seventeenth century when it was taken up by the royal family as a favourite form of entertainment. It is a highly stylised entertainment intended for the educated elite and filled with sophisticated symbolism. Tuong is to Vietnam what Noh is to Japan, or the Beijing Opera is to China.

It uses minimal props and relies on the imagination of the audience to create scenery, but the colourful costumes are also intricately embroidered and convey complex messages to an audience which needs to be educated to grasp their inferences. For instance, a general wears two flags on his back. If he also carries a fake whip in his hand, it means he is riding a horse.

During the performance Trish had noticed Lona Thwaites in the audience and, during the interval, managed to edge her away from the crowd and spring her little plan on her.

'Lona,' Trish tried to smile winningly, 'I know you are always flat-out busy, but I wondered if, given your journalistic background, you would be interested in finding time to do a bit of work at VOV5, to fill in there ... perhaps just until AVI get their act together and find replacements for us?'

In the cab on the way home we discussed the idea and the likelihood that, as an ambassador's wife, Lona may well not have enough time to devote to *What's On*.

'Perhaps she might take it on as a bit of light relief,' Trish said, 'because she agreed to at least come in and have a look at what's involved and, who knows, it could also be a good opportunity for their daughter, Anna.' Some months previously, at a careers day at the Hanoi International School, we had learned that Anna had an interest in journalism.

If we'd thought our afternoon participation in a session of karaoke and ballroom dancing was going to let us off the hook from further invitations, we were sadly mistaken. Thuy, from the administration office upstairs, had made vague noises during our visit to her house that we should join her and her husband again, this time at a proper ballroom.

So one Friday morning, when we were both in the office together to record *What's On*, she came up to us and, with Huan interpreting, asked us to join her at some place called the Discovery Club the following day, a Saturday, in the morning.

'Saturday morning? Ballroom dancing?' we queried her, through Huan.

'Yes,' he confirmed, after asking her. 'Apparently, a lot of people go dancing on Saturday morning.'

As Thuy was being very friendly about the whole thing, we felt under something of an obligation.

'It's airconditioned,' Huan assured us after she had told him some more about it, 'and very close to here. Only ten minutes from your place.' He wrote down the address she had given him.

'What time?' we asked.

'Nine-thirty,' Huan told us, and when we looked surprised he added, 'the club is open early to late every day of the year. They'll meet you inside.'

That's how it came about that at 9.30 the following morning we climbed the curving concrete outside staircase of the Discovery Club, next to the Youth Sports and Culture Palace, to the second floor, in through a gaudily decorated hallway, then through a heavy door and into a darkened ballroom with spotlights and rotating mirror balls.

It was like stepping into a parallel universe. Even at that early hour, it was already full of twirling couples for whom the dress code ranged from jeans and T-shirts through to up-market evening gowns, complete with diamanté hairclips, chokers and earrings, and evening stilettos.

Thuy and her husband emerged from the gloom to greet us. She was dressed to the nines; a picture of elegance in a long red gown. Her husband, who had a carefully coiffed shock of long white hair, scrubbed up pretty well too in black trousers, black shirt and a smart black and gold tie.

The fact that we were rather more casually dressed worried no-one and, almost immediately, they had grabbed us and hustled us out there onto the floor where we could strut our stuff ... well, sort of. You get the picture. We had a go at sambas, lambadas, salsas and tangos. Both of us found the whole thing rather amazing. There was no entry fee to the club, but they were doing a good trade in beer, wine and other liquor, even at that time of the morning. Also, for those women who had come with no personal dance partner, the club provided a group of young men, all dressed in black slacks, long-sleeved white shirts and sober ties, looking for all the world like a team of recently escaped Jehovah's Witnesses. And the whole thing was apparently all straight and above board.

After about an hour and a half, by which time we felt we'd done our duty, we said goodbye and staggered out into the morning sunshine and heat, feeling that perhaps you don't really qualify as a modern Hanoian until you've had a go at karaoke and Saturday morning ballroom dancing.

The general consensus in the office about Lona Thwaites stepping in to help with *What's On* was very positive. We warned them that it was still only a possibility, but they were so keen for it to happen that when Lona turned up to watch us do a recording, to get a feel for how things worked, she received a warm welcome. Which made it all the more embarrassing when the guard in the pillbox outside the adjoining building in which the studio was located refused her entry. Khoi, who had decided to accompany us on this occasion, as a mark of respect, did his best to persuade the uniformed official that it would be all right, no doubt adding that Lona was the wife of the Australian Ambassador. But to no avail. A form, signed by Madame Hue, was required. So we all hung around in the heat while Khoi dashed back to the office for the correct documentation.

Lona sat in the studio as we recorded our pieces and saw how we swapped over to work with Huan and Thi. Afterwards we talked about the scripts: what went into them and how we went about chasing up stories and information to go into the program. She was clearly interested and we hoped we might convince her to pick up some of the running when we left at the end of the month.

'It's all a matter of time,' she said. 'I'd love to do it, but …'

'Perhaps if you just do one day a week,' Trish suggested. 'On Wednesdays we usually do only one item. Perhaps you could do Wednesdays. You could do it all at home. You wouldn't need to come into the office, except to record.'

Lona nodded slowly and we could see she was thinking about it. 'Maybe …' she smiled.

Later, back in the office, Thi picked up a book of Vietnamese legends that Trish was reading and asked, 'Are you enjoying them?' Trish assured her that she was, even though they were for the most part so sad.

'When I was a small child,' Thi, who was now twenty-one, told her, 'I used to sit on the mat beside my grandfather, who was dying of cancer, and read them to him. The story of *Tam and Cam* was our favourite and I read it over and over.' *Tam and Cam* is the Vietnamese version of Cinderella, only with a great deal more pain and heartache. 'I would read at night by candlelight,' Thi told Trish. 'Times were hard and there was little money, but we always found some for books and I re-read them so many times I know many of the stories by heart.'

Still learning to be humbled by their personal histories, we had yet more to learn from Minh Ha, who had once again been laid low by giddiness, the cause of which continued to be undiagnosed. She also knew the legends by heart, but what she came to ask was what we would like as a farewell gift from the office. Minh Ha stood stony-faced as Trish blathered on about a gift not being necessary, but thank you very much and so on, and then said, 'When a Vietnamese asks you what gift you would like, it is impolite to refuse.' When she could see that Trish was embarrassed by her faux pas, she grinned and suggested she ask for something that would remind us of Vietnam. Trish agreed that would be excellent.

Trish's response, shortly afterwards, to the news that Huan and Thi had been accepted as full members of staff was to give them both a hug. This was probably seen as a particularly 'Western' reaction, but in the ebb and flow of what they had learnt from each other, it seemed to be acceptable. Trish knew how important this admittance into the sanctum of government service was as the first step onto the career ladder, which brought with it a degree of financial security. They, along with Tram, had been on a year's probation. Tram, who had taken four months' maternity leave in the middle of that time, was still anxiously waiting approval.

As a further gesture that he now really was a member of the team, Huan had been appointed representative of the Sports Section of the Youth League at Voice of Vietnam and in the middle of the day he asked Trish to join them for a game of badminton on the make-do court in the open-air office car park which fronted onto Ba Trieu.

'Why didn't we do this in the winter?' Trish asked, puffing and sweating as she ran about the court after the shuttlecock, providing, in the process, much amusement for passers-by who stopped to watch this foreigner make a fool of herself. At least she wasn't trying to play in high-heeled stilettos, like Tram, who was doing famously and not sweating at all.

'We couldn't afford the racquets then.'

'How much did they cost?' Trish asked.

'100,000 dong.' (A$10.00)

Back upstairs in the airconditioning, amusingly red-faced and dangerously overheated, Trish found a used nail-polish bottle holding a single tiny rosebud on her desk; a gift from dancer Thuy to say thank you for joining her and her husband on their Saturday morning ballroom excursion. And while we all hung about the central table, scoffing the chocolates and sweets that Khoi's wife had brought back on her recent return from six months in Japan, Huan, with a shy smile, presented Trish with his Youth League badge.

1. We needs in dendent and peace protetion and dynasty yours my minority in this highland.
2. We donot wants to subsic tence by Vietnamese government.
3. Let Vietnamese government to giving back of this highland to my minority peoples.

These demands, scrawled in large capital letters across a bedsheet-sized piece of material, and carried by tribespeople through the streets of Buon Ma Thuot, the capital of the central highlands province of Dac Lac, over the Easter weekend, went on:

4. We needs to have the presidnt and dynasty whose my minority in this Highland.
5. We wants the Vietnamese government to release all my minority peoples from the jail.
6. We wants all Vietnamese army and troops to get awty from this highlands.
7. We like Mr Kok Ksor to be presidents to protection and dynasty oursesin this highlands.

Although at first glance the fractured English made the sentences a little difficult to pick up, the overall message was clear. A photograph of this piece of material appeared in the Vietnamese-language newspaper *Thanh Nien* on 27 April, more than two weeks after the event. However, practically no news at all, let alone pictures, appeared in the English-language press.

The news of the 'unrest', as it was euphemistically called, in the central highlands of Vietnam over that weekend seeped out slowly. We suppose if we'd been listening to the BBC or following CNN more closely we would have picked up on it earlier. As it was, the first we knew of it was around the middle of the month, when news stories began to come across our desk for editing saying things like: 'A spokesman for the Ministry of Foreign Affairs, Le Dzung, yesterday confirmed that no-one was beaten to death during the recent protest meetings in Bon Ma Thuot ...' or: 'A government spokesman has denied reports that authorities violently suppressed demonstrators during recent incidents of unrest in the central highlands. Charges made by Amnesty International "are based on fabricated and ill-intentioned information", a government spokesman said.'

All of which, of course, was a dead giveaway that something important *had* happened and was difficult to deny. The US Embassy reported that a delegation of its officials, on a previously scheduled visit, had been prevented by police from entering the town of Buon Ma Thuot on that weekend. Their car was stopped en route from Ho Chi Minh City and they were told the area was 'not suitable for foreigners'. They were also told they could not visit Pleiku, another major city in the highlands.

There had previously been major unrest in the highlands in February 2001 over religious and property rights relating to loss of their ancestral lands, which were being taken up for use as coffee plantations by the majority Kinh people. The religious complaints had revolved around restrictions on their practice of an 'unsanctioned' form of Protestantism.

Reports about this latest event from different sources varied from 'Thousands of minority hill people, known as Montagnards, marched on government buildings ...' etc. to '"It was not a very big crowd," said one local policeman.'

The 'Mr Kok Ksor' mentioned on the protest sheet is known to be the leader of the US-based Montagnard Foundation, which was formed in South Carolina by members of a group of anti-communist Montagnard fighters who had been allied with the United States during the war in Vietnam and who the Vietnamese government blames for instigating protests and demonstrations amongst the hill tribes, with promises of asylum in the United States and money.

Up to 40 per cent of the residents of the highland provinces of Gia Lai and Dac Lac are members of ethnic minority groups, not necessarily all of the Protestant faith, but sufficient in number for them to be difficult for the government to ignore — particularly in the light of increasing international pressure from the European Union and human rights groups calling for observer and media access to the two provinces.

On a carefully arranged tour, a small group of foreign reporters eventually met with officials and people who had supposedly taken part in the protests.

'I'll never do it again. I've realised my mistake,' was the comment of a man called Chyam, from the Gia Rai ethnic group. Another insisted to the journalists that 'officials are very nice people, they educate us'.

There was little doubt that some sort of 'education' process had been under way. But there were still big differences left between the two versions of what had happened. According to officials, apart from three ringleaders, who would be charged with offences, other protesters, judged to have played only minor roles, were let off after conducting 'self-criticism'. On the other hand, Amnesty International claimed that at least eight Christians from the ethnic minority groups were killed in the clashes.

As is so often the case, the truth probably lies somewhere in between.

In the office, the boot was now very obviously on the other foot and Huan was not at all averse to putting it in. Much to our pleasure, though we humoured him by pretending to appear that we felt put upon, Huan would greet us every day with a demand that we get our *What's On* stories in to him pronto. He slipped so easily into the role of 'the boss' it was as if he was to the manner born.

Thi was powering too, especially pleased with herself when she interviewed a visiting Finnish painter and chopped up the recording to use as inserts in a piece for the program. The microphone technique and voice levels were correct, and the questions interesting because she listened to the answers.

With the two of them, we felt that our little creation was in good hands, but we had to admit that there were not enough hours in the day for us to get our *Personally Speaking* program up and running in a proper form. We had each recorded four or five different interviews over the preceding weeks, but with the pressure of other things and time running out, we could see there was no way we were going to get it to air on a regular basis, so we had to let it slide.

Tram, on the other hand, was extremely proud of her own successful production, her son Minh, who was doing all the things that young babies do, only of course he was doing them more quickly and showed signs of brilliance bordering on genius!

She brought in photographs of her darling boy. 'I sing him to sleep every night,' she smiled tenderly at his image, 'and I am going to do a piece, perhaps for the *Sunday Show*, on Eastern and Western lullabies. Please,' she asked Trish, 'would you record a few of the ones you used to sing to your children?'

Taking this as a challenge to the adequacy or otherwise of her mothering, and unwilling to reveal that she had bedded our rug rats down to a few bars of a Brahms lullaby, regurgitated in tinny tones over and over again by a music box, Trish couldn't immediately think of any lullabies, and turned desperately to the internet for assistance. Our children would have been amazed to have heard their mama's tender rendition of 'Rockabye Baby on a Treetop', 'Lavender Blue' and 'Here We Go Round the Mulberry Bush'. She did feel somewhat of a fraud and she certainly didn't try getting into explaining the political overtones of all these ditties.

On the domestic front, we were now beginning to think about the logistics and the practical side of finishing up our stint with VOV and the move back to Australia. In the house, we had collected all sorts of extra 'stuff' that we didn't want to cart along with us. Trish pointed out to Mai some of the things that we didn't want to take, like some bed linen, crockery and kitchenware such as a toaster and a small electric oven. There were also some clothes, pot plants, furniture and a bookcase. Mai was delighted to look through it all and happy to take everything we had mentioned to her, but she was adamant that she wanted to pay for the furniture — a cane lounge with two matching chairs. We argued for a while, but she was insistent.

We also told Mai that we would like to throw a party for all the people in the courtyard. This at first amazed her, but she quickly picked up on the idea and became the key person in organising it and spreading the word to let the other residents know that it would be on the following Sunday morning. It was still two or three weeks before we were due to finish at VOV, but we thought it best to get as much done as early as possible.

We wrote up an invitation in English, which we asked Huan to translate for us and which we had photocopied and gave to Mai to hand out to the residents. We also asked her to come with us while we arranged with the people from the local *bia hoi* on the corner to bring enough beer for up to about forty people. They said they could also provide a spread of food, from rice and noodles to spring rolls, fish and pork, as well as chicken and various vegetables.

We had no idea what sort of turn-up we'd get, but on the day we shifted all the furniture and chairs in the sitting room back up against the wall and put the oval-shaped kitchen table in the middle of the room, opened the two doors from the room onto the little ground-floor patio and then swung the metal security gate open to welcome whoever arrived.

As the new building being constructed at the end of the little alleyway was still going up at a hectic pace — already they were starting on the fourth floor — we thought that perhaps some of the workmen would also be coming along, but whether it had been arranged by the residents of the courtyard or someone else, there was no work under way on the house on this particular Sunday.

We'd suggested 11.00am and, sharp on 11.00, they began turning up, the men in smartly pressed shirts and ties, the women and children in their Sunday best. Unexpectedly, they had brought us several presents: a small carved wooden box with a hinged lid and a set of lacquer boxes as well as a framed lacquerware painting of the small temple in the centre of Hoan Kiem Lake. Many of them also carried their own personal versions of the tiny blue plastic stools seen all over the city. Taking off their shoes as they entered the sitting room, they placed their stools on the floor and sat down.

Rebecca, who had cycled across from West Lake, also came in to join us. There was lots of laughter and sign language as we tried

**The farewell party for our courtyard neighbours. Everybody was soon in high spirits.**

to communicate and ask them questions. None of our visitors spoke any English and our Vietnamese was not up to any form of sensible conversation. Nor were Mai's sporadic attempts at splintered English of much help, yet somehow we all managed perfectly. And, as the people from the *bia hoi* kept a running supply of draught beer flowing, everybody was very soon in high spirits.

One of the things that gave us a certain amount of pleasure was not so much the fact that they had all come on time, but that they had come at all. It was something we could not have anticipated when we first moved into the house in the courtyard. At that time, we were, we suppose, the foreign freaks who'd arrived to live in their midst. And despite the language barrier, over the months we had come to be accepted at a level of friendship that meant we had become a part of the small community. And we felt privileged to have bridged this gap. Eventually a couple of the men stood up and made speeches, most of which we didn't understand, but when everyone nodded and looked at us and smiled and then clapped enthusiastically, we assumed it was all okay. Iain responded with a brief thankyou.

And then, almost as suddenly as it all started, as if on an internal signal among our visitors, it all came to an end at 1.30pm. Some of the older residents stood up and said they must go and everyone else followed suit. We insisted that we must take a photograph and so, before everyone had gone, we mustered the central characters of our courtyard into a group and took a couple of shots that would remind us of them in time to come ... and them of us.

'Capitalism considers the market economy its goal, while socialism has always thought of it as merely a means.' Trish read on with her red pen poised. 'We are bypassing capitalism in a transition towards socialism, and globalisation is a period in capitalism on the road to true global socialism.

'From the lively practical experiences of seventeen years of renovation in the country, we can fully affirm that Vietnam is at present on the transitional development path toward socialism, bypassing the capitalist regime. This is a correct and creative application of Marxist Leninism and Ho Chi Minh Thought.'

Creative application, indeed, she thought, as she ploughed her way through the rhetoric of the last edition of the *Communist Party Review* with which we would ever be confronted. Who can be completely sure about the correct choice for a nation's political path? Capitalism has so many unacceptable faces; ask the women and underage children working for a pittance on the dangerously antiquated looms of factories in Bangladesh. So too does communism, as any Tibetan monk is aware.

'A disciplined democracy' is how Loc described Vietnam's present political status to us in the build-up to the upcoming People's Council elections. We had given up trying to work through the undercurrents and tones of language with Loc. Our energies were better spent on the younger ones with more open minds. Like the one who commented derisively, 'Central Committee of the Communist Party? We'd be doing better if there was a Central Reality Committee.'

Over the past few weeks we had noticed numerous small shophouses that had been given a red and gold makeover and morphed into small election booths. Posters depicting a young woman dressed in a white *ao dai* placing her vote in a ballot box were prominently displayed on sidewalk walls, and information trucks with loudhailers and the street public address systems went into hyper-drive, while the media went mad with statistics. Fifty-one million voters would cast their ballots in one of the 88,000 polling stations set up across the nation, to elect 311,000 people from among a total of 450,000 candidates, 32 per cent of whom were women, 21 per cent under thirty-five and, most significantly, 24 per cent of whom were not members of the Communist Party.

'Candidates,' according to Do Duy Thuong, a permanent member of the Presidium of the Vietnam Fatherland Front

Committee, 'had been selected, over five rounds of consultations, on the basis of their political credibility, ethics and lifestyle.' Mr Do went on to say that the Front, which had been responsible for choosing candidates from among those who had put themselves forward, 'is working to contribute to the elimination of bureaucracy and corruption and to successfully implementing the goal of creating a prosperous people, a strong country and a fair, democratic and civilised society.'

At five-thirty on the morning of the election Sunday, the loudspeakers began blaring their demand that the people give their vote. Fortunately it was 25 April, so the early call didn't worry us — we were already attending an Anzac Day Dawn Service in the grounds of the Australian Embassy at which a new poem by the distinguished Rhodes Scholar, naval officer, former ASIO Director and renowned poet, Michael Thwaites, who also happens to be the father of Ambassador Joe Thwaites, was read to the assembled throng. It was the same poem which some hours later would be recited at the recently inaugurated Australian War Memorial at London's Hyde Park Corner. In part, it reads:

> *... Here, racked with thirst, and dazed, and blind, and*
>   *sweating,*
> *Through pain, and dread, and ecstasy, and blood,*
> *Our flesh and bone climbed to their self-forgetting*
> *And in this place was born our nationhood ...*

Nguyen Quang, the Australian electrical engineer whom we met in February, and who also produced a TV science program for young people, phoned around this time to ask us to dinner at his home with his wife Chi and their two young sons. His seven-storey building on Mai Hac De Street, not far from our office, houses a small television production facility on the first floor, which Quang has set up to produce his weekly program. His own consulting business plus offices which are leased out to local and overseas businesses are on other floors. He and his family live in a luxurious apartment which occupies the top three floors of the building.

During our dinner with Quang and Chi we learnt that she was a concert violinist who had played with the Vietnam Symphony Orchestra.

'You must come to the Tang Yun concert with us,' Iain told them. 'He's the young Chinese violinist who is coming to Hanoi to play with the symphony orchestra. He is the lead actor in this new film called *Together*.'

They hadn't heard about it, so we talked for a while about the film and the concert and we could see a sort of nostalgic haze come over Chi's eyes, as if she was briefly back in the violin section of the orchestra, instead of tending to two young children and household chores.

'Yes, we'd love to,' Chi said, without any prompting from Quang.

Rising to the top in a pile of 1.2 billion people means you have to be a pretty impressive talent, which is what Chinese prodigy Tang Yun certainly is. Although only fifteen years old, he has already been playing the violin for over a decade. More than playing it, he has been caressing, coaxing and conning it into producing sounds of sublime beauty, such that make those fortunate enough to be within earshot shiver with delight.

We had met Tang Yun on the evening before his concert in the courtyard of Gerry's Cinematheque. We had also met his mother who, just as you would expect, was probably half the reason why Tang Yun had managed to scramble up the heap. The other half was more than likely due to her husband, who had stayed behind in Shanghai where the couple and their son now lived.

While her son challenged Iain to a yo-yo contest, Mrs Tang sat beside Ipa-nima bag-lady Christina Yu, who chattered away animatedly, no doubt happy to use her Mandarin skills. Mrs Tang smiled with gracious confident poise, but not for a second did she take her eyes off her teenage son. It had probably been like that ever since he was born, or at least since he was given his first violin when he was four, at which point it would have quickly become apparent that he was something out of the box.

We had just viewed, for the second time, the Chen Kaige film *Together*, which showcases Tang Yun's other talent, acting, and tells a story that somewhat echoes his own. Born in the provinces, the central character has a father who, on recognising his son's potential, concentrates his life in a determined drive to make it possible for the young boy's talent to receive the training and recognition it deserves. The film's violin prodigy struggles with the monkey grip of paternal care and love as the father pushes his son to fulfil his potential.

The following evening we crammed into a sold-out Opera House. Gerry had done a brilliant job of cross-promotion, having arranged for multi showings of the film *Together* with a follow-up visit by Tang Yun and his Opera House concert, so he had every right to look pleased with himself as he introduced the star of the show.

And what an occasion! Tang Yun's performance of Tchaikovsky's Concerto for Violin and Orchestra, Op. 35 in D major, was spectacularly well received with standing ovations for him, the conductor and the orchestra.

Later, at a reception which Gerry had laid on at the Metropole Hotel in honour of his special guest, we mingled with some of the friends we had made in Hanoi over the past year. Quang and Chi chatted animatedly with Christina Yu and Noel White, a friend visiting from Seattle. We spent time talking with Tran Thi Yen Lan, of whom we've spoken as the inspiring 'one-person NGO'. She was there with her nineteen-year-old daughter, who was also a student, but, on the flip side of the card, leant great support to her mother. Then there was Franz Xaver Augustin from the Goethe Institute, who had become one of our closest friends in Hanoi, who stood by the pool talking earnestly with Rebecca.

We felt there couldn't have been a better way for us to farewell Hanoi, but after a while we noticed that Gerry was not here amongst his friends, to share centre stage with Tang Yun. When he finally did arrive and we learnt the reasons, not only for his delay but for his facial expressions, which flashed between rage and distress, we all went into shock.

'They have closed down my cinema,' he sputtered distractedly. 'The government has closed down the Cinematheque.' His jaw worked furiously. 'They chose tonight, when they knew I would be at the Opera House, and they came ... these men, who said they were from the Finance Department, and they demanded to see the books and they made all sorts of outrageous accusations. And they demanded that the theatre be closed. Immediately.'

Against this depressing background of the threatened or impending closure of Gerry's Cinematheque, the last days of our contract with Voice of Vietnam came rolling on. The thirtieth of April was a Friday, which under normal circumstances would have been our final day, but as it also happened to be one of the most important days on the Vietnamese calendar, it had been declared a public holiday. It was Total Liberation Day, the day, in 1975, when Saigon fell to the invading forces from the North.

So, our last day would be the Thursday, 29 April. We recorded our final *What's On* program with Thi and Huan, not without a certain amount of emotion on everybody's part. Later, Huan and Tram asked us if we'd join them for lunch at a restaurant around the corner from the office. Thi had unfortunately gone home at the conclusion of her early shift.

'We'll go on our motorbikes,' Huan said. 'Iain can come with me. Trish, you go with Tram.'

The correlation and coincidence of two like events — one on the day of our arrival and introduction to Hanoi and the other, almost fourteen months later, on our last day at VOV — in the form of a pillion ride on a couple of motorbikes to a restaurant, was not lost on us. While of no real significance, it seemed to be a nice touch.

At the Paloma Café we had a small snack and talked nostalgically of events over the past year, then, at our suggestion, rode up around Hoan Kiem Lake to buy ice creams at Fanny's Ice Cream parlour on Le Thai Tho Street.

Our farewells to the rest of the staff were to be a drawn-out affair. We knew they wanted to take us out to dinner upon our return from the fiftieth anniversary celebrations at Dien Bien Phu, which we planned to attend on 7 May, but we also wanted to make a gesture of our own. So, we had organised a luncheon for all the staff, a few days previously, at a restaurant called Xua Nay, which means Past and Present.

At the end of the meal, we each gave a short speech saying how much we had both enjoyed our stint at VOV5 and valued the friendships we had made there. And it was here that we finally handed over the present that our American friends had brought in for us from San Diego — the *Times World Atlas*.

We handed it to Loc, as the most senior member, and when it was opened, it certainly brought the sort of reaction we had hoped for. Lots of 'oohs' and 'aahs' as it was passed around the table. The old *Philips School Atlas* had finally had its day.

And now, a few days later, here we were, at the end of that last working day, having said casual goodbyes to the others on duty, walking down the stairs to the ground floor and finding ourselves swept with unexpected emotions; a sense of loss and of the inexorable passing of time. Okay, it was our last day, but we knew we'd be seeing them all again during the following week and also after our visit to Dien Bien Phu, so why the unsettling feelings?

'We've had such great times with them all,' Trish said, as we slid into a taxi. 'Even the arguments . . .'

'A bit like the end of an affair, I suppose.'

'Or a little death.'

The taxi stopped for a red light and three motorbikes kept going, passing us and crossing against the red. We smiled at each other. Hanoi.

One of the troubles with getting older is that you start to look at things, or events, or experiences as if they can't ever be recaptured; as if it's the last time this will happen to you. And, while we had many ideas and plans bubbling away between us to find ways and means of returning to Vietnam to be able to contribute to the ongoing dynamics of the society, it was hard not to avoid the feeling that this had been one of those things in life which, while you can grab it with both hands and wring wonderful experiences from it, was also just 'joy as it flies'.

## *May*

# DIEN BIEN PHU AND AU REVOIRS

*'From defeat comes victory'*

In the first week of May, as we prepared to head off to Dien Bien Phu, there was another office party, this time thrown by the staff as VOV5's farewell dinner for us. It was held on the partly open rooftop of the popular Highway 4 Restaurant, a place named after the road running along the Vietnam–China border, which played such an important role in the campaign that led up to the decisive battle of Dien Bien Phu.

We all sat cross-legged on cushions around the low table as Minh Ha made a brief speech thanking us for what we had achieved at VOV5 and presented us with a gift, which she had obviously been instrumental in choosing: a beautiful hand-embroidered piece in a frame, showing two boys riding home through the paddy fields on the back of their buffalo; a quintessential Vietnamese scene.

We thanked them all and, as we were leaving in a welter of hugs all round, Huan informed Trish in a quiet aside, 'Your friend's Cinematheque has been closed. I'm not allowed to mention it any more in *What's On*.'

'Who told you that?' she asked sharply.

'Minh Ha. But it's also in the Vietnamese papers today.'

Trish had recently taken Huan along to Gerry's cinema to introduce him to the various people there. He had been nervous, thinking it was a place just for foreigners, and had been relieved to find just as many Vietnamese there.

'We'll talk about this when we get back from Dien Bien,' Trish said. 'But rest assured, it's not over yet.'

'Not until that fat lady sings …' He gave his winning grin, pleased with his assured use of English. 'Bloody hell, no!'

In the midst of all these farewells we had begun to pack. What to say about packing? It always seems to become an 'issue' — particularly when you stay in a place for more than a year. Generally, when we're on the road, either working or for pleasure, we travel quite light, with either just a small backpack or that plus one of those airline bags on wheels that you can fit in overhead lockers. But somehow, when we stay in a place for an extended time like this, we seem to collect unreasonable quantities of 'stuff'.

In this case the stuff included a large amount of research files that we needed to take back to Australia, but we had also collected some art material that had helped decorate the house in Hanoi and now, at the very last minute, we had made a decision we'd been pondering over for ages … to buy a pair of parallel sentences.

Parallel sentences? Well, parallel sentences have become, down through the ages, an integral part of Vietnamese culture. They are evident in virtually every pagoda or temple you might visit in Vietnam, usually in the form of vertical wooden panels, carved in Chinese or Nom characters, often painted in gold or red and placed on either side of a doorway or a temple altar. Modern Vietnamese have continued the tradition using their alphabetised tonal and monosyllabic script.

Throughout their long history, parallel sentences have often presented an opportunity for Vietnamese to confront and also affront authority publicly. In brief, they are two parts of a poem in which strict rules are followed. For example, the number of words in both sentences must be the same, the form must be the same — as in the placement of verbs, adjectives and nouns — and the content of each sentence must be significant, either as the antithesis or in the parallelism of ideas.

The poem, usually no more than half-a-dozen or a dozen words in each of the two stanzas, can be written by one person, or as is very often the case in famous versions, the first is spoken or written by one person and the other half is a response by another, usually required to be delivered on the spot . . . immediately.

The charm of parallel sentences doesn't translate readily to English, because of the need for more words and different sounds, but here's an example from history in which a bound man stands in front of the Emperor Minh Mang. The emperor says he will free the man if he can give an appropriate cross sentence in response to the emperor's verse. Spying a fish chasing a smaller one in the nearby pool, the emperor says, 'In clear water, fish eating fish.' Without hesitation, the captive replies, 'Under scorching sun, man tying man.' The emperor, astonished, releases him.

Not all endings were as happy. Others in history have been flogged to death for their responses. But the appeal of the sentences has never diminished. The subtleness of the phrases and of the figurative meanings within the Vietnamese language, coupled with the opportunity for irony, have assured their survival as a vibrant part of Vietnamese poetry and culture.

We had found our parallel sentences in the back of an old antique store on Yen Phu Street, which we'd explored with Rebecca on a couple of occasions. They were each about two metres long, made of wood painted black with the carved Chinese characters painted gold. The translation of our sentences, we would later find out, read, on the one panel:

*The young owners of the antique store in which we found our parallel sentences, an ancient form of clever verbal jousting which survived through the ages as an integral part of Vietnamese culture.*

'Presenting poetry, the court is filled with the fragrance of flowers.'

And on the other:

'The reading of a piece of literature is like the language of a myriad of birds.'

At the time, we're ashamed to admit, the messages were not the most important thing. We were obviously pleased with them, but in a much more pedestrian sense, there was now also the realisation that we suddenly had a couple of very awkward things to pack.

The Muong Thanh Hotel, where we had stayed on our previous visit to Dien Bien, was a very different scene from what it had been three months ago. It was crammed with guests, and in the lobby we immediately ran into a small bunch of international journalists, some of whom were exuding an air of self-importance and vying with each other over who had the latest on what was happening, where and when. This was, after all, still a communist country, which meant that any information is hard won. There was no official press kit or press conference. They frantically fed each other rumours and kept *xe oms* on stand-by, so they could dash off at a moment's notice to wherever they heard something was happening.

We walked back into the town, which this time was awash with visitors, including large numbers of minority tribespeople, with the women in their distinctive costumes. Some wore layers of full calf-length skirts, matching gaiters and loose, striped and appliquéd chemises, topped by headpieces either laden with table-tennis-ball-sized, bright orange-coloured woollen baubles, or row upon row of heavy silver coins which, on closer inspection, turned out to be currency from the period of French colonisation. Others wore full-length, tight wraparound skirts with closely fitted, spotless white long-sleeved blouses and a conical straw hat which sat above their heads on crowns of woven split cane. In all this constraining clothing they somehow managed to elegantly manoeuvre themselves through the crowd on bicycles. By comparison, their menfolk, who were dressed in regular shirts and trousers, looked extremely ordinary.

These were the people whose forebears had been as instrumental in winning the war against the French and the battle at Dien Bien Phu as other minority people had later been in the fight against the Americans. Unabashed, they stared at us as much as we stared at them. We were such a rarity among the many thousands of people we saw that afternoon that we caught a glimpse of only half-a-dozen or so other foreigners.

Caught up in the ebullient crowd, we trudged up a sealed roadway to the top of a hill overlooking the centre of town for a close look at the enormous new bronze sculpture whose recent cross-country journey had been covered extensively in the press. The structure, almost 13 metres tall, 10 metres long and weighing around 200 tonnes, had to be transported from Nam Dinh City, about 70 kilometres south-east of Hanoi, over 400 kilometres to the north-west, into and through the rugged mountain terrain to Dien Bien.

The statue, which is called 'Dien Bien Phu Victory', is overwhelmingly symbolic. It depicts three Vietnamese soldiers standing atop the bunker of the French commander, General Christian de Castries. A flag hoisted by one of the soldiers bears the motto *Quyet Chien, Quyet Thang* ('Determined to Fight, Determined to Win'). The second soldier holds an automatic weapon and the third carries on his shoulders a Vietnamese child of the ethnic Thai community, who holds aloft a bunch of flowers.

Trish has a weakness for such large-scale heroics and happily posed beside the giant muscled legs with the dozens of other groups having their photos taken and who now suddenly wanted to have one taken with a foreigner. Perhaps they thought she was a Frenchwoman come back to visit a place of ignominy. We took

**The statue to commemorate the Viet Minh's 1954 victory over the French at Dien Bien Phu. From this angle the third figure is obscured.**

scores of photographs of them too; resplendent in a wild collection of uniforms and *ao dai*, as well as traditional minority styles, often bedecked with medals. The atmosphere was one of great gaiety.

Not so at the enormous cemetery, a little further from the centre of town at the foot of hill A–1, or Eliane, which we had been to on our previous visit at the end of January. We got there in time for the arrival of an official wreath-bearing party led in by a couple of smart, goosestepping soldiers in white dress uniform. They marched down the central path, between row upon row of granite graves, all carrying the red star and marked with the title *Liet*, meaning 'Martyr'. On each one burnt a massive profusion of incense sticks, the perfumed smoke from which hung in a thick, heady pall. Behind the soldiers were men in sombre suits, followed by veterans and their families. Many of the old men had wispy Ho Chi Minh-style beards and were frail and bent. Some rested on the stronger arms of younger generations. Their chests too were laden with rows of medals — survivors of who knows what horrors. And what a lifeful of changes they had witnessed.

The heroically proportioned golden sculpture here, between two magnificent frangipani trees in full white bloom, was of a couple of graceful women, in flowing *ao dai* and in the gentle pose of a receptive embrace. Wreaths were laid, names read, incense lit. The old men stumbled over the gravel surrounding the graves and, indicating that they wanted their photographs taken, straightened up and stood tall ... a couple even saluted. Proud. This was their special day. It wouldn't come again.

That evening, over the only really awful meal we had throughout our time in Vietnam, we talked with Lona Thwaites, who had also made a special journey for the celebrations and who was staying at a brand-new, not yet finished, massive hotel complex which looked over Him Lam Hill, better known to the French as the fortified emplacement Beatrice.

Back at our hotel we bumped into Sam Taylor, the Hanoi correspondent for Deutsche Presse Agentur and Deutche Welle, the

German press and radio organisations. Sam was a Londoner, married to a Japanese, and he spoke perfect German. Now he was looking exhausted and a bit shaken up.

'I just did a long interview with a French veteran,' he seemed anxious to tell us. From his description, we recognised a man we had seen around the hotel and glimpsed briefly at the cemetery. He appeared to us to be in his late seventies, still dapper, with an obvious military bearing.

'He was a pilot here during the siege,' Sam explained. 'He told me he flew dozens of bombing sorties over the Viet Minh troops who were dug in around Dien Bien. He wanted to talk about his experiences, but then he suddenly started to cry.' Sam paused. 'He said this was the first time he had come back and that he felt a great sorrow for the people who had died ... on both sides. I didn't know what I could say to make him feel better.'

As we stood under the thatched roof of the small outdoor café at the front of our hotel, just before 7.00 o'clock the following morning, waiting for Lona to arrive in a cab, a steady rain was falling over Dien Bien. We were concerned that the weather would affect the ceremonies.

But, shortly after joining Lona for the ten-minute cab ride to the city's sports stadium, we could see that, as far as the Vietnamese were concerned, no-one was going to rain on *their* parade ... and if they did, it wasn't going to make a blind bit of difference.

The streets were filled with people making their way to the stadium. Alighting outside and protected by our $2 plastic cloaks and Lona's umbrella, we edged our way towards and straight through one of two big gates. We had no idea about ticketing, seating, or anything else and, as it turned out, there wasn't anything to know. It was Rafferty's rules, or 'first in, best dressed', as the entire surrounds of the stadium were rapidly filling up.

The main stand, where the VIPs and officials were under cover, was naturally enough completely occupied but, more or less by chance, we'd timed our arrival quite well and there was still some seating available around the sides and close to the low fence surrounding the field. 'Seating' is perhaps stretching it a bit. Broad, tiered concrete steps that doubled as seating ranged backwards, eventually elevating the back levels above the field by about 10 metres.

Laying claim to a short stretch of rain-soaked concrete on the second tier, we put down one of our plastic cloaks to sit on and then, stretching the other over the back of the three of us, we huddled as close as possible under Lona's umbrella — for about three-and-a-half hours!

This is not to say it wasn't worth it. It was. And at least the rain wasn't cold. So, relatively speaking, we had it easy. The many hundreds of people who participated in the extraordinary parade and then the complex theatricals that symbolically reproduced the battle of Dien Bien Phu stood out in the pouring rain during the first hour after we arrived, while the stadium filled and the rest of the VIPs arrived. Then they remained there, immobile, during another hour of speeches, until the main events got under way and they finally got to do their thing.

It was a bit like a mini-opening ceremony for the Olympics. There were soldiers marching, different ethnic groups in their ornate and highly coloured costumes, athletes, balloons, banners and complicated stage backdrops of mountains and houses. Then suddenly the mountains and houses began to morph into tanks and stylised military vehicles on wheels, with performers dressed as French soldiers atop the tanks. Others dressed in Viet Minh uniforms, with solar topee hats, pushed bicycles and pulled replica cannons through the jungle in intricately choreographed movements, all accompanied by smoke, sound effects and music.

And everywhere we turned, whether looking into the seated crowd or amongst those walking around the perimeter of the field, there were men to whom these theatricals must have seemed very strange, if not laughable — the old veterans of the real battle of half a century ago, laden down with their medals. But over it all, despite the rain, there was an incredible feeling of high spirits, enthusiasm and good will.

The rain had eased by the time it all wound up, so we walked the couple of kilometres back to our hotel along the crowded main thoroughfare, Him Lam Street. As on the previous day, there were large numbers of minority people and very few foreigners. We parted with Lona, who had a luncheon engagement, while we had a brief break at the hotel before charging out into the multitudes again; this time to the museum, which had been closed during our previous visit.

We weren't much more fortunate on this occasion. The museum was open, but the airconditioning had broken down and, with three or four hundred people inside, it was like an oven. We were only able to do a quick circuit before falling outside, drenched with sweat, to recover.

In the evening the rain held off while a massive outdoor concert, also with many hundreds of performers, was staged on the vast forecourt of the central government offices on the main street. Thousands of people turned out to stand shoulder to shoulder and probably 100 metres deep to watch the elaborately costumed performances.

When it was all over, the fireworks and the partying began. Not for us, though. We staggered back to the hotel where we were deep asleep within minutes of hitting the bed.

'I've been offered a job in Jordan,' Rebecca told us. 'What d'you think?'

Visions of Petra, 'rose red city, half as old as time', filled our minds.

'Go for it!' we said in unison.

We'd returned to Hanoi for our farewell with the young woman who had added an inestimable amount to our life in the city.

Keeping up with the extra three decades' worth of energy she had over us had been challenging. Keeping up with the rigours of her intellect had been equally so.

We had eaten together almost every day. Together we had visited museums, pagodas, art galleries, exhibitions, concerts and movies. We had played cards and Scrabble and devoured books, which we had then discussed. We had climbed mountains, walked national parks and done laps in the pool. And we never tired of talking and listening to each other's feelings and ideas; tossing around globalisation, sustainable development, international aid, volunteerism, religion, corruption, cultural similarities and differences, war, personal responsibility and how Trish could possibly like Charlene singing 'I've been to Paradise ... but I've never been to me'!

We had acted as debriefers for each other over our jobs — although we think Rebecca tolerated a disproportionate amount of ranting from us. We had developed an emotional circus act, catching each other mid-fall in inevitable downers. Rebecca's due in large part to the bewildering lack of eligible men. Ours caused by missing our grandchildren, and taking on a heavy workload. We looked out for each other. Perhaps best of all we laughed a lot as we teased each other over personal foibles.

Now the time had come to separate and it was hard, very hard.

The British Council had quickly picked up on Rebecca's obvious talents and now she was going to work for them as Teacher Training Coordinator, based in Amman. Another courageous leap into a very different culture. Another step along the road of what was certain to be a brilliant career. We were sad for us, but happy for her.

'Promise you will come and stay with me in Amman,' she demanded tearfully as we hugged on our little patio.

We promised. Rebecca got on her bicycle. 'I'll bring my Celine Dion collection with me,' Trish yelled as she began to pedal unsteadily away through the courtyard.

'Yippee,' she whooped and disappeared under the arch.

It was also time to say other goodbyes. We wrote a little 'thank you and goodbye' note, which Huan translated for us. We then handed copies of the note to people we had come to know on a friendly basis during the year. These included Huong, our regular *xe om* driver, the lady we bought flowers from, our barber and hairdresser, the shoeshine boys, and the owners of the local *bia hoi* and adjoining shops.

Then came our second and, in most cases, last round of goodbyes to the people in the courtyard. We went around to each place shaking hands and trying to say that we'd be back some time or, more importantly, that we'd like to come back.

The building at the far end of the courtyard was still going up. They were already working on the fourth floor, with at least another floor to go. They had only demolished the original house in the first week of March, less than two months previously. We weren't sure exactly which of our neighbours would be migrating into the new premises, but one thing was certain: they'd have a lot more room in the new place than they'd had before.

We also paid one last visit to the office and sat around the central table tossing back small glasses of Ming Manh wine, which seared the tonsils and brought tears to the eyes.

'Pity you are leaving us just as you learn our habits.' Tram squeezed Trish's arm. She had taken Trish aside as soon as we turned up, bursting to tell her the good news. 'I have been accepted as a permanent member of staff.' She beamed. 'I'm not reading the bulletins live yet, but that should happen soon.'

'Good on you,' Trish responded, knowing how important this was to Tram's sense of security, particularly as a new mum. 'Next time I see you you'll be head of the department.'

Tram shrugged, not entirely dismissing the idea.

'But you'll have to join the Party,' Trish added.

'Things are changing.' Tram was shaking her head. 'As you often say, changing very fast.'

*The new building under construction at the far end of our courtyard. After only two months they were working on the fourth floor.*

Minh Ha then insisted on interviewing us. It was as well she took us away to the deserted conference area, because all three of us found the talk and reminiscences quite confronting. Far easier to ask questions than to answer them.

'Everyone here will miss you,' Minh Ha turned off her tape-recorder and hugged us both. 'Me especially.'

'And you look after yourself,' we encouraged her, thinking of her dizzy spells.

She promised that she would and then, pushing our luck yet one more time, we hopped on the back of their motorbikes and drove in convoy to a café in the Old Town for a final meal together. When the time came to pay we remembered not to offer to put in. Another Vietnamese habit to which we had become accustomed. Invited guests do not offer to pay their share. 'You see,' Trish pointed out, 'we are learning.'

'When you have really learnt about us,' Huan commented sagely, 'you won't need to say so.'

How right he was, but how come he already knew that while, at three times his age, we were still learning?

Finally, our last night in Vietnam had arrived, but even now we could not avoid the type of combined cultural and political message that one becomes familiar with, but never quite inured to, in Vietnam and it came in the form of another piece of political censorship, or attempted censorship, of an art exhibition.

Our evening was also to be spent with someone who had become one of our closest friends in Vietnam, Franz Xaver Augustin. Throughout all of our time in Hanoi, he had been a constant pleasure — both as a friend and in a professional sense. He had worked tirelessly to develop, organise and promote the artistic, cultural and intellectual activities that were presented by the German cultural organisation the Goethe Institute.

On this occasion, it was the opening of an exhibition by Bangkok-based German photographer Ralph Tooten, in which he presented a wonderful collection of photographs he had taken all around the world of religious leaders of every denomination; fascinating photographs of monks and nuns and priests, popes and mullahs.

All of the photos had captions beneath them, saying who they were, except for three of the photographs: a big picture of a smiling Dalai Lama, one of a man who was obviously a Buddhist monk, and another of a woman who was equally obviously a Buddhist nun.

'The Ministry of Culture wanted to ban the shot of the Dalai Lama,' Xaver explained. 'I had to fight for it to be included. They said that China was their friend now, and that China and the Dalai Lama were not on good terms, so he had to go.'

He laughed. 'So I pointed out to them that China had also been a long-time foe of Vietnam ... and asked, "Does China respect you any more for falling over backwards to please them like this?"

'They agreed to let the picture stay, but without saying who it is. But they also said we couldn't have the shot of the Vietnamese Buddhist monk, Thich Nhat Hanh, who lives in France. He's a troublemaker, they insisted. Also the nun, Chiang Khong, who lives in France too.'

'Why didn't they want her?' Iain again asked.

'I posed the same question,' Xaver said. '"Don't you know who she is?" the guy said to me. "No," I replied. "She's Thich Nhat Hanh's lover ... that's who she is!"

'But eventually they also stayed ... without the captions, though. A compromise on both sides, I suppose.'

Very Vietnam and perhaps a fitting closure to our Vietnam experience. It didn't complete the picture by any means, but it was a reminder that Vietnam, although charging down the highway in the direction of a more free and democratic way of life, still has a way to travel.

Nevertheless, as we prepared to say 'Goodbye Hanoi', we both felt very privileged to have witnessed just a bit of its amazing journey.

Now it really was time to move on, to turn the page and begin the next chapter. We were formulating plans to return to Hanoi, hopefully to give workshops — expanded versions of the week-long modern newswriting seminar we had done for Nguyen Tien Long. But, as the Vietnamese say, you can never step into the same river twice, which though it may be sad, is perhaps just as well.

On the way to the airport we dropped by the Australian residence for a coffee and homemade Anzac biscuits with Lona and Joe and their daughters Anna and Julia. Just as we had hoped, Anna was planning to work alongside her mother at *What's On*. Perhaps the start of a career in journalism. We briefly discussed the idea of the ABC sending cadets to Hanoi on perhaps a three-month roster basis as a part of their training. It would bring an enormous benefit in understanding to both countries. One needs schemes and dreams.

It had been an exhilarating and challenging fifteen months. We hadn't anticipated the depth of the impact Vietnam and the Vietnamese people would have and we're not sure we can express why with mere words. It has to do with what we had seen of their admirable qualities. Resilience, perseverance, adaptability, courage, a capacity to love, accept, forgive and move on.

Whatever the evidence to the contrary, we'd like to believe there's a little bit of this Vietnam in all of us.

*Do you remember now the day you went away?*
*The apricot buds had barely opened to the western wind …*
*And I asked, dear, when would you come back?*
*And you assured me … when the peach trees bloom.*
*The peach blossom now is scattered on the wind.*
*Already faded petals strew the riverbanks.*

*From Chinh Phu Ngam*
(*Lament of a Wife whose Husband has gone to War*
by Doan Thi Diem, 1705–48)

# EPILOGUE

## WHERE ARE THEY NOW?

Iain and Trish have visited Rebecca at her British Council posting in Jordan and joined her on several short journeys in the Middle East, including one to the ancient city of Petra. They have also just completed a three-month return assignment in Vietnam, at the request of VOV, to help in planning the introduction of an all-English language radio network there.

**VOV Team**

Huan continued producing and hosting *What's On* along with his other work at VOV5. He has travelled as a translator for a government delegation to Hungary. His girlfriend has returned from Cuba and they are planning on marrying and having a family.

Terrific Thi also continued producing and hosting *What's On*, along with her other work at VOV5. She is married and pregnant.

Tram is now reading news bulletins on air and her son is thriving.

Hahn has given birth to a healthy baby daughter. She is now the team leader of the English-language section of VOV and has attended a course in production run by Dutch Radio in Holland.

Minh Ha is working as Press Assistant in the Hanoi office of Agence France Presse. She has been hospitalised twice with symptoms of dizziness, but has taken herself off medication and is hoping to have another child.

Khoi is working with his family's business, which now employs fifty people producing and installing, as well as exporting, rolling shutters and aluminium doors and windows. He is also studying accountancy at night. When he left his job at VOV he was expelled from the Communist Party. Having survived a hugely demanding learning curve, he has no regrets about his move into the private sector.

Quynh remains a happily married father of one, and managed to come out unscathed from a balance-of-power struggle within the team at VOV, following Khoi's departure.

Thuy continues at VOV5 and now has a longed-for son to join her daughter and complete her family.

Giang returned to VOV5 from a three-month BBC training course in radio production in Cardiff and Bristol. He is now married and has a son. He says his experiences in the United Kingdom have given him the confidence to 'survive anything anywhere'.

Phuong has a second daughter and remains part of the VOV5 team.

Madame Loc is retired from VOV, but is working as a consultant and language editor at the national English-language newspaper, the *Vietnam News*. She also does commercial translating.

Madame Hue is retired from VOV, but working as senior consultant to the Editorial Board of Voice of Vietnam and as an independent translator. Her job has been taken over by Mr Vu Hai.

Long has been promoted to the position of Director of the International Cooperation Department.

Huong continues to work as personal assistant to the Swedish Ambassador to Vietnam. Her son attends a private school in Vietnam.

Nam is still enjoying her retirement.

Ngan has returned VOV5 from another overseas training program. He has a second child, a son.

Madame Nguyet has taking an impressive step up the VOV corporate ladder to become one of four Deputy Director Generals of VOV.

## Outside VOV

Thi Yen Lan continues to run her one-person-NGO for ethnic minority women university students.

Trong Luan is still acting as a guide in Sapa.

Rebecca Hales is employed by the British Council as the Teacher Training Coordinator in Amman, Jordan. She has also conducted a course in Cairo and Kuala Lumpur and is considering professional opportunities in the Palestinian territories and the Sudan. She has completed her studies and gained an MA in International Relations.

Lona Thwaites continued to help out with *What's On* at VOV5 before returning to Canberra with her two daughters and husband, Ambassador Joe Thwaites. Joe has now left the Department of Foreign Affairs and Trade and is studying for his Diploma of Education.

Franz Xaver Augustin continues as Director of the Goethe Institute in Vietnam, but in 2007 will become overall Director of all nine Goethe Institutes in the Asia-Pacific region and will be based in Djakarta.

Sebastian Buckingham and his wife Hien now have a son and are living in Melbourne where Sebastian is studying for his MA. Hien is taking classes in English at Ballarat University and has established a company to import dolls and fabrics from Vietnam.

Jo Maloney is studying holistic medicine and teaching yoga in Fremantle, Western Australia.

John Sampson is working as a subeditor on *MX*, an afternoon newspaper in Melbourne.

Alison Hetherington is a Communications Officer with the Victorian Law Reform Commission.

Beverly Wickham has retired to Tairua on the Coromandel Peninsula, on the east coast of New Zealand's North Island.

David Payne and Ly are married. They both went to England where Ly studied drama. They have returned to Vietnam where David now heads up the UN program dealing with Bird Flu in Vietnam.

Patrick Burke is still working in HIV/AIDS programs in Vietnam. His area of responsibility has expanded to include India and several other South-East Asian nations.

Gerry Hermann's Cinematheque reopened and has gone from strength to strength.

Austereo did not proceed with its plans for a Vietnamese 'Easy Listening' FM radio network.

Australian Volunteers International renewed its contract with AusAID and is now actively seeking business and professional people who wish to be part of their new short-term placement program for volunteers. Melbourne radio journalist Collette Corr is currently filling one of the volunteer spaces at VOV5.

The parallel sentences now grace the main door to our little place in the bush. The piece of calligraphy celebrating our forty years together hangs alongside the embroidered picture of the buffalo boys given to us by the VOV5 crew.

Nam Cam was eventually executed by firing squad.

# BIBLIOGRAPHY

## General

Borton, Lady 2001 *To Be Sure: Work practices in Vietnam* Quaker Service Viet Nam, Hanoi
Burke, Patrick 1999 *Studies of Asia* Heineman, Australia
Heibert, Murray 1993 *Vietnam Notebook* Review Publishing Co. Ltd, Hong Kong
Huu Ngoc 1997 *Sketches for a Portrait of Vietnamese Culture* The Gioi Publishers, Vietnam
Huu Ngoc and Lady Borton 2003 *Betel and Areca* The Gioi Publishers, Hanoi
—— 2003 *Ceramics* The Gioi Publishers, Hanoi
—— 2003 *Cheo Popular Theatre* The Gioi Publishers, Hanoi
—— 2003 *Early Modern Vietnamese Painting* The Gioi Publishers, Hanoi
—— 2003 *Hanoi's Old Quarter* The Gioi Publishers, Hanoi
—— 2003 *Martial Arts* The Gioi Publishers, Hanoi
—— 2003 *Mid-Autumn Festival* The Gioi Publishers, Hanoi
—— 2003 *Royal Exams* The Gioi Publishers, Hanoi
—— 2003 *Traditional Medicine* The Gioi Publishers, Hanoi
—— 2003 *Vietnamese Lunar New Year* The Gioi Publishers, Hanoi
Karnow, Stanley 1983 *Vietnam: A history* Viking, New York
Kolko, Gabriel 1997 *Anatomy of a Peace* Routledge, London
Lamb, David 2002 *Vietnam Now* Public Affairs-Perseus Books Group, New York

Logan, William S. 2000 *Hanoi: Biography of a city* University of NSW Press, Sydney

McNamara, Robert S. 1995 *In Retrospect: The tragedy and lessons of Vietnam* Random House, US

National Political Publishing House, 2001 *Doi Moi and Human Development in Vietnam* Hanoi

Nha Xuat Ban My Thuat 2002 *Vietnam in 10 Years: My vision* Vietnam Fine Arts Association/ADB, Hanoi

Sheehan, Neil 1992 *Two Cities: Hanoi and Saigon* Jonathan Cape, UK

Sidel, Mark 1998 *Old Hanoi* Oxford University Press, Kuala Lumpur

Templer, Robert 1998 *Shadows and Wind* Little Brown & Company, Great Britain

1969 *An Introduction to Vietnam* The Vietnam Council on Foreign Relations, Saigon

1974 *Vietnam: A historical sketch* Foreign Languages Publishing House, Hanoi

1997 *Vietnam in the Past in French Engravings* Van Hoa Dan Toc (Publ.), Hanoi

2000 *The Vietnamese Government 1945 to 2000* National Politics Publisher, Hanoi

2000 *World Heritage Hoi An* Showa Women's University Institute of International Culture, Japan

2002 *Posters of Vietnamese Painters from 1945 to 2000* Bureau of Culture and Information, Vietnam

2003 *Through H'Mong Eyes* Vietnam Museum of Ethnology, Hanoi

2003 *Vietnam Arts Directory* British Council and Ministry of Culture & Information of Vietnam, Hanoi

## War

Brammer, Graham 1997 *Uncertain Fate* Allen & Unwin, Australia

Burchett, Wilfred 1965 *Vietnam: Inside story of the guerilla war* International Publishers, New York

Colonel Dang Van Viet 1990 *Highway 4: The border campaign (1947-50)* Foreign Languages Publishing House, Hanoi
Grenville, Kenneth 1972 *The Saving of South Vietnam* Alpha Books, Sydney
Herr, Michael 1968 *Dispatches* Alfred A. Knopf, New York
Kolko, Gabriel 1985 *Anatomy of a War* Phoenix, London
Murray, Robin (Ed) 1965 *Vietnam* Eyre & Spottiswoode, London
Sexton, Michael 1981 *War for the Asking: Australia's Vietnam secret* Penguin, Australia
Vo Nguyen Giap 1999 *Dien Bien Phu* The Gioi Publishers, Vietnam
1965 *The Real Facts about South Vietnam: A reply to the Liberal Party* Published by D.B. Young, Sydney
1965 *Why Vietnam* The White House, Washington DC
1979 *The Vietnam War: The illustrated history of the conflict in Southeast Asia* Salamander Books, Sydney
2000 *The War 1858-1975 in Viet Nam*, Van Hoa Dan Toc, Hanoi
2001 *Vietnam: A reporter's war* ABC, Sydney
2004 *Memoirs of Dien Bien Phu: History, impressions, memoirs* The Gioi Publishers, Hanoi

## Biography

Borton, Lady and Thomas, C. David 2003 *Ho Chi Minh: A portrait* Youth Publishing House, Hanoi
Bowden, Tim 1987 *One Crowded Hour: Neil Davis* Collins, Sydney
Chong, Denise 2000 *The Girl in the Picture* Simon & Schuster, London
Duiker, William 2000 *Ho Chi Minh* Allen & Unwin, Sydney
Hayslip, Le Ly 1990 *When Heaven and Earth Changed Places* Plume, New York
Ho Chi Minh 1961 *Selected Works*, 2 vols, Foreign Languages Publishing House, Hanoi
Pham, Andrew X 1999 *Cat Fish and Mandala* Picador, New York
Steinbeck IV, John 1968 *In Touch* Dell Publishing, New York

Swain, Jon 1996 *River of Time* William Heineman, London
2002 *Ho Chi Minh: The man who made a nation* The Gioi Publishers, Vietnam

### Fiction

Bao Ninh 1993 *The Sorrow of War* Secker & Warburg, UK
Duong Thi Huong 1994 *Paradise of the Blind* Penguin, UK
—— 1996 *Novel without a Name* Penguin, UK
—— 2000 *Memories of a Pure Spring* Hyperion East, New York
Green, Graham 1962 *The Quiet American* Penguin, UK
Grey, Anthony 1983 *Saigon* Pan, UK
Schultz, George F. 1965 *Vietnamese Legends* Charles Tuttle, Japan
2003 *Through Vietnam's Eyes: A selection of short stories from Vietnam News Sunday Edition* Vietnam News Agency Publishing House, Vietnam

### Travel/tourism

Cohen, Barbara & Kaplan, Fredric 1991 *Vietnam Guide Book* Houghton Mifflin, Boston
Friends of Vietnam Heritage 2001 *Bach Ma Temple* The Gioi Publishers, Hanoi
—— 2001 *Quan Thanh Temple* The Gioi Publishers, Hanoi
—— 2001 *Tran Quoc Pagoda* The Gioi Publishers, Hanoi
Pham Hoang Hai 2003 *Sa Pa: In the midst of clouds* National Political Publishing House, Vietnam
2000 *Vietnamese Phrasebook* Lonely Planet, Melbourne
2001 *Hanoi* Lonely Planet, Melbourne
2001 *Vietnam* Lonely Planet, Melbourne
2001 *Vietnam Administrative Atlas* Cartographic Publishing House, Vietnam
2001 *Travel Atlas* Cultural Information Publishing House, Vietnam
2003 *Hanoi Guide* Hanoi International Women's Club, Hanoi
*Impressions of Vietnam* Ministry of Culture and Information, Hanoi

## Movies

*The Boy with No Face* (Sweden)
*Buddhas and Genies* (French archival films)
*Cyclo* (France)
*Good Morning Vietnam* (US)
*Harmony in Hanoi* (US)
*Hearts and Minds* (US)
*In the Neighbourhood of Hanoi* (French archival films)
*Indochine* (France)
*Nostalgia for the Countryside* (Vietnam)
*The Quiet American* (US)
*Regret to Inform* (US)
*Scent of Green Papaya* (France)
*The Song of the Stork* (Vietnam)
*The Sorrow of War* (Vietnam)
*Through East German Eyes* (East German archives)
*Travelling the Tonkin Countryside* (French archival films)
*Vertical Ray of the Sun* (France)
*When Heaven and Earth Changed Places* (US)

# INDEX

Abortion 319
Agent Orange 59, 207, 296–7
Aid workers 219
Ananda, Roshni 322
*Ao dai* 65, 354, 367
Archaeology 57, 213–15, 252–5
Army Museum 74–5
Art Vietnam Gallery 105
Art-copying industry 50
Association of South-East Asian Nations (ASEAN) 172
Augustin, Franz Xaver 189–90, 357, 374–5
AusAID 198, 222, 225
Austereo 235–6, 285, 322
AusTrade 199
Australia Day 294–5
Australian Chamber of Commerce 246
Australian Embassy 137, 140, 182, 199, 205, 282, 334
Australian Trade and Aid 198
Australian Volunteers International (AVI) 1, 25, 126, 141, 152, 217, 221–2, 339
Avian flu 271–3

Ba Dinh Square 20–1, 148, 167, 169, 213
Babies 319–20
Bac Bo Gulf 218
Bach Dang River 86
Bach Ma Temple 93
Baguette et Chocolat 99
Balding, Russell 236
*Banh chung* 278
Bao Ninh 83
Ben Hai River 6
Best, Dave 76
Bi Doh (Red Pumpkin) Restaurant 4
Bias 331–2
Binh Soup Shop 123
Blair, Prime Minister Tony 312
Boat people 23
Bodhisattva Kwan Yin 198
Borton, Lady 169, 321–2
Briscombe, Alistair 199, 201
Broadcasting 9
Brudon, Dr Pascale 51
Buckingham, Sebastian 220
Buddha's birthday 40–1, 43
Buddhism 68, 197
Buddhist monks and nuns 41

Buddhist temples 92–3
Bui Nhat Quang 156
*Buon de* 320
Buon Ma Thuot 347–8
Burke, Patrick 46, 217, 233

Calligraphy 309–11
Cat Ba Island 223–4
Cat Ba langur 224
*Catfish and Mandala* 230–1
Catholicism 42–5, 245
Cau Giay 283
Censorship 122
Centre for Non-Government Organisations 220
Cha Ca Long Vong Restaurant 322
Chapman, George 236–7, 239, 322
Childbirth 17, 319
Children's Day 89
China 9, 50, 68, 213, 271, 297
Christianity 42–5
Christmas 259–61
Clinton, President 39, 208
CNN 8, 10, 18, 36
Communal outdoor kitchens 12, 13

Communist Party (Vietnamese) 33–5, 41, 78, 135
*Communist Party Review* 32, 34, 45, 72, 79, 104, 116, 126, 147–8, 163, 179, 354
Confucianism 64–5, 68
Cong Vi 128
Connell Wagner 314, 315
Corporate culture 291
Cuba 9, 16, 125, 144, 183
Cuc Phuong National Park 263–4
Cumquat trees 274–5
Currency 256–8

Dac Lac Province 347–9
Dakshin 188
Dang Mai Phuong 46, 115, 181, 194, 273
Dang Nhat Minh 328
Dao Nguyen 323–4, 330–1, 333
Dao Thi Thuy 68, 330
Davis, Peter 328
Day for the Pardoning the Sins of the Dead 150–3
Death sentence 95
Declarations of Independence 167, 186
Demilitarised Zone (DMZ) 6, 228
Dengue fever 199, 201
Department of Foreign Affairs (Vietnamese) 10
Dien Bien Phu 74–5, 186–7, 244, 286–9, 336, 339, 359, 361–70
Dien Bien Phu Victory 366
Dinh Thi Huong 46–7

Discovery Club 343
Do Duy Thuong 354
Do Troung Giang 48, 121, 127
Doan Thi Xuan Mai 14–15
Doi Moi reforms 117, 192, 203–4, 245
Downer, Alexander 138–41, 180
Drug addiction 228
Duc Pier 197
Dulles, John Foster 187
Duong Quynh Hoa 297
Duong Thu Huong 83
Dynasties 85, 214, 253

Ea Sola 80
Easter 41
Education 64, 225–7
English-language broadcasting 211–12
English Language Department 8, 35, 46, 126
European Jazz Festival 208
European Union Film Festival 81, 87

Fairhead, Paul 198, 200–2
Farewell party 351–3
Flowers 38
Forestry Science Institute of Vietnam 220
Foundation for the Peoples of Asia and the Pacific 199
Franco-Vietnamese Hospital 11, 111
Friends of Vietnam Heritage (FVH) 91, 197, 252, 309–10, 328–9
Frog markets 194–5
Funerals 248–51, 297–9

Gauci, Tim 198–9, 235
Gia Lac Province 349
Goethe Institute 189, 239, 242, 357, 374
'Golden Goat' 17–18, 111
Gordon, Pam 197
Gordon, Robert 197
Government 135
Government Education Bonds 225–6
Greene, Graham 43
Greve, RoseMarie 234
Griffith, Nanci 227–8

Ha Long Bay 185, 218, 222, 262
Ha Long City 219, 223
Ha Tay Province 300
*Hai Au* 218
Hai Duong Province 314
Hai Phong 27–8, 38, 54, 182, 188
Hales, Rebecca 25, 51, 53, 79–80, 82, 84, 103–4, 142, 157, 160, 163, 183, 208, 216, 218, 221, 225, 226, 248, 259, 261, 300, 352, 357, 363, 370–1
Hanoi 31, 33, 38, 54, 273
Hanoi Cinematheque 242, 255–6, 270–1, 327–9, 356, 358, 361
Hanoi Conservatory 190
Hanoi Film Club 328
Hanoi Hannah 57, 144
Hanoi International Women's Club 54
Hanoi Jazz Club 76
Hanoi Opera House 138–9
Hanoi Press Club 123
Hanoi Towers 39
Hartney, Terry 113, 123

Harvie, Peter 236–7, 239
Health system 110–11
Hebrad, Ernest 86
Henderson, Sandra 143, 182
Hermann, Gerry 242, 255–6, 270–1, 327, 358, 362
Heroic Mother's Day 130
Hetherington, Alison 221
Highlands outdoor restaurant 50
History 4, 57, 334–6
HIV/AIDS 46, 179, 219, 233–5
H'Mong people 99–100
Ho Chi Minh 20–2, 61, 68, 79, 148–9, 155, 167–9, 213, 227, 256, 317, 336
Ho Chi Minh City 12, 24, 27–8, 42, 122–3, 208, 210, 227, 242, 245, 273
Ho Chi Minh Offensive 61
Ho Chi Minh's Five Teachings 115
Hoa Lo Prison 38–40
Hoa Lu 262
Hoa Sua 90–1, 99
Hoan Kiem Lake 13, 61, 66, 165, 352, 359
Hoang Hoa Tham 128
Hoang Minh Nguyet 7, 15, 173, 175
Hoi An 185
Hong Dich Dong 198
Horowitz, Linda 190–1
Hospitals 110
*Hua* 310
Hung Kings 334–6
Hunger Eradication and Poverty Alleviation (HEPA) 191–3
Huu Ngoc 243–5, 282

Identity card 327
Ilich, Vladimir 33
Independence Day 165, 169
Institute for International Relations 3, 152
Institute of Archaeology 214, 253
International Day of the Disabled 235
International Relations Department of Radio the Voice of Vietnam 7, 15
International Women's Day 318–20
Interviews 332–3
Iraq War 4, 8–10, 18–19, 22, 26, 36, 55
Islam 225
Israel 225

Karaoke 307–9
Kayaking 218, 223
Kennedy, John F. 231
Kim Lien pagoda 79
Kirk, Dan 46, 216
Koto (Know One Teach One) 90–1

La Place 322
La Thi Kim Oanh 95
Lansdale, Colonel Edward 43
Lao Cai 99, 102, 104, 158, 162
Le Bach Duong, Dr 234
Le Nghiem 323, 330
Le Van Lan, Professor 55–7, 334–6
Lecht, Suzanne 105
Literacy 226–7
Long Bien Bridge 53–4, 188
Loseby, Frank 148–50
Luong Van Can 177
Ly Thai Phuong 323

McCain, John 38–9
McKenzie, Brian 132
'MacNamara Line' 229
Maconachie, Bill 107
Maloney, Joe 220
Man, Cardinal 245
Manguy, Jean Gabriel 236
Marchant, Ron 235, 256
Martyrs 59
Masion Centrale 38
Maya Bar and Nightclub 87
Médecins Sans Frontières 12
Media 116–18
Metropole Hotel 55, 357
Meyers, Richard 207
Military training 206
Mines Advisory Group (MAG) 229
Minh Luong prison and labour camp 231
Missing in Action (MIA) 207
Moca Café 83, 157
Montagnard Foundation 348
Moon cakes 176–7
Motherhood 52, 224
Motorbikes 1–2, 69, 71–2, 215–16
accidents 215–17
helmets 2–3, 128, 217
taxis 84
Mount Fanxipan 103, 154, 157–63, 299
Municipal Water Puppet Theatre 65–6
Muong Thanh Bridge 288
Muong Thanh Hotel 287, 364
Murphy, Paul 132
Museum of Ethnology 144
My Dinh Stadium 238

My Thuan Bridge 180, 201

Nam Dinh City 366
Nam Oum River 288
Names 3, 31–2
Nathan, Xavier 3, 5, 151–2
National Assembly 134–5
National Day for the People's Police 136
National Institute for Hygiene and Epidemiology 199
National Museum of Vietnamese History 85
National Opera and Ballet 190
National Public Radio 247
National Revolutionary Press Day 116
National Tuong Theatre of Vietnam 341–2
Nelson, Carol 91–3
Ngo Dinh Diem, President 232
Nguyen Ai Quoc 148–9, 167
Nguyen Dinh Thien 189
Nguyen Dy Nien 139
Nguyen, Felice 144–5
Nguyen Hoang Duong 3
Nguyen Hong Hanh 143
Nguyen Hong Ngan 193
Nguyen Quang 314–16, 355
Nguyen Quy Doan 116
Nguyen Tam Khoi 47, 77, 78, 94, 121, 290, 306, 317
Nguyen Thi Bao Tam 3–4
Nguyen Thi Hue, Madame 7, 17, 19, 32, 34, 35, 68, 122, 193, 240, 246

Nguyen Thi Loc, Madame 7–8, 35, 47, 72–3, 120, 136, 139
Nguyen Thi Phi 297
Nguyen Thi Thu 131
Nguyen Thi Tien 59
Nguyen Thi Van 151
Nguyen Tien Long, Mr 7, 35, 210, 323–4, 329, 375
Nguyen Trong Luan 100, 158, 299–305
Nguyen Van An 135
Nguyen Van Quy 297
1912 market 36–7
1945 August Revolution 154–6, 165, 168
Ninh Binh 261
*Nom* 145
Nong Duc Manh, Secretary General 135–6
North Korea 9, 213
Northrop, Sandy 329
Notre Dame Cathedral 245

Old Town 8, 48–51, 74, 76, 91, 93, 150, 157, 165–6, 177, 326, 373
*On-Line News* 46
Opera House 86
Operation Rolling Thunder 54
Operation Smile 179
Orphans 90
Overseas Vietnamese 23–4, 144, 280

Paloma Café 359
Parallel sentences 362–4
Payne, David 220
Peaceful evolution 118–19
Peach blossoms 274
People's Council elections 354–5

Perfume Pagoda 197–8
Petersen, Douglas ('Pete') 38–9
Pha Lai power plant 314
Pham, Andrew X. 230–1
Pham Dinh Tung 42
Pham Hong Hai 191
Pham, Jimmy 90
Pham Manh Hung, Professor 233, 235
Pham Thi Nam 35–6
Pham Thi Nhuong 248, 250
Pham Van Thong 231
Pham Van Tra 207–8
Phan Tai Duong 145
Phan Van Dong 187
Phan Van Khai, Prime Minister 135
Phan Xuan Quang 229
Phong Anh 47
Piracy 50, 82
Police 14, 136–7
Political structure 134–6
Pont Paul Doumer 54
Poverty reduction 222
Pregnancy 17, 29, 45–6, 124, 319
Presidency 135
Pronunciation 31
Prostitution 307

*Qi* 310
*Qin* 310
Quan Su Pagoda 40, 68, 153, 205
Quang An 79, 169
Quang Nam 131
Quang Tri City 229
Quang Tri Province 228
Quang Vinh 147
*Quoc Ngu* 145, 227
Quy Ho River 100
Quynh Van Minh 76

Rach Gia 231
Radio Australia 236

Rainy season 69
Rankin, Scott 217, 222
Rape 58, 282
Red Cross 219
Red River 53–4, 261
Red River Band 76
Refugees 23–4, 61
Respect 195–7
Retirement 35
Rowell, Andrew 199, 200
Royal Melbourne Institute of Technology (RMIT) 227
Rugby World Cup 188–9
Rumsfeld, Donald 207
Ryan, Ching 55–6
Ryan, Jordan 55–6, 233

Saigon 123
 fall of 74
*Saigon Times* 117
Salaries 126–7
Sampson, John 221
San Ho Restaurant 76
Sao Mai (Morning Star) kindergarten 62, 115
 swimming pool 79, 169
Sapa 99–104, 158, 299, 300
SBS 239–41
Securency 256
Severe acute respiratory syndrome (SARS) 10–11, 22, 25–6, 50–1, 55, 271
Sheppard, Dick 76
*Shu Fa* 310
Sin Chai 158
SMARTWork Vietnam 46
Soccer matches 246, 251–2
South-East Asian Games 146, 156, 235, 238–9, 242, 246

Soviet Union 3, 20, 30, 213, 318
Spotted Cow 106–7, 188
Squid 48
St Joseph's Cathedral 41–2, 322
Street children 90
Swedish Embassy 267, 306–7

Ta Van 102
*Tam and Cam* 345
Tam Coc 262
Tamarind Café 218
Tang Yun 356–8
Tao Quan, the Kitchen God 275–6
Taoism 65, 68
Taylor, Ben 322
Taylor, Sam 367–8
TB 269
Teachers' Day 226
Telstra 199–200
Temple of Literature 64, 66, 310
Terrific Thi 17, 137–8, 152–3, 273, 274, 297, 316
Terrorism 208
Tet Lunar New Year celebrations 273–82
Tet Offensive 1968 279–80
Thai Binh Province 297
Thang Long archaeological site 213–15, 252–5
 legend of 57
*Thanh Nien* 156, 347
Thanksgiving Mass 245
*The Boy With No Face* 81
Thich Nhat Hanh 375
Thien Tru Pagoda 197
*Thoi Su* 239–42
Thon Luu Xa 300

Thuy Anh Hotel 261, 263, 265
Thwaites, Ambassador Joe 55, 137–8, 170, 188, 198, 199, 283, 375
Thwaites, Lona 54, 243, 283, 342, 344–5, 368, 375
Thwaites, Michael 355
Tien Nguyen 241
*To Be Sure* 321–2
Tong Anh De 261
Tong Trung Tin 214, 253
Tonkin Café 307
Tooten, Ralph 374
Total Liberation Day 59, 61–3, 358
Tourism Day 121–2
Traffic 1–2
Tram 17, 44–5, 181–2, 194, 224, 240
Tran Duc Luong, President 135, 169, 281
Tran Fon Pass 159
Tran Ha Binh 5
Tran Ha Trang 3–5
Tran Hung Dao, General 86
Tran Le Chien 146
Tran Mai Hanh 26, 28–31, 36, 52, 86, 95, 108–9, 124, 128D–9
Tran Minh Ha 47, 94, 121, 283
Tran Quynh Hoa 3
Tran Thi Yen Lan 55, 57–8, 282–3, 357
Tran Trong Truy 217
Transparency in government dealings 200, 202–5
Trieu Phong 229
Truc Bac Lake 169, 260

Truong Van Cam (Nam Cam) 27–8, 56, 95
Tu Do 143
Tube houses 49
Turtles 65
Tyrell, Bob 132

Unexploded ordnance (UXO) 207, 228–9
United Nations Development Program (UNDP) 55–6, 233
United Nations International School (UNIS) 56
United States 207–8, 241–2, 296, 348
Unknown Soldier, monument to 253
Urbani, Dr Carlo 11–12
USS *Vandegrift* 208

Van Mieu 64–5
V.I. Le Nin 33
Viet Cong 122–3, 131, 280, 318
Viet Kieu 23–4, 144, 241, 280, 314
Vietnam
 independence 20
 Press Law 117
Vietnam Association of Victims of Agent Orange 297
Vietnam Australia Building Industry Services 189

Vietnam National University 55, 56, 80
*Vietnam News*, 10, 26, 82, 117, 191, 221, 243, 247, 294, 331
Vietnam Symphony Orchestra 255, 356
Vietnam Veterans Foundation of America 228
Vietnam Veterans Memorial Fund 229
Vietnam War 20, 59–61, 123–4, 131, 141, 207, 231–2, 282, 315
Vietnamese Army Museum 33
Vietnamese language 31
Vildieu, Auguste-Henri 38
Vo Nguyen Giap, General 74
Voice of Vietnam 4, 26, 141
 headquarters 6, 171
 language sections 8
 radio broadcasting facilities 8
 set-up at 9
VOV5 7, 29, 32, 45, 55, 67, 120–1, 212–13, 239–40, 285, 290, 314, 359
VOV-TV2 314
Vu Hoang Dung 28
Vu Nhat Quynh 67–8
Vu Sinh Nam, Dr 199, 201
Vu Van Hien 170, 173

Wage payment system 72–3, 126
War Invalids', Martyrs' and Heroic Mother's Day 130, 132
Water puppetry 65–7
Watkinson, Renate 76–7
Weisner, Mechtilde 190
West Lake 79–80, 260, 352
White, Noel 357
Wickham, Beverly 219
Wifedom 52
Wild Rice Restaurant 236
Winther, Mikael 55
Women 318–20
World AIDS Day 233–5
World Health Organization 296
World Heritage sites 218
World Trade Organization 10–11, 82, 201, 212

*Xe om* 84, 194, 325, 365, 372
Xua Nay Restaurant 359

Yen River 197
Yu, Christina 209–10, 356–7